STEPS IN SCALA
An Introduction to Object-Functional Programming

Object-functional programming is already here. Scala is the most prominent representative of this exciting approach to programming, both in the small and in the large. In this book we show how Scala proves to be a highly expressive, concise, and scalable language, which grows with the needs of the programmer, whether professional or hobbyist.

Read the book to see how to:

- leverage the full power of the industry-proven JVM technology with a language that could have come from the future;
- learn Scala step-by-step, following our complete introduction and then dive into specially chosen design challenges and implementation problems, inspired by the real-world, software engineering battlefield;
- embrace the power of static typing and automatic type inference;
- use the dual object and functional oriented natures combined at Scala's core, to see how to write code that is less "boilerplate" and to witness a real increase in productivity.

Use Scala for fun, for professional projects, for research ideas. We guarantee the experience will be rewarding.

CHRISTOS K. K. LOVERDOS is a research inclined computer software professional. He holds a B.Sc. and an M.Sc. in Computer Science. He has been working in the software industry for more than ten years, designing and implementing flexible, enterprise-level systems and making strategic technical decisions. He has also published research papers on topics including digital typography, service-oriented architectures, and highly available distributed systems. Last but not least, he is an advocate of open source software.

APOSTOLOS SYROPOULOS is a computer scientist. He holds a B.Sc. in Physics, an M.Sc. in Computer Science, and a Ph.D. in Theoretical Computer Science. His research interests focus on computability theory, category theory, fuzzy set theory, and digital typography. He has authored or co-authored six books, was co-editor of a multi-author volume, and has published more than 50 papers and articles.

STEPS IN SCALA

An Introduction to Object-Functional Programming

CHRISTOS K. K. LOVERDOS
APOSTOLOS SYROPOULOS

CAMBRIDGE
UNIVERSITY PRESS

CAMBRIDGE
UNIVERSITY PRESS

Shaftesbury Road, Cambridge CB2 8EA, United Kingdom

One Liberty Plaza, 20th Floor, New York, NY 10006, USA

477 Williamstown Road, Port Melbourne, VIC 3207, Australia

314–321, 3rd Floor, Plot 3, Splendor Forum, Jasola District Centre, New Delhi – 110025, India

103 Penang Road, #05–06/07, Visioncrest Commercial, Singapore 238467

Cambridge University Press is part of Cambridge University Press & Assessment, a department of the University of Cambridge.

We share the University's mission to contribute to society through the pursuit of education, learning and research at the highest international levels of excellence.

www.cambridge.org
Information on this title: www.cambridge.org/9780521762175

© C. K. K. Loverdos and A. Syropoulos 2010

First published 2010

A catalogue record for this publication is available from the British Library

ISBN   978-0-521-76217-5   Hardback
ISBN   978-0-521-74758-5   Paperback

Additional resources for this publication at www.cambridge.org/9780521762175

To Katerina, who is always here and is constantly making me a better person

CKKL

Στους γονείς μου Γεώργιο και Βασιλική και στον
γιο μου Δημήτριο-Γεώργιο

AS

Contents

Preface

What is Scala?

Scala is a relatively new programming language that was designed by Martin Odersky and released in 2003. The distinguishing features of Scala include a seamless integration of functional programming features into an otherwise object-oriented language. Scala owes its name to its ability to *scale*, that is, it is a language that can *grow* by providing an infrastructure that allows the introduction of new constructs and data types. In addition, Scala is a concurrent programming language, thus, it is a tool for today as well as tomorrow! Scala is a compiled language. Its compiler produces bytecode for the Java Virtual Machine, thus allowing the (almost) seamless use of Java tools and constructs from within scala. The language has been used to rewrite Twitter's[1] back-end services. In addition, almost all of Foursquare's[2] infrastructure has been coded in Scala. This infrastructure is used by several companies worldwide (for example, Siemens, Sony Pictures Imageworks).

Who should read this book?

The purpose of this book is twofold: first to teach the basics of Scala and then to show how Scala can be used to develop *real* applications. Unlike other books on Scala, this one does not assume any familiarity with Java. In fact, no previous knowledge of Java is necessary to read this book, though some knowledge of Java would be beneficial, especially in the chapter on GUI applications. On the other hand, the book assumes that readers do have a very basic understanding of programming concepts. In particular, we expect readers to be familiar with terms like compiler, interpreter, (character) string, etc. Thus, the book can be used by anyone who has done some high school computer programming. However, the book covers a number of subjects that are quite advanced and so are appropriate for readers with

---

[1] http://www.twitter.com (a.k.a. Twitter) is a free social networking and micro-blogging service.
[2] http://foursquare.com is a location-based social networking service.

a good background in both programming and mathematics. Sections describing such topics are marked with an asterisk (*).

The intended audience of this book includes computer science students as well as computing professionals. Obviously, students and practitioners of related fields and areas (for example, mathematics, physics, electrical and computer engineering, etc.) will find this book quite beneficial.

The book in detail

Essentially, the book is divided in two parts – the first seven chapters introduce most of the language constructs and related software modules, while the remaining six chapters present various applications of Scala. In particular, the first chapter of the book is an introduction to the basic ideas described in the rest of the book. In particular, it describes the basic ideas behind object-orientation, functional programming, and language extensionality, while it concludes with a comparison and discussion of programming languages similar to Scala.

In Chapter 2 we gradually introduce the various basic concepts and ideas of Scala. In particular, we present the "basic" data-types, classes and objects, methods and operators, and functions. Then we introduce some important predefined types-classes: sets, hash tables, lists and strings. In addition, we discuss other important features such as memo functions, regular expressions, annotations, etc.

Pattern matching is an another important feature of Scala that can be used to define useful structures like trees. In Chapter 3 we introduce traits in order to show how behaviors can be mixed in using them. Next, we discuss function objects. Polymorphism is an important characteristic of object-orientation and therefore is an important part of Scala. We discuss all aspects of Scala polymorphism, even higher-order polymorphism. We also discuss streams, setters and getters, memo functions, and we conclude with a discussion of monads.

Chapter 4 is about parser builders, that is, tools that can be used to implement language processors. After introducing the so-called basic parser combinators, we show how they can be used to build the interpreter of a relatively simple programming language. The chapter concludes with a short description of domain-specific languages and monadic parsing.

XML processing is a basic characteristic of Scala. In Chapter 5 we discuss how one can create and manipulate XML content using Scala. In addition, we show how to perform a number of important operations such as searching and printing. Also, we show how to produce XHTML content with Scala.

In Chapter 6 we show how to program GUI applications using Scala. In particular, we show how to use a number of GUI components such as frames, all sorts of buttons, labels, text fields, dialogs, menus, tabs, and tables. In addition, we show how to implement applets in Scala. The chapter concludes with a short discussion of functional graphics.

It was said above that Scala is a concurrent programming language in the sense that it includes a number of features that facilitate concurrent programming. Chapter 7 is dedicated to these facilities. In particular, we discuss threads and synchronization, animation using threads, mailboxes (a precursor of actors), and actors.

Chapter 8 deals with a ubiquitous abstraction, that of paths. Paths are used mainly to describe file locations. Although our design and implementation is heavily influenced by file-based APIs, we place paths in a more general algebraic context.

Chapter 9 moves from path modeling to file system hierarchies modeling by using the now widely accepted notion of a virtual file system (VFS). We build three VFS implementations: a traditional file system, one based on zip (compressed archives) files and finally a memory-based VFS.

Chapter 10 introduces the concept of file matching, inspired by Unix-related terminology and tools. But instead of just reproducing known behavior, we take full advantage of Scala's DSL definition abilities and make file searches more user-friendly than ever.

Chapter 11 extends the basic idea of the previous chapter, regarding the methodologies to search for the appropriate files. It presents two complementary techniques: one based on the classical notion of iteration and the other based on the emerging notion of traversal. During the course of study, we discover not so traditional ways to abstract over our data and clearly show how a pre-order depth-first search can share almost the same codebase with a breadth-first search. We conclude with a set of thought provoking remarks on the interplay between iteration and traversal.

Chapter 12 introduces and analyzes the expression problem, a not so widely known software design problem. Since its essence lies at the frontier of combining data with operations, we feel that this particular problem should be brought to the attention of a wider audience. Based on work by well-known researchers (including the creator of Scala, Martin Odersky) we build a small code library that follows a consistent set of naming conventions in order to help us tackle the expression problem.

Chapter 13 is a short chapter that shows how one can easily construct a relatively simple computer algebra system.

There are four appendices. The first one briefly discusses how one can construct multimedia applications with Scala. The second one shows how we can use the open-source tool Proguard to package Scala applications along with the Scala runtime in order to avoid any prerequisite when distributing Scala applications. The third appendix presents the Scala grammar. The fourth and last appendix presents the wealth of command line options of Scala's compiler and interpreter.

Each chapter contains a number of exercises that have been designed to help readers obtain a deeper understanding of the topics presented. There are no solutions to exercises, though in some cases material that follows the exercises contains the solution. In addition, there are some suggestions for programming projects. In most cases these are not easy and some of them are quite challenging.

In the book we use the term Unix, but since this may mean different things, we need to calarify the meaning. The term Unix means either the operating system originally created by Bell Labs or an operating system certified as Unix by the Open Group (for example, Solaris 10 is such a system). We use the term Unix to denote any system that seems sufficiently Unix-like (for example, OpenSolaris, Linux, MacOS, etc.) or is a certified Unix system.

All of the examples presented in the following pages have been tested to work under OpenSolaris and MacOS X [Snow] Leopard. We do not expect that readers who use different computer platforms will encounter any kind of problem, as long as they use the latest version of Java's JDK from Oracle. All examples are available from the book's web site.

Preparing the book

The book has been typeset using a Unicode-aware extension of LaTeX that runs atop of a novel typesetting engine created by Jonathan Kew. We have used Minion Pro to set the text of the book and GFS Neohellenic (by the Greek Font Society) to set captions. In addition, we have used UM Typewriter (created by Apostolos) to typeset code snippets. Asana Math (also by Apostolos) has been used to set mathematical text in this book. Our working platforms were MacOS X [Snow] Leopard (Christos) and OpenSolaris (Apostolos).

Thoughts before delving into the book

Sometimes, when introducing a new language, a new technology, a new approach, we may hear a great deal of technical arguments in favor. Scala can be introduced like that. For the reader who seeks technical ability and excellence in the everyday tools, Scala will provide a solid work-field. For the language enthusiast, the exploring student, the hobbyist programmer, the geek, the most important thing is that Scala can increase your enjoyment of programming. This has been our feeling while preparing this book and while using Scala in our everyday work.

Acknowledgments

First of all we would like to thank Heather Bergman, a former computer science editor of CUP's New York branch, who believed in this project. Heather has helped us during the writing of the book in every possible way! Also, we would like to thank Clare Dennison, our pre-production editor, and Jonathan Ratcliffe, our production editor. In addition, we would like to thank Michael Drig, Tony Morris, Bruno Oliveira, George Georgiou, and the anonymous reviewers for their help.

1

Introduction

Scala is a scalable object-oriented programming language with features found in functional programming languages. Nowadays, the object-oriented approach to software construction is considered the most succesful methodology for software design, mainly because it makes software reuse extremely easy. On the other hand, functional programming offers some very elegant tools which when combined with an object-oriented program development philosophy define a really powerful programming methodology. Generally, any programming language that can be extended seamlessly is called scalable. When all these ideas are combined in a single tool, then the result is a particularly powerful programming language.

1.1 Object orientation

The first object-oriented programming language was SIMULA [18], which was designed and implemented by Ole-Johan Dahl and Kristen Nygaard. The SIMUlation LAnguage was designed "to facilitate formal description of the layout and rules of operation of systems with discrete events (changes of state)." In other words, SIMULA was designed as a simulation tool of discrete systems. Roughly, a simulation involves the representation of the functioning of one system or process by means of the functioning of another. In order to achieve its design goal, the designers equipped the language with structures that would make easy the correspondence between a software simulation and the physical system itself. The most important of these structures is the *process*. A process "is intended as an aid for decomposing a discrete event system into components, which are separately describable." Processes, which nowadays are called classes, consist of two parts: a data part and a code part. In the data part, programmers can declare and/or define variables, while in the code part they can define actions (procedures) to process the data. Processes can be combined to describe the functionality of some system. *Elements*, which nowadays are called *objects*, are *instances* of processes, thus, for a single process there may be different instances. It turns out that these simple ideas are the core of what is now known as object-orientation. Nevertheless, the next major milestone in this technology was the design and implementation of Smalltalk (see [27] and [40] for an elegant and concise presentation of Smalltalk).

Smalltalk is an object-oriented programming language[1] designed and implemented by Alan Kay, Dan Ingalls, Adele Goldberg, Ted Kaehler, Scott Wallace, and several other people working at Xeror PARC during the 1970s. The basic design principle of Smalltalk was the idea that all data manipulated by a program are *objects*, that is, software entities capable of interacting with other similar objects. According to this view, the operation 3+4 is viewed as if the object 3 is sending the message + to object 4. Then, if object 4 understands the message +, it starts the execution of a method that specifies how to respond to this particular message. In this case, the method responds by sending back the object 7.

The paradigm shift pioneered by SIMULA and Smalltalk shaped the whole industry and this is evident in the number of object-oriented languages that emerged and their use in industry. For example, today any software engineer is fluent in at least one of the following object-oriented programming languages: C++ [70], Java [28], Eiffel [52], Self [74], Ruby [22], Python [49], Objective C [16], and Oberon [66]. But what are the reasons for the success of the object-oriented programming paradigm?

The reason for this success is that object-oriented languages implement a number of principles that make the software design and construction process much simpler and elegant when compared to "traditional" approaches. The four basic principles of object-orientation are described briefly below.

Abstraction Objects lie at the heart of object-oriented program design. A software object is an *abstraction* of a real-world object. An object has the essential characteristics of the real-world object that distinguish it from all other kinds of object. Thus, it is important to classify the various characteristics as essential or insignificant. This way the software becomes simpler and easier to understand.

Encapsulation An object is a software component that is characterized by its *state* and its *behavior*. Fields (think of them as placeholders that may hold numbers, words, etc.) are used to store its state, while its behavior depends on the actions its methods may take. Typically, the fields of an object are accessible only through its methods. In other words, one can either change the state of an object or become aware of its current state by invoking specific methods. This implies that the internal state of an object is not visible to anyone, thus providing a data protection mechanism. This property is known as *data encapsulation*.

Inheritance In general, objects are not independent software components. Usually, objects are related with an "isa" relationship, that is, if *A* and *B* are two objects such

---

[1] In fact, the designers of Smalltalk were the first to introduce the widely used object-oriented parlance that includes terms such as *object-oriented, method,* etc.

that B extends the functionality of A, then we say that B *is a* A. Object B may extend the functionality of A either by defining new fields and/or methods or by changing the actions taken by some methods. It is customary to say that B inherits A when B is an A. Objects may inherit characteristics from more than one object and in this case we talk about multiple inheritance, while if each object may inherit characteristics from only one object, we talk about single inheritance. When building new systems, it is not necessary to design all objects from scratch. Instead, one may opt to use existing objects and extend their functionality to suit one's own needs by designing new objects that inherit existing objects. In a nutshell, this is the essence of software reuse.

Polymorphism Seemingly different real-life structures may actually differ only in the items they process. So instead of defining an object for each instance of the real-life structure (something that is practically not possible), one can design a generic software module and then instantiate it to model particular real-life structures. For example, a stack consists of items that are put one atop the other and one can remove and/or add items only from/to the top of the stack. Thus, if we want a stack of integers or a stack of software modules modeling books, we can create a generic software module that will implement the functionality of any stack and then use particular instances of this software module to simulate stacks of integers and/or books. This marvelous capability is known as polymorphism. To put it very simply, a polymorphic software module is one that may have different instances with identical behavior.

Without worrying about the details, let us see by means of an example how these principles are realized in the language that is presented in this book.

Assume that we want to build a system simulating a zoo. In order to achieve this goal we need to build a hierarchy of classes that will describe the species living in the zoo. Naturally, we do not need to build a different class for each species since, for example, a bee is an insect and all insects are arthropods. Let us start by defining a class that describes arthropods:

```
class arthropod (NumberOfEyes: Int, NumberOfFeet : Int) {
  def numberOfFeet () = println(NumberOfFeet)
  def numberOfEyes () = println(NumberOfEyes)
}
```

We are not interested in every aspect of what makes an animal an arthropod. Instead, we center upon two quite important things: the number of eyes and the number of feet. Obviously, our choice is *subjective*, but it depends on the task we are trying to accomplish and this is exactly the essence of abstraction. Note that the values stored in the fields NumberOfEyes and NumberOfFeet cannot be changed.

An ant has six legs and let us assume it has two eyes. The declaration that follows creates an ant object that corresponds to an ant:

```
val ant = new arthropod(2,6)
```

Although we cannot alter the number of feet or the number of eyes of an ant object, we can inspect these values. Indeed, the commands

```
ant.numberOfFeet()
ant.numberOfEyes()
```

print the number of feet and eyes of an ant, correspondingly. Although we have used an indirect way to access the values of each field, one can use the fields directly to access or modify the corresponding values, However, one can also declare the fields in such a way that such operations are not directly possible, and this is a simple example of data encapsulation.

An insect is an arthropod with six feet. Instead of defining a new class for insects from scratch, we can *extend* the functionality of class `arthropod` to define a class for insects:

```
class insect (NumberOfEyes: Int)
    extends arthropod (NumberOfEyes, 6){ }
```

Creating and using `insect` is easy. The commands that follow

```
val bee = new insect(4)
bee.numberOfFeet()
bee.numberOfEyes()
```

create a new `insect` object (stored in variable `bee`) and print the numbers of feet and eyes of a bee. In this particular case, the numbers six and four will be printed on the computer screen. This very simple code shows the essence of inheritance. We extend the functionality of existing software modules by creating new software modules that inherit the properties of these existing modules and add new features making the resulting module more expressive. Although the examples presented are very simple, nevertheless, any real-world application uses inheritance in exactly the same way. The important benefit of the introduction of inheritance is that software modules become reusable. Thus, there is no need to invent the wheel every time one tries to solve a particular problem. And when a programming language is equipped with a huge library of such software modules, then it attracts many users. After all, this is just one of the reasons that the Java programming language has become so popular.

Although there are animals that change their forms entirely during their lifetime (think of butterflies for example), still it makes no sense merely to demonstrate polymorphism using such a complex example. Instead, we will use stacks to demonstrate polymorphism. As noted already, a stack is a structure where one can add/remove elements from its top. Let us first define a class that simulates a stack of integers:

```
class IntStack (n: Int) {
    private var S = new Array[Int](n)
    private var top = 0;
    private var TopElement;
    def push(elem: Int) {
        top = top + 1
        S(top) = elem
    }
    def pop () : Q = {
        var oldtop = top
        top = top - 1
        S(oldtop)
    }
}
```

Note that we have intentionally left out various checks that should be performed (for example, we cannot pop something from an empty stack) just to keep things simple. Creating new stacks is easy. We just specify the height of the stack as shown below:

```
var x = new IntStack(3)
x.push(3)
x.push(4)
println(x.pop())
```

The last command will print the number 4 on the computer screen. Suppose that we also need a stack of strings. The most "natural" thing to do is to define a StringStack by replacing all but the first occurrence of Int with String. Here the words Int and String are *data types* or just types. Roughly, a type is defined by prescribing how its elements are formed as well as when two elements are equal (see [64] for a practical account of type theory and [36] and the references therein for an account more suitable for theoretical computer scientists). With types one can distinguish between one as a natural number and one as a real number. In the simplest case, types may be seen as sets of data values. Thus, when one says $x : \mathbb{Z}$, where $\mathbb{Z}$ is the set of integers, one means that x can assume any value that is an integer number. Note that Int and String denote (a system dependent range of) integer numbers and finite character sequences, respectively. After this brief but necessary explanation, let us continue with our example. If one wants yet another stack structure, it can be defined in a similar way. Nevertheless, a far more elegant solution would be to define a parametric structure in which the type of its elements would be specified when a new instance of the structure is declared. Consider the following generic definition:

```
class Stack [γ] (n: Int) {
  private var S = new Array[γ](n)
  private var top = 0;
  def push(elem: γ) {
    top = top + 1
    S(top) = elem
  }
  def pop () : γ = {
    var oldtop = top
    top = top - 1
    S(oldtop)
  }
}
```

Here γ is a type variable, in other words, a variable whose values can be any type. This means that types are treated as values of the type of all types, usually called *Type*, and Stack[γ] is a generic type, that is, roughly a type pattern that can be used to specify particular types and, therefore, define particular objects of these particular types. In order to create a stack of integers, we need to declare an identifier to be an instance of Stack[Int]. In other words, by replacing γ with the name of a specific type (for example Int), we create a stack with elements of this particular type. Let us give some concrete examples:

```
var x = new Stack[Int] (3)
x.push(3)
x.push(4)
println(x.pop())
var y = new Stack[String] (4)
y.push("C++")
y.push("Java")
println(y.pop())
```

The really great benefit of polymorphism is that programmers do not have to spend time and energy defining similar things. On the other hand, finding the similarities between seemingly different structures is another problem that depends on the mathematical maturity of each person.

1.2 An overview of functional programming

A function can be viewed as a black box that maps elements drawn from a set (i.e., a collection of similar objects), which is called the *domain* of the function, into elements drawn from another set known as the *codomain* of the function. However, there is one restriction: no domain element can be mapped simultaneously to two or more different codomain elements. Let us consider a simple function that maps any integer number to an element of a set that consists of the words *minus, zero,* and *plus*. Obviously, the domain of the function is $\mathbb{Z}$ and its codomain is the three-word set {plus, zero, minus}. Function sign will map all negative integers to minus and all positive integers to plus. Finally, it will map 0 to zero. Verbal descriptions are not precise enough, so we need a more formal method to describe functions. One simple method is to write down a set of equations that specify which domain element is mapped to which codomain element. For example, the following equations can be considered to define function sign:

$$\vdots$$

$$\text{sign}(-3) = \text{minus}$$
$$\text{sign}(-2) = \text{minus}$$
$$\text{sign}(-1) = \text{minus}$$
$$\text{sign}(0) = \text{zero}$$
$$\text{sign}(1) = \text{plus}$$
$$\text{sign}(2) = \text{plus}$$
$$\text{sign}(3) = \text{plus}$$

$$\vdots$$

Another method to describe a function is to specify a single rule:

$$\text{sign}(x) = \begin{cases} \text{minus} & \text{if } x < 0 \\ \text{zero} & \text{if } x = 0 \\ \text{plus} & \text{if } x > 0. \end{cases}$$

The second definition can be easily coded into a Scala function:

```
def sign(x: Int) = if (x > 0)
                       "plus"
                   else if (x == 0)
```

```
                      "zero"
                    else
                      "minus"
```

Using the function is straightforward:

```
  println(sign(4))
  println(sign(-4))
```

Let us consider one more function. Assume that we want to define a function that computes the maximum of its two arguments. Clearly, if the first argument is greater than the second, then the first argument is the maximum. Otherwise, the second argument is the maximum. This function can be easily encoded as a Scala function as shown below:[2]

```
  def max(x: Int, y: Int) = if (x > y) x else y
```

Let us make our life a little bit more difficult and let us try to define a function that finds the maximum of three numbers. In order to solve this problem we need to check the various cases – if the first argument is greater than the second and the second is greater than the third, then the first argument is the greatest of all three, etc. Although this computes what we want, it does it in a very complicated way. A simpler approach is to compute the maximum of the second and the third argument and then the maximum of the first argument and the maximum of the second and the third argument, or in Scala

```
  def max3(x : Int, y : Int, z : Int) = max(x,max(y,z))
```

This is a form of function *composition*, that is, a process by means of which one can generate a new function from two or more other functions. In addition, *functional programming* can be defined as a programming discipline where programs are usually composite functions.[3] And this is the reason why functional programming

---

[2] This function is predefined in Scala, but we use it to demonstrate the notion of function composition.
[3] In a sense, this is similar to the *divide and conquer* programming methodology, that is, the decomposition of a particular problem to two or more simpler problems and the subsequent decomposition of these problems until we have problems that are simple enough to be solved directly. Then the composition of these solutions gives a solution to the original problem.

is particularly elegant. In order to ensure that procedure functions can be composed as their mathematical counterparts, one must avoid the so-called *side effects*. To understand what we mean by side effects, consider the following code:

```
var flag = true // a switch: can be either true or false
def f(n : Int) = {
  var k = 0 // local variable
  if (flag) k=n else k=2*n
  flag = ! flag // destructive assignment!
  k  // what the function yields
}
println(f(1) + f(2))
println(f(2) + f(1))
```

This code will print the numbers 5 and 4 on the computer screen. If f was a pure function, then the two commands would print exactly the same. The problem with this code is the *destructive assignment*, that is, a command that modifies the value of a variable. Programming languages that allow the use of such assignments are called *referentially opaque*. On the other hand, languages that do not permit the use of destructive assignments are called *referentially transparent*. In general, languages that are referentially transparent are purely functional languages like Haskell [38] and Erlang [5]. Obviously, one can keep side effects out of the programs in a referentially opaque language by deliberately avoiding the use of destructive assignments. Nevertheless, functional programming languages provide a number of tools (for example, pattern matching, algebraic types, that is, the disjoint union of several types) that greatly facilitate programming in these languages. But these are not the fundamental differences between an *imperative* language (i.e., nonfunctional for our purposes) and a functional programming language. The fundamental difference lies in the way solutions to problems are expressed. Typically, an imperative program is a sequence of "imperatives which describe *how* the computer must solve a problem in terms of state changes (updates to assignable variables)" while "a functional program describes *what* is to be computed, that is the program is just an expression, defined in terms of the pre-defined and user-defined functions, the value of which constitues the result of the program" [21].

1.3 Extendable languages

In October 1998, at the ACM Conference on Object-Oriented Programming, Systems, Languages, and Applications, Guy L. Steele Jr. advocated that "[A] language design can no longer be a thing. It must be a pattern – a pattern for growth – a pattern for growing the pattern for defining the patterns that programmers can use for their real work and their main goal" [69]. According to Steele there are two kinds of *growth* in a language – one should be able to change either the vocabulary or the rules that say what a sequence of words means (i.e., the *semantics* of a sequence of words). The essence of these two kinds of growth is that one should be able either to define new keywords or to change the meaning of operators and/or keywords. Similarly, there two ways by which a language can grow – either this can be done by a person, or a small group of persons (for example, a committee), or by a whole community. In the second case, members of the user community can actively participate in the extention of a language. Nevertheless, the development cannot be anarchical. For this reason a person or a small group of persons act as project coordinators. But how can a language be designed to be extendable?

Steele argues that the best way to make a language extendable is to include generic types, operator redefinition, and user-defined types of light weight, which could be used to define numeric and related types. In Section 1.1 we have discussed generic types, but we have said nothing about operator overloading and light weight user-defined types.

Instead of providing different predefined types for different kinds of numbers (for example, complex numbers, fractions, etc.), it is far better to provide an infrastructure by means of which one can easily implement such types. Many engineers need to be able to manipulate complex numbers easily, thus, the availability of a numeric type providing the functionality of complex numbers is a key factor in their choice of programming language. Defining a light weight user-defined type where ordinary arithmetic operators are redefined while their original meaning is not lost solves this problem, see Figure 1.1. Here a complex number is simulated by a class with two fields that can assume as values real numbers of double precision. Also, we (re)define the meaning of the operators +, −, *, and /. This way, we can write things like the following:

```
var a = new Complex (1.0, 3.0)
var b = new Complex (4.5, -2.5)
println ("a + b = " + (a + b) )
```

The last command will print "a + b = 5.5+0.5i" on the computer screen. Note also that in the last command the first + is used to concatenate character sequences and the second to add complex variables. And this is the reason we need the extra parentheses, or else we will get the following "erroneous" output

```
a + b = 1.0+3.0i4.5-2.5i
```

```
class Complex(val re: Double, val im: Double) {
  def + (x: Complex) =
    new Complex(re + x.re, im + x.im)
  // def + (x: Double) =
  //   new Complex(re + x, im)
  def - (x: Complex) =
    new Complex(re - x.re, im - x.im)
  def unary_- = new Complex(-Re, -Im)
  def * (x: Complex) =
    new Complex(re * x.re - im * x.im,
                re * x.im + im * x.re)
  def / (y: Complex) = {
    val denom = y.re * y.re + y.im * y.im
    new Complex((re * y.re + im * y.im) / denom,
                (im * y.re - re * y.im) / denom)
  }
  def ^ (exponent: Int): Complex =
    if(exponent == 0) Complex(1)(0)
    else if(exponent == 1) this
    else this * (this^(exponent-1))
  def toPolar = (radius, theta)
  private def radius = scala.Math.sqrt(Re*Re + Im*Im)
  private def theta = scala.Math.atan2(Re, Im)
  override def toString =
    if ( re == 0 && im == 0) "0"
    else if ( im == 0 ) re.toString
    else if ( re == 0 ) im + "i"
    else re + (if (im < 0) "" else "+") + im + "i"
}
object Complex{
  def apply(re: Double)(im: Double) = new Complex(re, im)
}
def zeroReal = Complex (0.0)
object i extends Complex(0.0, 1.0)
implicit def DoubleToComplex(d: Double) = Complex(d)(0.0)
```

Figure 1.1 A Scala light weight user-defined type implementing complex numbers.

In a nutshell, operator overloading is a facility that allows users to provide additional functionality for any existing operator. Going one step further, it is possible to define new literals as operators.

In Scala the symbols // start a comment that extends to the end of the current source line. Thus, the second definition of +, that is, the one that is commented out, should be useful when adding a variable that holds a complex number with a number literal (e.g., a+3). However, this approach cannot be used to handle the opposite case, that is, it cannot perform additions like 3+a. Fortunately, there are other better ways to handle problems like this. For example, it is possible to convert number literals implicitly to objects of the proper type by defining functions that do this conversion:

```
implicit def doubleToComplex(x: Double) : Complex   =
                                    new Complex(x, 0.0)
implicit def intToComplex (x: Int) : Complex =
                                    new Complex(x, 0.0)
```

Now the following commands

```
val i = new Complex(0,1)
var x = i+9.0; var y = -8+i;
println("x = " + x + " y = " + y)
```

will print the following on our computer screen:

$$x = 9.0+1.0i \ y = -8.0+1.0i$$

Here the keyword `val` signals that the value of the variable declared cannot be changed. On the other hand, variables declared with the `var` keyword are real variables, that is, they can change their value in the course of time.

Class `Complex` shows how easily one can define other numerical types. For example, a reader with some programming experience in any programming language should have no difficulty defining a light weight user-defined data type for quaternions (i.e., a noncommutative extension of complex numbers) and/or octonions (i.e., a nonassociative extension of the quaternions).

Although Steele would be really happy with a language that has the capabilities presented so far, it would be a great idea to be able to define new control structures. For example, although one can use a `while` to execute a block of code repeatedly, it would be nice to have a repetition construct, which is similar to the `while` construct but not the same. The `while` construct checks the truth of an expression and if it is true it executes a block of code, otherwise it aborts. Then it checks again the truth of the same expression and if it is again true it executes again the block of code, and so on, until the expression becomes false. Assume now that we want to construct a loop that should execute a piece of code, then examine a condition and if the negation of the condition is true, then it should execute a second block of code and repeat the same procedure, or else it should abort. This iteration construct, which was proposed by Dahl in [42], might have the following general form:

```
loop
    commands
until cond
    commands
repeat
```

In Scala it is not difficult to define a function that implements the functionality of this construct without adding syntactic sugar to the language. The trick is to employ *call-by-name* in the definition of a procedure:

```
def loop(pre: => Unit)(cond: => Boolean)
        (post: => Unit): Unit = {
  pre
  if (!cond) {
    post
    loop(pre)(cond)(post)
  }
  else
    ()
}
```

What is really surprising about this function is that when it is invoked, both `pre` and `post` can be pieces of real code! Here is a simple usage example of this function:

```
var x=6; var y=0
loop {
  x=x-1
  y=y+1
} (x == 0 ) { //cond must be on the same line
  println(x)  //as the closing curly bracket
  println(y)
}
```

When this code is executed it will print on the computer screen the numbers 5, 1, 4, 2, 3, 3, 2, 4, 1, and 5. Amazing, isn't it? But if one can define new control structures, would it not be nice to be able to change the semantics of a sequence of words? We do not believe this is a really good idea. For example, the following piece of code in the PL/I programming language shows exactly why changing the meaning of words is not a very good idea:

```
DO DO = 1 TO 10;
  CALL PRINT(DO);
END;
```

1.4 Scala: beyond the Java programming language

Admitedly, the Java programming language is a very popular programming language. The language owes its popularity to a number of reasons that include the following.

- Java is an object-oriented language.
- Java's compiler produces code for the Java Virtual Machine (JVM),[4] which has been ported to many and different computer architectures and platforms and is freely available, thus making programs really portable.
- Java has a huge application programming interface (API) that provides support from computer-telephony integrated call control to advanced image handling and mp3 playing.

The success of the Java programming language and its underlying technology had a profound effect on the development of programming languages. In particular, two basic design philosophies emerged. The first design philosophy is based on the idea of designing and implementing a new virtual machine similar to the JVM. C# [31] and the associated .NET framework (i.e., its virtual machine) are two examples. The second design philosophy is much cleverer – there is no need to re-invent the wheel, just use it! Thus, a host of programming languages were implemented atop the JVM, making the languages immediately available to a number of different computer platforms. In addition, language designers could opt to provide access directly to language users to the Java API, thus making these languages particularly powerful. This philosophy has been adopted by a number of programming languages that include Clojure,[5] which was developed by Rich Hickey, Groovy [8], which was based on ideas put forth by James Strachan, JRuby, a variant of Ruby that runs atop the JVM (Ruby was designed by Yukihiro "matz" Matsumoto), and Scala, which was designed by Martin Odersky.

In addition to the ideas presented so far, all these languages have in common some excellent design principles. For example, all values are objects and one can easily add methods to existing types, thus extending the functionality of these "values." Nevertheless, Scala is the only language that integrates these and a number of other important features in such a seamless way. Thus, Scala is the best example of what Stuart Halloway calls a "Java.next" language, in his blog. One may say that Scala is the Java.next, since it includes all features of the Java programming language, while it includes many features (for example, closures, traits, and pattern matching) that may find their way into future releases of Java. Since the designer of Scala has written two versions of the official Java compiler, Scala's compiler produces output that is as fast and reliable as the output produced by the official Java compiler. However,

---

[4] A virtual machine is a computer program that simulates a computer architecture and is able to run machine code for this particular computer architecture.
[5] See http://clojure.org/.

Scala can easily be used as a scripting language since Scala's distribution includes a compiler as well as an interpreter.

In Scala one can define classes or traits, that is, classes that cannot be instantiated but only inherited, that can be composed via mixins. Scala does not include the following *useless* Java features: static members, primitive types (everything is an object), break and continue commmands, special treatment of interfaces, wildcards, raw types, and enums. On the other hand, Scala has a *lightweight syntax*, that is, a simplified form of its basic syntax that comes from a number of features: semicolon inference, type inference, lightweight classes, extensible APIs, and closures, that is, special functions, as control abstractions. As a result, Scala programs tend to be shorter than their Java counterparts.

The *actor* model is a sort of object-oriented abstraction of concurrency [3]. An actor is an agent that has a mail address and, consequently, a mailbox and a behavior. Actors communicate by message passing and carry out their actions concurrently. Erlang was the first widely used programming language that provided an actor libary. Scala also provides an actor libary. However, the library has been implemented in such a way that users think it is part of the original syntax of the language. This is the best example of Scala's ability to grow as a language.

XML content can be used directly in Scala programs. For example, one can assign an XML tree to a variable as follows:

```
var person =
  <person>
    <name>
      <first_name>Alan</first_name>
      <last_name>Turing</last_name>
    </name>
    <profession>Computer Scientist</profession>
    <profession>Mathematician</profession>
    <profession>Cryptographer</profession>
  </person>
```

These and a number of other features have made Scala a popular programming language that is currently used by many enterprises. Our sincere hope is that this brief overview of the key features of Scala has whetted your appetite for more Scala!

2

Core features

Scala is a programming language designed in such a way that programs tend to be concise. Thus, it does not include many predefined data types and flow control constructs. Instead, it provides a small number of important predefined data types (for example, integers, float numbers, etc.) and flow control constructs (for example, while loops etc.), while it also provides tools that allow users to structure their programs in a way to suit their needs.

2.1 "Hello World!" in Scala

The standard Scala distribution includes an interpreter as well as a compiler. The compiler can be used to generate .class files, that is, binary files that can be executed by the JVM, while the interpreter can be used to execute source code contained in a text file or it can be used to work interactively with Scala. The program that follows is the customary "Hello World!" program in Scala, that is, a program that just prints the message "Hello World!" on the computer screen:

```scala
object HelloWorld {
  def main(args: Array[String]) {
    println("Hello, world!")
  }
}
```

The identifier args refers to the command line arguments (for an explanation see Section 2.9). Also, main is a predefined method (see Section 2.3). Let us assume this code is stored in a file named hello.scala. Note that, Java programs, Scala programs can be stored in files whose names are different from the name of the class/object that contains function main. The commands that follow show what should be done to compile and then to execute the resulting .class file:

```
$ scalac hello.scala
$ scala -classpath . HelloWorld
Hello, world!
$
```

Here the dollar sign represents the command line prompt. Also, -classpath is used to specify the location of one or more .class files. The period denotes the current working directory. Usually, people prefer to use the -cp switch, which has exactly the same functionality (see also the discussion in section 6.1). If one wants to use the interpreter and is working on a Unix system or a Unix-like system such as OpenSolaris or Linux, respectively, one has to type in either the following code

```
#!/bin/bash
exec scala "$0" "$@"
!#
println("Hello World!")
```

or the following code

```
#!/bin/bash
exec scala "$0" "$@"
!#
object HelloWorld {
  def main(args: Array[String]) {
    println("Hello, world! " + args.toList)
  }
}
HelloWorld.main(args)
```

in a text file, say hello. Then one has to change the attributes of this file and make it executable in order to be able to execute it:

```
$ chmod +x hello
```

The program can be executed by entering the following command:

```
$ hello
```

The two versions presented do not produce exactly the same output. For example, the second version will print the following message

```
Hello, world! List()
```

while the first will print just the message.

On Windows systems, users can get equivalent results by creating a text file, say hello.bat, which will contain the following lines:

```
::#!
@echo off
call scala %0 %*
goto :eof
::!#
rem *
rem Scala code follows
rem *
println("Hello World!")
```

This program can be executed from a CMD shell by entering a command like the following one:

```
C:\My Programs>hello.bat
```

Starting the Scala interpreter is easy: just type scala in your command prompt. The next few lines show a typical session with the Scala interpreter.

```
$ scala
Welcome to Scala version 2.7.7.final
(Java HotSpot(TM) Server 64-Bit VM, Java 1.6.0_18).
Type in expressions to have them evaluated.
Type :help for more information.

scala> 4+5
res0: Int = 9

scala> ("abcd").length
res1: Int = 4

scala> var x=4
x: Int = 4

scala> :quit
$
```

2.2 Scala's basic types

A typical Scala program describes the interaction between objects, which interchange messages. For example, things like numbers, character sequences, and character strings or just strings, are objects that can interact with other objects

Table 2.1 *Basic types supported by the Scala programming language*

Data type	Range of values
Byte	integers in the range from -128 to 127
Short	integers in the range from -32768 to 32767
Int	integers in the range from -2147483648 to 2147483647
Long	integers in the range from -9223372036854775808 to 9223372036854775807
Float	the largest positive finite float is 3.4028235×10^{38} and the smallest positive finite nonzero float is 1.40×10^{-45}
Double	the largest positive finite double is $1.7976931348623157 \times 10^{308}$ and the smallest positive finite nonzero double is 4.9×10^{-324}
Char	Unicode characters with code points in the range from U+0000 to U+FFFF
String	a (finite) sequence of Chars
Boolean	either the literal true or the literal false
Unit	corresponds to no value
Null	null or empty reference
Nothing	the subtype of every other type; includes no values
Any	the supertype of any type; any object is of type Any
AnyRef	the supertype of any reference type (i.e., nonvalue Scala classes and user-defined) classes

of the same or similar type. Objects with no internal *structure*, that is with no components, are said to be of a basic type. Table 2.1 presents the basic types supported by Scala. In what follows the Scala interpreter is used to demonstrate the properties of the basic types.

When declaring a variable or a constant, we write either the keyword var or the keyword val, the name of a variable or a constant, an equals sign (i.e., the symbol =), and then the value the variable or the constant will assume. Optionally, we can specify the type of a variable or a constant by writing, after its name, a colon (:) and then its type:

```
scala> val w : Byte = 32
w: Byte = 32
```

If the value does not agree with the type, a type error occurs:

```
val z : Byte = 567
<console>:4: error: type mismatch;
 found : Int(567)
 required: Byte
       val z : Byte = 567
                      ^
```

By default Scala assumes that an integer literal, that is, a sequence of digits possibly prefixed by a plus or minus sign, is of type Int:

```
scala> var x=3
x: Int = 3
```

An integer literal that is suffixed by an L or an l is assumed to be of type Long:

```
scala> var x=3l
x: Long = 3
```

Mixing an Int with a Long results in a Long:

```
scala> var y=x+1
y: Long = 5
```

In general, numbers can be written as decimal, octal or hexadecimal numerals. Octal numerals must be prefixed by the digit zero:

```
scala> 0755
res0: Int = 493
```

Hexadecimal numbers must be prefixed by 0x or 0X, that is, the digit zero and either the letter x or the letter X:

```
scala> 0x2009
res1: Int = 8201
```

Obviously, if one suffixes an octal or a hexadecimal numeral with an L or an l, then it is assumed to be of type Long:

```
scala> 0755l
res2: Long = 493
```

```
scala> 0x2009L
res3: Long = 8201
```

Under certain circumstances, every integer number is automatically transformed to its floating point equivalent:

```
scala> var x :Float = 1
x: Float = 1.0
```

A floating point number consists of an integral part and an optional decimal point (represented by a period character) that may be followed by an optional fractional part, an optional exponent and an optional type suffix. The exponent starts with either the letter E or the letter e and is followed by a signed integer, that is, an integer that may be prefixed by a plus or minus sign. The exponent designates that the number is multiplied by ten raised to the power specified by the number that comes after the letters e or E. The type suffix can be either the letters f or F or the letters d or D. The letters f and F denote a single precision floating point number, while the letters d and D are used to specify a double precision floating point number:

```
scala> 2.01
res4: Double = 2.01

scala> 14.4E100
res4: Double = 14.4E100

scala> 12e100f
<console>:1: error: floating point number too large
       12e100f
       ^

scala> 0.00000000000000000000029
res5: Double = 2.9E-22
```

A character corresponds to a number from 0 to 65535 and it must be enclosed in single quotation marks:

```
scala> var w = 'α'
w: Char = α
```

As it stands, one cannot assign to a character variable a single quotation mark:

```
scala> var v = '''
<console>:1: error: empty character literal
       var v = '''
       ^

<console>:1: error: unterminated character literal
       var v = '''
       ^
```

We can solve this problem by using an *escape sequence*, that is, a sequence of easily accessible characters that represent other characters. An escape sequence starts with a backslash (\) and it can be followed by (a) up to three octal digits representing characters with code points from 0 to 255 (0377 in octal), (b) a designated letter or character, or (c) the letter u followed by four hexadecimal digits representing

Table 2.2 *Escape sequences that Scala recognizes*

Escape sequence	Meaning
\b	backspace
\t	horizontal tab
\n	linefeed (new line)
\f	form feed
\r	carriage return
\"	double quote
\'	single quote
\\	backslash
ooo	o is an octal digit
uhhhh	h is a hexadecimal digit

Unicode characters having the corresponding code point (see Table 2.2):

```
scala> println('\'')
'
```

```
scala> println('\124')
T
```

```
scala> println('\u03ae')
ή
```

Note that `println` prints its arguments on the computer screen.

A `String` is a sequence of `Char`s that is enclosed in double quotes:

```
scala> "Scala"
res6: java.lang.String = Scala
```

For some reason the type of a string is not `String`, but `java.lang.String`, which is a Java type. In fact, each basic Scala type corresponds to an instance of a class of package `java.lang`, which makes implementation of the language easier. This description is actually an oversimplification of the actual situation, nonetheless, for the time being the newcomer should not care about what is really going on under the hood.

Multiline strings can be typed in using the \n escape sequence:

```
scala> println("This is a\nmultiline\nstring!")
This is a
multiline
string!
```

However, this is not convenient and so Scala provides a better way to type in multiline strings – one starts a string with three consecutive double quotes, then the string follows with embedded new lines and the string closes with three consecutive double quotes. For example, when executing the following program

```
println("""This is a
          multiline
          string""")
```

one gets the following output on the computer screen:

```
This is a
          multiline
          string
```

Not quite what we expected, right? To remedy this problem, programmers should type a "|" (vertical line) after the three consecutive double quotes and at the beginning of each line and append the string with .stripMargin:

```
println("""|This is a
           |multiline
           |string""".stripMargin)
```

This program will produce the expected result, try it! Note that stripMargin is a method that any object of type String has (this method strips whatever comes before the "|" character), but we will say more about objects and methods in the next section.

The literals true and false denote truth and untruth, respectively. These literals are the only values of type Boolean:

```
scala> val T = true
T: Boolean = true

scala> val F = false
F: Boolean = false
```

Type Unit has only one value, which is designated by two parentheses:

```
scala> var x = ()
x: Unit = ()

scala> print(x)
()
```

When a function does not return a result (for example, when it merely assigns values to variables), then it yields a value of type Unit.

Exercise 2.1 Which of the following declarations/definitions are illegal and why?

```
1. val x1 : Int = 3.14        2. var x2 : Short = 33000
3. var x3 : Byte = -12        4. var x4 : Char = "A"
5. var x5 : String = 'A'      6. var x6 : String = "Mike's Place"
7. var x7 : Boolean = 1>7     8. var x8 : Unit = println("OK")
```

Scala demands that each variable/constant gets a value when it is declared/defined. However, if one does not want to assign a particular value, then one can use the special value _, which forces Scala to assign some default value to the variable/constant being declared/defined. For numbers the default value is 0 or 0.0 depending on the type of number; for characters the default value is character NULL; and for all other objects it is the literal null. This value is of type Null and designates that an object of some nonbasic type is empty.

2.3 Classes and objects

A class is an archetypal software module that is used to create objects, that is, concrete instances of a class. Unfortunately, in Scala software modules are called objects which is quite confusing, especially for newcomers. In order to avoid confusion, when we have to refer to both software modules and objects, we will call the former class instances and the latter either objects or modules. A class definition is a detailed description of the elements of a new type and the operations these elements may perform. A class definition consists of *field* declarations and *method* definitions. Fields are used to store the state of an object and methods may provide access to fields, alter the state of an object, etc. Let us start with a simple example borrowed from [1]. Class cell describes a storage-cell with one field that is initialized to zero:

```
class cell {
    var contents : Int = 0;
    def get() = contents
    def set(n: Int) = {
        contents = n
    }
}
```

As is evident, the definition of a class begins with the keyword class, which is followed by the name of the class. The whole class definition is enclosed in curly brackets. This class definition includes the definition of one field, namely contents, and the definition of two methods, namely get and set. Although there is no rule about the order in which methods and fields must be defined, it is customary to write first the field definitions and then the methods definitions. In general, a field can be viewed as a variable and so it is declared in exactly the same way. Methods are defined in a similar way. As with variables, we use the keyword `def` to designate a method definition. This keyword is followed by the name of the method being defined. If the method takes arguments, we need to specify the name of each parameter and its type. These definitions are separated by commas. The whole parameter list is enclosed in parentheses. Even if a method takes no arguments but returns a value, then one should type the parentheses to designate exactly this. If a method returns a meaningful value, then one may specify its return type. As noted in the previous section, methods that do not yield a value, are assumed to return a value of type `Unit`. The code that will be executed each time the method is invoked is surrounded by braces, unless it is a simple expression. In the first case one can omit the equals sign. The return value of a method can be specified either implictly by letting it be the last expression of the method, or explicitly by using one or more `return` commands. In this case, it is mandatory to specify the return type of the method. For example, here is how method `get` from the previous example should be written:

```
def get() : Int = return contents
```

If the return type is omitted, then Scala infers the return type of the method by examining the body of the method.

Exercise 2.2 Now that you have a basic understanding of class definitions, write down the definition of a class `date`. The class should have three fields, namely `day`, `month`, and `year`, and two methods, namely `set` and `output` with obvious meaning. The initial value of each field should be zero. (Hint. If the expression $n + \sigma$, where n is a variable and σ a string, appears as argument of `println`, it outputs a string consisting of the value of n and σ side by side.)

Once a class is defined one should be able to construct objects of this class. New objects (or class instances) are constructed in the following generic way

```
var object-name = new class_name()
```

The expression `new` is used to construct an instance of a class. Note that in this case the parentheses are optional. For example, here is how one can construct a new object of class `cell`:

```
var c = new cell
```

Interestingly, we can create a new object and at the same time we can give values to fields. For example, the code that follows

```
var w = new cell { contents = 7 }
```

creates a new object and gives a specific value to a field. Furthermore, the following idiom

```
var w = new { contents = 7 }
```

creates an instance of (a subclass of) class `AnyRef`. Accessing individual methods and fields is easy: we write the object's name, a period, and then the name of the method or field. If a method takes arguments, we should specify them as well:

```
c.set(4)
println(c.get)
c.contents = 5
println(c.get)
println(w.get)
```

The last command will print the number 7.

Exercise 2.3 This example violates the principle of encapsulation, why?

To ensure that the value of a field cannot be directly modified or accessed, we need to declare it as `private`. For example, if the definition of field `contents` is modified as follows

```
private var contents : Int = 0
```

then the command that follows

```
println(c.contents)
```

will trigger Scala to print the error message:

variable contents cannot be accessed in cell.

Note that even methods can be declared as `private`, with the expected semantics.
If you did Exercise 2.2 you may have noticed that it is quite unnatural first to define an object and then to set the values of its fields. It is far more natural to set the value of its fields the very moment the object is *created*. Indeed, Scala offers this capability and the example that follows shows how one should define class `date`:

```
class date (var day:Int, var month:Int, var year:Int){
  def set(dd:Int, mm:Int, yy:Int) = {
    day = dd; month = mm; year = yy;
  }
  def output() = println(day+"/"+month+"/"+year)
}
```

Now one can define a new object as follows:

```
var today = new date(24,9,2008)
```

If we skip the keyword var, the fields are assumed to have been declared as constants. Naturally, one can use the keyword val for clarity.

Exercise 2.4 Modify the definition of class cell so that users are able to initialize its only field when creating a new object.

Although it is really important to be able to set the value of all fields during initialization, still it is equally important to be able to have some fields assume a default value. In Scala this can be achieved by specifying one or more definitions of a special function called this. Actually, this is what is commonly called in most object-oriented languages a *constructor*, that is, a function that creates new instances of a class. In Scala the default or primary constructor corresponds to the commands, definitions, and declarations that are specified in the body of the class. The following code shows how one could rewrite the definition of class cell:

```
class cell (private var contents : Int){
  def this()=this(0)
    . . . . . . . . . .
}
```

Of course, if there is more than one field, we can define alternative constructors as shown below:

```
def this (first: Int, third: Int) = this(first,10,third)
def this (third: Int) = this(5,10,third)
```

Exercise 2.5 Rewrite class date so that when an object is created without specifying initial values for its fields, it is assumed that they correspond to Christmas of 2009.

In certain cases it might be useful to have one or more methods and/or fields that are shared by all class instances. This means that if the value of a field is changed by one object, then the change will affect all objects. Such fields and methods are called *static*. Scala supports static fields and methods but there is no special field modifier to declare a field or a method as static. Instead one has to declare a *companion object*, that is, one has to define a structure that is similar to a class but whose declaration is introduced with object instead of class and which has the name of the class. This entity cannot be initialized, but its methods and fields are immediately available to the class that has the same name. Let us see a simple example that will make these ideas clear.

Assume we want to define a class of yellow fruits. Typically, one could come up with a definition like the following one:

```
class YellowFruit {
  var color = "yellow"
  def getColor = color
  def setColor (newColor : String) {
    color = newColor
  }
}
```

Since all fruits described by such a class are yellow, it makes no sense to specify the color of the fruit separately for each different fruit. This is exactly the case where a static field is an ideal solution. The definition that follows is a modified version of the previous class accompanied by a companion object where the static field is defined:

```
class YellowFruit {
  def getColor = YellowFruit.color
  def setColor (newColor : String) {
    YellowFruit.color = newColor
  }
}


object YellowFruit {
  var color = "yellow"
}
```

As in the previous case, for all objects that are instances of this class, method getColor will print yellow. Indeed, the following commands

```
var lemon = new YellowFruit
println("lemon color = "+lemon.getColor)
var banana = new YellowFruit
println("banan color = "+banana.getColor)
```

will print the following messages on the computer screen:

```
lemon color = yellow
banana color = yellow
```

Now, suppose that for some reason we alter the color of a lemon:

```
lemon.setColor("green")
```

This command will change the color of all objects old and new. Thus, the commands that follow

```
var quince = new YellowFruit
println("quince color = "+quince.getColor)
println("lemon color = "+lemon.getColor)
println("banan color = "+banana.getColor)
```

will print the following messages on our computer screen:

```
quince color = green
lemon color = green
banana color = green
```

The object that was presented in Section 2.1 has nothing to do with the companion object that has been described here. The former is a software module that is used to create a .class file that holds the body of a program. Any software module with a main method is the equivalent of a main program found in conventional programming languages.

2.4 Some basic operators

Previously, it has been stated that in Scala *everything is an object* and, thus, an operation between two objects is viewed as an invocation of a method of the first operand that sends a message to the second operand. In particular, the expression $\alpha \otimes \beta$ is actually a sugared form of the expression $(\alpha). \otimes (\beta)$. Obviously, different classes may include operator-methods with identical names (for example, think of the + method). This is a technique that is known as *operator overloading* (see Section 3.6 and in particular Section 3.6.2 for more details). For example, the operations $3 + 4$, $2 + 5.2$, and $1.2 + 3.3$ involve three different methods that have the same name. The basic arithmetic operators are: + (addition), − (subtraction), * (multiplication), / (division), and % (remainder). When one of the operands is a floating point number and the other a whole number, the result is always a floating point number. In other words, if we asssume that types are sets, then the following type hierarchy is predefined:

$$\text{Byte} \subset \text{Short} \subset \text{Int} \subset \text{Long} \subset \text{Float} \subset \text{Double}.$$

This implies that if $x : X$ and $y : Y$ and $X \subset Y$, then $x \otimes y : Y$. Here are some simple examples:

```
scala> 11 % 2
res7: Int = 1
```

```
scala> 5.0 % 2.0
res8: Double = 1.0

scala> 5+2.0
res9: Double = 7.0

scala> x=4*(3+4)
x: Int = 28
```

The last example is a typical example of an assignment command, that is, a command that *updates* the value of a variable. Note also that one can use parentheses for clarity or to override the default way operations are performed. But we will come back to this matter at the end of this section. An object of type Char is actually a number. Therefore, it does make sense to multiply or add characters. For example, the operation 'b'*'a' is valid and it is equal to 9506.

In the previous examples, the names of variables and constants consisted only of Latin latters. But Scala does not impose any artificial restriction and, thus, an *identifier*, that is, the name of class, an object, a variable, etc., can consist of any Unicode character that is used as a letter in some language as the following examples show:

```
scala> var τιμή = 3
τιμή: Int = 3

scala> var ЦЕННОСТЬ = 7
ЦЕННОСТЬ: Int = 7

scala> println (τιμή+ЦЕННОСТЬ)
10
```

In general, an identifier starts with a letter and can be followed by letters, digits, the symbol _ or any Unicode character in the range 0020–007F except square brackets, parentheses, and periods.

Quite frequently, people need to assign a new value to a variable that depends on the previous value stored in the variable. If one wants to add/subtract a number or to multiply/divide by a number, then it is far better to use the assignment operators: +=, -=, *=, /=, and %=. In general, the expression $v \oplus = n$ is shorthand for $v = v \oplus n$, where $\oplus$ is any of the five arithmetic operators described above.

The relational operators ==, !=, <, >, <=, and >= can be used to compare objects. In particular, the operators == and != can be used to check whether two objects are equal or not:

```
scala> ("wa"+"ter")=="water"
res10: Boolean = true

scala> true != false
res11: Boolean = true

scala> 'A' != 'A'
res12: Boolean = true
```

Exercise 2.6 Why do you think the last comparison does not evaluate to false?

If objects are comparable, then one can use the binary operators <, >, <=, and >= to see whether the left operand is less, greater, less than or equal to, or greater than or equal to the right operand. For `Strings` Scala uses the *usual* lexicographic order and for numbers the usual number order:

```
scala> "Ariel" > "Mimas"
res13: Boolean = false

scala> "Απόστολος" < "Χρήστος"
res14: Boolean = true

scala> 4 > 1
res15: Boolean = true
```

Exercise 2.7 What is the result of the following comparisons:

$$\text{"ΑΠΟΣΤΟΛΟΣ"} < \text{"ΑΠΟCΤΟΛΟC"} \qquad \text{"ΧΡΗΣΤΟΣ"} > \text{"CHRISTOS"}$$
$$\text{true} > \text{false} \qquad\qquad 5 == (6-1)$$

The logical operators &&, | |, and ! can be used to perform conjunction, disjunction and negation of `Boolean` variables and/or values. The binary operators && and | | are evaluated from left to right and evalution stops as soon as the result is known. In particular, the operation a && b is `false` if a is `false` and the expression a | | b is `true` if a is `true`. The following examples demonstrate exactly this:

```
scala> (1>0) || (1/0 >2)
res16: Boolean = true

scala> (0 == 1) && (0/0 == 7)
res17: Boolean = false

scala> (0 != 1) && (0/0 == 7)
java.lang.ArithmeticException: / by zero
```

Table 2.3 *Operator precedence and associativity*

Operator precedence of operator whose name starts with	Associativity of operators whose name ends with the corresponding characters
(all other special characters)	left to right
* / %	left to right
+ -	left to right
:	right to left
= !	left to right
< >	left to right
&	left to right
^	left to right
|	left to right
(all letters)	left to right

Note that the expressions 1/0 and 0/0 do not compute and thus force Scala to print a runtime error (see the next section for more details). Also, the two assignment operators &&= and ||= have the expected meaning.

There are four bitwise operators: ~ (bitwise negation), & (bitwise conjunction), ^ (bitwise exclusive disjunction), and | (bitwise disjunction). Given a whole number a, ~a=(-a)-1. Given two whole numbers a and b, then a & b, a ^b, and a | b perform the corresponding operation on each pair of the corresponding bit representations of equal length of a and b. In addition, there are three shift operators: << (bitwise left shift), >> (bitwise right shift), >>> (logical right shift). Assume the n and s are two whole numbers, then, $n << s = n \cdot 2^s$, $n >> s = \lfloor n/2^s \rfloor$ (where $\lfloor x \rfloor$ is the largest integer which does not exceed x), $n >>> s = n >> s$ if $n > 0$ and $n >>> s = (n >> s) + (2 << \sim s)$. There are also six assignment operators: &=, ^=, |=, <<=, >>=, and >>>=.

Roughly, operator precedence is the reason why the expression 5 + 3 * 2 is evaluated as 5 + (3 * 2), giving 11, and not as (5 + 3) * 2, giving 16. Also, operator associativity is the reason why the expression 2 + 3 + 4 is evaluated as (2 + 3) + 4. Table 2.3 describes the operator precedence and associativity of the operators supported by Scala.

2.5 Basic built-in control structures

Programming languages provide control structures and data structuring facilities. The former provide the means to express algorithms, and the latter provide ways to organize information. In Section 1.3 it was explained why Scala is an extendable language. In addition, it was explained that one can define new control structures, which clearly implies that Scala provides some *built-in* control structures. In this section, we are going to describe some basic built-in control structures.

A conditional control structure allows one to control the flow of the code that is executed based on different conditions in the program, input taken from the user, etc. On the other hand, a conditional expression is an expression one can use to select between values based on a condition. Scala provides a conditional control structure that can also be used as a conditional expression. The following example shows the *dual* nature of the `if` structure:

```scala
scala> var x = 5
x: Int = 5

scala> if (x > 0) println("positive") else println("negative")
positive

scala> println(if (x>0) "positive" else "negative")
positive
```

The general forms of the `if` structure are

```
if   (condition)              if   (condition)
       then-part                     then-expression
   else                          else
       optional-else-part            optional-else-expression
```

In both cases, the optional part appears only if the `else` keyword is present. In addition, in either part if one wants to execute more than one command, these commands must be enclosed in curly brackets. Also, note that if one wants to have more than one command in one line, these commands must be terminated by a semicolon (`;`). However, note that the last "command" of each clause of a conditional expression must be of the same type and they should yield a value not of type `Unit`. Clearly, if they return a value of type `Unit`, it is better to transform the conditional expression to a conditional command. Here is a relatively simple example that demonstrates these points:

```scala
var x = 6
var y = if (x >=6 ) {
            x += 1
            3
        }
        else {
            x += 2; 4
        }
println("x= "+x+" y= "+y)
```

Table 2.4 *Methods for reading values from the terminal provided by object* `Console`

Method	Explanation
readBoolean	Read a boolean value from the terminal
readByte	Read a byte value from the terminal
readChar	Read a char value from the terminal
readDouble	Read a double value from the terminal
readFloat	Read a float value from the terminal
readInt	Read an int value from the terminal
readLine	Read a full line from the terminal; returns null if the end of the input stream has been reached
readLong	Read a long value from the terminal
readShort	Read a short value from the terminal

Exercise 2.8 Can you say what the last command will print?

Suppose that we want to create a simple program that interactively inputs two numbers and prints their maximum. Clearly, finding the maximum of two numbers is easy – just compare the two numbers and print the largest. Nevertheless, the real problem is that we said nothing about interactive input. Scala provides a number of methods that can be used to input numbers, strings, etc. interactively. The most useful input methods are described in Table 2.4. Let us return to the original problem. Now it is very simple to write the program that computes the maximum of two numbers:

```
print("enter the first number...\n? ")
var x = readInt()
print("enter the second number...\n? ")
var y = readInt()
println("The maximum is ")
if (x >= y)
   println(x)
else
   println(y)
```

Note that method `print` does not add a new line character to the values being printed.

Suppose that we want to find the maximum of an indefinite number of comparable objects. Obviously, we need a repetitive control structure, that is, a control structure that executes a number of commands while some condition holds true. Scala has two basic repetitive control structures whose general form is shown below:

```
while (condition)          do {
    commands                   commands
}                          while (condition)
```

The structure on the left first examines the condition and if it is true, then it executes the commands, otherwise it stops; next it re-examines the condition and so on. The structure on the right is similar to the construct on the left except that it checks the condition only after it has executed the commands one time. Let us see how we can solve the problem we posed in the beginning of this paragraph: to find the maximum of an indefinite number of comparable objects. The code that follows solves this problem for integers:

```
var max : Int = 0
print("enter a number...\n? ")
var x = readInt()
while (x != 0 ) {
   if (x > max)
      max = x
   print("enter a number...\n? ")
   x = readInt()
}
println("The maximum is " + max)
```

Exercise 2.9 Rewrite this code so that it finds the "maximum" of an indefinite number of strings.

Exercise 2.10 Rewrite this code using a do-while construct.

In the previous example the user has to enter the number zero in order to stop the iteration. Nevertheless, when a user enters the end of file marker (usually Ctrl-D under OpenSolaris, Linux, etc. and Ctrl-Z under Windows) or even if the user enters a letter or some other symbol, the program will crash and it will print a message like the following one:

```
java.lang.NumberFormatException: For input string: "a"
        at java.lang.NumberFormatException.forInputString(. . .)
        at java.lang.Integer.parseInt(Integer.java:447)
        at java.lang.Integer.parseInt(Integer.java:497)
        . . . . . . . . . . . . . . . . . . . . . . .
```

The error was reported by the *runtime* environment which, in general, is a virtual machine state that provides software services for processes or programs. However, it is an indication of really poor program design to rely on the runtime environment to catch our programming errors. Scala provides a mechanism to handle errors like these. The `try` command encloses commands that are potentially dangerous (i.e., input commands) and it is accompanied by a `catch` clause that contains fallback code that is executed when an error occurs. In a pure object-oriented environment, even errors are objects and when they occur they send messages that are caught by the corresponding constructs. For now, errors will be identified with special cases of class `Exception`. New *exceptions* can be defined as follows:

```
class DivisionByZero extends Exception
```

Exceptions are sent with a `throw` command. For instance, the function definition shows a simple example that demonstrates how exceptions are thrown:

```
def div(x: Int, y:Int) : Int =
  if (y == 0)
    throw new DivisionByZero()
  else
    x / y
```

The careful reader may have noted that the `if` expression yields either an exception or an integer. Clearly, this is not correct since the `if` expression should yield an integer value in both cases. However, exceptions are of type `Nothing`, which is a subtype of every other Scala type. Thus, the whole expression is *well typed* (i.e., does not violate the type rules of Scala).

As was noted above, the `try` command is used to evaluate *dangerous* code. If the code triggers a runtime error, then execution is transferred to the `catch` clause. It should be obvious that there are different kinds of errors which demand different handling. For this reason, Scala provides a form of *pattern matching*, that is, a structure with which one can specify a number of different cases that are examined one after the other by the Scala implementation. For now, it suffices to say that the different cases are about similar objects. The various patterns are introduced with the keyword `case`. In the code that follows, the command in the `try` command triggers a runtime error that is handled in the `catch` clause:

```
try {
  println(div(3,0))
}catch {
  case e:DivisionByZero =>
    println("Impossible operation: Division by zero!")
}
```

The symbol `=>`, which is used to separate the pattern from what should be done if this pattern is matched, can be replaced by the symbol ⇒ (i.e., the Unicode character \u21D2). Although the control structures introduced so far are enough, at least from a theoretical point of view,[1] still there are some other constructs that are quite convenient. Such constructs allow programmers to specify how to stop the execution of a repetitive construct immediately. Since these constructs have no place in the world of functional programming, Scala's designer felt they should be excluded from the language. But this does not make the language less expressive. On the contrary, one can use Boolean variables to control the flow of control. This may seem *unnatural* in certain cases, nevertheless, it helps programmers write better and more readable code. Let us now proceed with a solution to our problem of finding the maximum of an indefinite number of interactively provided values. The code that follows solves this problem:

```
var max      = 0
var EOF      = false
var firstTime = true
var x        = 0
do {
  print("gimme a number...\n? ")
  try {
    x = readInt()
  }
  catch {
    case eof: java.io.IOException => EOF = !EOF
    case numFormat: java.lang.NumberFormatException => EOF = !EOF
  }
  if (!EOF) {
    if (firstTime) {
      max = x
      firstTime = !firstTime
    }
    if ( x > max )
      max = x
  }
} while (! EOF)
println("maximum is " + max)
```

Exception java.io.IOException has been especially designed for handling Input and Output errors while exception java.lang.NumberFormatException is caused when a nonnumber is given when a number is expected.

Exercise 2.11 Modify this code so it can compute the largest as well as the smallest numbers given.

---

[1] In particular, any programming language equipped with a repetitive and a conditional construct can be used to compute anything a fully fledged programming language can do.

2.6 Subclasses and inheritance

A subclass describes the structure of a set of objects. However, a subclass definition does so by describing extensions and changes to an existing class, which is called its *superclass*. All fields of a superclass are implicitly included in the subclass definition. Methods can be explicitly overridden or implicitly included, as is done with fields. When a method is overridden, it retains its name and possibly its type, but computes something different.

First let us define a very simple class that will be used to describe some aspects of *inheritance*:

```
class Fruit {
   def price() = 0.5
}
```

This class has no fields and only one method. A subclass of this class could include additional fields and/or methods or the modified versions of the original methods, or both. Assume that lemons cost 0.5 € each. Then the following is a subclass of class Fruit describing lemons:

```
class Lemon extends Fruit {
   def color = "yellow"
}
```

Note that the keyword extends is used to designate that class Lemon is a subclass of class Fruit.

Exercise 2.12 What will be printed on the computer screen when the commands

```
var l = new Lemon()
println("price: "+l.price()+" color: "+l.color())
```

are executed?

From this description one would conclude that a subclass definition is a convenient way to define new, unrelated classes from previous definitions without the need to repeat identical definitions. In fact, this is not true. Consider the following piece of code:

```
def worth(f:Fruit)=f.price()
var l = new Lemon()
var f = new Fruit()
f = l
println(worth(f))
```

Although f and 1 are of different types, nevertheless, Lemon is a *subtype* of type Fruit. In addition, Liskov's substitution principle [48] is the reason why the assignment f = 1 is meaningful. This principle can be stated as: If L is a subtype of F, then one can replace objects of type F with objects of type L without altering the meaning of a program. However, one should note that the assignment 1 = f is incorrect (why?).

Overriding a method means changing an inherited method in a subclass. For example, if a lemon costs 0.2 €, then this could be specified as follows:

```
class Lemon extends Fruit {
   override def price() = 0.2
   def color() = "yellow"
}
```

The keyword override is used to designate that the method definition that follows is not a new method definition but rather a method that is overridden. If 1 is of type Lemon and f is of type Fruit, then the following code

```
f=1
println("price: "+f.price())
```

will have as result the number 0.2 printed on the computer screen. Let us see one more example of a subclass.

We will define a subclass of class cell, which was presented on page 24. We call this new class reCell, for restorable cell, that is a cell that *remembers* its previous value:

```
class reCell extends cell {
   private var backup : Int = 0
   override def set(n: Int) = {
      backup = this.contents
      super.set(n) //this.contents = n
   }
   def restore() = contents = backup
}
```

The field backup is declared as private. Recall that class cell has a field called contents, which is also private. Also recall that private fields are nonaccessible. However, they are not only nonaccessible, but they also cannot be inherited by subclasses and they may not override definitions in parent classes. Thus, the previous definition is not correct, because the definition of class cell is practically nonextendable. To remedy this problem, we need to define field contents as protected. Such fields are not visible but are inheritable.

Exercise 2.13 Modify the definition of class `cell` so it can be extended.

Method `set` is overridden. Note that field `backup` is assigned the value of field `contents`, while this field gets its new value by invoking the method of the superclass – the keyword `super` refers to the superclass of the presently defined class.

Suppose we have opted to define class `cell` as follows

```
class newcell (protected var  contents : Int){
   def this () = this(0)
   def get() = contents
   def set(n: Int) = {
     contents = n
   }
}
```

Unfortunately, it is not that obvious how one can define a subclass of this class. Instead of explaining how one can specify a subclass of this class, let us give a simple example that will make all the relevant details clear:

```
class renewCell (x : Int) extends newcell(x) {
   private var backup : Int = x
   override def set(n: Int) = {
     backup = this.contents
     super.set(n)
   }
   def restore() = contents = backup
}
```

Here x is a dummy variable that refers implicitly to field `contents`.

Exercise 2.14 What will be the output of the following commands:

```
var C = new reCell(5)
println(C.get())
C.set(9)
println(C.get())
C.restore()
println(C.get())
```

We have seen what to do when declaring a subclass that has the same number of members initialized when constructing an object of this subclass. The question is: How can we declare a subclass with a different number of members which are initialized when constructing objects? Again, we answer this question by giving an example. The class that follows describes two-dimensional points:

```
class point(var x: Int, var y: Int) {
  def this() = this(0,0)
  def move(x1:Int, y1:Int) = {x=x1; y=y1}
  def translate(dx: Int, dy: Int) = {
    x += dx; y += dy;
  }
  override def toString = "("+x+","+y+")"
}
```

Method toString is overriden since all classes define this method implicitly. A proper subclass of this class is one that describes three-dimensional points. The following class is a subclass of class point:

```
class point3D(x2d: Int, y2d: Int, var z: Int)
                        extends point(x2d,y2d) {
  def move(new_x:Int, new_y:Int, new_z:Int) = {
    x=new_x; y=new_y; z=new_z;}
  def translate(dx: Int, dy: Int, dz: Int) = {
    x += dx; y += dy; z += dz;
  }
  override def toString = "("+x+","+y+","+z+")"
}
```

Note that methods move and translate do not override the corresponding definitions of point since they are different definitions (for example, the former take two arguments while the latter take three arguments). As is evident, one just adds the additional fields in the header.

Exercise 2.15 Assume that the following code

```
var p=new point(3,2)
println(p)
var q=new point3D(4,5,6)
p=q
println(p)
q.translate(1,1,1)
println(p)
p.translate(1,1)
println(p)
```

is included in a file together with the two definitions above. If this code is fed to Scala, as shown below, it will print the output that is shown below:

```
$ scala points.scala
(3,2)
(4,5,6)
(5,6,7)
(6,7,7)
```

Can you explain why the code is correct and why you get this output?

If we have two or more classes, it is not possible to create a new class that is a subclass of all these classes. Technically, Scala does not support multiple inheritance, nevertheless, it does support tools to achieve the same effect without the problems of multiple inheritance.

It is possible to create an extension of a class while creating an instance of an existing class. This can be achieved only for classes that do not have "parameters," like the following simple class:

```
class A{ var x = 7; var y =9 }
```

The following class instantiation shows exactly how this can be done:

```
val x = new A{ var z = 11 }
```

This facility is extremely useful and more realistic examples using this facility are presented in Chapter 6.

2.7 Functions

In Section 2.3 we briefly described how methods are declared and used. In Scala functions are first-class citizens since a function definition is equivalent to a module definition (see Section 3.5) and thus a function definition can appear anywhere in a source file. Unlike most programming languages that can be considered to descend from the C programming language, like C++ and Java, Scala permits *nested* function definitions, that is, function definitions inside other function definitions. This is a feature pioneered by Algol and followed by its ancestors like Pascal. There is nothing special about nested function definitions – one writes one function definition inside another function definition. The following function definition is a very simple example that demonstrates the use of this feature:

```
def E(x: Float) = {
  def F(y: Float) = x + y
  F(2*x)
}
```

The command `println(E(5))` will print the number 15.0. Note that parameter y is not visible in the body of function E, since it is defined in an inner definition. As a general rule, variables that are declared in an inner definition are not visible outside the *scope*, that is, the range in which a variable can be referenced, while all variables and parameters declared outside this scope are visible. In the case of name conflict, for example, where two or more variables have the same name but are declared in different scopes, then any use of these variables refers to the variable being declared in the current scope. For example, consider the following code snippet:

```
var a: Int = 1;
def P = {
   var b = 1;
   def Q = {
      var b = " b "; var c = 4;
      println(a+b+c)
   }
   Q
   println(a+b)
}
P
```

Here Q is not visible outside P. Thus, Q is invoked only when P is invoked and when it is invoked it will assign values to two variables and it will print the values of these variables. The effect of the command

```
println(a+b+c)
```

is to print the string 1 b 4, since b refers to the string variable that is declared inside the definition of Q. The command that follows the invocation of Q will print 2, since b refers now to the variable that has type `Int`. We will say more on scope later when we discuss inner classes in Section 2.17.

Generally speaking, most, if not all, functional programming languages provide two mechanisms to define functions – one that looks like Scala's mechanism to declare functions and one that is based on Alonzo Church's λ-calculus. The latter can be used to define anonymous function objects (remember: everything in Scala is an object). In the λ-calculus one deals with anonymous functions and their operations. Typically, an expression of the form $\lambda x.E$, where x is an identifier and E an expression that may contain x (for example, E can be the expression $x + 1$), is a λ-abstraction that defines an anonymous function. This function can be applied to an expression F, written as $(\lambda x.E)F$, as follows: first we substitute each occurrence of x in E with F and then we perform all remaining operations. For example, the application $(\lambda x.3 \cdot x + 1)4$ will yield the expression $3 \cdot 4 + 1$ which evaluates to 13.

Since Scala supports functional programming tools and methodologies to a great extent, one can easily "define" anonymous functions. For example, the following code snippet shows how to assign to an identifier an anonymous function that increases the value of its argument by one:

```
var inc = (x:Int) => x+1
```

Here x is the equivalent of the identifier in a λ-expression, the symbol => plays the role of the dot, and the expression after the symbol => is the expression that will be evaluated when the function value is applied to some other value. Variable inc is now a function that can be used the usual way:

```
var x = inc(7)-1
```

Obviously, one can define anonymous functions with two or more arguments. Here is an anonymous function definition that multiplies its two arguments:

```
var mul = (x: Int) => (y:Int) => x*y
println(mul(3)(4))
```

To be precise, here we define a function that takes one argument and returns a function that takes one argument. In other words, this is a *higher-order* function. And this explains why function mul is invoked this way. Since mul is a function that takes one argument and returns a function, the invocation mul(n) returns a function that multiplies its only argument by n. For example, the following definition

```
var mul3 = mul(3)
```

defines a function that multiplies its argument by three. Thus, the command

```
println(mul3(4))
```

will print the number 12.

Exercise 2.16 Write an anonymous function which will compute the maximum of three integer numbers.

There are two standard functions that can be used to transform functions accepting pairs or, more generally, *n*-tuples as arguments to functions that take one argument and return a function. These functions are the curried and the uncurried functions and they are defined in a class called Function.(To be precise Function is a *trait* not a class.) These definitions are not readily available and one has to *import* them. In certain cases, one has to import all definitions included in a package definition. A package is a collection of classes and related constructs that provide access protection and name space management. One can import the definition a of some class C from a package P with the command

```
import P.C.a
```

For example, one can import function `curried` with the following command:

```
import scala.Function.curried
```

Note that if the package identifier is omitted, then it is assumed to be `scala`. Thus, the previous import command could be written as follows:

```
import Function.curried
```

If one wants to import two or more definitions, one has to separate by a comma the definitions that are needed:

```
import Function.uncurried, Function.curried
```

More generally, one can import all definitions from a package with a command like the following one:

```
import Function._
```

Here the character _ plays the role of a wildcard character that can be substituted with anything. Now, let us present the functionality of `curried` and `uncurried`. Function `uncurried` takes a function that returns a function and transforms it into a function that takes as argument an n-tuple, as the following shows:

```
scala>  import Function._
import Function._

scala> var mul = (x: Int) => (y:Int) => x*y
mul: (Int) => (Int) => Int = <function>

scala> var mul_pair = uncurried(mul)
mul_pair: (Int, Int) => Int = <function>

scala> mul_pair(4,5)
res0: Int = 20
```

On the other hand, function `curried` does exactly the opposite. The following is a demonstration of its usage and its capabilities:

```
scala> def add(x:Int, y:Int) = x + y
add: (Int,Int)Int
scala> val addCurried = curried(add _)
```

```
addCurried: (Int) => (Int) => Int = <function>

scala> addCurried(3)
res1: (Int) => Int = <function>

scala> addCurried(3)(5)
res2: Int = 8
```

Observe that function `curried` actually takes two arguments, the second being the character _ because the function expects as argument a partially applied function.

At this point it is rather important to stress that Scala is a programming language where all *values* are first-class citizens. This means that all values have the same "rights" and the same "obligations." Thus, functions should be able to have functions as arguments and at the same time they should be able to return (or yield, if you prefer the term in this particular case) other functions. This capability is needed to implement a powerful feature: closures.

A *closure* is a function whose return value depends on the value of one or more variables declared outside this function. The following interaction with the Scala interpreter has been designed to make clear what we mean by the previous "definition":

```
scala> var m = 5
m: Int = 5

scala> var inc5 = (x:Int) => x+m
inc5: (Int) => Int = <function>

scala> inc5(7)
res0: Int = 12

scala> m = 10
m: Int = 10

scala> inc5(7)
res2: Int = 17
```

In words, when the value of m changes, the function changes its definition too. And this is exactly the essence of closures. However, the previous example is not realistic and it does not show all the capabilities of closures. A more realistic example is provided in the following code snippet:

```
def fmul(x:Double) = x*3
```

```
def derivative(f: (Double => Double), dx: Double) =
    (x: Float) => (f(x + dx) - f(x)) / dx

var der = derivative(fmul, 0.1)
```

Here der is a function that computes the expression

$$(fmul(x+0.1)-fmul(x))/0.1$$

This happens because the variables f and dx do not cease to exist even when the function that creates the closure finishes its computational task. For example, the expression der(5) will compute the number 2.9999999999999893.

Exercise 2.17 The following definition is a closure:

```
def sayHello2(n : String) : Unit =
    return println("Hello "+n)
```

Can you explain what it does?

Alternatively, one can define function der as follows:

```
var der = derivative(((x:Double) => x*3), 0.1)
```

In other words, there is no need to define an argument separately if it happens to be a function – the whole function definition can be supplied as argument.

As was noted in Section 1.2, functional programming can be viewed as the discipline of defining and composing functions.[2] In order to make pure functional composition available to Scala users, the language provides the operator compose. The operator behaves like its mathematical counterpart (i.e., the operator "o"). For example, consider the following definitions:

```
val f = (x: Int) => x + 1
val g = (x: Int) => x * 3.3
val h = (x: Double) => x + 0.1
```

One can compose all these functions and the following code snippet shows how this can be done:

```
val result = h compose g compose f
println(result(4))
```

The last command will print the number 16.6.

---

[2] Given a function $f : A \to B$, that is, a map of elements of set A to elements of set B, and a function $g : B \to C$, the function $g \circ f : A \to C$ maps elements of A to elements of C and is defined by $(g \circ f)(x) = g(f(x))$.

Exercise 2.18 Given a function $f : A \rightarrow B$ its inverse, if it exists, is a function $f^{-1} : B \rightarrow A$ such that $f^{-1}(f(x)) = x$. In other words, the composition of a function and its inverse is the identity function $1_A : A \rightarrow A$. Define a function and its inverse and verify that their composition is the identity function.

2.8 Arrays and tuples

The array is the most common data structure. It consists of a collection of elements that have the same type. Elements are associated with an index, usually an integer, which is used to access or replace a particular element. In fact, an array is implemented as a number of consecutive memory locations indexed by consecutive numbers. Most programming languages provide arrays as an elementary way to structure data, and Scala is no exception. In Scala arrays are objects and, thus, have a number of methods associated with them. Basically, there are two ways to define an array: either one specifies the total number of elements and then assigns values to the elements, or one specifies all values at once. Naturally, these values can change provided we have declared the identifier as a variable. Let us see how we can define a simple array:

```
var z:Array[String] = new Array[String](3)
```

Here z is declared as an array of `Strings` that may hold up to three elements. In most cases we can simplify the declaration as follows:

```
var z = new Array[String](3)
```

If one wants to assign values to individual elements or to get access to individual elements, one can do so by using commands like the following:

```
z(0) = "Java"; z(1) = "Scala"; z(4/2) = "Oberon"
println(z(2))
```

The index of the first element of an array is the number zero and the index of the last element is the total number of elements minus one. The last example shows that in general the index can be any expression that yields a whole number. Let us now see how one could write the same commands in a more compact way. The code that follows shows an alternative way to define an array:

```
var langs = Array("Java", "Scala", "Oberon", "Self")
println(y(2))
```

As is evident, in this case we simply specify the elements after the keyword `Array`. Note that the elements are separated by commas and they are enclosed in parentheses.

Exercise 2.19 Define and initialize an array of Doubles that contains five elements.

Most programming languages that support arrays provide a control construct that is used mainly for the processing of arrays. Scala does provide a very generic construct that can be used to process arrays concisely. In particular, a *for comprehension* processes ranges of values and since arrays are ranges of values they can be processed with such structures. The *for comprehensions* are so called because they are reminiscent of *set comprehensions*, which is a mathematical notation for describing sets by stating what properties each member of a particular set satisfies. For example, the set comprehension $\{x \mid x \in \mathbb{R} \wedge x > 0\}$ describes the set of all positive real numbers. The command

```
for (l<-langs) println(l)
```

will print out all the elements of the array langs. In the expression e <- ℓ cs the fresh variable e runs through all values of the list of values ℓ at each step the variable can be used in the "cs." The symbol <- separates the fresh variable from the list of values. Also, we may opt to use the symbol ← instead of the "symbol" <-.

Assume that A and B are two arrays that represent two vectors. Then the code that follows computes their scalar product:

```
var sprod = 0
for ( (a, b) <- A.zip(B) ) sprod += a * b
```

Here A.zip(B) yields a new array of *pairs*, where the first element comes from A and the second from B. Note that Scala supports an *n*-tuple type, which is a very common type in functional programming languages. An *n*-tuple contains *n* elements each having its own type. Although the elements of an array can be modified, the elements of a tuple cannot. For each TupleN type, where $1 \leq N \leq 22$, Scala defines a number of element-access methods. Given the following definition

```
val t = (4,3,2,1)
```

the method _*n*, where $1 \leq n \leq 4$, can be used to access the *n*th elements of t. For example, the following expression computes the sum of all elements of t:

```
t._1 + t._2 + t._3 + t._4
```

If we have a tuple T that has as elements only integers and we want to compute their sum, then we should use the following code snippet:

```
for (i <- 0 to t.productArity - 1 ) {
  sum += (t.productElement(i)).asInstanceOf[Int]); }
```

Method `productArity` returns the number of elements of a tuple, which are indexed like an array. Variable `i` assumes as values all the values in the specified range. Actually, the expression

$$0 \text{ to } t.\text{productArity} - 1$$

is syntactic sugar for the expression

$$0.\text{to}(t.\text{productArity}() - 1)$$

which yields a `Range` object. If we replace method `to` with method `until`, we can safely delete the minus one part. This method produces a range that does not include the last element. To return to the original example, method `asInstanceOf` is a method that performs *type casting*, that is, a method that changes an object of one data type into another. Actually, this is not an arbitrary method that changes any type to any other type. On the contrary, the two classes should be related with the subclassing relationship (see Section 3.6.6). Method `productElement` yields objects of type `Any`, which explains why we need typecasting.

Exercise 2.20 Why is the following code correct?

```
var sprod = 0
for ( (a, b) <- A zip B ) sprod += a * b
```

Another way to merge two arrays is by using the `++` operator, which creates a new array that consists of all elements of the first array followed by all elements of the second array. Again, the expression `A++B` is syntactic sugar for `A.++(B)`.

In the examples using the `for` comprehension we had to process all elements of a range. However, there are cases where one needs to process only some elements that have some property in common. For example, the double factorial of an integer n which is defined as follows

$$n!! = \begin{cases} n \cdot (n-2)\ldots5 \cdot 3 \cdot 1 & n > 0 \text{ odd} \\ n \cdot (n-2)\ldots6 \cdot 4 \cdot 2 & n > 0 \text{ even} \\ 1 & n = -1,0 \end{cases}$$

is such a function.

Exercise 2.21 Write a function that can be used to compute the double factorial of any integer number.

Some readers may come up with a solution that uses `while` commands, whereas others may have opted to use the `for` command with some test in the body of the command. However, it is possible to attach the tests to a `for` command as our solution to this problem shows:

```
def dfact(n: Int): Int = {
  var prod: Int =1
  if (n > 0) {
    if (n % 2 == 0)
      for(i<-2 to n if n % 2 == 0) prod *= i
    else
      for(i<-1 to n if n % 2 != 0) prod *= i
  }
  return prod
}
```

It is possible to attach more than one *filter* (i.e., a condition) to a `for` command, since filters are separarted by semicolons and each filter starts with the keyword `if` and is followed by some conditional expression.

Exercise 2.22 Write a `for` command that sums up all even integers from 1 to 1000.

If you try to use the function `dfact` to compute the double factorial of 21 or 22 you will discover that Scala will print two negative integers! The truth is that,

$$21!! = 51,090,942,171,709,440,000$$

$$21!! = 1,124,000,727,777,607,680,000$$

and these numbers are far bigger than the largest positive `Long`. In order to be able to solve this and other similar problems, Scala provides the types `BigDecimal` and `BigInt`, which are "infinite precision" decimals and integers with the number of digits only limited by the available computer memory and CPU time. Therefore, if one wants to be able to compute the double factorial of (almost) any integer, one has to change the definion of `dfact` as shown below:

```
def dfact(n: Int): BigInt = {
  var prod: BigInt =1
  . . . . . . . . . .
  return prod
}
```

The arrays we presented so far are unidimensional (i.e., their elements are not arrays). However, there are many applications, especially numerical, where one needs to be able to define and use multi-dimensional arrays (i.e., arrays whose elements are arrays). For example, matrices and tables are examples of structures that can be realized as two-dimensional arrays. Scala does not directly support multi-dimensional arrays. Instead, one can define arrays that have as elements other arrays, which may have as elements other arrays, etc. Currently, Scala supports arrays with up to nine dimensions. If one wants to define a matrix, one can use a declaration like the following one:

```
var A = new Array[Array[Int]](3,3)
```

This is an array that has three elements each being an array of integers that has three elements. The code that follows shows how one can process a multi-dimensional array:

```
for (i <- 0 to 2) {
   for ( j <- 0 to 2) {
      if (i == j)
         A(i)(j)=1
      else
         A(i)(j)=0
   }
}
```

The expression `A(i)(j)` refers to the `j`th element of the `i`th array. Since `A(i)` is an array, the following assignment is legal:

```
A(1)=Array(2,2,2)
```

Exercise 2.23 Write a `for` command that prints all the elements of array A. You should consider printing it as a real matrix, that is, one row on each line.

Given two arrays A and B that have elements of the same type, then the expression A ++= B appends to A all the elements of B:

```
scala> var A = Array(1,2,3)
A: Array[Int] = Array(1, 2, 3)

scala> A(5)
java.lang.ArrayIndexOutOfBoundsException: 5
 .  .  .  .  .  .  .  .  .  .  .  .  .

scala> var B = Array(5,6,7)
B: Array[Int] = Array(5, 6, 7)

scala> A ++= B

scala> A(5)
res2: Int = 7
```

The ++= operator can also be used for other random access structures and lists (see Section 2.13).

2.9 Command line arguments

Scala has a predefined array called `args` that can be used to process command line arguments (i.e., strings supplied to the program through the command line). Each element of this array contains a command line argument. The array is initialized the very moment Scala starts executing our code. To keep things simple, we will use only the interpreter. Assume we want to write a simple program that prints the phrase "Hello CLA!" for each command line argument CLA. Before presenting the solution to this problem, let us say that method `length` returns the total number of elements of an array. Since we have no idea how many command line arguments there will be in any case, we definitely need to use this method. Let us now see how we can solve our little problem. The code that follows does exactly what we have asked for:

```
for ( i <- 0 to args.length - 1)
  println("Hello "+args(i)+"!")
```

Surprisingly, the same problem can be solved with the following expression:

```
args.foreach((CLA:String)=>println("Hello "+CLA+"!"))
```

Here we use method `foreach`. The argument of this method is a form of pattern matching. Here variable CLA, which has to be declared in parentheses, assumes the values of all elements of the array and for each such value the code after the => symbol is executed. If A is an array of integers defined as follows

```
var A=Array(1,2,3,4,5,6,7,8,9,10)
```

then we can print all of its elements with the following command:

```
A.foreach(println)
```

The example presented above shows the basic characteristics of array `args` as well as a simple usage example. However, it would be far more interesting to present an example where the command line argument is processed.

Assume that the word "tato" is an acronym that expands to "tato and tato only," which in turn expands to "tato and tato only and tato and tato only only," etc. Our problem is how to write a Scala program which will take a number from the command line and print the corresponding expansion of the "tato" acronym. The most difficult part is how to generate an expansion of the acronym. The most natural solution to problems like this is to define a *recursive* function, which is a function that is defined in terms of itself. To understand what recursion is all about, consider the sum of the n first positive integer numbers, which we will denote as $s(n)$. Obviously,

$$s(n) = 0 + 1 + 2 + \ldots + (n-1) + n.$$

Suppose that we have at our disposal a procedure to compute the sum of all positive integers up to $n-1$, then $s(n) = s(n-1) + n$. Clearly, $s(n-1) = 0 + 1 + \ldots + (n-1)$ which implies that $s(n-1) = s(n-2) + (n-1)$. By following this way of thinking we end up with a trivial case, that is, the sum of all integers from zero to zero which is equal to zero or, formally, $s(0) = 0$. In conclusion, the sum of the positive integers up to some positive integer n can be defined as a recursive function as follows:

$$s(n) = \begin{cases} n + s(n-1) & n > 0 \\ 0 & n = 0. \end{cases}$$

Note that the first case is called the *recurrence relationship* while the second case is called the *termination condition*. In general, each problem can be expressed as a recursive function or procedure by employing a design analysis similar to the one presented in this paragraph. Let us now see how we can define a recursive Scala function that solves the "tato"-acronym problem. The easiest part is to identify the termination condition. When n is equal to one, the function should just print out the word "tato." In all other cases, we need to expand the two occurrences of the word "tato" to the phrase

"tato and tato only."

Thus each occurrence of the word "tato" should be replaced by a recursive call, or in Scala:

```scala
def tato(n:Int): Unit = {
  if (n==1) {
    print("tato")
  }
  else {
    tato(n-1)
    print(" and ")
    tato(n-1)
    print(" only")
  }
}
```

What is left is to show how one should handle the command line argument. Obviously, the user has to specify only one command line argument which has to be a positive integer. For reasons of simplicity let us assume that the user may enter only

Table 2.5 *Methods that parse a string as a literal of some basic type and return an object of this type*

Method	Explanation
toByte	Parses a string object as a Byte and returns this number
toShort	Parses a string object as a Short and returns this number
toInt	Parses a string object as an Int and returns this number
toLong	Parses a string object as a Long and returns this number
toFloat	Parses a string object as a Float and returns this number
toDouble	Parses a string object as a Double and returns this number
toBoolean	Parses a string object as a Boolean and returns this truth value

positive integers. The code that follows handles the cases just described:

```
if (args.isEmpty)
   println("Usage: tato number")
else if (args.length > 1)
   println("Usage: tato number")
else
   tato(args(0).toInt)
```

Here isEmpty returns true if the the array contains no elements. Method toInt is one of a family of methods that parse a string as a literal of some basic type and return an object that corresponds to this literal (see Table 2.5).

Exercise 2.24 The following code handles better the command line argument:

```
var l = 0
if (args.isEmpty)
   println("Usage: tato number")
else if (args.length > 1)
   println("Usage: tato number")
else
   try {
     l = args(0).toInt
   }catch{
     case e : Exception => l=0
   }
if (l>0)
   tato(l)
else
   println("Invalid command line argument.")
```

Explain what this code does.

2.10 Sets

By following a tradition pioneered by Pascal, Scala provides sets as predefined structures. Technically, a set is a collection of pairwise different elements of the same type. In other words, there are no duplicate elements in a set. A set is either empty or it has elements. One can declare an empty set as follows:

```
var y : Set[Int] = Set()
```

The type annotation is necessary as the system needs to assign a concrete type to variable y. On the other hand, when declaring a nonempty set, the type annotation is not necessary:

```
var x = Set(1,3,5,7)
```

Given two sets, one should be able to compute their union and their intersection.[3] Also, one should be able to check whether a set is empty or not and whether a set is a subset of another set (i.e., whether all elements of the first set are elements of the second set):

```
scala> var A = Set(1,3,5,10)
A: scala.collection.immutable.Set[Int] = Set(1, 3, 5, 10)

scala> var B = Set(0,2,4,10)
B: scala.collection.immutable.Set[Int] = Set(0, 2, 10)

scala> A ** B //intersection
res0: scala.collection.immutable.Set[Int] = Set(10)

scala> A ++ B //union
res1: scala.collection.immutable.Set[Int] = Set(0, 5, 10, 1, 2, 3)

scala> A subsetOf B //subsethood
res2: Boolean = false

scala> A.isEmpty
res3: Boolean = false

scala> A.contains(5)
res4: Boolean = true
```

Variables A and B are of type Set[Int]. The operators ** and ++ denote set intersection and set union, respectively. As expected, operator subsetOf checks whether the left operand is a subset of the right operand; method isEmpty returns

---

[3] Given two sets A and B, their union, $A \cup B$, is a new set that contains the elements of both sets, while their intersection, $A \cap B$, is a new set that contains all elements that belong to both sets.

Table 2.6 *Methods of class* `scala.util.Random`

Method	Explanation
nextBoolean	Returns the next pseudorandom boolean value
nextBytes	Generates random bytes and places them into a user-supplied byte array
nextDouble	Returns the next pseudorandom double value between 0.0 and 1.0
nextFloat	Returns the next pseudorandom double value between 0.0 and 1.0
nextInt	Returns a pseudorandom integer value between 0 and the specified value
nextLong	Returns a pseudorandom integer value between 0 and the specified value
setSeed	sets a new seed for the random number generator

true when a set is empty; and method `contains` returns true only if an element belongs to a set. It is also possible to create a set by successively adding elements to it as the following example shows:

```
var A : Set[Int] = Set()
for (i<-1 to 20; if i % 2 != 0) A += i
```

The rest of this section presents two simple set manipulation examples.

Assume that we have a skiing competition[4] and we want to determine the order in which contestants will set off. In the code that follows a set is used to hold the contestants. In addition, we use a (pseudo-)random number generator to solve our problem. Class Random, which is part of package `scala.util`, can be used to compute a sequence of pseudorandom numbers. Table 2.6 describes the methods this class defines. There are two ways to construct a new pseudorandom number generator: either by providing a seed or by not providing a seed. In the former case, every time we execute the code, it will produce the same "random" sequence. On the other hand, when we do not explicitly provide a seed, we get a different sequence each time the code is executed. Having said enough about "random" numbers, let us present a solution to the problem we posed at the beginning of this paragraph:

```
import scala.util.Random
var B : Set[Int] = Set()
for (i<-1 to 50) B = B ++ Set(i)
var position = 0
var rnd = new Random()
```

---

[4] In Greece, owing to the greenhouse effect, we do not expect to see much snow in the years to come. In fact, we are more likely to see warm winters and very hot summers. If humanity as a whole does not understand the severity of the current situation, and if therefore drastic measures are not taken, we will only be able to dream of winters, snow, and skiing competitions.

```
do {
  var entrant = rnd.nextInt(50)+1
  if ( B.contains(entrant) ) {
    position += 1
    print(position); print(" ");
    println(entrant)
    B -=  entrant
  }
} while (! B.isEmpty)
```

The expression B -= entrant removes the element on the right from the set on the left.

Exercise 2.25 Can you explain why we have used rnd.nextInt(50)+1 instead of rnd.nextInt(50)?

Exercise 2.26 In the previous example, people are identified with numbers. Modify the code so that B becomes a set of strings that are input interactively from the computer keyboard.

An integer number p is called *prime* if its only divisors are the numbers 1 and p. For example, numbers 5 and 7 are prime numbers while 4 and 9 are not (4 is divisible by 2 and 9 is divisible by 3). The *sieve of Eratosthenes* is an efficient algorithm that can be used to generate the prime numbers that are less than or equal to a positive integer N. The algorithm has as input a set of numbers that includes all integers greater than 1 and less than or equal to N. Then we gradually remove all numbers that are multiples of other numbers. For example, if the set contains p, then we should remove $p^2, p^2 + 2p, \ldots$ provided that all these numbers are less than or equal to N. The following program implements this idea and is based on a Pascal program presented in [4]:

```
var N = 100
var sieve = Set(2)
var n = 3
while (n <= N) {
  sieve = sieve + n
  n += 2
}
var p = 3
while (p*p <= N) {
  var step = p + p
  var s = p * p
```

```
  while (s <= N) {
    sieve = sieve - s
    s += step
  }
  do {
    p += 1
  }while (!sieve.contains(p))
}
println(sieve)
```

Exercise 2.27 The previous program is static, that is, every time it is executed it will print the same output. Make it dynamic.

2.11 Hash tables

Many popular languages, like Perl and Ruby, provide a generalization of arrays that are called hash tables. Instead of having as index only natural numbers, hash tables can have as index strings or any other object. Note that in Perl indices can only be strings while in Ruby any kind of object can serve as an index. In Scala hash tables can have objects of any type as indices, but, obviously, all indices have to have the same type. For some reason hash tables are called maps in Scala, but we will stick to the generally accepted term.

We can initialize hash tables either by creating an empty table or by initializing a new table. The following command creates a new empty hash table whose keys are strings and whose values are integers:

```
var A:Map[Char,Int] = Map()
```

Obviously, the following structure

```
var B:Map[Int,String] = Map()
```

is not particularly useful, unless we need to map specific numbers and not just a range of numbers to some strings. If we want to add a key-value pair to a hash table, we can use the operator +. As an example, suppose that A has as keys Greek Acrophonic Attic digits and as values the corresponding Arabic numerals. Then hash table A should be initialized as follows:

```
A += ('I' -> 1)
A += ('Γ' -> 5)
A += ('Δ' -> 10)
A += ('H' -> 100)
```

```
A += ('X' -> 1000)
A += ('M' -> 10000)
A += ('𝔽' -> 50)
A += ('𝔽' -> 500)
A += ('𝔽' -> 5000)
A += ('𝔽' -> 5000)
```

Exercise 2.28 If you try this code, you will discover that Scala will complain about some illegal characters. Which are these illegal characters and why are they illegal?

Now if we want to find to which number corresponds a Greek Acrophonic Attic numeral, we can define a function as the following one:

```
def GAA2arabic(x:String): Int = {
  var sum = 0
  x.foreach(d => sum += A(d))
  return sum
}
```

Here method `foreach` scans all keys, thus, d takes the value of all keys in the table. Obviously, it is very straightforward to use this function as the following usage example shows:

```
println(GAA2arabic("ΔΠΙ"))
```

This command will print the number 16. Note that we have used the character Π instead of the character Γ, since Scala does not understand Unicode characters whose code point is above 65535.

Assume that we are developing an application that generates web pages. Since color is an important aspect of every serious web page, we could define a hash table to hold an association between names of colors and their hexadecimal representation like the following one:

```
var colors = Map("red"   ->  "#FF0000",
                 "azure" ->  "#F0FFFF",
                 "peru"  ->  "#CD853F")
```

Method `size` returns the number of key-value pairs. For example, the code snippet that follows:

```
colors += ("indigo" -> "#4B0082")
println(colors.size)
```

will print the number four. One can check whether there is a particular key by using method `contains` as shown in the example that follows:

```
if (!colors.contains("green"))
  println("Error: \"green\"  is not defined!\n")
```

If we want to remove one or more pairs from a hash table, we can use the operator minus as is shown in the example that follows:

```
colors -= "azure"
if (!colors.contains("azure"))
  println("Pair for \"azure\"  has been removed.\n")
```

The condition evaluates to `true` and, consequently, a message is printed on the computer screen. Although it is not particularly useful to delete all entries from a hash table, the following code achieves this task:

```
colors.keys.foreach( c => colors -= c )
```

Method `keys` generates a special data structure from all the keys of the table. One can easily process the elements of such a data structure, which is known as an *iterator* exactly for this reason. In fact, even a hash table is an iterator, but one that returns pairs. Thus, the code that follows does exactly what the previous command does:

```
colors.foreach( c => colors -= c._1 )
```

If a hash table is empty, then method `isEmpty` will return `true`. For example, if the following code is executed after the previous command has been executed

```
if (colors.isEmpty)
  println("Hash table is empty.")
```

the condition will evaluate to `true` and the corresponding message will be printed on the computer screen. Method `values` returns an iterator data structure that contains all values that are stored in a hash table.

Exercise 2.29 The expression `x.toInt` yields the Unicode code point of a `Char` object `x`. Create a hash table that has as keys the letters of a string and as values their Unicode code points.

Assume that the hash table from the previous exercise is called `letters`. Then the following code sums up the values of the table:

```
var sum = 0
letters.values.foreach(v => sum += v)
println(sum)
```

Method `elements` creates an iterator that consists of all pairs that make up a particular hash table. Following the previous example, we can print all pairs of table `letters` with this command:

```
letters.elements.foreach(println)
```

Let us conclude this section with an interesting example that we have borrowed from the *Rosetta Code* web page[5]: Given two arrays of equal length, create a hash table which has as keys the elements of the first array and as values the elements of the second array. The code snippet that follows solves this problem:

```
val keys = Array(1, 2, 3)
val values = Array("A", "B", "C")
val hash_table = Map(keys.zip(values) : _*)
```

Note that expression `keys.zip(values)` creates an array of pairs, while on the other hand `Map` expects a sequence of pairs. By now, it should be obvious that the symbol : is used to specify the type of a variable or expression. In this case the type is `_*` which is read as `Seq[_]`, that is, a finite sequence of elements of any (compatible) type. In general, if `T` is a type name, then `T*` is a shorthand of `Seq[T]`. This is the trick employed to declare a function or a method with a variable number of arguments or *varargs*, as they are usually called in computer jargon. In the example above, using this trick we make the language processor "think" that the array of pairs is actually a sequence of pairs, which is exactly what `Map` expects. Roughly, we can say that sequences, that is, objects of type `Seq[T]`, are generalized lists. Therefore, we will not say much more about them.

2.12 Memo functions

A memo function is one that "remembers" values it has already computed. Typically, memo functions involve some "benign side effects" [15, 39], though they can be implemented in purely functional languages (see section 3.10*). In Scala the easiest way to implement the equivalent of a memo function is to define a class which computes the required value by looking up a hash table that is defined in the companion object of the class. Hash tables are ideal since their keys can assume any possible value and are dynamic in the sense that their size is not predefined. As an example, we show how to write a memo function that computes any Fibonacci number. The Fibonacci numbers are a sequence of numbers that was discovered by the Italian mathematician Leonardo Fibonacci.

---

[5] See http://www.rosettacode.org/wiki/Creating_a_Hash_from_Two_Arrays.

The first number of the sequence is 0, the second number is 1 and each subsequent number is equal to the sum of the previous two numbers of the sequence, that is, $F_n = F_{n-1} + F_{n-2}$, where F_i is the ith Fibonacci number. Let us now provide a concrete implementation of a memo function in Scala.

First we define the companion object where we define the hash table where our program stores the Fibonacci numbers computed so far. We know the first and the second numbers and the third number is obviously equal to the second, so initially we store these three numbers in the table:

```
object Fibonacci {
    var F = Map(0 -> 0,
                1 -> 1,
                2 -> 1)
}
```

Our class will have only one method and no fields. We have chosen to implement a simple algorithm and leave any possible improvements as an exercise to the reader. First we check to see whether the requested number has been computed or not. If it has not been computed, then we find the first number in the sequence that has not been computed. Obviously, this number is less than or equal to the requested number. Next, we compute all numbers that are less than or equal to the requested number using the formula $F_n = F_{n-1} + F_{n-2}$. In the end, the method returns the requested Fibonacci number. The code that corresponds to this discussion is shown in Figure 2.1.

```
class Fibonacci {
    def num(n : Int): Int = {
        if (! Fibonacci.F.contains(n) ) {
            var k = 3
            while ( Fibonacci.F.contains(k) ) {
                k += 1
            }
            while ( k <= n ) {
                Fibonacci.F += (k -> (Fibonacci.F(k-1) +
                                      Fibonacci.F(k-2)));
                k += 1
            }
        }
        return Fibonacci.F(n)
    }
}
```

Figure 2.1 A memorized version of a function that computes the Fibonacci numbers.

Now consider the following commands:

```
var A = new Fibonacci
println("fib(12)="+A.num(12))
println("fib(6)="+A.num(6))
println("fib(4)="+A.num(4))
```

The last two commands compute nothing since the corresponding Fibonacci numbers had been computed by the second command.

Exercise 2.30 Write a memo function that computes the factorial of an integer number, that is, given a number n the function should compute the product $1 \cdot 2 \cdot 3 \cdots (n-1) \cdot n$.

2.13 Lists

Lists are the most important data structure of functional programming languages. Also, Lisp is a programming language where programs as well as data are represented as lists. Strictly speaking, Lisp's programs and data are both s-expressions, which is a form of tree structure (see Definition 2 on page 101). Roughly, a list of objects of some type A is a data structure that is either empty or else it is nonempty and consists of an object, called the *head* of the list, and another list of objects, called the *tail* of the list. The empty list is specified by Nil, which is an object that represents any empty list. An entity, for example the number one, and the empty list make a list with only one element. The method : :, pronounced *cons*, transforms an object and a list into a new list whose head is the object and whose tail is the first list. Thus, the code

```
var A = 1::Nil
var B = 2::A
var C = 1::2::3::Nil
println(A)
println(B)
println(C)
```

will print

```
List(1)
List(2, 1)
List(1, 2, 3)
```

Alternatively, one could use the following definitions for variables A, B, and C:

```
var A = List(1)
var B = List(2,1)
var C = List(1,2,3)
```

Writing down explicitly the elements of a list is not the best way to create a list. As an alternative solution, one can use a `for` comprehension to specify the elements of a list implicitly. For example, the following code creates a list that contains all whole numbers from one to ten:

```
var A:List[Int] = Nil
for(i<- 10 to 1 by -1) A = i::A
```

Here the keyword by is used to specify the iteration step. If we print list A, we will get

```
List(1, 2, 3, 4, 5, 6, 7, 8, 9, 10)
```

An easier way to create the same list is shown below:

```
var A = range(10,1,-1)
```

Function `range` creates a sorted list of integers in a specified range. The third argument is the step. If we omit the third argument, this function creates a sorted list of *all* integers in the specified range.

Exercise 2.31 Consider the following code snippet:

```
var B:List[Int] = Nil
for(i<- 0 to 20 by 2) B = i::B
println(B)
```

After the execution of this code, what will be printed on the computer screen?

In general, when processing a list, one first needs to specify how the head of the list will be processed and then how the tail will be processed. Since the tail is a list, this implies that the processing will stop once we have to process an empty list. This implies that the most natural way to process a list is by using a recursive procedure. As a first example, let us see how one can compute the length of a list of integers:

```
def Length(A:List[Int]):Int =
   if (A.isEmpty)
      0
   else
      1+Length(A.tail)
```

Given a list A, its length is computed by `A.length`, nevertheless, we present this example for purely pedagogical reasons. This function examines the list and if it is empty (method `isEmpty` returns `true` if the list is empty), it returns zero since the length of an empty list is zero. If the list is not empty, then it returns one plus the length of the tail. Methods `head` and `tail` return the head and the tail of a list, respectively. Although this function is correct, its definition seems *unnatural* to people with a background in functional programming. In a typical functional programming language, someone would program this simple function using pattern matching. When using this approach, one presents a number of general *structural cases* that are matched by concrete instances. For example, when dealing with lists there are two general structural cases: either the list is empty or it is nonempty. The match command, or expression if you find this term more appropriate, is used to examine an object against such structural cases. Before giving some of the relevant details, let us see how we could reprogram our function using pattern matching:

```
def Length(A:List[Int]):Int =
  A match {
    case Nil   => 0
    case x::xs => 1+Length(xs)
  }
```

In a match expression we specify first an object, then the keyword match and then the structural cases. Each structural case starts with the keyword case followed by a pattern and the command or commands to be executed if the pattern is matched. The symbol => separates a pattern from the command or commands. In this particular example, we have two such cases: when the list is empty this is denoted by Nil and when it is not empty this is specified by the x::xs expression. Here x denotes the head of the list and xs denotes its tail.

Exercise 2.32 Write down a function that sums up the elements of a list of integers.

Let us try to solve a slightly more difficult problem: how to reverse only lists that contain only two elements. This problem is not really hard, but it gives us the opportunity to present various forms of patterns. Before proceeding, try to solve the problem without using pattern matching. The empty list, a singleton list (i.e., a list with only one element) and a list with more than two elements should be returned intact. A singleton list is one whose tail is the empty list, thus, the pattern x::Nil should be used to capture this case. Alternatively, one could use the pattern List(x), but we do not recommend the use of such patterns as they cannot express really general cases. A list with two elements is described by the pattern x::y::Nil. The last case can be described by a similar pattern. The following function does exactly what we asked for:

```
def revereseTwo(A:List[Int]): List[Int] =
  A match {
    case Nil        => Nil
```

```
    case x::Nil        => List(x)
    case x::y::Nil     => List(y,x)
    case x::y::z::ws => x::y::z::ws
  }
```

Let us now see a more challenging problem: to write a function that reverses the order of the elements in a list. One way to solve this problem is by thinking that the head of the list has to be the last element of the list and this would apply to the head of the tail of the list, etc. In order to implement this idea, we need to use the :: : operator, which is pronounced *prepend*. The result of the expression A: : :B is to have A *prepended* to B (remember that all operators whose name ends with : are right-to-left associative, see Table 2.3; this implies that A: : :B is syntactic sugar for B. : :: (A)). We are now ready to present a solution to our problem:

```
  def Reverse(A:List[Int]): List[Int] =
    A match {
      case Nil    => Nil
      case x::xs => Reverse(xs):::List(x)
    }
```

Unfortunately, this solution is not optimal and this is the reason most functional programming languages provide an alternative implementation of this function. In order to define such an alternative implementation in Scala we need to introduce some important notions. However, before proceeding with the presentation of these notions, we will present some (predefined) methods that each List object can use.

Assume that A is a list defined as follows:

```
  var A = List(5,4,3,2,1)
```

The expression A(n), where $n \geq 0$, yields the $(n+1)$th element of the list, thus, the command

```
  println(A(4))
```

will print the number 1 on the computer screen. The method count returns the number of elements of a list that have a particular property. The following command prints the number of even elements of A:

```
  println(A.count(e => e % 2 == 0))
```

Variable e is a dummy variable that successively assumes the value of each element of the list, examines the condition that follows the => symbol and if it yields true, then it increases the value of a hidden counter. In the end, it returns the value of this counter.

Exercise 2.33 Define a list of strings and print the number of strings that contain only two characters. (Hint: If A is a string, then A.length returns its length, that is, the number of characters it contains.)

The methods take, drop are used to take from a list a specific number of consecutive elements. Sometimes it is more convenient to view certain methods as operators and this is just one such case. The left operand of take is a list L and the right operand is an integer number n. The expression "L take n" returns a sublist of L that consists of the first n elements of L. If n is greater than or equal to the length of L, it returns L. Similarly, the operator drop has as operands a list L and an integer number n and the expression "L drop n" returns a sublist of L that consists of all but the first n elements of L. Finally, the expression "L splitAt n" returns a pair of lists defined as follows:

$$L \text{ splitAt } n = (L \text{ take } n, L \text{ drop } n).$$

Here are some simple usage examples:

```
scala> var A = List(1,2,3,4,5)
A: List[Int] = List(1, 2, 3, 4, 5)

scala> A take 2
res18: List[Int] = List(1, 2)

scala> A drop 2
res19: List[Int] = List(3, 4, 5)

scala> A splitAt 2
res20: (List[Int], List[Int]) = (List(1, 2),List(3, 4, 5))
```

Lists cannot be altered in any way. This means that if for some reason we need to modify a list we practically have to create a new list from the original. Now, if we want to remove a number of consecutive elements from the right-hand side of a list, we can use the method dropRight. This method takes one argument which is the number of elements to be removed. For example, the following commands

```
var B = A.dropRight(2)
var C = Reverse((Reverse(A)).drop(2))
```

create two indentical lists: List(5, 4, 3). Method exists can be used to check whether some element of a list has a particular property. For example, the expression

```
A.exists(e => e > 6)
```

evaluates to `false` since no element of A is greater than six. On the other hand, method `forall` examines all elements of a list and if all of them have a property, then it returns `true`. For example, the expression

```
A.forall(e => e < 10)
```

evaluates to `true` since all elements of A are less than 10. Method `filter` yields a list that includes all elements that have a particular property. For instance, the following code snippet

```
var B = A.filter(e => e % 2 == 0)
println(B)
```

will print the list `List(4, 2)`, that is, a list that contains all even elements of A. Method `filter` may have many applications. For example, the following function implements the *quicksort* sorting algorithm of Tony Hoare. The function that follows is not really quicksort, but in a way looks like quicksort. The reason is that quicksort relies on destructive assignments, while the style of this function is functional. At any rate, this function does what it claims to do – it returns a list that contains the elements of its argument sorted.

```
def qsort(A: List[Int]): List[Int] =
  if (A.isEmpty)
    Nil
  else {
  val m = A.head
  (qsort(A.tail.filter(e => e >= m))).:::(
      (List(m)).:::(
         (qsort(A.tail.filter(e => e < m)))))
  }
```

Expressions like `A:::B:::C` must fit on one line. Since the corresponding expression of the function definition above would not fit on one line of this book, we had to transform it into an expression of the following form:

```
(C).:::((B).:::(A))
```

This alternative form can span over several lines.

Exercise 2.34 Rewrite function `qsort` using pattern matching.

Method `foreach` has the same functionality as the corresponding method used by arrays. However, method `map`, which functions as method `foreach`, takes as argument a function that returns a type other than `Unit`, which is the type of all arguments of `foreach`. Here is an example that shows exactly what we mean:

```
var A = List(5,7,9,10,11,13)
var B = A.map(_ + 2)
var sum = 0
A.foreach(sum += _)
println(B)
println(sum)
```

Here the character _ stands for an anonymous variable that is supplied to this function by the operator from the list. The code just presented will print the following values:

```
List(7, 9, 11, 12, 13, 15)
55
```

In certain cases, instead of the foreach method one can use a *for expression*. A for expression differs from a for comprehension in that the former yields a value. For example, the following shows how one can use a for expression:

```
scala> var A = range(1,6)
A: List[Int] = List(1, 2, 3, 4, 5)

scala> for (x<-A) yield x*2
res5: List[Int] = List(2, 4, 6, 8, 10)
```

Note that if the *generator*, that is, the expression x<-A, is of the form i <- 1 to 10, then the result is not a list but a more general structure – a random access sequence. We will say more about for expressions that yield lists in Section 3.13*.

Method reverse returns the elements of the list with their order reversed. Method remove yields a list that does not contain the elements that satisfy a certain condition. For example,

```
var B = A.remove(e => e % 2 == 0)
println(B)
```

will print the list List(5, 3, 1).

If we want to take the largest prefix of a list that satisfies a particular property, then we should use method takeWhile. This method can be used just like most of the methods described above. Let us see a simple example:

```
scala> var A = List(5,7,9,10,11,13)
A: List[Int] = List(5, 7, 9, 10, 11, 13)

scala> A.takeWhile(e => e % 2 != 0
res21: List[Int] = List(5, 7, 9)
```

Obviously, one can use this method as an operator. However, one can use closures, in order to make the definition look more natural:

```
scala> A takeWhile ( _ % 2 != 0)
res22: List[Int] = List(5, 7, 9)
```

A prefix of a list is a list of elements at the beginning of the list that satisfy a certain property. Method dropWhile returns what is left from a list when the largest prefix of a list is removed from the list:

```
scala> A dropWhile (_ % 2 != 0)
res23: List[Int] = List(10, 11, 13)
```

Method init returns all but the last element of a list, or in Scala parlance:

```
A.init == A.reverse.tail.reverse
```

Let us repeat that two objects are equal when they have exactly the same structure. Obviously, if they have different types, the comparison is always false, unless the type of one is a subtype of the other. And this is the reason why 1.0 == 1 is true. Method last returns the last element of a list, or in Scala parlance:

```
A.last == A.reverse.head
```

Although it is uncommon to ask for the *n*th element of some list, Scala provides the method apply which can be used to obtain an arbitrary element of some list:

```
scala> var A = List('a','b','c','d','e')
A: List[Char] = List(a, b, c, d, e)

scala> A.apply(3)
res24: Char = d

scala> A apply 3
res25: Char = d
```

Method zip takes as argument a list and creates a new list that consists of pairs: the first element from this list and the second from the argument list. If one list is shorter than the other, the resulting list has the length of the shorter list. For example, the following code

```
var A = List(11,12,13,14,15,16)
var B = List('a','b','c','d')
println(A.zip(B)); println(A zip B)
```

will print "List((11,a), (12,b), (13,c), (14,d))" two times.

If we have a list whose elements are lists, then function `flatten` can be used to concatenate the elements of this list as shown below:

```
scala> import List._
import List._

scala> var A=List(List(1,2),List(3,4))
A: List[List[Int]] = List(List(1, 2), List(3, 4))

scala> flatten(A)
res3: List[Int] = List(1, 2, 3, 4)
```

In addition, method `flatMap` concatenates the elements of a list of lists but first it applies to each element a function. For example, if `double` is a function that multiplies by two each element of a list, then one can use this function as shown below:

```
scala> A.flatMap(double)
res4: List[Int] = List(2, 4, 6, 8)
```

The method `toString` is used by any object to create a canonical string representation of this object. The `List(. . .)` representation is the canonical representation of lists. Since it is not possible to redefine this method, Scala's implementor has equipped lists with the `mkString` method. This method has three arguments – the first specifies the delimiter that opens a list, the second specifies a symbol that will be used to separate elements, and the third specifies the delimiter that closes a list. For example the code that follows

```
var B = List('a','b','c','d','e')
println(B.mkString("[",",","]"))
```

will print the string `[a,b,c,d,e]`, which is the standard representation of lists that is employed by most programming languages.

Exercise 2.35 Explain how one could obtain the standard Scala string representation of lists using `mkString`.

In certain cases it would be useful to be able to copy a list to an array. Method `copyToArray` has two arguments – an array and the starting position, which implies that we can copy part of a list. The following is a typical usage example:

```
scala> var B = List('a','b','c','d','e')
A: List[Char] = List(a, b, c, d, e)
```

```
scala> var A = new Array[Char](10)
A: Array[Char] = Array(, , , , , , , , )

scala> B.copyToArray(A,0)

    scala> A
res26: Array[Char] = Array(a, b, c, d, e, , , , , )
```

The functions foldl and foldr are used very frequently in functional programming to compute various things. Typically, these operators are defined as follows:

$$\text{foldl } f \ y \ [x_1, x_2, \ldots, x_n] = f\left(f\left(\ldots f\left(f(x_1, y), x_2\right), \ldots\right), x_n\right)$$

$$\text{foldr } f \ y \ [x_1, x_2, \ldots, x_n] = f\left(x_1, f\left(x_2, f\left(\ldots, f(x_n, y)\ldots\right)\right)\right).$$

Here f is a binary operator and y a sort of unit element of the operator (for example, if the operator is $+$, then $y = 0$). In Scala the foldl and foldr operators are "called" `/:` and `:/`, respectively. Let us see how we can use these operators. Suppose we want to define a function that computes the sum of any list of integers. Then we can define this function using foldl as follows:

```
def sum(A: List[Int]): Int = (0 /: A)(_ + _)
```

Exercise 2.36 Assume that prod is a function that computes the product of all elements of a list of integers. Define function prod using foldl.

Let us now define function reverse as it is actually defined in Scala:

```
def rev(A: List[Int]) = (List[Int]() /: A) { (A,a) => a::A}
```

Note that List[Int]() is an annotated version of Nil, the empty list.

Exercise 2.37 Explain why function rev computes the reverse of a list.

As a final example, let us present a function that can compute the first n prime numbers using the sieve of Eratosthenes:

```
var A : List[Int] = List()
for (i<-2 to 100) A = A ++ List(i)
def sieve (B:List[Int]) : List[Int] =
  B match {
    case Nil   => Nil
    case x::xs => x::sieve(xs.filter(e => e % x > 0))
  }
```

```
val primes = sieve(A)
println(primes)
```

This algorithm was invented by David Turner and first appeared in his unpublished *SASL Language Manual.*

2.14 Strings

In Scala, as in Java, a string is an *immutable* object, that is, an object that cannot be modified. On the other hand, objects that can be modified, like arrays, are called *mutable* objects. Each element of a string is associated with an index number. The first character is associated with the number 0, the second with the number 1, etc. Since strings are very useful objects, in the rest of this section we present the most important methods class `java.lang.String` defines.

length Returns the number of Unicode code units in a string. For example, the following code

```
var A = "Наталья"
println(A.length)
```

will print the number 7.

isEmpty Returns `true` if method `length` returns the number 0.

charAt This method has as argument an index number and returns the `Char` at the specified index. The expression `A.charAt(5)` returns the character ь.

codePointAt Returns the Unicode code point at the specified index. For instance, the command

```
println(A.codePointAt(5))
```

prints the number 1100.

startsWith Tests whether this string starts with the argument of this method. The command that follows

```
println(A.startsWith("H"))
```

wil print `true` since the string Наталья stars with a Н.

endsWith Tests whether this string ends with the argument of this method. The command that follows

```
println(A.endsWith("a"))
```

wil print `false` since the string Наталья does not end with an a.

indexOf Returns the index within this string object of the first occurrence of the string argument. For example, the commands that follow

```
println(A.indexOf("я"))
println(A.indexOf("та"))
```

will print the numbers 6 and 2.

lastIndexOf   Returns the index within this string object of the last occurrence of its Char or string argument. In the case of strings, the rightmost empty string "" is considered to occur at the index value that is equal to the length of the string. For instance, the command that follows

```
println(A.lastIndexOf("a"))
println(A.indexOf("ал"))
```

will print the numbers 3 and 3.

substring   Returns a new string that is a substring of this string. It may take one or two arguments. In the case that the method takes one argument, then the substring begins with the character at the specified index and extends to the end of this string. In the case that the method takes two arguments, the substring begins at the index specified by the first argument and extends to the character at the index specified by the second argument. For example, the commands that follow

```
println(A.substring(2))
println(A.substring(2,4))
```

will print талъя and та, respectively.

concat   This method appends its argument to this string. For instance, the commands that follow

```
A = A.concat("Дериева"); println(A)
```

will print Наталья Дериева.

contains   With this method we can examine whether a string contains a particular substring or not. For example, the code snippet

```
if (A.contains("ри")) println("OK")
```

will print the word OK.

replace   This method takes two arguments and returns a new string resulting from replacing all occurrences of the first argument in this string with the second argument. For example, the code

```
println(A.replace('a','o'))
```

will print Нотолъя.

toLowerCase   This method converts all of the characters in this string to lower case. The command

```
println(A.toLowerCase())
```

prints the string Наталья.

toUpperCase This method converts all of the characters in this string to upper case. The command

```
println(A.toUpperCase())
```

prints the string НАТАЛЬЯ.

trim Returns a copy of the string, with leading and trailing whitespace omitted.

toCharArray This method transforms a string into an array. The code snippet that follows

```
var A = "Наталья"
var B = A.toCharArray()
B(1)='α'; B(3)='α'
B.foreach(print)
```

will print Нαтαлья.

Exercise 2.38 Write a function to recognize palindromes, that is, words that read the same backwards as forwards. Some examples are: a, madam, Anna, and revivider. Extend the function to allow palindromic sentences. For example,

```
A man, a plan, a canal: Panama!
Evil rats on no star live.
```

Hint: Use replace to eliminate all punctuation marks, transform all sentences to lowercase, and use the fact that for any string A:

```
A.reverse.reverse != A   but   A.reverse.reverse.trim == A.
```

This is a known bug in the language implementation and springs from Scala's dependence on Java's basic types and the desire of Scala's designers and implementors to provide a really complete set of methods for each basic type.

2.15 Regular expressions

Regular expressions are used by many editors and other programs to search, edit, or manipulate text and data. A regular expression is a way of describing a set of strings using common properties (for example, strings that start with an "A" and end with an exclamation mark). Although Scala provides a package that can be used to create regular expressions and use them, we will show how to use the corresponding standard Java libraries. The libraries are actually a reimplementation of Perl's regular expressions engine. Before describing how to specify regular expressions, let us first see how we can use them.

Since regular expressions are like tiny language processors, it is far better to compile them into some internal representation and then use them. The following

Table 2.7 *Special characters that can appear in regular expressions*

Character	Meaning
x	The character x
\\	The backslash character
\0n	The character with octal value 0n ($0 \leq n \leq 7$)
\0nn	The character with octal value 0nn ($0 \leq n \leq 7$)
\0mnn	The character with octal value 0mnn ($0 \leq m \leq 7, 0 \leq n \leq 7$)
\xhh	The character with hexadecimal value 0xhh
\uhhhh	The character with hexadecimal value 0xhhhh
\t	The tab character ('\u0009')
\n	The newline (line feed) character ('\u000A')
\r	The carriage-return character ('\u000D')
\f	The form-feed character ('\u000C')
\a	The alert (bell) character ('\u0007')
\e	The escape character ('\u001B')
\cx	The control character corresponding to x

recipe describes what has to be done:

(i) turn the string representation of a regular expression into a `Pattern` object;
(ii) create a `Matcher` object from the object created in the previous step that applies to a particular string;
(iii) apply the various methods of the `Matcher` object to the particular string.

These steps can be expressed in Scala as follows:

```scala
import java.util.regex.{Pattern,Matcher}
. . . . . . . . . . . . . . . .
val p = Pattern.compile("regularExpression")
val m = p.matcher(String)
var foundMatch = m.find()
```

The most simple regular expression is a sequence of characters (for example, the string bar) that will match any substring that contains the characters of the pattern in this order. Thus, the pattern bar will match the "bar" in string Babar. If for any reason we cannot directly type a particular character or need to use a character that has a reserved meaning, then one should consult Table 2.7. This table explains how to enter almost any character.

Character classes Assume we want to check whether a string contains either the string bar or the string par. In other words, we want to check whether a string contains a substring that starts with either "b" or "p" and ends with "ar." Thus, it would be extremely useful to be able to specify this in a compact way, or else our task would be very difficult. To handle cases like this, one can use *character classes* that describe a set of characters and one can use them to check whether a character belongs to this set. All elements of a character class are enclosed in square brackets. Thus, we can use the following code to solve our little problem:

```
val p = Pattern.compile("[bp]ar")
```

By placing the symbol ^ just after the left square bracket we specify that we are looking for strings that do *not* contain the characters in the character class. Thus, the following

```
val p = Pattern.compile("[^f]ar")
```

will match all three letter substrings that end in "ar" but do not start with an "f." A range of characters is a special character (sub)class that consists of a sequence of characters whose code numbers form consecutive numbers. Ranges are specified by writing the first character of the range, a dash, and then the last character of the range. For example, the following regular expression

```
val p = Pattern.compile("[1-5]00")
```

will match the number 500 in "it costs 500 Euros." Actually, the notation $[a_1-a_n]$ is a shorthand for $[a_1 a_2 \ldots a_n]$. Also, if one wants to specify the union of two ranges, one can use either the notation $[a_1-a_n[b_1-b_m]]$ or the simpler notation $[a_1-a_n b_1-b_m]$. Thus, the regular expression

```
val p = Pattern.compile("[1-57-9]00")
```

will not match any string in "it costs 600 Euros." By putting the symbol && between ranges or character *subclasses*, the result is a character class that consists of the characters common to the two subclasses. For instance, the pattern specified in the command

```
val p = Pattern.compile("[[1-5]&&[5-9]]00")
```

is actually equivalent with the pattern specified in the following command:

```
val p = Pattern.compile("500")
```

The character class $[[a_1-a_n]\&\&[^b_1-b_m]]$ includes all characters a_i that are not included in the range b_1-b_m. Finally, there are a few predefined character classes which are shown in Table 2.8.

Quantifiers In many cases we do not want the regular expression engine to perform an exhaustive search of the string and match against all possible substrings. Instead,

Table 2.8 *Predefined character classes*

Character class	Meaning
.	Any character (may or may not match line terminators)
\d	A digit, shorthand for [0-9]
\D	A nondigit, shorthand for [^0-9]
\s	Shorthand for [␣\t\n\x0B\f\r] (i.e., a whitespace character)
\S	A nonwhitespace character, shorthand for [^\s]
\w	A word character, shorthand for [a-zA-Z_0-9]
\W	A nonword character: [^\w]

Table 2.9 *Quantifiers for regular expressions*

Quantifiers			
Greedy	Reluctant	Possessive	Matches X...
X?	X??	X?+	one or zero times
X*	X*?	X*+	zero or more times
X+	X+?	X++	one or more times
X{n}	X{n}?	X{n}+	exactly n times
X{n,}	X{n,}?	X{n,}+	at least n times
X{n,m}	X{n,m}?=	X{n,m}+	at least n but not more than m times

we may need to specify the number of occurrences to match against. Quantifiers can be either greedy, reluctant, or possessive as shown in Table 2.9.

Let us first briefly discuss the difference between these quantifiers. As expected, the following code will find two instances of "o" in the corresponding string:

```
val p = Pattern.compile("o")
val m = p.matcher("Απόστολος")
var found = false
while (m.find()) {
  print("I found the text \""+ m.group())
  print("\" starting at index " + m.start())
  println(" and ending at index " + m.end())
  found = true
}
if (!found)
  println("No match found.%n")
```

Method `find` attempts to find the next subsequence of the input sequence that matches the pattern. It returns `true` if the attempt is successful, false otherwise. Methods `start` and `end` return the start index of the previous match and the offset after the last character matched. If we change the pattern to `"o?,"` then this pattern will be matched ten times! This happens because it may match one or zero times. This explains the nine times. But since empty strings are matched also, this explains the tenth time. Similar results will be delivered if we change the pattern to `"o*."` However, if we change the pattern to `"o+,"` then the pattern will be matched exactly two times.

A greedy quantifier checks first whether the entire string matches the regular expression. If it does not, then the matcher pushes back one character and examines the resulting string. It repeats this process until a match is found or there are no more characters to push back. A reluctant quantifier works in the opposite way: it starts by examining the first character and depending on the success or failure of the examination it stops or consumes one more character until it finds a match or there are no more characters to consume. A possessive quantifier consumes the whole string and tries once and only once to find a match. To see the difference between these three approaches to pattern matching, assume that we want to find all the "α" letters that are preceeded by any sequence of letters in the word "Αναστασία." First, we need to write the patterns:

```
val p1 = Pattern.compile(".*α")
val p2 = Pattern.compile(".*?α")
val p3 = Pattern.compile(".*+α")
```

Exercise 2.39 Write down the corresponding matcher definition and a while-loop like the one in the previous paragraph for each pattern.

The greedy matcher will find the text *"Αναστασία" starting at index 0 and ending at index 9*; the reluctant matcher will find the text *"Ανα" starting at index 0 and ending at index 3, the text "στα" starting at index 3 and ending at index 6, and the text "στα" starting at index 6 and ending at index 9*. Finally, the possessive matcher will find nothing.

Groups What if we want our regular expression to include subpatterns which can be referred to directly? Such a subpattern is called a group and it is specified by enclosing it in parentheses. As a trivial example, if we want to check whether a string contains the syllable "στα," we could use the regular expression `"(στα)."` It is quite possible to have nested groups. In this case, if it is necessary to know what did any subgroup match, we have to invoke methods `group`, `start`, and `end` with the group's number as their only argument. To find a group's number just count the left parentheses that preceed a particular subgroup and subtract one, as the whole regular expression is in group zero. Thus, in the expression ((A)(B(C))), the subexpression B(C) is in group 2.

Exercise 2.40 Assume we have the following regular expression and input string:

```
val p1 = Pattern.compile("(([^bp])(ar))+")
val m1 = p1.matcher("on mars there are no cars")
```

What do you expect to see on your computer screen when the code

```
while (m1.find()) {
  print("I found the text \""+ m1.group(2))
  print("\" starting at index " + m1.start(2))
  println(" and ending at index " + m1.end(2))
}
```

is executed?

We can specify alternatives with classes, but we can employ a special notation involving groups. In particular, we can specify the alternatives in a group where alternatives are separated by the symbol |. For example, the pattern (\+|-)? will match either a plus or a minus sign. If we place a backslash (\) in front of any special character, then it is turned into a normal character. Also, if for some reason we want to refer to a subpattern that forms a subgroup and which has been matched already, then we can do so by using \n, where n is the subgroup's number. Note that everything that has been matched is stored in memory for future reference.

Boundary matchers These are special symbols that should be used when it matters where the string that will be matched is located. For example, when one analyzes an input string it matters whether some *token* is in the beginning or the end of the string. The various boundary matchers that are available are shown in Table 2.10.

Compiler flags The regular expression compiler can be invoked with an extra argument as shown below:

```
val p1 = Pattern.compile("(([^bp])(ar))+",
                         Pattern.CASE_INSENSITIVE)
```

This extra argument is a flag that can be either one of the following symbols or a combination of them using bitwise conjunction and/or disjunction.

Pattern.CANON_EQ Enables canonical equivalence. Unicode "composite" characters (e.g., å) are considered equivalent to their constituents (e.g., a and °).

Table 2.10 *Boundary matchers supported by Scala*

^	The beginning of a line
$	The end of a line
\b	A word boundary
\B	A nonword boundary
\A	The beginning of the input
\G	The end of the previous match
\Z	The end of the input but for the final terminator, if any
\z	The end of the input

Table 2.11 *Embedded flag expressions for regular expressions*

Constant	Equivalent embedded flag expression
Pattern.CANON_EQ	none
Pattern.CASE_INSENSITIVE	(?i)
Pattern.COMMENTS	(?x)
Pattern.MULTILINE	(?m)
Pattern.DOTALL	(?s)
Pattern.LITERAL	none
Pattern.UNICODE_CASE	(?u)
Pattern.UNIX_LINES	(?d)

Pattern.CASE_INSENSITIVE Enables case-insensitive matching.

Pattern.COMMENTS Permits whitespace and comments in pattern.

Pattern.DOTALL Enables dotall mode.

Pattern.LITERAL Enables literal parsing of the pattern.

Pattern.MULTILINE Enables multiline mode.

Pattern.UNICODE_CASE Enables Unicode-aware case folding.

Pattern.UNIX_LINES Enables Unix lines mode.

There are some embedded flag expressions, shown in Table 2.11, that can be used inside a regular expression. This way, one can avoid specifying the flags presented above.

Replacing text There are two methods that can be used to replace text that matches a given regular expression. Method `replaceFirst` replaces the first occurrence while method `replaceAll` replaces all occurrences. The following code shows how these methods can be used:

```
var REGEX = "foo"
var INPUT = "The town has foos. All towns have foos."
```

Table 2.12 *Special noncapturing constructs*

Construct	Meaning
`(?:X)`	X as a noncapturing group
`Y(?=X)`	A zero-width positive lookahead; matches a Y that is not followed by an X.
`Y(?!X)`	A zero-width negative lookahead; matches a Y and a trailing X while disregarding it from the final result
`(?<=X)Y`	A zero-width positive lookbehind; matches an X followed by a Y while disregarding X from the final result
`(?<!X)Y`	A zero-width negative lookbehind; matches a Y that does not follows an X.
`(?>X)`	Pattern equivalent to `(?=(X))\1`, where `\1` is a backreference

```
var REPLACE = "bar"
val p = Pattern.compile(REGEX)
val m = p.matcher(INPUT) // get a matcher object
INPUT = m.replaceAll(REPLACE)
println(INPUT)
```

Although we have used a simple word as a regular expression, the most interesting cases are those where "real" regular expressions are involved. As an example consider the following piece of code that transforms any sequence of digits into one with commas. For example, it will transform the string 1234 to string 1,234:

```
var REGEX = "(\\d)(\\d\\d\\d)(?!\\d)"
var INPUT = "123456789"
var REPLACE = "$1,$2"

val p = Pattern.compile(REGEX)
var m = p.matcher(INPUT)
while (m.find()){
  INPUT = m.replaceFirst(REPLACE)
  m = p.matcher(INPUT)
}
println(INPUT)
```

First note that we need to escape the backslash. Second, the group `(?!\\d)` is a special group that does not count when numbering groups. This group is used when we want to make sure a specific pattern is not followed on another specific pattern (see Table 2.12 for more details). The symbols `$1` and `$2` refer to what the first and the second groups have matched. If you wonder why we need the repetition command, the answer is very simple: in order to apply the replacement to all possible cases even after one replacement has been applied.

Exercise 2.41 The following regular expression can be used to match float numbers:

$$((\backslash+|-)?\backslash d+(\backslash.\backslash d+)?([eE](\backslash+|-)?\backslash d+)?)$$

Explain why it does so.

2.16 Scientific computation with Scala

The term scientific computation refers to the use of computers to compute numbers and functions important to sciences and engineering. Scala has not been designed as a tool for scientific computation, but provides rudimentary support for it. Scala defines an object that contains fields and methods that can be used to perform basic numeric operations such as the elementary exponential, logarithm, square root, and trigonometric functions. Object Math defines a number of methods that are described in Table 2.13. Note that there are four different versions of max, min, abs, and signum: one for each number type. In all other cases, methods expect arguments of type Double and return values of the same type. Obviously, one can import all methods defined by this object. However, in certain cases it is better to use only the methods that are needed. For example, if a and b are the lengths of the catheti of a right triangle, then the expression

```
Math.sqrt(a*a+b*b)
```

computes the length of its hypotenuse. Object Math also defines a number of fields that are described in Table 2.14. The NaN fields represent something that is not a number. For example, 0/0 is such a value. Unfortunately, we cannot use these fields to test whether an expression evaluates to a value that is not a number. For instance, in the code

```
var zero:Double = 0;
if ((0 / zero) == Math.NaN_DOUBLE)
    println("0 / 0 can be tested with NaN_DOUBLE.")
else
    println("0 / 0 cannot be tested with NaN_DOUBLE")
```

the expression will evaluate to false. Fortunately, there are some methods, which have found their way into Scala through the Java programming language, that can be used to test whether an expression evaluates to a value that is neither a number nor a finite number. The example that follows shows how these methods can be used:

Table 2.13 *Methods defined by object* Math

Method	Meaning
IEEEremainder	Computes the remainder of its two Double arguments
abs	Returns the absolute value of its argument
acos	Computes the inverse cosine; returns the value in radians
asin	Computes the inverse sine; returns the value in radians
atan	Computes the inverse tangent; returns the value in radians
atan2	Converts rectangular coordinates (x, y) to polar (r, θ)
ceil	Returns the smallest integer not less than its argument
sin	Computes the sine
cos	Computes the cosine
tan	Computes the tangent
exp	Computes the expression e^x, where x is its argument and e the base of the natural logarithm
floor	Returns the largest integer less than or equal to its argument
log	Computes the natural logarithm of its argument
max	Returns the maximum of its two arguments
min	Returns the minimum of its two arguments
pow	Computes the value of the first argument raised to the power of the second argument
round	Returns the Long that is closest to its argument
rint	Like round except that it returns a Double
signum	Returns the sign of its argument
sqrt	Computes the square root of its argument
toDegrees	Takes an angle expressed in radians and computes its equivalent in degrees
toRadians	Takes an angle expressed in degrees and computes its equivalent in radians

Table 2.14 *Fields defined by object* Math

E	e, the base of the natural logarithm
Pi	The number π
MIN_INT	The smallest value of type Int; for all other numeric types similar fields exist
MAX_INT	The greatest value of type Int; for all other numeric types similar fields exist
EPS_FLOAT	The smallest Float that is greater than zero
EPS_DOUBLE	The smallest Double that is greater than zero
NEG_INF_DOUBLE	Negative infinity of type Double
POS_INF_DOUBLE	Positive infinity of type Double
NEG_INF_FLOAT	Negative infinity of type Float
POS_INF_FLOAT	Positive infinity of type Float
NaN_DOUBLE	"Not a number" of type Double
NaN_FLOAT	"Not a number" of type Float

```
if ( (0 / 0.0).isNaN )
  println("NaN")

if ( (1 / 0.0).isInfinity )
  println("Infinity")

if ( (-1 / 0.0).isNegInfinity )
  println("-Infinity")

if ( (+1 / 0.0).isPosInfinity )
  println("+Infinity")
```

Assume we have to write a function that increments a Double number by EPS_DOUBLE. At first this may seem a trivial task, but it is not. First, we need to check whether the argument is an infinity or a nonnumber. Clearly, in this case the function must return its argument intact. If the number is not infinity and it is a number indeed(!), then we transform it to a 64-bit two's complement integer representation just because Longs can hold any Double. The n-bit two's complement representation of a positive integer is the base 2 representation of the integer with 0s added to the left to give a total of n-bits. To transform back and forth we need to use some methods available only to the corresponding Java objects. As for the rest of the code, we leave it to the reader to find out what it does.

```
def Increment(value: Double): Double = {
  if( value.isInfinity || value.isNaN )
   return value
  var signed64: Long =
     java.lang.Double.doubleToRawLongBits(value)
  if ( signed64 < 0 )
    signed64 -= 1
  else
    signed64 += 1
  if ( signed64 == Math.MIN_LONG ) //= "-0", make it "+0"
   return 0;
  var tmp_value = java.lang.Double.longBitsToDouble(signed64)
  if ( tmp_value.isNaN )
    return Math.NaN_DOUBLE
  else
    return tmp_value
}
```

The following two tests will both print OK, thus verifying that our function works as expected:

```
if ( (Increment(Math.MAX_DOUBLE)).isInfinity )
  println("OK")
else
  println("error")

if (Increment(0.0) == Math.EPS_DOUBLE)
  println("OK")
else
  println("error")
```

2.17 Inner classes

Classes and traits (see Section 3.3) can be declared inside other classes and/or traits and are called *inner*. With inner classes it is possible to "connect logically related objects simply and effectively" [6]. In order to demonstrate the inner workings of inner classes, we will borrow the bank account example from [6]. In this example, the last action is always expressed as an instance of an inner class. The code in Figure 2.2 shows a version of a very simplified bank account class that implements exactly this functionality.

The first thing one should note in inner class definitions is that they introduce a scope. All fields and methods defined outside the inner class are accessible from within the inner class, however, methods and fields defined inside an inner class

```
class BankAccount(val number : Long) {
  private var balance = 0L
  private var lastAct: Action = null

  class Action(val act: String, val amount: Long) {
    override def toString =
      number + ": " + act + " " + amount
  }

  def deposit(amount: Long) {
    balance += amount
    lastAct = new Action("deposit",amount)
  }

  def withdraw(amount: Long) {
    balance -= amount
    lastAct = new Action("withdraw",amount)
  }
}
```

Figure 2.2 A simple class implementing bank accounts.

are not visible outside the class. Thus, if we add a field `act` in class `BankAccount`, then the name `act` inside `Action` will not refer to the field of class `BankAccount`. One could say that the definition inside the inner class *hides* or *shadows* the corresponding definition that occurs just outside the inner class. Shadowing occurs also when a field or a method is inherited by an inner class. Thus, when using simple names in an inner class they refer to the members of the inner class whether they are declared or inherited. The members of the enclosing class can be accessed explicitly with a qualified-`this` expression. In particular, if class `Z` defined inside class `Y` has a method `m`, then if class `Y` has a method defined or inherited with the same name it can be referred to in code inside `Z` with `Y.this.m`. For example, if the following definition is part of class `BankAccount`

```
val act = "surprise!"
```

then it can be accessed inside `Action` with the following expression:

```
BankAccount.this.act
```

Similarly, if class `Y` extends class `X`, then we can refer to the superclass implementation of the method `m` in code defined in `Z` with `Y.super.m`.

2.18 Packages

Packages are used to group classes and, thus, they can be used to separate source code in several source files. Scala packages are similar to Java packages. A package name consists of words separated by periods. The first part of the name of a Java package represents the organization which created the package while the rest of the name reflects the contents of the package. In addition, a Java package name also reflects its directory structure. Roughly, this is true even for Scala packages. For example, the following declaration

```
package scala.util.logging
```

implies that the directory `scala/util/logging` is where this package resides. But Scala packages differ from Java packages in that Scala has incorporated ideas borrowed from C#. In particular, it is possible to declare one package inside another, thus forming a hierarchy of nested packages. Each nested declaration is enclosed in curly brackets:

```
package A {
   package B {
      class a(x:Int) {
         def get = x
      }
   }
}
```

When this code is compiled, it will create a directory called A and inside this directory it will create another directory, B, which will contain the file a.class. Similar to inner classes, nested packages and/or classes define a scope, thus affecting the "visibility" of classes and/or class members. Consider the following sample code:

```
package A {
   package B {
      class a(x:Int) {
         def get = x
         def obj2 =  new A.C.a("OK")
      }
   }
   package C {
      class a(x: String) {
         def get = x
         def obj3 = new _root_.C.a(4.0)
      }
   }
}
package C {
   class a(x: Double) {
      def get = x
   }
}
```

Observe that method obj3 returns an instance of class a which belongs to package C that is at the same level as package A. In addition, observe that the class name is prefixed by the the symbol _root_, which is the name of the *root* package, that is, the package that is at the top of the package hierarchy. It is a Scala feature that if one defines a class on the top level, one cannot use it inside another class that bears the same name. Scala will complain that *type α is not a member of package <root>*.

Packages may affect the visibility of members of a class in a different way. When a member of a class is declared as private[this], this means that it can be accessed only from the object that contains it. If instead of this we use a package name, then this member can be accessed by this package and packages declared inside this package. For example, if we use the access modifier private[parsing] and we have the following package hierarchy

```
scala.util
scala.util.parsing
scala.util.parsing.combinator
```

then the method or field will be accessible only from the last two packages.

Classes declared inside packages can be *imported* by using the import command, as has already been explained. The command offers some options that can be used to control which classes, methods, objects, etc., will be imported. In the simplest case, we can specify exacly what to import. For example, with the command

```
import A.a, b
```

we ask Scala to load exactly two members. In addition, it is quite possible to give a new name to a member as shown below:

```
import A.a => {α, b}
```

Now, α will stand for A.a. The underscore serves as wildcard and one can use it to import everything. Nevertheless, the following "idiom"

```
import A.{a=>_,_}
```

will import all members except a. The last thing one should know about the import command is that one can have imports anywhere in a source file.

2.19 Documentation comments

As was noted in Chapter 1, one can place comments in code by placing the symbol // anywhere in the source code. In addition, by enclosing code segments between the symbols /* and */ one can force Scala to ignore this code segment completely. In general, comments can be used to force a language processor to ignore a section of the source code and/or to include text that of course is ignored but explains the functionality of the source code. In many cases, these comments serve as a basis for the construction of a reference manual. To facilitate the construction of such documents, the designers of the Java programming language introduced the so-called *documentation comments*, or just *doc-comments*. These are comments that allow programmers to include reference comments directly in their code which can be used to generate reference documentation. Scala provides support for doc-comments à la Java and source code that contains such comments can be processed with the `scaladoc` utility. The result of the processing is a set of HTML files.

A doc-comment opens with the symbols `/**` and closes with the symbols `*/`. Doccomments describe identifiers whose declaration immediately follows the comment. In a doc-comment, whatever comes before the first period is considered a summary for the identifier. Of course it is a matter of style what one considers a good summary, so we will not make any attempt to dictate to the reader what to write in doc-comments. One can add HTML tags inside a doc-comment to enhance readability, to provide links to documents that may contain specific details, etc. Leading asterisk (`*`) characters, tabs and spaces are discarded. Furthermore, one can use a number of different tags inside a doc-comment. These tags can hold particular kinds of information.

The `@author` tag can be used to specify the author of a class or a trait. If there is more than one author, then one should specify each author with a different `@author` tag. The `@version` tag should be used to specify the version number of a class or a trait. Since different versions of the same software may introduce new features, add or remove functionality, etc., it is quite useful to keep track of when particular changes took place. This necessity is served by the information stored in a `@since` tag. The `@param` tag can be used to explain the functionality of parameters. For each parameter there should be a corresponding tag line. Each such line should have the tag followed by the name of the parameter followed by a description. The `@return` tag should be used to describe what a method returns. The `@see` tag provides a means to have references in the final documentation. If the tag is followed by simple text, then the tag will be replaced by a "**See Also:**" and the text of the tag will appear on the next line. The text can be normal text (for example, the title of a book), an HTML hyperreference tag, or something like the text in the following tag:

```
@see package.class#member   label
```

where `package.class#member` is any valid name in Scala that is referenced and `label` is text that appears in the hyperreference that is constructed. The `@throws` adds a "Throws" subheading to the generated documentation. Finally, the `@deprecated` tag followed by text adds a comment indicating that what is commented should no longer be used. A relatively complete example of class definition with doc-comments is shown in Figure 2.3, while the rendered output can be seen in Figure 2.4.

```
package Cell
/** Package <code>Cell</code> defines class
 * <code>cell</code>.
 */
/** Class <code>cell</code> implements a simple
 * storage cell into which one can store numbers.
 * The class can be instantiated by either supplying
 * an initial value or by assuming its initial value
 * is  equal to zero.
 *
 * @author Dimitrios-Georgios Syropoulos-Harissis
 *
 * @version 1.0
 */
class cell (protected var  contents : Int){
/** Creating a new instance of this class with no value
 * specified implies that the number 0 is to be stored
 * in the object.
 */
 def this () = this(0)
/** Method <code>get</code> should be
 * used to retrieve the value currently
 * stored in the storage cell.
 *
 * @return The current contents of the cell.
 */
 def get() = contents
/** Method <code>set</code> should be
 * used to alter the contents of the cell.
 *
 * @param n The new value to be stored
 * in this storage cell.
 */
 def set(n: Int) = {
   contents = n
 }
}
```

Figure 2.3 A simple Scala package/class with doc-comments.

2.20 Annotations

Annotations are comments of a special kind that do not directly affect the intended meaning of any program, but they supply information about how a program should be compiled, deployed or executed. In a way, annotations complement doc-comments. For example, the annotation @deprecated before a method as shown below

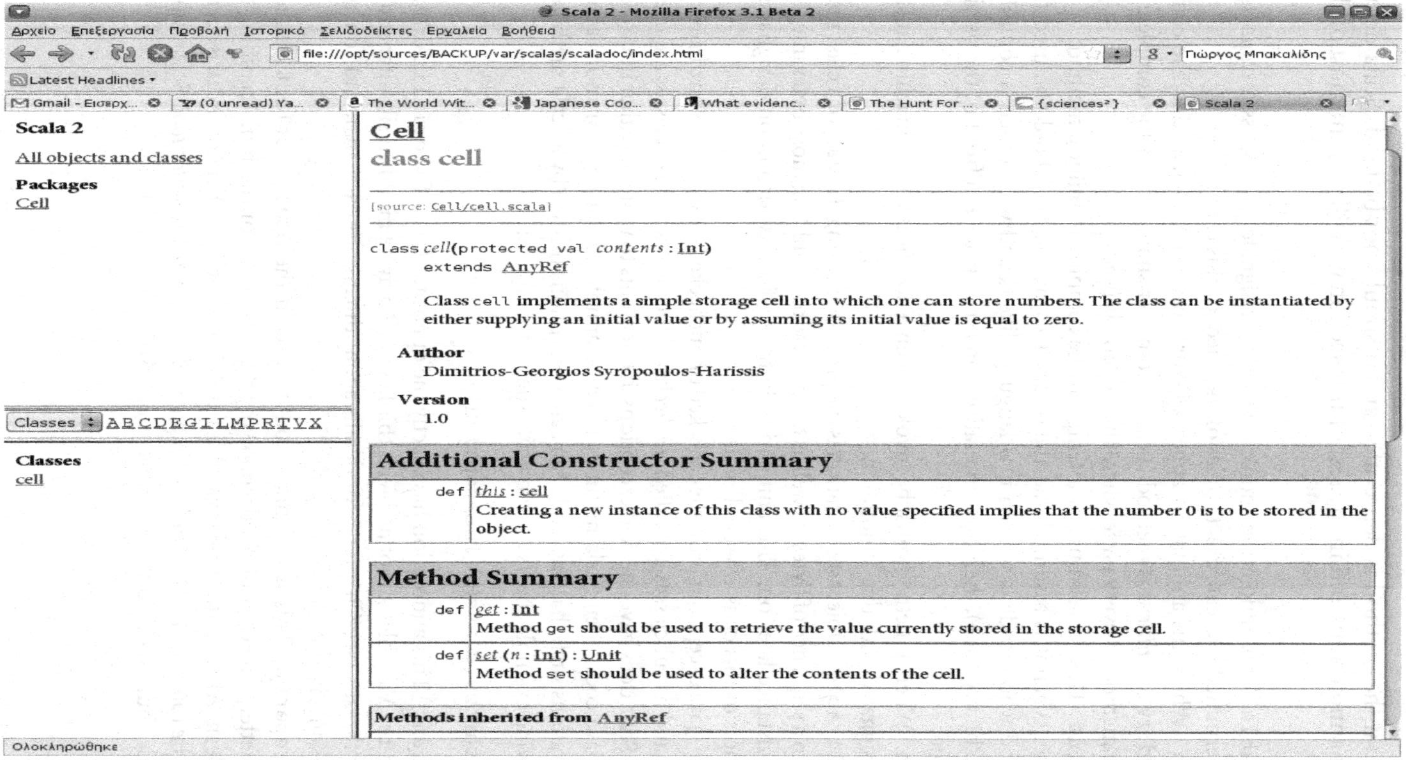

Figure 2.4 The reference documentation produced by the code in Figure 2.3.

```
@deprecated def deprecatedMethod() { }
```

indicates that the method is deprecated and it should not be used. Scala defines a number of annotations and in the rest of this section we will present most of them.

@cloneable   This annotation should be used to designate that a class is *clonable* (i.e., it is permitted to create exact copies of instances of this class).

@inline   When this annotation appears before method, it signals that the compiler should try to *inline* this method (i.e., the compiler should insert the complete body of the method in every place where the method is used).

@noinline   This cancels out any attempt by the compiler to inline a method.

@native   When it is assumed that the body of *native* method should be used (i.e., a method whose code is written in a language like C and which then is compiled in native binary code), then this annotation should be placed in front of the particular method.

@remote   When a method must be invoked from a nonlocal virtual machine, it should be designated with this annotation.

@serializable   Object serialization is the process of saving the state of a class instance state to a sequence of bytes, as well as the process of rebuilding those bytes into a "live" class instance later on. This annotation in front of a class definition designates that instances of this class are serializable.

@throws   Java exceptions are either checked or unchecked – exception RuntimeException and its subclasses are called *unchecked*. All other exception classes are checked. Since Scala does have checked exceptions, if one wants to write code that interoperates with Java code, then Scala methods must be annotated with one or more @throws annotations such that Java code can catch exceptions thrown by a Scala method. The following example shows how to write such annotations:

```
@throws(classOf[IOException])
```

@transient   This annotation has exactly the opposite effect of @serializable.

@volatile   Variables annotated with this keyword may be modified simultaneously by other threads (see Chapter 7 for details about threads, in particular, and concurrent processing, in general).

@BeanProperty   This is an annotation defined in the scala.reflect package. It adds setter and getter methods following the JavaBeans convention. According to the JavaBeans API specification (available from Oracle's web site): *A Java Bean is a reusable software component that can be manipulated visually in a builder tool.* Scala supports this idea but follows different conventions (see Section 3.12).

3

Advanced features

The constructs that have been presented in the previous chapter are enough for the creation of simple software systems. On the other hand, it is quite possible to create very complex software systems with these constructs, but the design and implementation processes will be really difficult. Fortunately, Scala provides many *advanced* features and constructs that facilitate programming as a mental activity. In this chapter we will describe most of these advanced features, while a few others like parsing combinators and actors will be presented thoroughly in later chapters.

3.1 Playing with trees

In the previous chapter we presented many important data types, but we did not mention trees, which form a group of data types that have many uses. Also, from the discussion so far, it is not clear whether Scala provides a facility for the construction of *recursive* data types, that is data types that are defined in terms of themselves. For example, a binary tree is a typical example of a recursively defined data structure that can be defined as follows [4].

Definition 1 Given the type *node*, a *binary tree* over the type node is defined in the following way.

(i) An empty set of elements of the type node is a binary tree.
(ii) If T_1 and T_2 are binary trees over the type node, then so is the triple (n, T_1, T_2), where n is an element of the type node. T_1 and T_2 are called the left and right subtrees of the tree (n, T_1, T_2).

Typically, when using an imperative programming language like C, one has to use records and *pointers*, that is, values that point to elements of some type T that are stored somewhere in a computer's memory using their memory address, to define recursive data types. Admittedly, this is a low-level mechanism and one that has no place in a high-level language like Scala. On the other hand, when programming in a functional programming language, one can use algebraic data types to define recursive data types. Roughly, an algebraic data type is a type where it is necesary to specify the "shape" of each of its elements. In particular, an algebraic data type is defined as an alteration of *constructors* of the type. For example, one could specify a binary tree over integers using a hypothetical data type specification command as follows (the vertical bar is pronounced *or*):

```
datatype BinTree = Empty | Node(Int, BinTree, BinTree)
```

Scala is an object-oriented programming language and its main data structuring facility is the class. Since algebraic data types are particularly elegant and useful, Scala allows its users to define class hierarchies that mimic algebraic data types. More specifically, the type itself is declared as an *abstract* class and all the forms of the type are declared as subclasses of the abstract class. A type is called abstract if its identity is not precisely known. When it comes to classes, one is termed abstract when its body is partially defined or completely empty. The definition that follows is the Scala equivalent of the previous definition:

```
abstract class BinTree
case class EmptyTree() extends BinTree
case class Node(elem : Int,
                left : BinTree,
                right: BinTree) extends BinTree
```

The keyword `case` is used to introduce the various forms of the type. Note that the same keyword was used to present the various cases in the various list manipulation algorithms which were expressed with pattern matching. In general, but not always, the cases in a match command correspond to the cases introduced in a case class definition. Note that it is the same to declare a class without a body and to declare it with an empty body, that is, `{ }`. Also note that the two subclasses of `BinTree` are proper classes; nothing is special about them. Although the definition of `BinTree` is correct, since the instantiation of class `EmptyTree` is actually restricted to one object, that is, there is only one empty tree, it is better to follow the singleton design pattern and define it as an object:

```
abstract class BinTree
case object EmptyTree extends BinTree
case class  Node(elem : Int,
                 left : BinTree,
                 right: BinTree) extends BinTree
```

Once we have defined a case-class hierarchy, we can construct instances of these classes without using the new command. For example, the following commands create an empty tree and a tree with only one node:

```
var t1 = EmptyTree
var t2 = Node(4,EmptyTree,EmptyTree)
```

Instances of recursive data types are easily manipulated with recursive functions. If we want to list the nodes of a binary tree, there are three different strategies. Informally, these strategies can be described as follows:

- visit the topmost node, visit the left subtree, and visit the right subtree;
- visit the left subtree, visit the topmost node, and visit the right subtree;
- visit the right subtree, visit the topmost node, and visit the left subtree.

These strategies are known as pre-order, in-order, and post-order tree traversals. It is not difficult to design a function that will *flatten* a binary tree into a list using, say, the in-order tree traversal strategy. Indeed, the following function accomplishes this task:

```
def inOrder(t: BinTree): List[Int] =
  t match {
    case EmptyTree   => List()
    case Node(e,l,r) => inOrder(l):::List(e):::inOrder(r)
  }
```

Here we have used pattern matching since this is the easiest way to solve such problems. Previously, we stated that in most situations the cases in a match command correspond to the cases introduced in a case class definition. However, in certain cases this is not true. For example, consider the following function definition that computes the depths, that is, the longest path from the topmost node to the lowermost node:

```
def depth(t: BinTree): Int = {
  t match {
    case EmptyTree => 0
    case Node(_,EmptyTree,r) => 1 + depth(r)   // case 2
    case Node(_,l,EmptyTree) => 1 + depth(l)   // case 3
    case Node(_,l,r) => Math.max(depth(l),depth(r)) + 1
  }
}
```

We could leave out the cases marked as case 2 and case 3, but we have introduced them because they make the code more efficient.

Exercise 3.1 Write two functions that implement the pre-order and post-order tree traversal strategies.

Although it is interesting to see how one can manipulate binary trees or, more generally, recursive data types, it is equally important to show how one can construct such structures. Instead of showing how one can build any binary tree, we will show how to build binary search trees. Roughly, a binary search tree is a tree such that given a node n its left subtree contains only values less than the node's value and its right subtree contains only values greater than the node's value. In addition, we demand that no two different nodes can hold the same value. Clearly, we do not need to provide a special definition for these trees – the one given above is OK. Interestingly, if we traverse and print each element stored in a binary search tree using the in-order tree traversal strategy, the elements will be printed in ascending order. In other words, building a binary search tree and then traversing the tree can be considered as a sorting algorithm.

We assume that we are going to build a binary search tree from data that are stored in a list. The following code shows how one can build a list from data that are supplied interactively by a user. On page 37 we showed how one can write a loop that inputs from the keyboard a sequence of numbers. The skeleton code snippet that follows shows how we can build a list from input supplied from the keyboard:

```
var x:Int = _ // variable used to input numbers
var In:List[Int] = List()
do {
   .  .  .  .  .  .
  if (! EOF) {
     In = x::In
  }
} while (! EOF)
```

Now that we have a list, the next thing is actually to build the tree. For this we need a function that will insert one element at a time into the tree. This function will be used repeatedly by another function that will insert all elements of the list into the tree. The code in Figure 3.1 shows how this can be done. Note that we have a nested function definition. We have opted to define function mkTree this way in order to keep things simple, at least for the user. The recursive function insert has two arguments: the element to be inserted in the tree and the tree itself. If the tree is empty, it just returns a new Node. Otherwise, if the element is less than the element stored in the current node, it returns the current node with the element inserted in the left subtree of the tree; if the element is greater than the element stored in the current node, it returns the current node with the element stored

```
def mkTree (l:List[Int]): BinTree = {
  def insert(x:Int, t:BinTree) : BinTree = {
    t match {
      case EmptyTree    => Node(x,EmptyTree,EmptyTree)
      case Node(y,l,r) => if (x < y)
                             Node(y,insert(x,l),r)
                          else if (x > y)
                             Node(y,l,insert(x,r))
                          else
                             EmptyTree
    }
  } // end of insert
  l match {
    case Nil => EmptyTree
    case x::xs => insert(x,mkTree(xs))
  }
}
```

Figure 3.1 A function that builds a binary search tree from a list.

in the right subtree of the tree. Finally, if the element is equal to the element of the list it is disregarded and this is the reason the function returns an empty tree. Function mkTree first creates an empty tree and then it inserts the elements of the list in reverse order into the tree. In order to help the reader fully grasp the way function mkTree operates, we provide a full trace of an invocation of this function in Figure 3.2.

Exercise 3.2 Write a function `reflect` that will take a binary tree and return a second binary tree whose left subtree is the right subtree of the original tree and whose right subtree is the left subtree of the original tree.

Exercise 3.3 A linked list is a data type that can be defined in Scala as follows:

```
abstract class LinkedList
case object EmptyList extends LinkedList
case class  Node(elem: Int, next: LinkedList)
```

Write functions that create a linked list, delete a particular element from a list, and add an element in a specific position.

A problem whose solution is reminiscent of in-order tree traversal is the problem of the *Towers of Hanoi*. This problem can be stated as follows (see Apostolos's web page for more information).

```
mkTree([1,3,2])  =  insert(1,mkTree([3,2]))

                 =  insert(1,insert(3,mkTree([2])))

                 =  insert(1,insert(3,insert(2,insert(Nil))))

                 =  insert(1,insert(3,insert(2,EmptyTree)))

                 =  insert(1,insert(3,Node(2,EmptyTree,EmptyTree)))

                 =  insert(1,Node(2,EmptyTree,insert(3,EmptyTree)))

                 =  insert(1,Node(2,EmptyTree,Node(3,EmptyTree,EmptyTree)))

                 =  Node(2,insert(1,EmptyTree),Node(3,EmptyTree,EmptyTree)))

                 =  Node(2,Node(1,EmptyTree,EmptyTree),Node(3,EmptyTree,EmptyTree))
```

Figure 3.2 Full evaluation of mkTree([1,3,2]).

There are three poles and a tower of disks on the first pole, with the smallest on the top and the largest on the bottom. The purpose of the puzzle is to move the whole tower from the first pole to the second, by moving only one disk each time, and by observing the rule that a larger disk cannot be placed atop a smaller one.

The problem can be solved by a simple problem-reduction approach. One way of reducing the original problem, that is, that of moving a tower of n disks from pole A to pole B by using pole C, to a set of of simpler problems involves the following chain of reasoning.

(i) In order to move all of the disks to pole B we must certainly move the largest disk there, and pole B must be empty just prior to moving the largest disk to it.
(ii) Now looking at the initial configuration, we cannot move the largest disk anywhere until all the other disks are first removed. Furthermore, the other disks should not be moved to pole B since then we would not be able to move the largest disk there. Therefore we should first move all the other disks to pole C.
(iii) Then we can complete the key step of moving the largest disk from pole A to pole B and go on to solve the problem

In this way we have reduced the problem of moving a tower to the problem of moving a tower with height one less and that of moving the largest disk. This solution can be most effectively rendered as a recursive function. Function hanoi implements the recursive solution suggested by the solution above:

```
def hanoi(n:Int):List[String] = {
    def move(A: String, B: String) = List(A+B)
    def _hanoi(n: Int, A: String,
                        B: String,
                        C: String):List[String] =
        if (n>1)
            _hanoi(n-1,A,C,B):::move(A,B):::_hanoi(n-1,C,B,A)
        else
            List()
    _hanoi(n,"A","B","C")
}
```

Let us now see how we can handle s-expressions. An s-expression is a data structure which forms the basis of pure Lisp.

Definition 2 Assume that T is a simple type whose elements are called *atoms*. Then the set of s-expressions is defined as the smallest set such that:

(i) atoms are s-expressions,
(ii) if s_1 and s_2 are s-expressions, then so is the pair (s_1, s_2).

It is not difficult to define a character s-expression as follows:

```
abstract class SExp
case object NilSExp extends SExp
case class Atom(elem: Char) extends SExp
case class Pair(left : SExp,
                right: SExp) extends SExp
```

Obviously, there are many ways to construct an s-expression. Nevertheless, the function that follows can be used to build an s-expression interactively:

```
def createSExp() : SExp = {
  println("Enter choice...")
  println("0 for NIL");
  println("1 for ATOM");
  print("2 for PAIR\n? ");
  val choice : Int = readInt()
  if (choice == NIL)
     return NilSExp
  else if (choice == ATOM) {
     print("Enter atom...\n? ");
     val s : Char = readChar()
     return Atom(s)
  }
  else
     return Pair(createSExp(),createSExp())
}
```

Exercise 3.4 Write a function printSExp that will print its only argument fully parenthesized. For example, if it has as argument the s-expression

```
Pair(Atom("a"),Pair(Atom("b"),Atom("c")))
```

it has to print (a, (b, c)).

Exercise 3.5 Tradionally, the Lisp programming language includes three operators: car, which returns the first element of an s-expression, cdr, which returns the rest of an s-expression, and cons, which takes two s-expressions and creates a new one. Write three functions that implement the functionality of these operators.

3.2 More about pattern matching

In the previous chapter, in general, and the previous section, in particular, we discussed the various forms of patterns, without giving the whole picture. In this section, we are going to present systematically all types of patterns as well as sealed classes and optional values.

3.2.1 Types of patterns

The simplest pattern is the *wildcard* pattern _, that is, a pattern that matches anything. For example, here is a simple function that examines whether a binary tree is empty or not:

```
def IsEmpty(t: BinTree): Boolean =
   t match {
     case EmptyTree => true
     case        _   => false
   }
```

Also, this pattern can be used as a "don't care" pattern. For example, if we want to print the information stored in the topmost or *root* node of a binary tree, we could use the following function:

```
def rootElem(t: BinTree): Unit =
   t match {
     case Node(e,_,_) => println(e)
     case EmptyTree   => println("empty tree!")
   }
```

When a pattern is a constant, then it matches only itself. For example, the following function has as argument trees and returns the numbers 3, 5, 7, 11, and −1 if the number stored in the topmost node of its argument is either 3 or 5 or 7 or 11 or any other number, respectively:

```
def constMatch(t: BinTree): Int =
   t match {
     case Node(3,_,_)  => 3
     case Node(5,_,_)  => 5
     case Node(7,_,_)  => 7
     case Node(11,_,_) => 11
     case       _       => -1
   }
```

The following code snippet will print the numbers 3 and -1, respectively:

```
var t1 = Node(3,EmptyTree,Node(2,EmptyTree,EmptyTree))
var t2 = Node(13,EmptyTree,EmptyTree)
constMatch(t1); constMatch(t2)
```

Identifiers are like the wildcard pattern except that the values that are matched are stored in variables that have these names. We have seen usage examples in the previous section. However, these variables cannot be used to alter the corresponding value. For example, the following function definition

```
def modifyRoot(t: BinTree): Unit =
  t match {
    case Node(r,_,_)   => r *= 2
    case      _        => println("empty tree")
  }
```

will not be accepted by Scala and the compiler/interpreter will issue a *reassignment to val* error message. A rather interesting problem is this: Since identifiers are actually wildcard patterns and as such match anything, what happens if we use as identifier the name of a field? The answer is that it first checks whether an identifier is the name of some field and if this is true, then it matches only the value that this field corresponds to. For example, consider the following code snippet:

```
import Math._
print("gimme a number...\n? ")
var x:Long = readLong()
x match {
  case MIN_LONG => println("the smallest long")
  case MAX_LONG => println("the largest long")
  case    _     => println("an ordinary long")
}
```

If we run this code and enter the number 9223372036854775807 when prompted to enter a number, Scala will "recognize" that this number is actually the largest long and, consequently, it will print the appropriate message. If we comment out the first line, then Scala will complain that MIN_LONG and MAX_LONG are undeclared values. However, this contradicts what was said above, that is, that identifiers are like wildcard patterns. Unfortunately, we *forgot* to mention that only identifiers that start with a lowercase letter are treated as wildcard patterns. Now, there is another problem: What if a field starts with a lowercase letter? How can we match such a field? The language designer suggests that the easiest way to tackle this problem is to prefix the identifier with a class or an object name. However, we have noticed that in certain cases this fails. Thus, the language designer suggests enclosing the identifier in backticks (the patterns are called *stable identifier* patterns, see Section 6.7.1 for an explanation and a real usage example). Unfortunately, even this fails in certain cases. Thus, it is wise to plan ahead before attempting to use bare identifiers in pattern matching. Fortunately, things are clearer when one uses identifiers in constructors of case classes. We have presented many usage examples of this kind in the previous section, so there is no reason to present more examples.

Patterns can also be used to process lists as was explained in Section 2.13. However, what we did not mention is how to specify patterns that, for example, match a list whose second element is the number two while we do not care whether it is followed by zero, one or more elements. Cases like this can be specified with the pattern _*, which is like _ except that it may match any number of elements within a list. However, note that this pattern must be used only in cases like the one demonstrated in the code snippet that follows:

```
var A = List(1,2,3)
A match {
  case List(_,2,_*) => println("matches")
  case       _      => println("failure")
}
```

The code will print "matches" since A is a list whose second element is the number two. In conclusion, the pattern _* cannot be used with general patterns that involve the :: operator.

We can even use tuples as expressions to be matched by and tuples patterns to match expressions. The following function shows how this works:

```
def isTall(x:Tuple3[String,Int,Double]) : String =
  x match {
    case (x,_,z) if z >= 1.65 => x + " is tall"
    case (x,_,_)              => x + " is not tall"
  }
```

This function takes as argument a triple, that is, a tuple that consists of three elements. In general, the type of tuple is specified as follows

$$\text{Tuple}n[T_1, T_2, \ldots, T_n],$$

where T_i is the type of the ith element of the tuple. Another interesting thing about this function is the use of *pattern guards*. This is a feature of Scala that is activated if a pattern is matched. In this case, some additional tests are performed and depending on the outcome of the test, the pattern matches or fails. Thus, only if the value of the third element of the triple is greater than or equal to 1.65, does the pattern match, otherwise it fails. Pattern guards always start with the keyword `if`. Assume that we have the following definitions

```
var M = ("Mary",1970,1.70)
var C = ("Chanelle", 1975,1.75)
var S = ("Sophie", 1980, 1.63)
```

Then the commands that follow will print the messages "Mary is tall," "Chanelle is tall," and "Sophie is not tall," respectively.

```
println(isTall(M))
println(isTall(C))
println(isTall(S))
```

Another type of pattern is the so-called typed pattern. This is a type of pattern that can be used to match not only values but also types. This is achieved by attaching a type to the pattern. For example, the following function can be used to check whether its argument is a number or not:

```
def isNum(a : Any) =
  a match {
    case i : Int    => true
    case l : Long   => true
    case f : Float  => true
    case d : Double => true
    case     _      => false
  }
```

Note that the argument of this function is of type `Any`, since any object is of this type. The expression `ifNum(M)`, where M is the triple from the previous example, evaluates to `false`, while `isNum(4)` evaluates to `true`.

Exercise 3.6 Write a function that returns the length of (a) strings, (b) hash tables, and (c) lists. (Hint: You do not need to care about the type of hash tables and lists.)

Let us now see whether we can write a function that tests whether its argument is a list of integers or something similar. Unfortunately, the obvious solution that follows does not work:

```
def isIntList(a:Any) =
  a match {
    case h: List[Int] => true
    case    _         => false
  }
```

The reason is that Scala, following the lead of the Java programming language, "forgets" the type of elements that make up a structured type. The language remembers only the structure not the type. After all, if the program has passed the type-checking phase,[1] there is no reason to "remember" the types. Thus, it is almost impossible to have some sort of type violation. Therefore, function isIntList will always return true whenever it is supplied with *any* list structure.

There are cases where one wants to be able to match a part of a constructor, but then needs to refer to this part as a single entity. For instance, assume that we have a tree and we want to obtain its left subtree only if in the topmost node is stored a number less than zero. A solution to this problem follows:

```
var t1 = Node(3,Node(-2,EmptyTree,EmptyTree),EmptyTree)
var t3= t1 match {
        case Node(_,Node(x,y,z),_) if x < 0 => Node(x,y,z)
        case   _ => EmptyTree
    }
```

The designer of Scala observed that there are many cases like this and so he decided to provide *variable bindings*, that is the capability to refer to a subpattern by prefixing this subpattern with an identifier that is followed by the @ symbol. For example, if we opt to use this feature here is how the previous code snippet might look:

```
var t3= t1 match {
        case Node(_,t@Node(x,_,_),_) if x < 0 => t
        case   _   => EmptyTree
    }
```

3.2.2 Sealed classes

Although the examples presented so far are simple and they do not involve many cases, still in most *real-world* applications a case-class will have many subclasses. In situations like this, one needs to make sure that in a typical match expression all possible cases are covered. However, this is not always easy. For this reason, the designer of Scala introduced the notion of a sealed class. In order to play with sealed classes all we have to do is to declare the top class as such. Here is how we could declare binary trees:

```
sealed abstract class BinTree
```

---

[1] Canonically, a compiler goes through a number of phases like grammatical and syntactical analysis, and type-checking is one of these phases. A program is type-correct if the type-checker cannot find inconsistencies, for example multiplying an integer with a string. Remember that Scala allows mathematical operations between characters and numbers, since characters are represented by integers. However, more strict language designs do not allow the mixing of characters with numbers.

The really great benefit of using sealed classes is that the compiler detects whether there is a problem in some match expression. For example, consider the following function:

```
def printRoot(t: BinTree):Unit =
  t match {
    case Node(x,l,r) => println(x)
  }
```

If this function is included in a file where the definition of a binary tree is included, then the compiler will produce the following warning message:

(fragment of tree.scala):70: warning: match is not exhaustive!
missing combination EmptyTree

. . . .

However, if we define the same function in a file where binary trees are defined as a nonsealed class hierarchy, then the compiler will not produce any warning at all. Unfortunately, there can be no good without evil and this applies even to sealed classes. In situations where we are absolutely sure that all cases are covered, Scala will warn about cases that may not be covered in a particular match expression. The solution to this problem is to use the @unchecked annotation as shown below:

```
(t : @unchecked) match {
    case Node(x,l,r) => println(x)
  }
```

The meaning of this annotation is that an exhaustive check of the patterns that follow is turned off.

3.2.3 Optional values

If you enter in the Scala interpreter the expression 3/0, the interpreter will print a */ by zero* error message. However, it is an indication of poor program design, when a program relies on the language runtime system to detect rare and exceptional errors. A better way is to use exceptions, but another way is to use optional values. Typically, an optional value can be either None or Some(v), where v is a value of some type T while the type of both None and Some(v) is Option[T]. Here is a function definition that computes the quotient of the division of two whole numbers a and b:

```
def div(a:Int, b:Int): Option[Int] =
  if (b = 0)
    None
  else
    Some(a/b)
```

Another common use of optional values is in the definition of the method by which it is possible to obtain the value that corresponds to a particular key of some hash table. In particular, method get returns a None if no value corresponds to a key and a Some (v) if the value v corresponds to a key k:

```scala
scala> var A=Map("Greece" -> "Athens", "Italy" -> "Rome")
A: scala.collection.immutable.Map[java.lang.String,java.lang.String]
= Map(Greece -> Athens, Italy -> Rome)

scala> A.get("Athens")
res3: Option[java.lang.String] = None

scala> A.get("Greece")
res4: Option[java.lang.String] = Some(Athens)
```

Once we have defined functions that yield optional values, the next question is how do we use these values? The "obvious" answer is: with pattern matching. Here is how it is possible to print the result of function div:

```scala
div(3,0) match {
    case Some(x) => println(x)
    case None    => println("Problems")
}
```

In this case the result will be the word problems, while the expression

```scala
div(25,5) match {
    case Some(x) => println(x)
    case None => println("Problems")
}
```

will print the number 5.

3.3 Traits and mix-in composition

As was explained in Section 2.6, any class can inherit any other class. However, no class can inherit methods and fields from more than one class. This is commonly known as single inheritance. On the other hand, when a class can inherit methods and fields from more than one class, then we are talking about multiple inheritance. Obviously, single inheritance is too restrictive, nevertheless, multiple inheritance can be a problematic feature since it increases complexity (i.e., lack of simplicity) of the resulting program, while the order of inheriting classes may affect the features and the behavior of the new subclass. A much cleaner way to solve the problems of multiple inheritance while avoiding the disadvantages of single inheritance is *mix-in* composition. But what exactly is mix-in composition?

First of all mix-in composition[2] is made possible by mixing in traits,[3] that is a class that defines a number of methods and/or fields, but which is not meant to stand alone. On the other hand, traits can be *mixed in* a class. In other words, several traits can be used to extend the behavior of a class. In order to illustrate the usefulness of traits we will borrow an example that was presented in [23] (for reasons of completeness let us note that this example was originally described in [24]). Assume we are implementing a maze adventure game (think of Doom or Quake for example). A player moves a virtual character from one virtual room to another through virtual doors. Clearly, if all locations in the virtual world of the game were exactly the same, the game would not be interesting, nevertheless, all similar components that make up the virtual world (walls, doors, floors, ceilings, etc.) share a number of properties although they may have different behavior. For example, there are many kinds of doors – open doors, locked doors, magic doors, electronic doors, etc. A naive way to implement these different kinds of doors is to implement each different door as a different subclass of a basic class. For example, the code in Figure 3.3 shows how one could implement a class describing a locked door and a class describing a short door. Unfortunately, this design approach does not make it straightforward to define a class that describes a door that is both short and locked – one has to define a new class. Traits solve this problem by allowing the user to define behaviors that can be mixed in with the behaviors of existing classes, thus making the definition of a class that describes a locked and short door easy. For example, the code in Figure 3.4 shows exactly how one can define some behaviors and how they can be mixed in. Note that in this example the curly brackets that surround some white space denote that there is no addition behavior defined. Clearly one can omit them, but we have included them just to stress this point. Also, both definitions in Figures 3.3 and 3.4 assume that we have defined a class that describes persons. For reasons of completeness one can assume that persons are described by a rudimentary class like the following one:

```
class Person(val height:Int, val name:String, val key:Int) {
    def hasKey(checkKey: Int) = key == checkKey
}
```

As noted above, traits are a mechanism to define behaviors that cannot stand alone, nevertheless, traits are a mechanism that is based on the observation that an "object (type) may be a synthesis of several component abstractions, being able to do the job of its components and more" [17, p. 2]. In Scala traits are introduced using a *trait* declaration. The code in Figure 3.4 shows how one can define and use

---

[2] Mix-in composition was first introduced as a programming pattern in the Flavors [54] programming language and became widely available through the CLOS [43] programming language.

[3] It seems that traits is a relatively old idea that was first used in the construction of the "Star WS" software (a form of text editing software) running on Xerox Star 8010 workstations [17].

```
class LockedDoor extends Door {
    def canOpen(p: Person): Boolean =
        if (!p.hasItem(theKey) {
            println("You don't have the key")
            return false
        }
        println("Using key...")
        return super.canOpen(p)
    }
}
class ShortDoor extends Door {
    def canPass(p: Person): Boolean {
        if (p.height() > 1) {
            println("You are too tall")
            return false
        }
        println("Ducking into door...")
        return super.canPass(p)
    }
}
```

Figure 3.3 Single inheritance makes it impossible to create a class that describes a locked and short door.

traits. Obviously, a trait's definition starts with the keyword `trait` which is followed by the trait's name. In addition, one or more traits can *extend* the behavior of a specific trait. When extending the behavior of a class with the behaviors described by a trait, one should use the keyword `with` followed by the trait's name. If one trait extends the behavior described by another trait, then one should specify this using the keyword `extends`. Moreover, if more than one trait extends the behavior of another trait, the first is preceded by the keyword `extends` and all others by the keyword `with`. Let us see a simple example. Consider the class Lemon defined in Section 2.6. Assume that we define the following almost trivial trait:

```
trait gustation {
    var taste = "sour"
    def has_taste(): String = {
        return taste
    }
    def set_taste(newtaste: String) = {
        taste = newtaste
    }
}
```

```
trait Door {
  def canOpen(p: Person) : Boolean =
    return true
  def canPass(p: Person) : Boolean =
    return true
}

trait Locked extends Door {
  override def canOpen(p: Person): Boolean = {
    if (!p.hasItem(theKey)) {
      println("You don't have the Key")
      return false
    }
    println("Using key...")
    return super.canOpen(p)
  }
}

trait Short extends Door {
  override def canPass(p: Person): Boolean = {
    if (p.height > 180) {
      println("You are too tall")
      return false
    }
    println("Ducking into door...")
    return super.canPass(p)
  }
}

class LockedDoor extends Door
                 with Locked { }
class ShortDoor extends Door
                with Short { }
class LockedShortDoor extends Door
                      with Locked
                      with Short { }
```

Figure 3.4 Mix-in composition allows the composition of classes and traits and so one can describe locked doors, short doors, and locked doors that are short too.

Then we can redefine class Lemon so as to extend its behavior as shown below:

```
class Lemon extends Fruit with gustation {
  override def price() = 0.2
  def color() = "yellow"
}
```

Obviously, it is possible to make the color a behavior that is added by some trait. First let us define this new trait:

```
trait yellow_color {
  var color = "yellow"
  def get_color(): String = {
    return color
  }
  def set_color(newcolor: String) = {
    color = newcolor
  }
}
```

Class Lemon can be redefined as follows:

```
class Lemon extends Fruit with gustation with yello_color {
  override def price() = 0.2
}
```

So far we have showed how to extend the behavior of a class, but nothing has been said or even implied about the ability to extend the behavior of objects (i.e., class instances). Not so surprisingly, Scala makes it easy to extend the behavior of objects. Of course one should not get too excited as the behavior of objects cannot change while they are in use. To make things clear, let us give a simple example.

Assume we want to define a set of strings where each element is a string that contains only lowercase characters. The trait definition in Figure 3.5 defines the required behavior. Here we redefine three operators and, unlike what happens in many other programming languages, there is nothing special about the definitions here. Also note that it makes no sense to redefine the removal operator since all elements of a set are already in lowercase form, nevertheless, it was included for reasons of completeness. Having defined the additional behavior, here is how we can actually use it:

```
val lcSet = new HashSet[String] with LowerCaseSet
lcSet += "Scala"
lcSet += "Java"
println(lcSet)
```

The last command will print the following on the computer screen:

$$\text{Set(scala, java)}$$

Note that we have defined an object of a particular class where, at the same time, its behavior is augmented by the behavior defined in the trait. Not surprisingly,

```
import scala.collection.mutable._

trait LowerCaseSet extends HashSet[String] {

    override def +=(e: String) = {
        super.+=(e.toLowerCase)
    }

    override def contains(e: String) = {
        super.contains(e.toLowerCase)
    }

    override def -=(e: String) = {
        super.-=(e.toLowerCase)
    }
}
```

Figure 3.5 A trait that defines a set of strings that can have as elements lowercase strings only.

one can even extend objects as software modules, but we will say more on this in Chapter 6.

It is possible to prefix the definitions and the declarations of a trait or a class by a definition whose most general form is as follows

$$identifier: type \;\Rightarrow$$

or by its simpler form in which we just do not specify the *type*. This is known as a *self type* declaration. This declaration enables one to redefine the type of this (i.e., the trait or class being defined). This is a particularly useful "trick" as we will see in Chapter 6.

If we use the simpler form, then the *identifier* is can be used in place of this in the body of a trait, class, or object. If we use the full version of the definition, then if the *type* is T and the type of the trait, class, or object is C, then the type the keyword this is referring to is another type S such that $S \subset T$ and $S \subset C$, where $A \subset B$ denotes that A is a subclass (subtype) of B. The example in Figure 3.6 shows how one can use self-types to rewrite the example in Figure 3.4. Assume that the following class describes persons:

```
class Person {
    var name = "Μήτσος"
    var _height: Int = 180
```

```
trait _Block {
  def canOpen(p: Person) = false
  def canPass(p: Person) = false
}

trait Door extends _Block {
  override def canOpen(p: Person) : Boolean =
    return true
  override def canPass(p: Person) : Boolean =
    return true
}

trait LockedDoor extends _Block {
  this: Door =>
  override def canOpen(p: Person): Boolean = {
    if (!p.hasItem(theKey)) {
      println("You don't have the Key")
      return false
    }
    println("Using key...")
    return super.canOpen(p)
  }
}

trait ShortDoor extends _Block {
  this: Door =>
  override def canPass(p: Person): Boolean = {
    if (p.height > 180) {
      println("You are too tall")
      return false
    }
    println("Ducking into door...")
    return super.canPass(p)
  }
}

class LockedShortDoor extends Door
      with LockedDoor with ShortDoor
```

Figure 3.6 Using self-types to redefine the door hierarchy.

```
def hasItem(key:Int): Boolean =
  if (key == 1)
    true
  else
    false
  def height = _height
}
```

Also suppose that we have the following declarations:

```
val theKey = 2
val door = new LockedShortDoor
val μήτσοσ = new Person
```

Then the following method invocations

```
door canOpen μήτσος
door canPass μήτσος
```

will print the following text on the computer screen:

```
You don't have the Key
Ducking into door...
```

The self-type of a trait, class, or object must not differ from the corresponding self-types of the objects, classes, or traits that are inherited by the type used in the self declaration. It is quite possible to specify only a class or trait name (i.e., a type) followed by the symbol =>. In this case, the specified type will become the type of this.

3.4 Sorting objects

In many cases when declaring a new class it is imperative to be able to *compare* instances of this particular class. However, it is not at all obvious how one can implement a generic method by which object comparison can be a straightforward task. Fortunately, one can use Scala's trait mechanism to implement such a mechanism. In fact, the standard Scala implementation provides a trait that provides the required functionality. Every class becomes comparable when it mixes in with trait Ordered. To understand how this trait achieves this remarkable functionality, it is necessary to study its source code:

```
trait Ordered[α] {
  def compare(that : α) : Int

  def <  (that : α) : Boolean = (this compare that) <  0
  def >  (that : α) : Boolean = (this compare that) >  0
  def <= (that : α) : Boolean = (this compare that) <= 0
  def >= (that : α) : Boolean = (this compare that) >= 0
  def compareTo(that : α) : Int = compare(that)
}
```

Variable α is a type variable. When the trait is mixed in with a class, α should be substituted with the name of this class (type). As is evident, all method definitions depend on the definition of method compare. Thus, one might think that it is necessary to define this method. Indeed, this is the case. In addition, one has to define method equals. As a simple example, consider the following definition of class Person:

```
class Person(val firstName: String, var lastName: String,
             val nameOfFather: String,
             var age: Int) extends Ordered[Person] {
  def compare(that: Person) = {
    if ( lastName < that.lastName ) -1
    else if ( lastName > that.lastName ) 1
    else if ( firstName < that.firstName ) -1
    else if ( firstName > that.firstName ) 1
    else if ( nameOfFather < that.nameOfFather ) -1
    else if ( nameOfFather > that.nameOfFather ) 1
    else 0
  }
  override def equals (that: Any) =
    that match {
      case that: Person => compare(that) == 0
      case      _       => false
    }
}
```

Note that here we assume that persons are sorted alphabetically using first their last names, then their first names and lastly the names of their fathers. Also, note that a person is "equal" to another person if their first names, family names, and their fathers' names are equal. If you run the following code, the symbol < will be printed on the computer screen:

```
var john_smith1 = new Person("John", "Smith", "Jack", 18)
var john_smith2 = new Person("John", "Smith", "Steve", 19)
if (john_smith1 < john_smith2)
  println("<")
else
  println(">")
```

Exercise 3.7 Fruits can be sweet, bitter or sour. Define a class Fruit that has as fields a fruit's name, its color, and its taste. In addition, this class should be mixed in with trait Order so as to define the following order between class instances: first compare taste using bitter ≤ sour ≤ sweet, and then the colors in alphabetic order and lastly the names.

3.5 More on functions

Functions in Scala are modules that have a special `apply` method. In addition, an application of a function is actually a method invocation. For instance, consider the following simple function:

```
def double(x : Int) = 2 * x
```

This definition is completely equivalent to the following module definition:

```
object double {
  def apply(x: Int) = 2 * x
}
```

That the two definitions are completely equivalent means that once we have defined the module `double`, we can compute the double of, say, the number three as follows:

```
println(double(3))
```

In addition, to all these we can *overload* method `apply` (i.e., we can provide multiple definitions of the same method; see Section 3.6 for more details), thus allowing the use of the same function in different cases. For example, if we want to be able to compute the double of integers, long integers, floats, double floats, and strings, we should redefine our module as follows:

```
object double {
  def apply(x: Int) = 2 * x
  def apply(x: Long) = 2 * x
  def apply(x: Float) = 2 * x
  def apply(x: Double) = 2 * x
  def apply(x: String) = x + x
}
```

With this definition we can easily compute the double of different values:

```
val x:Long = 3
val y:Float = 3.14f
println(double(x))
println(double(y))
println(double("Scala"))
```

As was explained in Section 2.7, there are two ways to define functions of two parameters and more for functions of more parameters. Similarly, one can define a function of two arguments as an object in two different ways. Unfortunately, the two definitions cannot coexist in a single object definition since they *have [the] same type after erasure* (see Section 3.6.12), thus the first definition is commented out:

```
object D {
  //def apply(x: Double, y: Double) = Math.sqrt(x*x+y*y)
  def apply(x: Double)(y: Double) = Math.sqrt(x*x+y*y)
}
```

As expected, D can be invoked as shown below:

```
println(D(2)(3))
```

Assume that one wants to pass the object just defined to a function that has as parameter a function that takes two double precision float numbers as arguments and returns a double precision float number. The following function is an example:

```
def someMethod(f : Function2[Double, Double, Double],
               x : Double, y : Double) = f(x,y)
```

Unfortunately, we cannot use our function as an argument of this function! The reason is that the language processor cannot correctly deduce the type of the function object, something that should not be taken as a language deficiency, but, rather, as an open problem. And this is exactly why the language processor complains about a *type mismatch*. To solve this problem we need to specify which Function trait our object extends. Before presenting the new definition of D, let us say that Scala currently supports traits Function0 through Function22, where, in general, Function*N* denotes a function that takes *N* arguments. The following definition is a revisited definition of our object according to the solution just described:

```
object D extends Function2[Double, Double, Double] {
  def apply(x: Double,y: Double) = Math.sqrt(x*x+y*y)
}
```

Now, it is legitimate to use D in commands like the following one:

```
val x = someMethod(D,3,4)
```

An alternative way to specify the type of a function object is to use the "symbol" => or its equivalent. In general, an expression of the form S=>T denotes a function whose domain consists of all elements of type S and whose codomain consists of all elements of type T. Thus, the type expression R=>S=>T, where R is yet another type, is the type of some higher-order function. A function that takes two arguments is one that actually takes one argument which is a pair (i.e., a 2-tuple), thus, its type is (R,S)=>T. Now let us see how we could rewrite the definition of object D:

```scala
object D extends ((Double, Double) =>Double) {
    def apply(x: Double,y: Double) = Math.sqrt(x*x+y*y)
}
```

Using this notation one can easily specify the type of parameters of higher-order functions. For instance, let us define a higher-order function and use it:

```scala
scala> def f(g:Int=>Int,n:Int)=2*g(n)
f: ((Int) => Int,Int)Int

scala> val x = (a:Int)=> a+5
x: (Int) => Int = <function>

scala> var y = f(x,7)
y: Int = 24
```

A list, a set or a hash table is an instance of some predefined class and as such it should be created using new command. Nevertheless, when creating lists, sets or hash tables we do not use this command. Thus, either this is an exception to the general rule, which is most unlikely, or somehow the use of the command is made implicit, which seems to be the case. Indeed, for each such class definition, there is a companion object in which there are one or more definitions of method apply. These method definitions invoke the class constructor passing their arguments to the actual constructor. For example, here is how we could solve the problem of Exercise 2.2 on page 25:

```scala
class date (day:Int, month:Int, year:Int){
    def output() = println(day+"/"+month+"/"+year)
}
object date {
    def apply(d:Int, m: Int, y: Int) = new date(d,m,y)
    def apply(d: Int, m: Int) = new date(d,m,2009)
}
```

Now that we have defined this class and its companion object, we can create instances of this class and use them as shown below:

```scala
scala> var today = date(24,9,2008)
today: date = date@e77781
```

```
scala> today.output
24/9/2008

scala> var yesterday = date(23,9)
yesterday: date = date@1703484

scala> yesterday.output
23/9/2009
```

Another example of this particular use of the companion object is class `Complex` described in Figure 1.1 on page 11.

Exercise 3.8 Redefine the companion object of class `Complex` so as to allow the creation of ordinary complex numbers and complex numbers whose imaginary part is equal to zero.

Parameter passing Arguments are passed to functions which use them to compute a number, a string, etc. Although this is absolutely obvious, it is not obvious at all how these arguments are passed to functions. There are several ways to pass arguments to a function, but we will discuss only those relevant to Scala. In fact, Scala supports only two methods.

by-value When a function is invoked, the language processor creates for each argument a local variable to which it assigns the value of the corresponding argument. Upon termination these variables are destroyed for ever.

by-name In effect, passing an argument by-name is equivalent to the textual substitution of the formal parameter by the argument itself in the body of the function. This implies that an argument may never be evaluated or it may be repeatedly evaluated. Typically, when a variable is passed by-name, it can be both accessed and updated, nevertheless, Scala does not allow variables to be updated, thus avoiding side effects.

In order to designate that a formal parameter should be passed by-name, we prefix its type designation by the symbol =>. For instance, the following inter-action with Scala's interpreter shows the difference between call by-value and call by-name:

```
scala> def const1(x:Int)=1
const1: (Int)Int

scala> const1(1/0)
java.lang.ArithmeticException: / by zero
        at .<init>(<console>:6)
        . . .. . . . . . . .
```

```
scala> def const1(x: =>Int)=1
const1: (=> Int)Int

scala> const1(1/0)
res1: Int = 1
```

Note that the symbol => must be separated by at least one space from the colon that follows a parameter's name. A more interesting example is the definition of function loop on page 13. This function takes three arguments which are passed by-value. The first and the third are of type Unit (i.e., one can pass as arguments Scala commands and expressions) and the second is a boolean expression. Since each argument is re-evaluated each time it is needed, it perfectly simulates the behavior of the corresponding loop construct.

Now let us discuss an interesting case. Consider the following Scala code snippet:

```
class X(var x : Int)
var y = new X(3)
println(y.x) // First output command
def p(a : X) = { a.x = 2*a.x }
p(y)
println(y.x) // Second output command
```

As expected the first output command will print the number 3 on our computer screen, but what will the second output command print? The reader may think that the answer is again 3 since in Scala objects are passed by-value, however, the correct answer is 6! The reason is that the language passes by-value the *reference* to the object, that is it passes the address of the memory location that holds the particular object. Thus, all changes made to the local copy are actually global changes. However, one cannot use the same "trick" when the objects are "simple" objects like numbers and strings. For example, Scala cannot compile the function

```
def q(a : String) = { a += "a" }
```

it will complain that there is an error: *reassignment to val*. Although this may seem strange, the truth is that it is not! In the first case, we alter members of the object while in the second we try to alter the whole object which is not possible.

Functions as patterns In Section 3.2.1 we presented the various forms of patterns supported by Scala, but we did not say anything about functions. Unfortunately, functions are not represented by case classes and this prohibits their use as patterns.

On the other hand, functions are first-class values and so it should be possible to use them in pattern matching. Method unapply solves this problem in a very elegant way. First of all let us explain what this method does. This method is called an *extractor* because it can be used to extract parts of a type. In the case of function objects, if we have such an object and a particular value of this function, then it is possible to obtain the arguments of this function. For example, consider the following two modules:

```
object fivetimes {
  def apply(x : Int) = x * 5
  def unapply(z : Int) = if(z % 5 == 0) Some(z/5) else None
}

object threetimes {
  def apply(x : Int) = x * 3
  def unapply(z : Int) = if(z % 3 == 0) Some(z/3) else None
}
```

Here method unapply implicitly introduces case classes since Some and None are a case class and a case object, respectively. The following code snippet shows how these two function-objects can be used:

```
val x = threetimes(4)
x match {
  case fivetimes(y)  => println(x+" is 5 times "+y)
  case threetimes(y) => println(x+" is 3 times "+y)
  case _             => println(x+" is something else")
}
```

When the language processor "sees" a function call as a pattern, then it invokes its corresponding unapply method, provided that the function has been defined as a function object. As noted above, this method returns a case class object that is used in the pattern matching. Thus, the expression above will print the message "*12 is 3 times 4.*" In addition, method unapply as well as method apply can be used even when dealing with case classes. In this case, one can specify an easy way to create and to decompose objects. For example, think of a case class that encodes a multiplication between two factors, then the unapply method will yield the two factors.

Partial functions A partial function is a function that is not defined for all possible values. For example, the reciprocal of a real number x is the number $\frac{1}{x}$, which is undefined when $x = 0$. In general, partial functions are usually undefined for a few arguments, nevertheless, there are some cases where a function is defined for a few arguments only. In the first case, one can define a function so it can handle these few exceptional arguments for which it is undefined. For example, here is how one could define a function that computes the reciprocal of a whole number:

```
def R(x:Long) = if (x == 0)
                    Math.POS_INF_DOUBLE
                else
                    1.0 / x
```

Unfortunately, we cannot use the same technique to define a function that is defined for a few arguments only. Instead, one can use the PartialFunction trait to define such a function. The following example shows how we could define a partial function that computes the reciprocal of some whole numbers:

```
val R : PartialFunction[Long,Double] = {
  case 0  => Math.POS_INF_DOUBLE
  case 1  => 1.0
  . . . . . . . . . .
  case 9  => 1.0/9.0
  case 10 => 0.1
}
```

Note how one has to specify the value of each argument that is defined. The keyword case is followed by a value, for which the function is defined, while the "symbol" => separates the argument's value with the result of the "computation." Also, one can define partial functions that take two arguments, but then again two arguments can be viewed as one:

```
val Q : PartialFunction[Tuple2[Long,Long],Double] = {
  case (1,2) => 5.0
  case (2,3) => 13.0
}
```

The predefined method isDefinedAt should be used to check whether a partial function is defined for some particular value. For instance, the code snippet

```
if (R.isDefinedAt(11))
  R(11)
else
  println("not defined for this value")
```

will print the message *not defined for this value* for obvious reasons. Suppose that someone has defined another partial function that can compute the reciprocal of 11 and 12:

```
val S : PartialFunction[Long,Double] = {
   case 11 => 1.0 / 11
   case 12 => 1.0 / 12
}
```

Then we can define a new composite function using the `orElse` method as shown below:

```
val P = R orElse S
```

The resulting partial function will use R when invoked, and only when R is not defined for a particular value will it invoke S.

3.6 Polymorphism

As was explained in Chapter 1, polymorphism is one of the four basic principles of object-orientation. Although we have briefly explained what polymorphism is and we have shown how it can be used in Scala, still it is necessary to give a thorough description of polymorphism, in general, and how it is realized in Scala, in particular. In the next few pages, we present the various forms of polymorphism and how these have been incorporated into the Scala programming language.

3.6.1 Types of polymorphism

When a programming language has functions, methods, structures, etc., that can have a unique type, they are called *monomorphic*. On the other hand, if a programming language has functions, methods, procedures, etc., whose arguments can have more than one type not at the same time but at different moments, then they are called polymorphic. For example, Pascal and FORTRAN are monomorphic programming languages while Java and Haskell are polymorphic languages.

As is noted in [13], Christopher Strachey, who was a pioneer in programming language design, distinguished two major kinds of polymorphism – *parametric* and *adhoc* polymorphism. A parametric polymorphic function or procedure is one that works uniformly on a range of types, which normally exhibit a common structure (for example stacks). On the other hand, an ad hoc function or procedure is one that works, or at least appears to work, on several different and possibly unrelated types and which may behave in different ways for each specific type. Luca Cardelli and Peter Wegner [13] refined Strachey's classification by adding *inclusion*

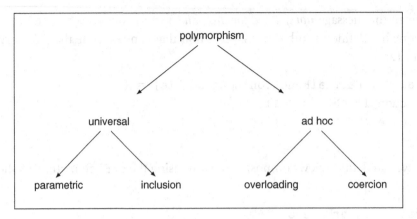

Figure 3.7 Variants of polymorphism.

polymorphism, *overloading*, and *coercion*, see Figure 3.7. Inclusion polymorphism was introduced to model subtypes and inheritance, which are necessary to deal with object orientation.

Parametric polymorphism achieves uniformity by using the idea of type parameters, nevertheless, this is not the only way to achieve uniformity and in this respect parametric polymorphism is a special case of universal polymorphism. For example, inclusion polymorphism assumes that an object belongs to many different classes that may form a hierarchy of subclasses. Note that functions, methods, procedures that exhibit parametric polymorphism are usually characterized as *generic*. A typical example of a generic method is the `length` method that computes the length of any list structure.

When we say that a function or an operator is overloaded, then we typically mean that the same name or operator symbol is used to denote different functions and it depends on the context to say which particular function or operator is denoted. A coercion is the operation of converting an argument or an operand to the type expected by a function or an operator, where otherwise a type error would have been detected. To understand the difference between overloading and coercion, consider the following operations:

```
4 * 5
4.0 * 5
4 * 5.0
4.0 * 5.0
```

The first of these operations will yield an `Int` and the others will yield `Double`s. This is justified since classes `Int` and `Double` provide among others the following overloaded definitions of operator *:

```
def * (arg0 : Int)     : Int
def * (arg0 : Int)     : Double
def * (arg0 : Double)  : Double
def * (arg0 : Double)  : Double
```

Thus, Scala defines all possible cases and no coercion is needed. However, class Complex, which is defined in Section 1.3, does not include an exhaustive set of overloaded definitions and thus coercion is employed to solve this problem. This is exactly what the functions doubleToComplex and intToComplex do. To summarize, coercion is the implicit type conversion when needed and overloading allows the use of the same name for different semantic objects.

Subtyping is a form of inclusion polymorphism and, roughly, the idea that some type is a subtype of another type. We have encountered this notion already when we talked about the type hierarchy of numerical types in Section 2.4. In addition, since any class is a type, a subclass of some class is a subtype of this type.

In certain programming languages the same constant value is shared by a number of different types. For example, in the C programming language the symbol 1 denotes the true truth value, the integer 1, and the START OF HEADING character, while the symbol NULL is a pointer value that is shared by all pointer types. This type of polymorphism, which is known as *value sharing*, is a special case of parametric polymorphism.

To summarize, both parametric and inclusion polymorphism, which are called collectively *universal* polymorphism, can be thought of as forms of *true* polymorphism, whereas adhoc polymorphism can be thought of as *apparent* polymorphism, that is, polymorphism that is valid within a restricted range. Thus, subtyping is an example of true polymorphism whereas parametric polymorphism is the purest form of polymorphism.

3.6.2 Overloading

Most widely used object-oriented programming languages provide facilities to overload operators and functions. Nevertheless, languages like C++ make a distinction between operators and functions. In Scala everything that can perform an action is a method and, thus, operators are methods. This obviously simplifies the way an operator is overloaded. To see the difference compare the following definition in C++

```
complex complex::operator+ (const complex& c) const {
    complex result;
```

```
    result.real = (this->real + c.real);
    result.imag = (this->imag + c.imag);
    return result;
}
```

with the corresponding definition in Scala (see also Figure 1.1 on page 11):

```
def + (another: Complex) =
    new Complex(Re + another.re, Im + another.im)
```

Since we have already presented a complete example of operator overloading, we will use this example to describe the various aspects of operator overloading in Scala.

First of all, let us repeat that operators are methods. In particular, the expression 3+4 is syntactic sugar for the expression (3).+(4). Thus, when a binary operator is overloaded, it is like defining a function that takes one argument. This argument corresponds to its right operand while its left operand is an instance of the class in which this operator is overloaded. Naturally, things exchange roles when a right-associative binary operator is overloaded. When a unary operator ⊛ has to be overloaded, then it should be redefined as a function whose name is unary_⊛. For example, here is how one could redifine the unary minus operator:

```
def unary_- = new Complex(-Re, -Im)
```

Exercise 3.9 Overload the operator ~ so that it computes the complex conjugate of a complex number (i.e., given a complex number $a + bi$, its conjugate is the number $a - bi$).

In mathematics, quaternions are a sort of hypercomplex numbers that extend complex numbers and their arithmetic. Briefly, a quaternion is a number $a + bi + cj + dk$, where $i^2 = j^2 = k^2 = ijk = -1$. Obviously, a class defining quaternions must first extend a class that defines complex numbers and second it must overload the various operators. Note that in Scala one can overload operators in any subclass of a class or to its superclass.

Exercise 3.10 Define a class Quaternion that overloads the following operators: +, binary -, *, and /.

3.6.3 Implicit conversion: a form of coercion

In general, a real number, and for that matter an integer number, is a complex number whose imaginary part is equal to zero. Thus, an expression of the form

4+b where b is an instance of class `Complex` will cause the language interpreter to complain about a *type mismatch* error. This problem can be solved with *implicit type conversions*.

A function that performs an implicit conversion is a map by which elements of one type are mapped to elements of another type. For example, it is possible to map integer and real numbers to strings in an obvious way. A Scala function that is designed to perform such a mapping must be prefixed by the `implicit` keyword. For example, the following function transforms integers to complex numbers:

```
implicit def DoubleToComplex(d: Double) = Complex(d)(0)
```

Whenever the user specifies an operation between a `Double` and a `Complex`, the language processor will perform an implict transformation of the `Double` to a `Complex` whose imaginary part is equal to zero. An interesting question is what should happen when one attempts to multiply a complex number by an integer. The answer is that Scala will complain since the language processor does not know how to handle the multiplication of any complex number by any integer number. The simplest solution to this problem is to add one more implicit value converter:

```
implicit def intToComplex(i: Int) =
  Complex(int.toDouble) _
```

One may wonder how the language processor *knows* which type transformer to apply. A naive answer would be that it checks the name of each value converter. However, the names of the implicit conversion functions have been chosen so as to reflect the functionality of these functions and there is nothing special about them. So how does the language processor choose the proper converter? The answer is simple: it checks the type of all functions that have been declared as implicit and chooses the one that matches a particular case.

In the example that we study, the implicit function definitions appear outside the class definition but are part of a file that can be fed to the language interpreter. In general, the best place to define these implicit definitions is the companion object. For instance, here is how we could declare two implicit type converters:

```
object Complex{
  def apply(re: Double)(im: Double) = new Complex(re, im)
  implicit def doubleToComplex(d: Double) = Complex(d) _
  implicit def intToComplex(int: Int) =
    Complex(int.toDouble) _
}
```

Now, if one includes the revised code of class `Complex` in a file and appends a command like the following

```
println((5 + 3.0*i) * (3 - 4*i) + (3 + 5*i))
```

the language processor will complain that *overloaded method value * with alternatives (Double)Double <and>...cannot be applied to (this.i.type).* This is really strange because we have already specified what to do when an integer must be multiplied by a complex number. The solution is to bring the definition into scope via an import command, though it is actually in scope. Thus, by adding the command

```
import Complex._
```

into our source file and then by feeding the resulting file to Scala, we will get:

```
30.0+-6.0i
```

Exercise 3.11 The output we get is not aesthetically correct. Rework method `toString` to remedy this problem.

One should avoid defining two or more implicit value converters that perform the same conversion. If by mistake one has defined two value converters, then the language will complain that *implicit conversions are not applicable because they are ambiguous.* Last but certainly not least, one must note that value conversions are applied only if they are necessary. In other words, the expression 4+3 is a valid Scala expression, so there is no reason to convert the two integers to complex numbers. Nevertheless, the value converters are called in all instances where they are needed, such as the following command:

```
var a : Complex = 15
```

Implicit function parameters are parameters that are implicitly inserted in argument lists. The trick to defining implicit parameters is to make a function definition as if it is a special function. For instance, here is a function that may have an implicit parameter:

```
implicit def Sum(a : Long)(implicit b : Long) = a+b
```

Once we have defined a function with an implicit parameter, we need to specify the implicit value of this parameter. Here is how this can be done:

```
implicit val B : Long = 4
```

Note that the name used in this definition can be anything and so it may seem as if it is completely irrelevant. Now that we have defined our function and the value of its implicit parameter, let us use it. The following two examples show how this can be done:

```
println(Sum(4))
println(Sum(5)(9))
```

If we want to have more than one implicit parameter, then we have to declare them in a similar way and make sure they all have different type. Otherwise, the language processor will complain about *ambiguous implicit values*. Here is an example of a function with three implicit parameters:

```
implicit def IMP(a:Int)(implicit b : Int,
                c : Float, d : Double) = a+b+c+d
```

Obviously, it is now necessary to define the value of the three implicit parameters:

```
implicit val imp3         = 5
implicit val imp4 : Float = 6.0f
implicit val imp5  :Double = 7.0
```

When using this function, we can either specify all four arguments or just the first one as shown in the example,

```
x = IMP(0) + IMP(1)(2,2,2)
```

As a more realistic example, here is how one could modify the definition of the companion object of class Complex:

```
object Complex{
  def apply(re : Double)(implicit im : Double) =
    new Complex(re, im)
  implicit val imzero : Double = 0.0
  implicit def doubleToComplex(d : Double) = Complex(d)
  implicit def intToComplex(int : Int) =
    Complex(int.toDouble)
}
```

3.6.4 *Parametric polymorphism*

Let us start with a simple problem: how to write down a Scala function that takes a list and returns its last element. A possible solution to this problem is the function definition that follows:

```
class EmptyList extends Exception
def last(l : List[Int]) : Int =
```

```
l match {
  case  Nil      => throw new EmptyList()
  case  List(x) => x
  case  x::xs    => last(xs)
}
```

Although this solution shows how the problem can be solved, still it cannot be used when one wants to obtain the last element of a list of strings or characters – one has to rewrite this function so as to be able to handle strings or characters. This means that the solution is not general enough. In order to provide a pragmatic solution to this problem we have to write a similar function for each possible list type we are going to use. Unfortunately, it is not possible to write an infinite set of functions which implies that this solution is not general enough either. A far better solution would be to define a function that could handle every possible type of list. In other words, what we are looking for is a truly polymorphic function. But how can we implement such a truly polymorphic function in Scala? We can use parametric polymorphism or *generics*. Instead of defining a function that takes a list of integers, we will define a function that takes a list of objects of some generic type λ. Here is a function defined along these lines:

```
def last[λ](l : List[λ]): λ =
  l match {
    case  Nil      => throw new EmptyList()
    case  List(x) => x
    case  x::xs    => last(xs)
  }
```

This definition differs from the previous in that there is, just after the function name, a generic type name, enclosed in square brackets, which is subsequently used in the specification of the return type and the type of the argument. This generic type is instantiated the very moment one uses this particular function with a proper argument (i.e., a list of something not an array of something). In the following examples we define two lists of different type and use the same function to compute their last element:

```
scala> val l = List(1,2,3,4,5)
l: List[Int] = List(1, 2, 3, 4, 5)

scala> last(l)
res0: Int = 5

scala> val ll = List("a","b","c","d","e")
ll: List[java.lang.String] = List(a, b, c, d, e)
```

```
class Stack [γ] {
    private var S = List[γ]()
    def push(elem: γ) {
        S = elem :: S
    }
    def pop () : γ =
        if (S.isEmpty)
            throw new EmptyList()
        else {
            val q = S.head
            S = S.tail
            return q
        }
    override def toString =
        S.mkString("[",",","]")
}
```

Figure 3.8 A generic implementation of stacks using lists.

```
scala> last(ll)
res1: java.lang.String = e
```

A more interesting application of generics is the definition of new classes and/or traits. For instance, in Section 1.1 we presented a simplified version of a generic stack. A far more readable and slightly better definition of a generic stack is shown in Figure 3.8. Here we have opted to use lists instead of arrays since lists support the basic operations needed to implement stacks. As was explained in Chapter 1, γ is a *type parameter* that has to be instantiated when creating new instances of this class. And this is exactly why new stacks are instantiated as shown below:

```
var x = new Stack[Int](3)
```

If we leave the [Int] part out, the language processor will complain that a *type mismatch* occurred.

Exercise 3.12 A queue is an ordered list in which insertions are made at one end, called the *rear*, and deletions are made at the other end, called the *front*. Define a generic class that implements queues.

The solution presented depends on another fundamental data structure and it contains many destructive assignments (i.e., it is not functional). Wouldn't it be nice to be able to define a purely functional stack structure? The following specification shows the basic properties of such a purely functional structure:

```
datatype Stack[γ] = EmptyStack | StackC[γ](γ, Stack[γ])
```

A simple way to define such a structure is to use case classes that define each part of the specification. However, in this case we demand that all basic stack manipulation functions be defined as methods.

Case classes are a convenient tool to define algebraic data types implicitly, but they are also ordinary classes. Thus, they can have (private) fields and/or methods. The abstract class definition that follows includes the definition of three abstract methods, that is methods that have not been initialized yet. Nonabstract classes must properly define abstract methods and fields. Method push is supposed to insert an element onto the stack, while method pop is supposed to delete the top-most element from the stack. Method top is supposed to return a copy of the topmost element of the stack:

```
abstract class Stack[γ] {
  def push(x : γ) : Stack[γ]
  def pop : Stack[γ]
  def top : γ
  def IsEmpty : Boolean
}
```

As is evident, an abstract class definition is a bare bones definition. As in the case for trees, an empty stack will be modeled by an object not a subclass. In the definition that follows, only function push is redefined to do something meaningful since it makes sense to push an element onto an empty stack, while it makes no sense to delete an element from an empty stack or to print the topmost element of an empty stack.

```
case object EmptyStack extends Stack[Any] {
  def push(x: Any) = new StackC(x,this)
  def pop:Stack[Any] =
    throw new NoSuchElementException("stack underflow")
  def top:Any =
    throw new NoSuchElementException("top of empty stack")
  def IsEmpty : Boolean = true
}
```

The exception used in the previous class definition is a standard Java exception that can be used in any Scala program. The empty stack is a subtype of Stack[Any] since we want this value to denote an empty stack of any possible type. Surprisingly, the easiest part is to define the class that describes the real action:

```
case class StackC[γ](e: γ, s: Stack[γ]) extends Stack[γ] {
  def this(e : γ) = this(e,
```

```
                          EmptyStack.asInstanceOf[Stack[γ]])
    def push(x : γ) = new StackC[γ](x, this)
    def pop = s
    def top = e.asInstanceOf[γ]
    def IsEmpty : Boolean = false
}
```

Now that we have defined the functional data structure let us play with it. The reader can type in the definitions given above in a source file and then append the code snippet that follows:

```
val q0 = new StackC[Int](5)
val q1 = StackC(3,StackC(4,q0))
println("q1 = " + q1)
val q2 = q1.pop
println("q2 = " + q2)
val q3 = q2.pop
println("q3 = " + q3)
val q4 = q3.push(9)
println("q4 = " + q4)
var x = 7 + q4.top
println("x = " + x)
val s1 = new StackC[String]("a")
val s2 = s1.push("b")
println("s2 = " + s2)
```

When the final file is fed to the language processor, the following output will be printed on the computer screen:

```
q1 = StackC(3,StackC(4,StackC(5,EmptyStack)))
q2 = StackC(4,StackC(5,EmptyStack))
q3 = StackC(5,EmptyStack)
q4 = StackC(9,StackC(5,EmptyStack))
x = 16
s2 = StackC(b,StackC(a,EmptyStack))
```

So far we have used abstract classes to define the topmost type in the type hierarchy of a particular set of case classes. However, it does make sense to use a trait instead of an abstract class. For instance, here is how we could rewrite the abstract class Stack[γ] as a trait:

```
trait Stack[γ] {
    def push(x: γ):Stack[γ]
```

```
    def pop:Stack[γ]
    def top:γ
    def IsEmpty:Boolean
}
```

Exercise 3.13 Define purely functional queues using the following data type specification:

```
datatype Queue δ = Queue List[δ] List[δ]
```

3.6.5 More on implicit parameters

Assume we are asked to write a generic function that can sum up the elements of any list. A function implementing this functionality is one that understands how to add two objects having the type of the elements of the list and also which is the unit element of the addition (i.e., which is the element that does not affect addition, just as 0 does not affect the addition of integer numbers). Obviously, it is difficult, if not impossible, to implement such a function mainly because we cannot cover all possible cases. However, a better solution would be one that takes an implicit parameter that contains the relevant information about the type of the elements of the list. In fact, Odersky and his colleagues [58] have shown us how this function can be implemented in Scala and in the rest of this section we are going to describe it. The first step involves the definition of a generic type that abstractly defines the unit element and how addition is performed:

```
trait Monoid[α] {
  val unit :α
  def add(x:α, y:α):α
}
```

Clearly, when this abstract behavior is mixed in with a concrete class or module, one needs to make concrete its members. This means that we "specialize" the generic type α and then initialize the members of the trait. Thus, if we want to define a module that describes how strings are added and what is the unit element of string addition, we need a definition like the following one:

```
implicit object strMonoid extends Monoid[String] {
  val unit = ""
  def add (x: String, y: String) = x.concat(y)
}
```

Observe that the unit element is the empty string and addition is string concatenation. Similarly, we can define the required behavior for integers as follows:

```
implicit object intMonoid extends Monoid[Int] {
  val unit = 0
  def add (x: Int, y: Int) = x+y
}
```

Exercise 3.14 Define a boolMonoid object for Booleans.

The next step is to define a function that can sum up the elements of a list.

```
def sum[α](A:List[α])(implicit m:Monoid[α]):α =
  A match {
    case Nil   => m.unit
    case x::xs => m.add(x,sum(xs)(m))
  }
```

We can now use this function in the following way:

```
val res1 = sum(List(1,2,3,4,5))(intMonoid)
```

However, it is possible to omit the second argument of the function, since the language processor can automatically infer which object it has to use. Thus, the following command

```
var res2 = sum(List("a","b","c","d","e","f"))
```

will correctly sum up the list of strings. The reason is that the proper value is chosen from those available. We treat the concept of monoid again in Section 8.10.2 when dealing with the path abstraction.

3.6.6 *Inclusion polymorphism*

As was noted previously, subtyping is a form of inclusion polymorphism, though this is valid only if a class definition is actually a type definition. The essence of subtyping is that if C' is a subclass of C and O' is an instance of C', then O' is an instance of C. Assume that A and B are two types, then $A <: B$ denotes that A is a subtype of B. Using this notation, we can express subtyping as: if $C' <: C$ and O'.isInstanceOf[C'], then O'.isInstanceOf[C], where isInstanceOf is a Scala method that returns true if an object is an instance of some class. For example, class reCell (see page 39) is a subclass of class cell (also see page 39), thus, the following code will print Ok:

```
var Oprime = new reCell(5)
if (Oprime.isInstanceOf[cell])
  println("Ok")
else
  println("Error!")
```

In general, relation <:, which is termed the *conformance* relation, must satisfy the following properties.

- Nothing <: T <: Any, for all class types T.
- T <: AnyRef and $T \nless:$ NotNull, then Null <: T, for all class types T. According to the Scala API documentation NotNull is a "marker trait for things that are not allowed to be null."
- If $a : A$ and A <: B, then $a : B$.
- C' <: C iff C' is a subclass of C.

The second property is called *subsumption* and its introduction creates a new problem. Instead of describing the problem, let us illustrate it by borrowing a simple example from [1]. Consider the following code snippet:

```
var y = new reCell(5)
def g(x: cell) = x.set(3)
g(y)
```

In this example, the formal parameter of function g has to be of type cell, but when the function is invoked the argument is of type reCell, which is a subtype of cell. The question is: Which method is called when function g is invoked? Obviously, there are two answers to this question: the function will invoke either the method of class cell or the method of class reCell. If a programming language behaves as in the first case, then it supports *static dispatch*; otherwise it supports *dynamic dispatch*. All object-oriented programming languages support dynamic dispatch.

3.6.7 Covariance, contravariance and invariance

A type operator is an operator or, more generally, a mechanism that can be used to map one or more types to a third type. For example, tuples, arrays, and functions can be considered to belong to types generated by type operators. An interesting question is this: If A <: A' and B <: B' and $\otimes$ is a type operator, then what can be said about the relationship between $A \otimes B$ and $A' \otimes B'$? The answer depends on whether the operator is *covariant, contravariant* or *invariant*:

covariance If A <: A' and B <: B', then $A \otimes B$ <: $A' \otimes B'$.
contravariance When A' <: A and B <: B', then $A \otimes B$ <: $A' \otimes B'$.
invariance If $A = A'$ and $B = B'$, then $A \otimes B$ <: $A' \otimes B'$.

When defining a new polymorphic type, it is possible to specify its *variance*. More specifically, a plus sign before a type denotes that the type varies covariantly, a minus sign before a type denotes that the type varies contravariantly, and when there is no plus or minus sign, this denotes that the type varies invariantly. An example of a covariant class declaration is the standard Scala class `Tuple2`:

```
case class Tuple2[+T1, +T2](val _1 : T1, val _2 : T2)
    extends Product2[T1, T2]
```

Note that `ProductN` is a trait that defines a cartesian product of N elements. Also, an example of a contravariant trait definition is the standart Scala trait `Function1`:

```
trait Function1[-T1, +R] extends AnyRef
```

But why is such the variance of these classes? The reason is explained by the following two short arguments.

Covariance of pairs Assume that there is a pair `(a,b)` whose type is `Tuple2[A,B]`. Obviously, the type of its first component is `A` and the type of its second component is `B`. Also, suppose that `A <: C` and `B <: D`. Then, by subsumption, a is also of type `C` and b is also of type `D`. This implies that `(a,b)` is also of type `Tuple2[C,D]`. In other words,

$$\texttt{Tuple2[A,B]} <: \texttt{Tuple2[C,D]}$$

when `A <: C` and `B <: D`.

Contravariance of functions Assume we have an object `f` of type `Function1[A,B]`. If `B <: D`, then, by subsumption, `f` produces also results of type `D`. Assume that `C <: A`. By subsumption, `f` accepts also arguments of type `C`. This means that

$$\texttt{Function1[A,B]} <: \texttt{Function1[C,D]}$$

if `C <: A` and `B <: D`.

Exercise 3.15 How do you think the types vary of a function with two arguments, that is, of type `Function2[T1, T2, R]`?

Invariance of mutable pairs A mutable pair is one whose components can be updated. A simple definition of such a mutable pair follows:

```
class mTuple2[T1,T2](private var x: T1, private var y: T2){
    def _1: T1 = x
    def _2: T2 = y
    def s_1(x : T1) = this.x = x
```

```
    def s_2(y : T2) = this.y = y
    def productArity : Int = 2
}
```

This definition uses *setters* and *getters* (see Section 3.12), thus, we do not expect readers to understand everything. For the time being, it suffices to say that these are method definitions that look like fields when used. In this definition the type parameters are invariant. If one tries to declare them as covariant, then the language processor will complain with the following message: *covariant type T1 occurs in contravariant position in type T1 of parameter of setter x_ =.* Note that if a type cannot vary covariantly or contravariantly, then even if we "force" it to vary in a specific way the language processor will detect this and signal an error message as happened in this case. Now, if one tries to declare the parametric types as contravariant, then the language processor will complain as follows: *contravariant type T1 occurs in covariant position in type => T1 of method x.*

Exercise 3.16 Provide a simple argument for the invariance of mutable pairs.

3.6.8 Bounded polymorphism

It is not unrealistic to demand to be able to express some assumptions or restrictions on type parameters. For instance, defining a function that sorts collections of elements means that the elements are comparable. Also, a matrix multiplication method of a matrix class is applicable only to matrices of numbers. This situation is quite common and it is known as bounded polymorphism [13]. Scala supports bounded polymorphism by allowing type constraints on type parameters. Let us see how one can specify contraints and how they affect the structure of classes. Assume we are building a class hierarchy that is supposed to describe seats in air carriers. Typically, passengers who travel in coach class sit in cradle seats, but if one is lucky enough one may get a better seat.[4] Here is a skeleton class describing coach class:

```
class CoachClass[θ >: Cradle_seat] {
    . . . . . . .
    def can_sleep(seat : θ) : Comfort = {
```

---

[4] Here is an anecdote that proves this claim: More than fifteen years ago A.S. and a girlfriend of his visited a friend who at that time was a Ph.D. student at UCLA (this friend was a hearing impaired person at that time, but thanks to a medical "miracle" he can now hear again normally). On their return date, their friend drove them to the airport, but they arrived almost 30 minutes before the flight's departure. Unfortunately, there were no remaining seats in coach class, which meant they could not travel! Fortunately, their friend had a plan – he "explained" to the manager that all three of them were hearing impaired persons! The manager was shocked! He apologized to all for his behavior and found for A.S. and his girlfriend two seats in business class. So this was the first and until now the only time A.S. traveled business class.

```
    . . . . . .
  }
}
```

The relation θ >: `Cradle_seat` specifies that type θ will have as *lower* bound type `Cradle_seat`. In other words, `Cradle_seat` must be a subtype of θ. Practically, this means that a passenger traveling in coach class can travel by sitting in a seat that is at least as comfortable as a cradle seat. Here `Comfort` is an enumeration type (i.e., a set of named constants that may be assigned to a variable). In Scala enumerations can be defined as follows:

```
object Comfort extends Enumeration {
  type Comfort = Value
  val NotComfy, . . . , VeryVeryComfy = Value
}
```

The `type` declaration can be used to define new names, but it can be used to do more interesting things. We will present these additional capabilities in the next few sections. Let us turn our attention back to our example. The class that describes business class is more interesting:

```
class BusinessClass [Cradle_seat <: θ <: Angled_lie_flat] {
  . . . . . . .
  def can_sleep(seat : θ) : Comfort = {
  . . . . . .
  }
}
```

In this example, we specify that the passenger can travel by sitting in a seat that is at most as comfortable as an angled lie-flat seat, which is specified by relation θ <: `Angled_lie_flat`], and at least as comfortable as a cradle seat. In other words, we specify that θ is a subtype of `Angled_lie_flat`. At the same time `Cradle_seat` must be a subtype of θ. Practically, this means that passengers traveling in business class will sit in all types of seats that are more comfortable than a cradle seat but which are less comfortable than an angled lie-flat seat. Obviously, angled lie-flat seats are an *upper* bound for all seat types. The last example specifies that a passenger traveling business class must sit in a seat that is at least as comfortable as a full-flat seat:

```
class FirstClass [θ >: Full_flat] {
  . . . . . . .
  def can_sleep(seat : θ) : Comfort = {
  . . . . . .
```

```
        }
    }
```

The `type` command can be used either to define a *type alias* or to declare a *bounded* abstract type. The most general form of a bounded abstract type declaration is

```
    type θ[tps] >: L <: U
```

Note that everything except θ is optional. If θ is a parametric type, then the letters *tps* denote type parameters. For instance, the following are legal type declarations:

```
    type MyIterable[+ξ] <: Iterable[ξ]
    type α[-γ,+β] >: ε[γ,β] <: ζ[γ,β]
```

Basically, bounded abstract types are used in the declaration of abstract types. For example, here is how one would define an abstract class for cells:

```
    abstract class ABSTRACT_CELL {
        type α
        var x : α
        def get() : α
        def set(y : α) : Unit
    }
```

Type α should become concrete in any class that extends this class. Also, note that the methods are just declared and not defined. This is something one should expect as, in the most general case, it does not make sense to program with *abstract* values. The following class extends the abstract class just declared and apart from type definition there are also method definitions:

```
    class Int_CELL extends ABSTRACT_CELL {
        type α = Int
        var x : α = 0
        def get() = x
        def set(y : α) = x = y
    }
```

As was shown in the previous example, in a type definition one writes first the new type and then an equals sign that is followed by a predefined or user-defined type. In the most general case, one may specify type parameters and any other information that is necessary. For example, the following type definitions are valid:

```
type Hash = Map[Int,String]
type Hash[α] = Map[Int,α]
type Pair[+α, +β] = Tuple2[α, β]
```

The last example is interesting because `Tuple2` is a case class and not so surprisingly the type definition introduces a new case class. Also, after a new type has been introduced with a type definition, the language interpreter will consider it as a normal type. For example, if one types in the following definition in the Scala interpreter,

```
var x : Hash = Map(3 -> "red", 4 -> "blue")
```

the interpreter will not respond with the following message

```
x: scala.collection.immutable.Map[Int,java.lang.String]
= Map(3 -> red, 4 -> blue)
```

but with the following one

```
x: Hash = Map(3 -> red, 4 -> blue)
```

In other words, it will not try to "expand" type names.

3.6.9 *Views and view bounds*

A *view* is another form of implicit conversion. An implicit function parameter of type α=>β or (=>α)=>β (i.e., a function that has one argument that is passed by-name) defines a view from type α to type β. The notation α <% β is used to specify views from α to β. In particular, instead of defining a function the "normal" way

```
def f[α]{a :Int)(implicit v: α => β): γ = . . .
```

we can define it more compactly using views as follows:

```
def f[α <% β]{a :Int): γ = . . .
```

There are two situations in which views are applied.

(i) Assume that an expression *e* is of type α and that α does not conform to the expression's expected type β. Then, the language processor searches for an implicit type convertor *v* that is applicable to *e* and whose result type conforms to β. When it is found, it is applied to *e*.

(ii) Assume that *e* is of type α. Also, assume that *e.m* is a selection and that *m* does not denote a member of α. Then the implicit convertor, *v*, is searched and when found it transforms *e* in order to make the selection meaningful. In other words, the selection is performed to $v(e).m$.

If α is a type parameter of a method or a class but not of a trait that has view bound $\alpha <\% \beta$, then α can be instantiated to any σ provided that σ can be converted by a view to the bound β. The most common view bound is $\alpha <\%$ `Ordered[α]`.

In Section 2.4 we talked about a subset relationship between basic Scala types. The truth is that there is no such relationship. Instead, for all basic numerical types the following view bounds hierarchy is predefined:

`Byte <% Short <% Int <% Long <% Float <% Double.`

In addition, `Char <% Int`.

3.6.10 Existential types

We have learned how to define classes, traits, and methods that are parametrized by some type. Thus, we can define a stack that can contain elements of some type α. Unfortunately, everything we have said so far cannot be used to define a stack that can have elements of any type. In other words, if Scala had provided us with tools to define heterogeneous lists what would be the type of these lists? First of all, the good news is that Scala provides a facility to define such heterogeneous types. And this is achieved by using *existential* types. The easiest way to define a heterogeneous list is by defining it as follows:

```
val A:List[_] = List(1,"Scala",1.0,true,'X')
```

Here the wildcard type _ is a shorthand for the most simple existential type:

```
α forSome type α
```

This means that the previous definition of the heterogeneous list is completely equivalent to the following definition:

```
val A:List[α forSome type α] = List(1,"Scala",1.0,true,'X')
```

Note that one could easily define the same heterogeneous list as follows:

```
val A:List[Any] = List(1,"Scala",1.0,true,'X')
```

However, if one tries the following code

```
val A:List[Any] = List(1,"Scala",1.0,true,List(1,2,3))
```

one will discover that it is not correct (Scala will complain that *implicit conversions are not applicable because they are ambiguous*), but the following code does not exhibit this problem:

```
val A:List[_] = List(1,"Scala",1.0,true,List(1,2,3))
```

Naturally, replacing Any with AnyRef does not solve the problem (try it!).

Assume one wants to define a heterogeneous list that contains only elements which are numbers. In this case one needs to put restrictions on α:

```
val C : List[α forSome type α <: Double] = List(1,'α',1.0)
```

Similarly, if we want to create a list that has as elements lists that can have *at most* long numbers, then we should define our list as shown below:

```
val D : List[List[α forSome { type α <: Long }]] =
    List(List(1,2,3),List(10,20))
```

More generally, the following type definition

```
B[α] forSome { type α <: β }
```

is type constructor B of type α which is a subtype of β. Even more generally, the following type definition

```
B[α] forSome { type α >: β <: γ }
```

is type constructor B of type α which is a subtype of γ and β is a is a subtype of α. If the lower bound is omitted, it is assumed to be Nothing. When the upper bound is omitted, it is assumed to be Any.

Now that we have an understanding of Scala's existential types let us see some other interesting examples. First of all let us define a function that takes an argument of any type and returns something of any type. Obviously, this is an ideal job for existential types and here is how we can define this function and, moreover, how this function can be used:

```
type β = α forSome { type α }
type γ = β => β
def id(x: β): β = x
def f(A: γ ) = (A(3),A('x'))
```

An even more interesting example is the following case class hierarchy that can be used to implement an algebraic type that can be either a generic value or a pair that consists of a function that can take any kind of argument and returns a value of some generic type and a value of this generic value:

```
trait Expr[α]
case class Val[α](x: α) extends Expr[α]
```

```
case class Apply[α,β](a: (α=>β), b:α) extends
    Expr[α forSome { type α }]
```

If we enter these definitions into the Scala interpreter, then we can experiment with these definitions:

```
scala> type β = α forSome {type α }
defined type alias β

scala> def id2(x : β) = 4
id2: (β)Int

scala> val y = Apply(id2,"help")
y: Apply[java.lang.String,Int] = Apply(<function>,help)

scala> println(y.a(y.b))
4
```

The part of existential type that appears in curly brackets is called the *binding clause*. The binding clause can contain more than one type declaration that must be separated by semicolons. In addition, a binding clause may also contain value declarations. In particular, the existential type

```
α forSome { P; val x : λ; Q}
```

is completely equivalent to

```
β forSome { P; type t <: λ with Singleton; Q}
```

Here t is a new type name while β is obtained by replacing every occurrence of x.type with t. Here a.type is a *stable* type, that is either a singleton type or one that conforms to Singleton.

The Singleton type is a type that has two values: null and the single value stored to a variable p. Here is a simple variable initialization:

```
var x : Singleton = 4
```

Alternatively, we can define a variable having a *singleton* type with an initialization like the one shown at the end of the following interaction with the language interpreter:

```
scala> class X(var x : Int)
defined class X

scala> val a = new X(4)
a: X = X@1c71508
```

```
scala> a.x)
res0 : Int = 4

scala> var b : a.type =a
b: a.type = X@1c71508
```

3.6.11 *Type projections*

Given a class C that defines some type α, then the expression C#α is a way to refer to this particular type member. The following, completely useless, example demonstrates how type projections can be used:

```
trait B {
    type P
}

trait A extends B {
    type Q
}

class C extends A {
    type X1 = A#P
    type X2 = A#Q
}
```

3.6.12 *Type erasure*

Currently, there is a disparity between Scala and the JVM: Scala supports generic types but, unfortunately, the current version of the JVM does not.[5] This implies that generic types exist during compilation but they are omitted from the generated byte-code, for the reason just explained. This phenomenon is known as *type erasure.*The upcoming new major release of the JVM, code named the *Da Vinci Machine* and also known as the *Multi Language Virtual Machine* (MLVM), will include support for the compilation of dynamic languages. Thus, once Scala is moved to MLVM, type erasure will no longer be a problem. On the other hand, when a language has access to information about generic types at run time, we say that the generic types are *reified*.

Because of type erasure the implementors of Scala devised a mapping from generic types to nongeneric types in order to ensure the proper functionality of any

---

[5] If you wonder what types have to do with machines and machine code, let us remind you that the JVM is a high level virtual machine. In addition, it is possible to define a typed assembly language even for ordinary hardware like the x86 architecture. In fact, Greg Morrisett [56] and his colleagues have defined and implemented a typed assembly language.

program. Assume that α denotes a generic type. Then ⦃α⦄ will denote its erasure. In particular, this mapping from generic types to nongeneric types is defined as follows.

- The erasure of an abstract type is the erasure of its upper bound.
- The erasure of `Array[α]` is `Array[⦃α⦄]`.
- The erasure of every other parameterized type α`[β,..,ζ]` is ⦃α⦄.
- The erasure of α `with ... with ζ {. . . }` is ⦃α⦄.
- The erasure of α `forSome {Ξ}` is ⦃α⦄.

Scala provides a method to reify types that is based on *manifests*. To use this feature, one has to add an implicit parameter of type `scala.reflect.Manifest[α]`, where α is a generic type that appears in the method definition and which is supposed to be reified. For example, here is a trivial use of this technique:

```
scala> def name[α](implicit m: scala.reflect.Manifest[α]) =
     | m.toString
name: [α](implicit scala.reflect.Manifest[α])java.lang.String

scala> name[Int=>Int]
res0: java.lang.String = scala.Function1[int, int]
```

In addition, one can use method `erasure` that returns an object that corresponds to the run time erasure of the Scala type represented by the manifest:

```
scala> def etype[α](implicit m: scala.reflect.Manifest[α]) =
     | m.erasure
etype: [α](implicit scala.reflect.Manifest[T])java.lang.Class[_]

scala> etype[Int=>Int]
res1: java.lang.Class[_] = interface scala.Function1
```

Also, the operators `<:<` and `>:>` can be used to test whether the type represented by the manifest on the left of the operator is a subtype/supertype of the type represented by the manifest on the right of the operator.

3.7 Nominal and structural typing

Instead of giving a formal description of nominal and structural typing, let us show their differences with a simple example. Consider the following two class definitions:

```
class ClassA {                   class ClassB {
    private var name = "A"           private var name = "B"
    def getName = name               def getName = name
    def setName(y: String) =         def setName(y: String) =
        name = y                         name = y
}                                }
```

At first, one can say that both definitions have exactly the same structure, but they introduce two different types since they have different names. On the other hand, one would claim that both types are equivalent since their structure is identical. The first view is in accordance with nominal typing, while the second view is in accordance with structural typing. Scala honors structural typing and so these two classes are of the same type. Structural typing allows one to relax type requirements in value and function declarations. For example, the following defines a list of objects that have at least a method called getname that simply returns a string:

```
val A = List[ def getName: String ](new ClassA, new ClassB)
```

Similarly, the following type definition introduces a new class type that has a method named setName:

```
type Setname = { def setName(y: String):Unit }
```

It is very important to note that the type is deduced from the header of a function definition.

Another aspect of structural typing is subtyping. Again, consider the following class definition:

```
class ClassC {
    private var name = "Class C"
    private var backup = name
    def getName = name
    def setName(y: String) = name=y
}
```

The question is whether ClassC is a subclass of ClassB. According to structural typing the answer is affirmative: yes ClassC is a subclass of ClassB. For instance, the following code

```
def FF(x:{ def getName: String }) = println(x.getName)
var A = new ClassC
FF(A)
```

will compile and it will print the message *Class C*.

3.8* Higher order polymorphism

Although one can define classes, traits, and methods that are polymorphic, still it is not clear whether it is possible to have functions that can have types as parameters and which might be able to return types as results. In other words, it is not clear whether Scala provides facilities that allow its users to write programs that are parametrized by a datatype (for example, a list or a tree). Fortunately, Scala provides all the necessary facilities for *data generic programming*, that is for writing programs that are parametrized by datatypes. In other words, Scala is a language that provides the necessary facilities for *higher order* polymorphic programming. In order to illustrate Scala's expressive power we will show how to encode *hylomorphisms*. But first we need to explain what hylomorphisms are and what is the general idea behind them.

Hylomorphisms are recursive functions whose invocation tree (i.e., the graphical representation of the various invocations involved in a particular function invocation) is *isomorphic* to that of a function that processes lists. Roughly, two entities (for example, collections of things, invocation trees, etc.) are isomorphic when there is a resemblance between these two entities and one can be taken for the other. The term hylomorphism (Greek ὑλο-hylo-, "matter" + morphism < Greek μορφή, morphē, "form") refers to the philosophical theory, originating with Socrates, that conceptually identifies substance as matter and form. A hylomorphism can be viewed as the composition of an *anamorphism* (from Greek: ἀνά, upwards, + morphism) that builds the invocation tree as an explicit data structure and a *catamorphism* (from Greek: κατά, downwards or according to, + morphism) that *reduces* the data structure to a required value. The notion of hylomorphic recursive functions was introduced by Erik Meijer, Maarten Fokkinga, and Ross Paterson [51].

The idea behind hylomorphisms is to be able to express (functional) programs as instances of common patterns, rather than inventing the wheel every time we have to solve a particular problem. After all, this is the idea behind design patterns. Thus, one could say that hylomorphisms are a sort of design pattern for functional programming. Since Scala is both an object-oriented and a functional programming language, both hylomorphisms and design patterns should matter for the Scala programmer. In order to give a practical account of hylomorphisms, we will borrow an example from Jeremy Gibbons' [25] lucid account of hylomorphisms (see also [26] for a thorough description of various techniques and methodologies employed in functional programming). Gibbons prefers the term *origami programming* (from origami (from oru, folding, + kami, paper) the Japanese art of paper folding) over hylomorphism.

In the examples below we will use lists to show what hylomorphisms can achieve. The function that follows is a typical example of a catamorphism:

```
def foldL[α,β](f: (α, β) => β)(e: β)(l: List[α]): β =
  l match {
```

```
    case  Nil  => e
    case x::xs => f(x, foldL(f)(e)(xs))
}
```

Note that although we use lists this definition works for any other isomorphic data structure. Also, this function does exactly what the :/ (foldr) operator does. The next function is a typical example of an anomorphism:

```
def unfoldLa[α,β](f: β => Option[Tuple2[α,β]])
                 (u: β):List[α] =
  f(u) match {
    case None        => Nil
    case Some((x,v)) => x::(unfoldLa(f)(v))
  }
```

This function can also be written as follows:

```
def unfoldL[α,β](p: β => Boolean)
                (f: β => α)(g: β => β)
                          (b: β):List[α] =
  if (p(b))
    Nil
  else
    (f(b))::(unfoldL(p)(f)(g)(g(b)))
```

Exercise 3.17 Provide a definition of unfoldL in terms of unfoldLa.

Let us see a first example that shows the power of these functions. The function that follows implements the insert sort algorithm for lists:

```
def isort[α](l: List[α])
          (implicit orderer: α => Ordered[α]): List[α] =
  foldL(insert[α])(Nil)(l)
```

Function insert is defined as follows:

```
def insert[α](y:α, xs:List[α])
          (implicit orderer: α => Ordered[α]):List[α] =
  xs match {
    case Nil    => List(y)
    case x::xss => if (y < x)
                     y::x::xss
                   else
                     x::(insert(y,xss))
  }
```

The implicit parameter is used to describe the ordering of αs. Thus, the following commands give the expected results because for many simple types there is a predefined method `orderer`:

```
val L = List(3,9,5,7,4,1,2,6)
val L2 = isort[Int](L)
```

After executing these two commands, list L2 will contain the elements of list L sorted in ascending order. As a second example, let us see how we can implement bubble sort. First, we need to define the following function:

```
def step[α](x: α, y: Option[Tuple2[α,List[α]]])
            (implicit orderer: α => Ordered[α]) :
                    Option[Tuple2[α,List[α]]] =
   y match {
      case None            => Some((x,Nil))
      case Some((z,zs))    => if (x < z)
                                 Some((x,z::zs))
                              else
                                 Some((z,x::zs))
   }
```

Function `bubble` is the one that places an element in the proper position:

```
def bubble[α](l: List[α])
              (implicit orderer: α => Ordered[α]) :
                    Option[Tuple2[α,List[α]]]  =
   foldL(step[α])(None)(l)
```

Function `bsort` can be used to sort a list using the bubble sort algorithm:

```
def bsort[α](l: List[α])
             (implicit orderer: α => Ordered[α]) : List[α] =
   unfoldLa(bubble[α])(l)
```

The following command creates a new list that contains the elements of list L sorted using bubble sort:

```
var L3 = bsort[Int](L)
```

As noted above, if we compose the fold and the unfold functions, we get a hylomorphism. A simple example of a hylomorphism is given by a function that computes the factorial of some integer *n*:

```
def fact(n: Int) =
  foldL( (_:Int) * (_:Int) )( 1 )
       ( unfoldL( (_:Int) == 0 )( id )( pred )( n ))
```

In a real source file the second and the third lines must appear on the same physical line or else the language processor will "find" errors. Also, function `id` returns its argument and function `pred` returns its argument, if it is equal to zero, or its argument reduced by one if it is greater than zero.

Exercise 3.18 Use function `fact` to compute the factorial of 5.

We can encode the natural numbers using a data structure that is similar to lists. In fact, we are going to encode numbers as defined in Peano's arithmetic, named after Giuseppe Peano. In this arithmetic all numbers are expressed in terms of the constant zero and the successor function. Thus, one is the successor of zero and two is the successor of one or the successor of the successor of zero. In order to complete our task we need to write the corresponding fold and unfold functions. But instead of writing such functions for each different data structure, one could write one folding and one unfolding function that could be used in every possible case. This is the essence of data generic programming. Before we proceed with the really generic solution, let us see how we can encode natural numbers and how we can write the corresponding fold function. We start with the datatype definition:

```
trait Nat
object Zero extends Nat {
   override def toString = "Zero"
}
case class S(n:Nat) extends Nat
```

For example, number 3 can be encoded as S(S(S(Zero))). The following function is the fold function for natural numbers:

```
def foldN[α](z : α)(s: α => α)(n: Nat): α =
  n match {
     case Zero => z
     case S(a) => s(foldN(z)(s)(a))
  }
```

Exercise 3.19 Define a simple function `succ` that takes a natural number and returns its successor.

Now we can define addition of natural numbers as follows:

```
def add(n: Nat, m: Nat): Nat = foldN[Nat](n)(succ)(m)
```

For instance, the code that follows

```
var w1=S(S(S(Zero)))
var w2=S(S(S(S(Zero))))
println(add(w1,w2))
```

will print S(S(S(S(S(S(S(Zero))))))). Although it is straightforward to implement the two forms of the unfold function for natural numbers, we leave it as an exercise for the reader to implement these two functions.

It is clear that the two versions of function fold are quite similar (as they are the corresponding forms of function unfold). In fact, one could say they are almost identical, thus, one is tempted to ask whether it would be possible to write very generic fold and unfold functions applicable to any kind of relevant data type. This and other similar ideas are akin to higher order polymorphism. Apparently, there are different forms of polymorphism. In simple type theory one can build types from atomic types (for example, Int is an atomic type) using type constructors like → (for functions), × (for tuples), etc. In first order polymorphic type theory one can also use type variables α, β, γ,... to build types. In second order polymorphic type theory one may abstract type variables as for example is done in the following function definition:

```
def id[α](x : α) = x
```

In higher order polymorphic type theory one can create functions and tuples of *kinds*. Mathematically speaking, one could say that if types are sets, then a kind is a category of these sets and the (constructors of the) various higher order types are endofunctors of this category (see Section 3.13* for an explanation of what a category is). In simpler words, if types are sets, then a collection of all these types is a kind. If we view all these types as elements of a set and then define a "function" from this set to itself (for example, the negation or the addition of two integers are functions from integers or a pair of integers to integers, respectively), then we are practically defining a higher order type. Although one can construct collections of kinds, this is something no one has considered from a practical point of view.

Although Scala does not directly support kinds, still Adriaan Moors, Frank Piessens, and Wouter Joosen were the first to describe a library for datatype-generic programming in Scala [55]. In fact, they have translated a library written in Haskell to Scala. Not surprisingly, the resulting library is more in spirit with the philosophy of object-oriented programming than with that of functional programming. Nevertheless, later on Bruno Oliveira and Jeremy Gibbons presented a version of the

```
def id[α](x: α) = x

case class Fix[F[_,_],α](out:F[α,Fix[F,α]])

trait BiFunctor[F[_,_]] {
  def bimap[α,β,γ,δ]:
    (α => β) => (γ => δ) => F[α,γ] => F[β,δ]
  def fmap2[α,β,γ]: (β => γ) => F[α,β] => F[α,γ] =
    bimap(id[α])
}


def cata[α,β,F[_,_]] (f: F[α,β] => β)
                     (t: Fix[F,α])
                     (implicit ft: BiFunctor[F]): β =
  f(ft.fmap2(cata[α,β,F](f))(t.out))


def ana[α,β,F[_,_]](f: β => F[α,β])
                   (x : β)
                   (implicit ft: BiFunctor[F]): Fix[F,α] =
  Fix[F,α](ft.fmap2(ana[α,β,F](f))(f(x)))


def hylo[α,β,γ,F[_,_]](f: α => F[γ,α])
                      (g: F[γ,β] => β)
                      (x: α)
                      (implicit ft: BiFunctor[F]): β =
  g(ft.fmap2(hylo[α,β,γ,F](f)(g))(f(x)))


def build[α,F[_,_]](f: {def apply[β]:(F[α,β] => β) => β} ) =
  f.apply(Fix[F,α])
```

Figure 3.9 A "library" for datatype-generic programming in Scala.

same library [61] which is closer to the spirit of the initial Haskell library. The result is shown in Figure 3.9. The reader should be aware that since Scala does not support higher-ranked types, they have been encoded by wrapping methods in objects.

Figure 3.10 shows how one can use this library to encode lists. The shape of lists is described by a case-class hierarchy. The object biList defines a method to process list structures. The function that follows can be used to sum up the elements of a

```
trait ListF[α,β]
case class Nil[α,β]() extends ListF[α,β]
case class Cons[α,β](x:α, xs:β) extends ListF[α,β]

implicit object biList extends BiFunctor[ListF] {
    def bimap[α,β,γ,δ] = f => g => {
      case Nil()            => Nil()
      case Cons(x,xs)  => Cons(f(x),g(xs))
    }
}


type List[α] = Fix[ListF,α]
def nil[α]:List[α]    = Fix[ListF,α](Nil())
def cons[α]    = (x:α) =>
                          (xs : List[α]) =>
                          Fix[ListF,α](Cons(x,xs))
```

Figure 3.10 Defining lists using the library for datatype-generic programming in Scala.

list of integers:

```
def sumList = cata[Int,Int,ListF]  {
    case Nil()        => 0
    case Cons(x,xs) => x + xs
  } _
```

The following command shows how to write down lists using this new tool and how the function can be used:

```
var x = sumList(cons(1)(cons(2)(nil)))
```

Exercise 3.20 Define Peano numerals using the library for datatype-generic programming and then define a function that sums up two such numerals.

3.9 Streams are "infinite" lists!

There are cases where one has to use the first n numbers of an infinite sequence of numbers (like the Fibonacci numbers for example) but, unfortunately, there is no way to determine how many members of the sequence will be actually needed. Obviously, it makes no sense to start computing a large number of consecutive elements since the *large* may turn out to be too large or even too little. A better "solution" would be to compute all elements of the sequence and use as many as we want. Although the computation of infinite sequences of numbers in finite time is not impossible (see [72] for more details), still the computers on which Scala runs cannot perform such a task. But Scala offers an even better solution – the ability to define infinite sized data structures (for example, a list that holds all Fibonacci numbers) whose elements are computed on demand. These peculiar data structures are called streams. A stream is a list whose elements are not computed *eagerly*, but rather lazily. Eager evaluation means that a function first evaluates its arguments and then it uses them, while lazy evaluation means that an argument is evaluated only when it is needed. Obviously, lazy evaluation and call by-name are strongly connected. In order to understand how one can create and use "infinite" lists, we will present a simple example. Assume we want to create a stream that consists of all integer numbers. The code that follows can be used to create such a stream:

```
def numsFrom (n :Int):Stream[Int] =
              Stream.cons(n,numsFrom (n+1))
```

cons is the stream equivalent of the : : operator. Now we can create an "infinite" stream using the following command:

```
lazy val N = numsFrom(0)
```

The keyword lazy designates that the value assigned to the constant N should not be evaluated. By entering the expression

```
N take 10 print
```

the language processor will print out the following output:

```
0, 1, 2, 3, 4, 5, 6, 7, 8, 9, Stream.empty
```

Streams have their own print method that outputs elements of this stream one by one and separated by commas. If for some reason we need a different separator symbol, we can supply one as an argument of method print. In addition, methods foldRight and foldLeft are the stream equivalents of /: and :/. Also, one can get a list from a stream using the force method.

In most cases, we need to define some function that will create an "infinite" stream, still in some simple cases there is no need to define such a function. For example, the following constant definition creates an "infinite" list of ones:

```
lazy val Ones: Stream[Int] = Stream.cons(1,Ones)
```

Exercise 3.21 Write an expression that will create a list that consists of five ones.

Exercise 3.22 Define a Scala stream that computes the Fibonacci numbers. Hint: Construct a stream whose first two elements are the first two elements of the Fibonacci sequence. Then define recursively the tail of the tail of this stream by zipping the stream with its tail and then by replacing each pair with the sum of its elements.

3.10* More on memo functions

The discussion on memo functions presented in Section 2.12 can be seen as a general recipe to construct memo functions. Nevertheless, one cannot automatically generate memo functions – one has to construct each function manually. In his blog (michid@wordpress), Michael Dürig presented a solution that can be used to create memo functions automatically. His solution, which is shown in Figure 3.11, is a direct generalization of trait Function1. Method Y should be used to generate a recursive memo function. This method corresponds to the *fixed point* combinator or operator Y of the λ-calculus (see [9] for more details). This operator is used to

```scala
class Memo1[-α, +β](f: α => β) extends (α => β) {
    import scala.collection.mutable
    private[this] val vals = mutable.Map.empty[α, β]

    def apply(x: α): β = {
        if (vals.contains(x)) {
            vals(x)
        }
        else {
            val y = f(x)
            vals + ((x, y))
            y
        }
    }
}

object Memo1 {
    def apply[α, β](f: α => β) = new Memo1(f)
    def Y[α, β](f: (α, α => β) => β) = {
        var yf: α => β = null
        yf = Memo1(f(_, yf(_)))
        yf
    }
}
```

Figure 3.11 A generic representation of a memo function of one argument.

compute the fixed point of a function, that is, given a function f, x is its fixed point
if $f(x) = x$. In general, for any function f it holds that:

$$Yf = f(Yf).$$

A function may have more than one fixed points, but the expression Yf computes
the *least fixed point* of f. The Y combinator is used in the untyped λ-calculus to
define recursive functions.

Assume we want to create a memo function to compute the factorial of a positive
integer. Then in order to compute the factorial using a recursive algorithm, we have
to first define a function whose fixed point is the memorized factorial function.
Feeding this function to the fixed point combinator will then yield the desired
memorized factorial function:

```
def facRec(n: BigInt, f: BigInt => BigInt): BigInt = {
  if (n == 0) 1
  else n*f(n - 1)
}

val fac = Memo1.Y(facRec)
```

We use `BigInts` to avoid integer overflows. Also, in order to be able to store the
intermediate results, we need to make them available outside the function. This is
exactly why we had to introduce the extra parameter in the function definition. The
next thing is actually to use `fac` to compute the factorial of some numbers:

```
for (k <- 201 to 0 by -1)
  println(fac(k))
```

Programming project 3.1 Define a class `Memo2` and use it to compute the first
hundred Fibonacci numbers.

3.11 Assertions

Assertions are used to check *invariants*, that is, conditions that should always be true.
If at any given moment an assertion does not hold and the program detects this,
an exception is thrown. Assertions can be used as internal invariants, control-flow
invariants, preconditions, postconditions, and class invariants. Internal invariants
are assertions that replace comments that would have been written to assert an
invariant. Control-flow invariants are assertions placed at any location of the code
one assumes will not be reached. A precondition describes what must be true when
a method is invoked while a postcondition describes what must be true after a

method completes successfully. Finally, class invariants describe what must be true about each instance of a class.

In Scala preconditions and postconditions can be asserted with the two forms of the `assume` method:

```
assume(x > 2)
assume(x > 2, "x must be greater than 2")
```

The following example shows how this method can be used:

```
assume(x <= 0)
x = x*x
assume(x >= 0)
```

The invariants can be better served with the two forms of method `assert`:

```
assert(false)
assume(false, "unreachable location!!!")
```

The following example shows how one could use method `assert`:

```
assume(i>=0)
if (i % 3 == 0) {
    . . . . . . . . . .
} else if (i % 3 == 1) {
    . . . . . . . . . .
} else {
    assert(i % 3 == 2)
    . . . . . . . . . .
}
```

Unrecoverable situations can be "handled" with method `error`. This method takes a string as argument and aborts program execution by throwing an exception which curries its only argument. For example, if the reader feeds to the language interpreter a file containing the following line

```
error("this can't happen!")
```

the computer screen will show an error message like the following one (not all lines shown):

```
java.lang.RuntimeException: this can't happen!
        at scala.Predef$.error(Predef.scala:76)
        . . . . . . . . . . . . . . . . . . . . .
```

Finally, method `exit` should be used to stop program execution. This is useful if there is no other way to stop program execution. These two methods have nothing to do with assertions, but they are presented here for reasons of completeness.

By default assertions are on, that is, their conditions are examined and if they fail an exception is thrown. However, the following command line option

```
-Xdisable-assertions
```

informs both the compiler and the interpreter to ignore all assertions.

3.12 Setters and getters

JavaBeans are Java classes that, among others, provide getter and setter methods for accessing its properties. In Scala whenever one defines a nonprivate field, the language processor automatically creates a getter method, which is used to access the value of the field, and a setter method, which is used to alter the field's value. For example, for the following class

```
class A {
    var a: Int = _
}
```

the compiler will generate the following output (using the −Xprint:sup command line option, see Appendix C for more on command line options):

```
class A extends java.lang.Object with ScalaObject {
    def this(): A = {
      A.super.this();
      ()
    };
    private[this] var a: Int = _;
    def a(): Int = A.this.a;
    def a_=(x$1: Int): Unit = A.this.a = x$1
}
```

This is an internal representation of the source code above. Ignoring all the incomprehensible symbols, one may note towards the end of the code that there are two method definitions – method a and method a_= (both the underscore and the equals sign are part of the method's name). Obviously, the first method is the getter and the second one is the setter.

A rather interesting aspect of getters and setters is that one can define them manually and then use the variable that would correspond to these methods. The following class shows how this can be implemented:

```
class price {
  var euros : Double = _
  def dollars = euros * 1.36296
  def dollars_=(d: Double) =
    euros = d * 0.73370
  override def toString =
    "%.2f EUR/%.2f USD".format(euros,dollars)
}
```

Objects of this class hold prices in both EUR and and USD. Before we explain the functionality of this class, let us explain what method toString returns. This method returns a string, in which the values specified as arguments of method format are formatted according to the formatting instructions contained in the string object. Each formatting instruction starts with the % symbol that is followed by a conversion character, which denotes how the corresponding value should be formatted. Between the symbol % and the conversion character one can specify a number, which specifies the minimum number of characters that have to be used to represent the corresponding value, a period, which separates the width from the precision, and a number, which is the precision, that is, the maximum number of characters that have to be used to represent the information after the period. Table 3.1 shows the basic formatting conversions. In our example, we do not specify a number after the %, which means that we do not care about the number of characters that will be used to represent the two numbers. However, we want each number to have only two decimal digits.

Assume that we create an instance of class price. Then every time we assign a value to "field" dollars the method dollars_= is invoked and the value that is assigned to the "field" is passed to this method. Thus, by defining a getter and a setter method for a particular "field," we can implicitly specify actions that should be taken every time the "field's" value changes. Obviously, this is not something one could do with ordinary fields:

```
scala> var c = new price
c: price = 0,00 EUR/0,00 USD

scala> c.euros = 400

scala> c
res0: price = 400,00 EUR/544,56 USD
scala> c.dollars = 500
```

Table 3.1 *Basic formatting conversions*

Character	Printed as
s, S	String
c, C	Unicode character
d	Decimal integer
o	Unsigned ictal integer
x, X	Unsigned hexadecimal number (without leading 0x)
e, E	Decimal number in computerized scientific notation
f	Decimal number
g, G	Either computerized scientific notation or decimal format, depending on the precision and the value after rounding
a, A	Hexadecimal floating-point number with a significand and an exponent
%	The literal %
n	Line separator

```
scala> c
res1: price = 367,27 EUR/500,00 USD
```

Exercise 3.23 Make class `price` more useful by adding support for more currencies (Japanese yen, Canadian dollars, etc.).

3.13* Monads

Monads are mathematical structures that were introduced in homological algebra and later they were introduced in category theory. Eugenio Moggi [53] was probably the first researcher who used monads in structuring semantic descriptions of features such as state and exceptions. Philip Wadler [76] established a connection between list comprehensions and monads that led to a generalization of list comprehensions to an arbitrary monad. This feature was employed to express concisely in pure functional programming languages programs that handle exceptions, parse text files, etc. Although it is not necessary to have a solid background in category theory in order to understand the various ideas described in the rest of this section, still we believe it is better to be familiar with some basic notion of category theory. In this section we will introduce the reader to these ideas. Readers who are either familiar with category theory or simply do not want to bother with these mathematical notions, can safely skip this section and ignore all future references to categories.

Categories in a nutshell Categories were first introduced by Samuel Eilenberg and Saunders Mac Lane. In a nutshell, a category can be viewed as a *mathematical universe*. There are many categories and each of them consists of entities, which have the same nature, and ways to pass from one entity to another. Also, there are ways to pass from one category to another. In addition, it is possible to transform these ways from one category to another while preserving their internal structure.

Definition 3 A category consists of *objects* (i.e., mathematical structures like sets) and morphisms (i.e., maps between objects). Each morphism f has a *domain* (i.e., the object that is mapped by the morphism) and a *codomain* (i.e., the object to which the morphism maps). When a morphism f has as domain the object A and as codomain the object B, we write $f : A \rightarrow B$. For each object A there is an identity morphism $\mathrm{id}_A : A \rightarrow A$. Also, for each pair of morphisms $f : A \rightarrow B$ and $g : B \rightarrow C$ a composite morphism $g \circ f : A \rightarrow C$ can be defined. Morphism compositions must satisfy the following rules:

(i) if $f : A \rightarrow B$ is a morphism, then $\mathrm{id}_B \circ f = f$ and $f \circ \mathrm{id}_A = f$; and
(ii) if $f : A \rightarrow B$, $g : B \rightarrow C$, and $h : C \rightarrow D$ are morphisms, then $(h \circ g) \circ f = h \circ (g \circ f)$.

Examples The collection of all sets and functions between them with the usual function composition make up the category **Set**. Consider the set $\mathbb{N}$ of all positive integer numbers including zero and the usual numerical ordering, $\leq$, of integer numbers. Then we can define a category whose objects are the elements of $\mathbb{N}$ and given two numbers n and m there is a morphism from n to m if $n \leq m$ (as an exercise explain why each object has an identity morphism, how morphism composition is defined, and whether morphism composition satisfies the rules of morphism composition).

   A *functor* is a way to go from one category to another that preserves the categorical structure of its *domain*.

Definition 4 Given two categories $\mathscr{C}$ and $\mathscr{D}$ a functor F is a map that assigns to each $\mathscr{C}$-object A a $\mathscr{D}$-object $F(A)$ and to each $\mathscr{C}$-morphism $f : A \rightarrow B$ a $\mathscr{D}$-morphism $F(f) : F(A) \rightarrow F(B)$ such that

(i) the identity morphism on A is assigned the identity morphism on $F(A)$, and
(ii) $F(g \circ f) = F(g) \circ F(f)$, whenever $g \circ f$ is defined.

A functor $T : \mathscr{A} \rightarrow \mathscr{A}$ is called an *endofunctor*. Also, any endofunctor $T : \mathscr{A} \rightarrow \mathscr{A}$ has composites $T^2 = T \circ T : \mathscr{A} \rightarrow \mathscr{A}$ and $T^3 = T \circ T \circ T : \mathscr{A} \rightarrow \mathscr{A}$.

Exercise 3.24 Why does a function from the set of even numbers (with the usual numerical ordering) to the set of natural numbers define a functor?

The next notion that we need to introduce is the *natural transformation*. Assume that $\mathscr{A}$ and $\mathscr{B}$ are two categories and that $\mathscr{B}^{\mathscr{A}}$ is the collection of all functors from $\mathscr{A}$ and $\mathscr{B}$. Then if we form a category whose objects are the functors that belong to $\mathscr{B}^{\mathscr{A}}$, the morphisms of this category are natural transformations.

Definition 5 Given two functors $F, G : \mathscr{C} \to \mathscr{D}$ a natural transformation $\tau : F \to G$ is a map that assigns to each $\mathscr{C}$-object A a $\mathscr{D}$-morphism $\tau_A : F(A) \to G(A)$, such that for any $\mathscr{C}$-morphism $f : A \to B$ $\tau_B \circ F(f) = G(f) \circ \tau_A$.

Now we are ready to define monads.

Definition 6 A monad in a category $\mathscr{C}$ is a triple $\langle T, \eta, \mu \rangle$, where $T : \mathscr{C} \to \mathscr{C}$ is a functor and $\eta : \mathrm{id}_{\mathscr{C}} \to T$ and $\mu : T^2 \to T$ are natural transformations, such that

(i) $\mu \circ T\mu = \mu \circ \mu T$, and
(ii) $\mu \circ T\eta = \mathrm{id}_T = \mu \circ \eta T$

where $T\mu_A : T^3(A) \to T^2(A)$ and $\mu T_A = \mu_{T(A)}$.

Readers with a strong mathematical background can consult [50] for a thorough discussion of category theory. However, we suggest [45] to anyone willing to learn the basics of category theory in a systematic but accessible way.

Monads in Scala Method map (see Section 2.13) has some really interesting properties. Before discussing these properties, it is better to review the following interaction with Scala's interpreter:

```
scala> val double = (x:Int) => x*2
double: (Int) => Int = <function>

scala> val triple = (x:Int) => x*3
triple: (Int) => Int = <function>

scala> var A=List(1,2,3,5)
A: List[Int] = List(1, 2, 3, 5)

scala> A.map( double compose triple )
res0: List[Int] = List(6, 12, 18, 30)

scala> val B = A.map(double)
B: List[Int] = List(2, 4, 6, 10)
scala> B.map(triple)
```

```
res1: List[Int] = List(6, 12, 18, 30)

scala> val id = (x:Int) => x
id: (Int) => Int = <function>

scala> A.map(id)
res2: List[Int] = List(1, 2, 3, 5)
```

This interaction with Scala's interpreter shows that this method maps a list to another list. In general, the two lists can have different types as there is no restriction on this. Also, if the only argument of this method is an identity function, then the result is as if one has applied the identity function for lists of a specific type to this particular list. In addition, we see that if the argument of map is the composition of two functions, then by successively applying map with the first function as argument and then with the second function we observe that the results are the same. Let us summarize these properties:

$$\text{map id} = \text{id} \tag{3.1}$$

$$\text{map}(g \circ f) = (\text{map } g) \circ (\text{map } f) \tag{3.2}$$

It is not difficult to see that map is a functor.

Method flatten is a function that has an interesting property:

```
scala> var A=List(List(1, 2), List(3, 4))
A: List[List[Int]] = List(List(1, 2), List(3, 4))

scala> flatten(A.map(e => e.map(double)))
res3: List[Int] = List(2, 4, 6, 8)

scala> (flatten(A)).map(double)
res4: List[Int] = List(2, 4, 6, 8)
```

This code reveals that in general the following holds

$$(\text{map } f) \circ \text{flatten} = \text{flatten} \circ \text{map}(\text{map } f), \tag{3.3}$$

where f is just a normal function that maps elements of one type to elements of another type. Note that this equality cannot be expressed directly in Scala. Another function that has a similar property is function unit that takes an object and returns a singleton list with this object as its only element. The following shows the essence of this property of unit:

```
scala> def unit(x:Int) = List(x)
unit: (Int)List[Int]

scala> (unit(3)).map(double)
res5: List[Int] = List(6)

scala> (unit(double(3))
res6: List[Int] = List(6)
```

Mathematically, the property can be expressed as follows:

$$(\texttt{map f}) \circ \texttt{unit} = \texttt{unit} \circ f. \tag{3.4}$$

In categorical terms, `flatten` and the `unit` are natural transformations. And the more interesting thing is that these two functions and the method `map` form a monad. To be precise, these three functions do not form a monad but a *strong monad* in a *cartesian closed category* (CCC). Roughly, a strong monad is a monad $\langle T, \eta, \mu \rangle$ together with a natural transformation $t_{A,B}$ from $A \times TB$ to $T(A \times B)$ that satisfies some properties (see [53, p. 74]). If A and B are two objects (types) of some CCC, then there is an object $[A \to B]$ that represents the collection of all morphisms (functions) from A to B. The object $[A \to B]$ is called the *exponential* object. This object is associated with a special morphism ev $: [A \to B] \times A \to B$, where $F \times G$ is the categorical product of these objects, which in the case of sets is the cartesian product of sets, with the property that $ev(\langle f, x \rangle) = f(x)$. Also, what makes CCC interesting is that if we view a category as a formal system, then a CCC is a type of category that has the same expressive power as a typed λ-calculus (see [44] for a discussion of the connection between CCCs and typed λ-calculi).

Examples of monads List comprehensions, that is, `for` comprehensions that create lists, can be expressed in terms of the monad presented above:

$$\texttt{for (x<-u) yield t} \equiv \texttt{u.map(x => t)} \tag{3.5}$$

$$\texttt{for (p; q) yield t} \equiv \texttt{flatten(for (p) yield} \tag{3.6}$$

$$\texttt{(for (q) yield t))}$$

In other words, we can have `for` expressions for free with monads! Also, the type `Option` is a monad (can you see why?). However, a more interesting example involves the representation of *continuations* as a monad. But first let us say a few things about continuations. The discussion that follows is based on the presentation found in [21], but the reader should also consult [37] for a discussion of the use of continuation in partial evalauation.

   Continuations are a programming technique by which a recursive function which is not *tail recursive* (i.e., a recursive function whose result in the nonbase case is determined solely by the result of recursively calling the function) can be transformed into a tail recursive function. Roughly, a continuation is a mapping which is applied to a partially evaluated result to yield the fully evaluated result. The goal is to find a sequence of partial result/continuation pairs that can be used to obtain the final result by applying the continuation to the partial result. Furthermore, one may say that these pairs define the basic property of an iterative process and hence the tail recursion. In general, every recursive function can be transformed into a tail recursive one using a particular technique, but the resulting function is far more complex than the original. The transformation technique involves the definition of a function that has as argument another function. Assume that $f : A \to B$ is a recursive function defined as follows:

$$f(x) = \begin{cases} q & \text{if } p \\ E & \text{otherwise.} \end{cases}$$

Then its tail recursive version will be a function $f_{\text{tr}} : A \to (B \to C) \to C$. Initially, f-tr is applied to the argument of f and a simple continuation, such as the identity function:

$$f(x) = f_{\text{tr}}(x, \text{id}).$$

In the base case, the result is simply an application of the continuation, γ, to what f might have returned in the base case: $\gamma(q)$. We assume that the expression E in the nonbase case has a single occurrence of f that is applied to a subexpression $s(x)$, where x is the formal parameter. Also, let $r = f(s(x))$ and $E_r = [r/f(s(x))]E$, that is, the expression E in which each occurrence of $f(s(x))$ is replaced by a w. Then the continuation function is defined as follows:

$$f_{\text{tr}}(x, \gamma) = \begin{cases} \gamma(q) & \text{if } p \\ f_{\text{tr}}\Big(s(x), \big((r : C) \Rightarrow \gamma E_r\big)\Big) & \text{otherwise.} \end{cases}$$

Let us apply this technique to a specific example. Consider the following nontail recursive function that appends two lists:

```
def append[α] (A:List[α],B:List[α]):List[α] =
    A match {
        case Nil   => B
        case x::xs => x:: append(xs,B)
    }
```

Note that here $s(A, B) = (\text{tail}(A), B)$ and by applying the technique just described we create a tail recursive version of this function:

```
def append[α](A: List[α], B: List[α]): List[α] = {
  def append2[α,β](A: List[α], B: List[α],
              cont: (List[α] => β) ):β =
    A match {
      case Nil   => cont(b)
      case x::xs => append2(xs,B,
                        ((r:List[A]) => cont(x::r)))
    }
  append2(A,B,((r: List[α]) => r))
}
```

Exercise 3.25 Define a tail recursive version of the following function:

```
def Reverse[α](A:List[α]): List[α] =
  A match {
    case Nil   => Nil
    case x::xs => Reverse(xs):::List(x)
  }
```

We proceed to present a monad for continuations. Wadler [76, p. 486] presented a monad of continuations which can be expressed in Scala pseudocode as follows:

$$\text{object Cont}(x : (\alpha \Rightarrow \rho) \Rightarrow \rho)$$

$$\texttt{def map}^{\text{Cont}}(f, \bar{x}) = k \Rightarrow \bar{x}\left(x \Rightarrow k(f(x))\right)$$

$$\texttt{def unit}^{\text{Cont}}(x) = k \Rightarrow k(x)$$

$$\texttt{def flatten}^{\text{Cont}}(\bar{\bar{x}}) = k \Rightarrow \bar{\bar{x}}\left(\bar{x} \Rightarrow \bar{x}(x \Rightarrow k(x))\right)$$

$$\texttt{def callcc}(g) = k \Rightarrow g(x \Rightarrow (k' \Rightarrow k'x))k.$$

Here $\bar{x}$ is a continuation of type x and $\bar{\bar{x}}$ a continuation of a continuation of type x. Translating this pseudocode into real Scala code is not a trivial task. Figure 3.12 shows an implementation of this pseudocode in Scala designed by Tony Morris. Recall that new {D}, where {D} is a class body, is equivalent to the creation expression new AnyRef{D}. A more general solution to the construction of monads and many other useful computational objects is provided in the scalaz package[6] whose main contributor is Tony Morris.

---

[6] See http://code.google.com/p/scalaz/.

```
import Cont.cont
sealed trait Cont[ρ,α] {

    def apply(f: α => ρ): ρ

    def map[β](f: α => β) =
        cont[ρ,β](k => apply(k compose f))

    def flatten[β](xc: α => Cont[ρ,β]) =
        cont[ρ,β](k => apply(xc(_)(k)))


}


object Cont {

    def cont[ρ,α](g: (α => ρ) => ρ) = new Cont[ρ,α] {
        def apply(f: α => ρ) = g(f)
    }

    def unit[ρ] = new {
        def apply[α](x: α) = cont[ρ,α](k => k(x))
    }

    def callcc[ρ,α,β](g: (α => Cont[ρ,β]) => Cont[ρ,α]) =
        cont[ρ,α](k => g(1 => cont(x => k(1)))(k))


}
```

Figure 3.12 An implementation of the continuation monad in Scala.

Programming project 3.2 Wadler [76, p. 486] presented the following definition of a "continuation-comprehension":

$$\texttt{for}(x \leftarrow \overline{x};\ y \leftarrow \overline{y})\ \texttt{yield}\ (x,y) \equiv k \Rightarrow \overline{x}\Big(x \Rightarrow \overline{y}\big(y \Rightarrow k(x,y)\big)\Big).$$

Extend Morris's code and implement "continuation-comprehensions."

4

Parser builders

A parser is a piece of software capable of resolving a string into *tokens* and then checking whether the string belongs or not in a particular (formal) language. Constructing a parser from scratch is an interesting problem. However, a more interesting problem is that of constructing a particular parser from other (pre-defined?) parsers rather than from scratch. This problem can be solved by using *parser builders*. In the end, some of these parser builders have to be constructed from scratch, but all the complex parsers can be built from the other parser builders that parse components. Scala includes a rich library for building parsers using parser builders. In this chapter we first give an overview of some relevant notions, then we describe the library and finally we use this library to construct an interpreter for a simple programming language.

4.1 Language parsers

Given an *alphabet* (i.e., a set of symbols or characters), the closure of this alphabet is a set that has as elements all strings that consist of symbols drawn from this particular alphabet. For example, the digits 0 and 1 form an alphabet and the closure of this alphabet consists of "numbers" like 000, 101, 11, etc. A language can be considered a subset of the closure (including the empty string) of an alphabet. The language that is the closure of an alphabet is not particularly interesting since it is too large. Programming languages are also languages in the sense just described, thus, we need tools to define the set of valid strings that make up any particular programming language.

In simple cases, it is possible either to enumerate the strings that belong to a language or to write down a set-comprehension that describes the elements of a language. For example, the following set includes all the sequences of zeros followed by ones:

$$L = \left\{ 0^i 1^j \mid i \neq j \text{ and } i, j > 0 \right\}.$$

Here 0^i denotes a sequence of i zeros. Unfortunately, in most cases this is not a realistic way to describe a language. A more realistic way is to specify the *grammar* of a language. A grammar consists of a finite set of *production rules* that specify the syntax of the language. A production rule is a formula like the following one:

$$\alpha = \beta\gamma.$$

This formula means that the symbol α consists of a symbol β followed by the symbol γ. The symbol on the left of the equals sign (i.e., the symbol α) is a *nonterminal* symbol (i.e., it can be expanded into other symbols) while the symbols on the right of the equals sign might be either terminal (i.e., they cannot be expanded further) or nonterminal symbols. Terminal symbols, which are also known as *tokens*, are enclosed in quotation marks to distinguish them from nonterminal symbols. In addition, there is a unique nonterminal start symbol (for example, a symbol that denotes a program, a module, etc.).

Definition 1 A grammar is a quadruple $G = (T, N, S, P)$, where

- T is the set of terminal symbols,
- N is the set of nonterminal symbols,
- S is the start symbol, and
- P is the set of productions.

Productions are specified using a number of *metasymbols*. The equals sign is such a metasymbol whose functionality was explained above. Instead of giving the exact definition of each metasymbol, we will provide simple examples that demonstrate their use. Consider the following two production rules:

$$D = \texttt{"0"} \mid \texttt{"1"}$$

$$B = BD \mid D.$$

The metasymbol "$\mid$" denotes choice, that is, $\texttt{"0"} \mid \texttt{"1"}$ denotes a choice between the token $\texttt{"0"}$ and the token $\texttt{"1."}$ Thus, these production rules specify that a B is a B followed by a D or just a D, where D is either the token 0 or the token 1. In other words, a B is a sequence of binary digits.

A major problem of rules like the second one is that they cannot be used for the construction of a parser. Thus, we need a way to eliminate *left recursion* from production rules. An easy way to eliminate left recursion is to replace it with *right recursion* and by introducing a rule that expands to nothing:

$$B = DB \mid \varepsilon,$$

where ε denotes the empty string. In order to eliminate the use of the special symbol ε, we introduce the metasymbols "{" and "}."

These symbols enclose terminal or nonterminal symbols that can be repeated zero or more times. Thus, a far more readable way to specify the above production is the following formula:

$$B = D\{D\}.$$

When one needs to specify that some symbols may occur one or zero times, then one can enclose these symbols in the symbols "[" and "]." For instance, the following production rule specifies that any sequence of binary digits may be preceded by an optional plus or minus sign:

$$B = ["+" \mid "-"]D\{D\}.$$

Assume that we want to expand the grammar so as to allow a "decimal" part. The following rule describes exactly this requirement:

$$B = ["+" \mid "-"]D\{D\}["."\{D\}].$$

However, if we have to allow both the period and the comma as decimal points, then we need to introduce an extra rule, unless we use the metasymbols "(" and ")." The symbols can be used to group alternatives. Thus, the new production rule can be written as follows:

$$B = ["+" \mid "-"]D\{D\}[("."\mid",")\{D\}].$$

Exercise 4.1 Give examples of strings that belong to the language described by the following rule:

$$L = \{a \mid b\}[c].$$

The *metanotation* introduced so far is known as *EBNF* and it was invented by Niklaus Wirth [77]. This metanotation can be used to describe the grammar of any programming language.

To be fair, it is a fact that the syntax of common programming languages like Java, Perl, and Haskell cannot be described completely by a metanotation like the EBNF. For example, one cannot specify that an array index should stay within specific bounds or the requirement that the invocation of a method or a function contains exactly as many arguments as there are parameters in the definition of the method or function. Unfortunately, although there are some techniques for handling these additional requirements, still there are no truly successful realizations of them. And this is the reason why the report of any programming language is given in two parts: one that specifies the general syntax and one that describes these additional constraints.

There are several conventional techniques that can be used to construct a parser. For example, the reader may consult [78] for a lucid account of parser construction.

One drawback of all these techniques is that they do not clearly reflect the grammar of any given language. Nevertheless, another major problem is that one has to construct any particular parser from scratch – an exercise well suited only for experienced programmers. A better idea is to use existing parsers, which can parse specific constructs, to build a new parser. Obviously, even in this case one has to build a number of simple parsers since one cannot know a priori which symbols will have a particular significance. For example, the symbol ":=" is used in Pascal as an assignment operator while other programming languages use the symbol "=" for the same thing. Fortunately, the construction of this simple parser is a trivial task as we will see later on.

4.2 Scala's parser builders

Parser builders or *parser combinators*, as they are also known, are an intelligible way to build parsers. In a nutshell, parser builders are operators that replace the metasymbols in an actual grammar (for example, the braces, the square brackets, etc.). If an input string matches a grammar,[1] then the parser will produce a list of strings which will contain all symbols matched. Otherwise, it will produce some error message and it will fail. This scheme is based on ideas put forth by William H. Burge [11] and Philip Wadler [75]. Table 4.1 describes the parser builders that Scala offers. In addition, there is a small number of additional "parsers" that can be used to recognize identifiers and numbers (see Table 4.2).

Given the grammar *G* of some language *L*, one can use the parser builders to build a parser for *G*. In general, for any grammar that can be specified with the EBNF metanotation, one can build a parser with Scala's parser builders. Nevertheless, special care should be taken to avoid grammars that are left recursive. The reason left recursiveness is a bad thing is that most parser combinators cannot properly handle such grammars. In some cases, if a Parser implements left recursive productions, it will loop forever and this is something no one wants!

When defining a parser with parser builders, one must closely follow a particular grammar and this is a particularly interesting feature. Let us make clear what exactly we mean with a simple example. Consider the following simplified production rule that describes an assignment command:

$$\text{assignment} = \text{id} \text{ ":="} \text{ integer ";"}$$

We can construct a parser, which can recognize assignment commands, using parser builders as follows:

```
def assignment = ident ~ ":=" ~ wholenumber ~ ";"
```

---

[1] If you have guessed that regular expressions are a kind of parser builder, then you have guessed correctly. In fact, all regular expressions can be described with EBNF.

Table 4.1 *Basic Scala parser builders*

Combinator	Meaning
p ~ q	Succeeds if p succeeds and q succeeds on the input left over by p
p ~> q	Same as p ~ q but keeps only the right result
p <~ q	Same as p ~ q but keeps only the left result
p ~! q	Same as p ~ q but in case of failure no back-tracking is performed
p | q	Succeeds if either p or q succeeds
p ||| q	Succeeds if either p or q succeeds; if both p and q succeed, the parser that consumed the most characters is chosen
p ^^ f	Succeeds if p succeeds and returns f applied to the result of p
p ^? (f, error)	Succeeds if p succeeds and f is defined at the result of p. Moreover, it returns f applied to the result of p. If f is not applicable, error (the result of p) should explain why
p ^^^ q	A shorthand for p ^^ (x => q)
rep1(p)	p is used repeatedly to parse the input until it fails, however, it must succeed at least once
repN(n, p)	p is used exactly n times to parse the input
rep1sep(f, p, q)	First use f and then repeatedly use p interleaved with q until p fails; f must succeed
opt(p)	Returns Some(x) if p returns x and None otherwise
rep(p)	Repeatedly uses p to parse the input until it fails.

Table 4.2 *Basic generic scanners*

Combinator	Scans...
ident	identifiers
wholeNumber	integers
decimalNumber	decimal numbers
stringLiteral	string literals
floatingPointNumber	floating point numbers

The symbol ~ is used to specify succession or concatenation while it keeps track of what symbols have been parsed successfully so far. In this example, an identifier is followed by the symbol :=, which in turn is followed by a whole number, which is followed by a semicolon. Here the semicolon is part of the command. However, in a number of cases some symbols are just needed to separate or group syntactic entities, and once it is understood what these symbols separate or group, there is absolutely no need for them. This means that it makes no sense to keep track of them. For this reason one should use the combinators ~> and <~, which disregard the symbols they parse. For example, consider the following production rule:

$$factor = \text{``(''} \; expression \; \text{``)''}$$

The obvious way to write a parser for this production follows

```
def factor = "(" ~ expr ~ ")"
```

but as explained this parser will store the parentheses somewhere, which is not necessary. A better way to achieve the same functionality without the drawback just mentioned is:

```
def factor = "(" ~> expr <~ ")"
```

Note that fixed literals are specified as string literals.

Assume that our language uses only natural numbers (i.e., whole numbers that are greater than or equal to zero). Unfortunately, we cannot use the predefined parser that recognizes whole numbers since this will accept even a negative number. Fortunately, we can define a little parser to recognize natural numbers as follows:

```
def naturalNumber: Parser[String] =
  """\d\d*""".r
```

The only thing one has to do in order to define such little parsers is to change the regular expression enclosed in three pairs of double quotation marks. As a second example, the following code defines a parser that can parse octal numbers:

```
def octalNumber: Parser[String] =
  """0[01234567][01234567]*""".r
```

Exercise 4.2 Define a little parser that can recognize hexadecimal numbers.

When one wants to specify a rule with alterations, that is, a rule for which there are different possibilities to choose from, one has to use the | operator. For example, in the toy parser shown in Figure 4.1, we are specifying that a D is either the digit 0 or the digit 1 with the following definition:

```
def D = "0" | "1"
```

If we want to specify repetition, we need to use the **rep** parser combinator. For example, the following rule

```
def B = D~rep(D)
```

specifies that a B should expand to a D that is followed by zero or more occurrences of D. Once one has defined a parser, the next question is can one use it?

As shown in Figure 4.1 a parser is defined as a set of methods that are defined in a subclass of a class `JavaTokenParsers`. The special method `parseAll` is the one that must be used to invoke the parser. This method takes two arguments: the first

```
import scala.util.parsing.combinator._
class BinDigit extends JavaTokenParsers {
    def D = "0" | "1"
    def B = D~rep(D)
    def parse(text : String) = parseAll(B,text)
}

var P = new BinDigit
println("input : "+args(0))
println(P.parse(args(0)))
```

Figure 4.1 A toy parser that accepts binary numerals.

is the parser that should be invoked in order to decide whether a particular string, which is the second argument, belongs or not to the language.

Exercise 4.3 The functions that make up a parser can be defined in an object instead of being methods of a class. Rewrite the code of Figure 4.1 so that class BinDigit becomes an object.

4.3 An interpreter for a toy language

Although the example shown in Figure 4.1 shows how one could define a parser for a real language, still there are a number of details that are not covered. For example, it is not clear how one could build a parse tree (i.e., a tree that faithfully represents the original source code) or how optional nonterminals and/or terminals should be treated. In this section we explain how to write an interpreter of a simple imperative programming language. We have opted to describe the interpreter of RAM++ which is a relatively simple language that includes some of the features common to almost every programming language. The grammar of RAM++ is shown in Figure 4.2 (the grammar as well as a language interpreter for this toy language were first described in [71]). The various commands have the intended meaning and each variable is assumed to be initially equal to zero. In addition, the value of each variable can be any integer number greater than or equal to zero.

Exercise 4.4 Write a "parser" that will recognize RAM++'s identifiers.

Programming in RAM++ is not difficult but it is tricky because one cannot assign to a variable any value. In fact, one can only increment or decrement by one the value of any variable. Nevertheless, the language is *Turing complete*, which means that it can be used to compute anything a Turing machine can. Strictly speaking

program	=	commands
command	=	{ command }
command	=	if-command
	|	while-command
	|	assignment-command
	|	input-command
	|	output-command
if-command	=	"if" check "then" commands
		["else" commands]
		"end"
while-command	=	"while" check" do"
		commands
		"end"
assignment-command	=	variable ("++" | "--")
input-command	=	"read" variable
output-command	=	"write" variable
check	=	variable "=" "0"
variable	=	letter {letter | digit}
letter	=	"a" | . . . | "z" | "A" | . . . | "Z"
digit	=	"0" | "1" | . . . | "9"

Figure 4.2 The grammar of RAM++.

the language is more *expressive* since it allows *interaction* with the environment, something no Turing machine can do. The following RAM++ program reads two numbers and computes their sum:

```
read x read y
if x=0 then
   write y
else if y=0 then
   write x
else
   while z=0 do
     x++
     y--
     if y=0 then
        z++
     end
   end
   write x
end
end
```

As was noted above, programming in RAM++ is tricky! Let us now describe how we can implement an interpreter for RAM++ in Scala.

The first thing one has to do is define the structure of the parse tree. The definitions that follow define structures that can represent the original code:

```
trait Command
case class Commands(cmds: List[Command]) extends Command
case class IFcomm(cond: String,
                  then_part: Commands,
                  else_part: Commands) extends Command
case class WHILEcomm(cond: String,
                     do_part: Commands) extends Command
case class WRITEcomm(outvar: String) extends Command
case class READcomm(invar: String) extends Command
case class ASSIGNMENTcomm(ass_var: String,
                          action: String) extends Command
```

There are five different kinds of commands, therefore, for each command we need to define a different case-class that can keep the essential information of each kind of command. For example, the IFcomm case-class has three fields that correspond to the variable that is used in the condition, the commands in the "then" part, and the commands in the "else" part, which might be empty. Since a program is just a sequence of commands, there is no need to have a separate structure to hold a whole program. In our case, a list of commands is the ideal structure to hold a complete program. The next step is to define an object where all parser-related definitions will be placed. In fact, this object will be the parser of a particular language. Figure 4.3 shows the definition of a Scala parser for RAM++.

The rep combinator returns a list that contains objects of the same type, thus, the RAM++ parser will return a list each element of which will correspond to the commands that make up a RAM++ program. In addition, this parser shows how one can use the ˆˆ parser combinator. This combinator takes an anonymous function and passes the result of the parse into the anonymous function as a parameter. For example, in the following definition

```
def commands = rep(command) ˆˆ {case cmds => Commands(cmds)}
```

the result of the parse, which is a list of objects representing commands, is passed to an anonymous function that uses it to build an appropriate object that represents a sequence of commands.

Another interesting thing about the RAM++ parser is that it shows how one can handle optional syntactic constructs. By inspecting the parser's code, the reader may notice that the optElse parser returns either a None value or a Some(m) value, where m is what the parser has actually matched. A `None` value indicates that an optional construct was not there and, obviously, a `Some` value indicates that the parser has found the optional syntactic structure.

If the parser encounters an opening left parenthesis, it will print the error message *unexpected symbol*, because it was instructed to do so. In general, when a parser must choose from a number of alternatives, it is better to issue a specific error message if the parser fails. This can be achieved by adding an alternative that has the following form:

$$\texttt{failure("error message")}$$

Obviously, the `error message` must be informative and explain why the parser has failed.

Typically, a language evaluator executes source code stored in some input file after verifying that it is at least syntactically correct. The parser in Figure 4.3 can be used to verify whether some input is correct or not. Thus, we need to define a function that will evaluate the output generated by the parser. Since our language supports variables, we need to define a structure that will hold the variables as well as their corresponding values. Obviously, the natural choice is to use a hash table:

```scala
var ST: Map[String,Int] = Map()
```

```scala
import scala.util.parsing.combinator._

object RAMparser extends JavaTokenParsers {
    def commands = rep(command) ^^ { case cmds => Commands(cmds) }
    def command =
        ifcommand | whilecommand | writecommand | readcommand | assignment |
        failure("unexpected symbol")
    def ifcommand: Parser[Command]  =
        ("if" ~ ident ~ "=" ~ "0" ~ "then" ~ commands ~ optElse ~ "end") ^^
        { case "if" ~ id ~ "=" ~ "0" ~ "then" ~ thenpart ~ elsepart ~ "end" =>
            IFcomm(id,thenpart,elsepart)}
    def optElse: Parser[Commands]  =
        opt("else"~commands) ^^ { case None => Commands(Nil)
                                  case Some("else"~cmds) => cmds}
    def whilecommand: Parser[Command]  =
        ("while" ~ ident ~ "=" ~ "0" ~ "do" ~ commands ~ "end") ^^
        {case "while"~id~"="~"0"~"do"~cmds~"end" => WHILEcomm(id,cmds) }
    def writecommand =
        ("write" ~ ident) ^^ { case "write"~id => WRITEcomm(id) }
    def readcommand =
        ("read" ~ ident) ^^ { case "read"~id => READcomm(id) }
    def assignment =
        (ident ~ ("++" | "--")) ^^ { case id~op => ASSIGNMENTcomm(id,op) }
}
```

Figure 4.3 A parser for RAM++ defined using Scala's parser builders.

The general structure of the program evaluator follows:

```
def eval(commands: List[Command]): Unit = {
  if (! commands.isEmpty) {
    commands.head match {
      . . . . . . . . . .
    }
    eval(commands.tail)
  }
}
```

If the list is not empty, the evaluator needs to find what kind of command represents the head of the list (i.e., the first command of the program) and then to evaluate it. In the end, the program evaluator recursively evaluates the rest of the program. Let us now see how each case should be handled. We start by showing how an output command should be implemented:

```
case WRITEcomm(myvar) => if (! ST.contains(myvar) )
                            ST += (myvar -> 0)
                          println(ST(myvar))
```

Since variables are not declared, it is quite possible that some variable is used for the first time in the output command. Therefore, we need to add into the symbol table variables that have not been used before. The next step is simple: just print the value of the variable.

As shown below, the code for the ouput command is more complicated:

```
case READcomm(myvar)   =>
          if (! ST.contains(myvar) )
            ST += (myvar -> 0)
          print("? ")
          var x = readInt()
          if (x < 0) {
            println("***ERROR: Number cannot be negative")
            return
          }
          else
            ST += (myvar -> x)
```

As in the case of the output command, it is necessary to ensure that the variable used is in the symbol table. Next, we use a standard Scala method to input the value of the variable which must be an integer greater than or equal to zero.

Exercise 4.5 Instead of relying on `readInt`'s way to deal with erroneous input, use method `readLine` and a regular expression to verify that the user enters only valid input.

There is nothing special about the "assignment" command except that when a variable is equal to zero, its value cannot be decreased further:

```
case ASSIGNMENTcomm(invar,act) =>
        if (! ST.contains(invar) )
          ST += (invar -> 0)
        if (act == "++")
          ST += (invar -> (ST(invar)+1))
        else
          if ( ST(invar) > 0 )
            ST += (invar -> (ST(invar)-1))
```

The if-command together with the while-command are the only choice and repetition constructs available in RAM++. Their meaning is standard and so their implementation is almost straightforward. Let us start with the if-command:

```
case IFcomm(condvar,thenPart,elsePart) =>
        if (! ST.contains(condvar) )
          ST += (condvar -> 0)
        if ( ST(condvar) == 0 )
          eval(thenPart.cmds)
        else
          eval(elsePart.cmds)
```

The code does the usual check and then checks whether the variable is equal to zero. If it is, the then-part of the command is executed. Otherwise, the else-part of the command is executed.

Exercise 4.6 If the `elsePart.cmds` is an empty list, then `eval` is invoked with an empty list and so it does nothing. Modify the code to avoid this unnecessary recursive invocation.

The implementation of the while-command is very simple – it is implemented by a while loop as shown below:

```
case WHILEcomm(condvar, doCMDs) =>
        if (! ST.contains(condvar) )
          ST += (condvar -> 0)
        while ( ST(condvar) == 0 ) {
          eval(doCMDs.cmds)
        }
```

```
import java.io.FileReader
if ( args.length != 1 )
    println("Usage: ramint input-file")
else {
    try {
        val reader = new FileReader(args(0))
        val result =
            RAMparser.parseAll(RAMparser.commands, reader)
        if ( result.successful) {
            val parseTree = result.get
            eval(parseTree.cmds)
        }
        else
            println(result)
    } catch {
        case e : Exception =>
            println("File "+args(0)+" does not exist")
            exit()
    }
}
```

Figure 4.4 Putting together the RAM++ parser and the evaluator.

We defined the parser as well as the evaluator of RAM++. The next step is to put these things together in order to build a RAM++ interpreter. We will proceed by assuming that the name of the file that contains the RAM++ source code will be given as a command line argument (see Section 2.9). The "main" program of the RAM++ interpreter is shown in Figure 4.4.

The input file is opened using an instance of the standard Java `FileReader` class. This is a class that can be used to read files that contain only characters, that is, files that do not contain raw bytes. Since the name of the input file is supplied as a command line argument, we need to make sure that one and only one command argument is supplied. Otherwise, the interpreter must print some error message. Of course, the fact that some user has supplied a command line argument does not mean that this argument is the name of an existing file. Thus, we need to make sure that Scala can open and read the contents of the file. This is exactly why the code that opens and reads the input file is inside a try-block. The commad that follows

```
val result = RAMparser.parseAll(RAMparser.commands, reader)
```

creates an object either of type `Success[δ]` or of type `Failure`. Both types are case classes in a class hierarchy in which the top class is trait `ParseResult`. The flag field `successful` is used to determine whether the parser has succeeded or not. If the parser has successfully parsed the input file, then method `get` should be used to store the parse tree in a variable. Finally, the parse tree is fed to function `eval`.

Programming project 4.1 X [37] is a tiny imperative programming language whose syntax is described by the following grammar:

$$
\begin{array}{rcl}
\text{program} & = & \text{"read" "X" ";"}\\
& & \text{cmd ";"}\\
& & \text{"write" "X"}\\
\text{cmd} & = & \text{"X" ":=" expr}\\
& | & \text{cmd ";" cmd}\\
& | & \text{"while" expr "do" cmd}\\
\text{expr} & = & \text{"X"}\\
& | & \text{"hd" expr}\\
& | & \text{"tl" expr}
\end{array}
$$

A program has only variable "X" whose value is a list of strings. The expressions `hd e` and `tl e` compute the head and the tail of `e`, respectively. The only variable can be initialized from input. A while loop `while e do c` first evaluates `e` and if its value is `["nil"]`, the loop terminates. Otherwise, it computes `c` and starts over again. The command `X:=e` assigns the value of `e` only to variables of the language. The semicolon is a statement terminator.

Write an interpeter for X in Scala.

4.4 Domain-specific languages

Roughly, a domain-specific language (DSL) is a notation that is designed to describe solutions to problems of a very specific nature. In other words, a DSL is a special-purpose programming language designed to express solutions to problems that belong to a particular problem domain. The canonical example of a widely used DSL is the "language" used to express the various calculations and contents of the cells in a spreadsheet. The opposite of a DSL is a general purpose language (GPL) like Java and Scala. In principle, a GPL can be used for just about any purpose, from creating a role playing game to programming a system to solve chemical problems. Unfortunately, GPLs have drawbacks simply because they are very general tools. For example, if one wants to perform a number of actions on a database and all one has at one's disposal is a GPL, then it is necessary to write a computer program for each task. However, the real problem is that for similar tasks one cannot use any previous program, unless one decides to create a DSL. This DSL could be used to drive the programs to perform a number of generic tasks. And this is exactly why

SQL, the structured query language, is considered by many a DSL. Similarly, HTML and XQuery/XPath are DSLs.

A DSL can be easily implemented using Scala's parser builders. To make the general idea clear, assume that we have created a program that allows users to load images. Users can instruct the program to generate a web page which will show the image as if there is a camera that maneuvers above it (this camera is usually called a viewport and this is basically something like the virtual camera system of many video games). Now, a user can specify the viewport size, the initial camera position as well subsequent moves with commands like the following set of commands:

```
viewport is 400 by 300
position at 100,100
left 200
up 100
down 250
right 40
```

Clearly, it is not difficult to write a grammar to describe these commands and from this grammar to write a parser using Scala's parser builders. The resulting parser can be used to generate a web page with the intended behavior. For example, a grammar for this particular DSL is given below:

program	=	view position commands
view	=	"view" "is" number "by" number
position	=	"position" "at" number "," number
commands	=	{ command }
command	=	"up" number I "down" number I "left" number I "right" number

Exercise 4.7 Extend the DSL presented above with repetition commands. For example, one could add a command to repeat a number of commands a specific number of times.

4.5 Monadic parsing

Graham Hutton and Erik Meijer [34] have demonstrated how monads can be used to build *recursive descent* parsers. Roughly, a parser is called recursive descent when for each nonterminal symbol there is a procedure (i.e., a method that returns Unit) that handles the corresponding nonterminal symbol. In their work, Hutton and Meijer describe how they have used the Haskell type classes to build a parser monad. In Scala, instead of defining a parsing monad from scratch, it is better

to define one using the scalaz library. The following code shows how one could
implement a basic parser:

```
import scalaz.control._
trait Parser[α] extends Monad[List] {
  def return_(a:α) = pure((cs : String) => List(Pair(a,cs)))
  def parse[α] (p : Parser[α]) = p match {
                              case List(a) => a
              }
. . . . . . . . . . . . . . . . . . . . . . . . . . . . . . .
}
```

Here we use trait Monad as basis. Method pure plays the role of method unit. In
order to define choice combinators one needs structures that go beyond monads. In
fact, one needs a *monad with a zero* and a *monad with a zero and a plus*. The scalaz
library defines the MonadEmpty and the MonadEmptyPlus traits that implement
exactly these monads. Therefore, it would be an interesting exercise to implement
a parsing library based on the work of Hutton and Meijer and scalaz.

5

XML processing

XML, the eXtensible Markup Language, is an industry standard for document markup. XML has been adopted in many fields that include software, physics, chemistry, finance, law, etc. XML is used to represent data that are interchanged between different operating systems while most configuration files in many operating systems are XML files. The widespread use of XML dictated the design and implementation of tools capable of handling XML content. Scala is a modern programming language and so it includes a standard library for the manipulation of XML documents. This library, which was designed and implemented by Burak Emir, is the subject of this chapter.

5.1 What is XML?

A markup is an annotation to text that describes how it is to be structured, laid out, or formatted. Markups are specified using *tags* that are usually enclosed in angle brackets. XML is a *meta-markup* language, that is, a language that can be used to define a specific set of tags that are suitable for a particular task. For example, one can define tags for verses, stanzas, and strophes in order to express poems in XML. When a specific set of tags is used to describe entities of a particular kind, then this set is called an XML application. For example, if one precisely specifies tags suitable to describe poems and uses them only for this purpose, then the resulting set of tags is an XML application. The following lines show the use of a hypothetical set of tags designed for the representation of poems:

```
<poem>
<title xml:space="preserve"> Magic Everywhere </title>
<poet> Yannis Papadopoulos </poet>
<stanza>
<verse xml:space="preserve">There's magic everywhere</verse>
```

```
<verse xml:space="preserve">When I see your eyes</verse>
. . . . . . . . . . . . . . . . . . . . .
</stanza>
</poem>
```

Whatever is delimited by start-tags like `<title>` and end-tags like `</title>` is an *element*, while whatever is in between the start-tag and end-tag is the content of the element. In general, white space is ignored but here it cannot be ignored so we explicitly specify that it should be preserved. There are tags that do not have content. Such tags begin with `<` but end with `/>`.

Most, if not all, XML applications assume that data are organized in a hierarchical data model, that is, data are organized in a tree-like structure. For example, consider a set of tags designed to describe people. The description of any person will form a structure of XML tags that will form a hierarchy, which is just a general tree structure.

XML elements may have *attributes*. An attribute is a piece of information expressed as a name-value pair attached to the start-tag of an element. For example, `xml:space` is a standard XML attribute whose possible values are "default" and "preserve." Note that the value of all attributes must be enclosed in quotation marks. Also, when writing songs, that is, poems of a special kind, there are usually refrain verses and/or stanzas. Using attributes we can describe refrains as shown below:

```
<verse refrain="yes">Sha la la la la la</verse>
```

Unicode is the default character set of XML. Almost every legal Unicode character may appear in an XML document. However, not all characters can be used in all different cases. An element name as well as any other XML name may contain any alphanumeric character. This includes the letters used in Latin-based alphabets, the Greek letters, the Cyrillic letters, Chinese ideograms, etc. Also, it includes the digits 0 through 9, any other symbol representing a digit, an underscore (_), a hyphen (−), and a period (.).

There are a few characters whose use is reserved and, therefore, they cannot be used for any other purpose. If it is absolutely necessary to use these characters, then one should use an *entity reference*. The following table summarizes the most common entity references:

character	<	&	>	"	'
entity reference	&lt;	&amp;	&gt;	&quot;	&apos;

In case it is absolutely necessary to include some XML markup verbatim in another XML document, then one can use a *CDATA* section. A CDATA section begins with `<![CDATA[` and ends with `]]>`. Also, let us say, in passing, that comments begin with `<!-` and end with `->`.

Usually an XML document starts with a line that has either the form

```
<?xml version="1.1" standalone="yes"?>
```

or the form:

```
<?xml version="1.1" standalone="no"?>
<!DOCTYPE svg PUBLIC "-//W3C//DTD SVG 1.1//EN"
   "http://www.w3.org/Graphics/SVG/1.1/DTD/svg11.dtd">
```

The DOCTYPE information depends on the *document type definition* (DTD) being used. In the second example, the header is the header of an SVG file. SVG is an XML application that is used to describe two-dimensional graphics. Specifying a DTD for a relatively simple XML application is not a difficult task, nevertheless, the reader interested in learning more about DTDs, in particular, and XML, in general, should consult a good refence book (for example, see [30]).

It is not out of the question to ask for the design of a new XML application that defines one or more elements that have already been defined in some other XML application. At the same time, it makes no sense to demand that each new XML application should include names that are unique. In order to overcome this problem, the designers of XML have included a provision for *namespaces*. Roughly, a namespace is a mechanism by which elements and attributes from different applications can be distinguished. Also, namespaces can be used to group related elements and attributes from a particular application so that software applications can recognize them. In general, namespaces are specified by prefixing each element and attribute with a label, which is mapped to a URI by an `xmlns:label` attribute. A URI is a Uniform Resource Identifier that includes URLs (Uniform Resource Locator, which include web addresses, etc.) and URNs (Uniform Resource Name).

5.2 Basic XML content manipulation

The easiest way to have XML content in a Scala program is to assign some XML content directly to a variable. The following piece of code shows how this can be done:

```
var poem  =
    <poem>
    <title> Magic Everywhere </title>
```

```
<poet realname="yes"> Yannis Papadopoulos </poet>
<stanza>
<verse> There's magic everywhere  </verse>
</stanza>
</poem>
println(poem)
```

Here we have started the XML content on a separate line purely for aesthetic reasons. The XML content is not stored as a long string, but as an instance of class scala.xml.Elem. The definition of this class is roughly as follows:

```
class Elem(val prefix: String,
           val label: String,
           val attributes: MetaData,
           val scope: NamespaceBinding,
           val child: Node*) extends Node { . . .}
```

Here prefix is a namespace prefix which may be null, but not an empty string; label is the element name; attributes is a linked list of attributes (see Exercise 3.3 on page 99); scope is the scope containing the namespace bindings; and child is the children of this node. Class MetaData holds an attribute (i.e., both the name of an attribute and its value) and a linked list of attributes. Every instance of class MetaData is either an instance of

```
UnprefixedAttribute(key,value,Null)
```

or an instance of

```
PrefixedAttribute(namespace_prefix,key,value,Null)
```

or just Null, that is, the empty attribute list. Having explained the use of the fields of class Elem, it would be interesting to see how one can encode XML content as an Elem object. The code snippet that follows shows how the XML content representing a poem can be represented as an Elem object:

```
import scala.xml._
var poem2 =
  Elem(null, "poem", Null, TopScope,
      Elem(null, "title", Null, TopScope,
          Text("Magic Everywhere")),
      Elem(null, "poet",
          new UnprefixedAttribute("realname","yes", Null),
          TopScope, Text("Yannis Papadopoulos")),
      Elem(null, "stanza", Null, TopScope,
          Elem(null, "verse", Null, TopScope,
```

```
              Text("There's magic everywhere")),
         Elem(null, "verse", Null, TopScope,
              Text("When I see your blue eyes"))
    )
)
```

We have presented two different ways by which XML content can be readily used in
a Scala program, however, the question is: Is there any difference between the two
ways? The only way to tell is by printing the variable and inspecting the output. In
the first case, the output will look exactly like the following:

```
<poem>
    <title> Magic Everywhere </title>
    . . . . . . . . . . . . . . . . .
</poem>
```

However, in the second case the output will look quite different:

```
<poem><title>Magic Everywhere</title><poet realname="yes". . .
```

In other words, white space before and after element content has been removed and
the whole content is printed on one line. Although this is not human readable, one
should bear in mind that XML has been designed to be processed by machines not
humans.

As it stands one can create XML content dynamically only by defining it using
`Elem` objects. Fortunately, it is possible to embed Scala expressions into pure XML
content by enclosing any Scala expression in curly brackets inside some XML content. For example, the code that follows shows exactly how one can mix Scala
expressions with XML content:

```
var title = "Magic "
poem   =
    <poem>
        <title>{title + "Everywhere"} </title>
        . . . . . . . . . . . . . . . . .
    </poem>
```

Obviously, this example is not very dynamic, but the following code snippet is more
dynamic (can you guess what will be the result in either case?):

```
var z = if (n > 9) { Some(Text("Darkness")) } else { None }
poem   =
    <poem>
        <title subtitle={z}>Magic Everywhere</title>
        . . . . . . . . . . . . . . . . .
    </poem>
```

If n is greater than 9, then the second line of the result will be transformed to

```
<title subtitle="In the Dark">Magic Everywhere</title>
```

On the other hand, if n is less than or equal to 9, then the same line will look as follows:

```
<title >Magic Everywhere</title>
```

As is obvious, if z evaluates to None, then the attribute is not included since it makes no sense to have an attribute with no value. In the second case the attribute is included since it takes a valid value.

If for some reason we need to have curly brackets in a tag or attribute, then we have to write the curly brackets twice, as, for example, is shown below:

```
scala> var x = <tt> {{ x++ }}</tt>
x: scala.xml.Elem = <tt> { x++ }</tt>
```

There are a few other classes that can be proved useful in certain cases. Class Atom should be used when raw text that contains no tags and no children elements has to be used somewhere. Here is a simple usage example:

```
<year>{ new Atom(1942) }</year>
```

As was noted above, everything that goes between the symbols <!-- and --> is ignored by all applications that manipulate XML content. Class Comment can be used to embed comments in XML content. For example, the following

```
{new Comment("This is a comment!")}
```

will generate this comment:

```
<!--This is a comment!-->
```

Similarly, one can use class EntityRef to specify entity references. If we use the following code snippet in our code

```
{new EntityRef("lt")}
```

the result will be the symbols <. The class Unparsed should be used when it is absolutely necessary to leave as is some entity. Finally, class Group should be used to make a list of elements. A nonsensical usage example follows:

```
{new Group(List(new Atom(3),new Comment("OK")))}
```

Exercise 5.1 Can you say what this example will produce?

5.3 Producing XHTML content with Scala

According to the World Wide Web Consortium (W3C), XHTML is "a family of current and future document types and modules that reproduce, subset, and extend HTML 4." In other words, XHTML refers to a family of XML applications that have been designed to have stricter and cleaner versions of HTML. Since XHTML is an XML application, one could use Scala's XML manipulation library to generate XHTML content. Indeed, in this section we will show how to generate XHTML content using this library. In particular, we will show how to use Scala to generate an XHTML file which when viewed with a browser will show all files that are contained in a directory that has been supplied by the user. Figure 5.1 shows a typical XHTML file that our application has to generate.

First of all there are two problems that must be solved in order to implement our solution. The first problem regards the first four lines of the XHTML source

```
<?xml version="1.0" encoding="UTF-8"?>
<!DOCTYPE html
PUBLIC "-//W3C//DTD XHTML 1.0 Strict//EN"
"http://www.w3.org/TR/xhtml1/DTD/xhtml1-strict.dtd">
<html xml:lang="en" lang="en" xmlns="http://www.w3.org/1999/xhtml">
    <head>
        <title>Directory /opt</title>
    </head>
    <body>
      <h2>Directory /opt</h2>
      <ul>
          <ul>gnu</ul>
          <ul>SUNWtvnc</ul>
          <ul>bordeaux</ul>
          <ul>SUNWvgl</ul>
          <ul>VirtualBox</ul>
          <ul>VirtualGL</ul>
          <ul>staroffice8</ul>
          <ul>netbeans-6.5ss</ul>
          <ul>SUNWjavadb</ul>
          <ul>SSX0903</ul>
          <ul>Adobe</ul>
      </ul>
    </body>
</html>
```

Figure 5.1 A typical XHTML source file.

file. This particular problem can be solved with tools provided by the XML library, nevertheless, here we solve it using alternative tools in order to show how to solve such problems generally. The tags in the first four lines are not normal tags and so need special treatment. For example, if we assign to a variable the first line of any XHTML file, the language interpreter will complain that *xml is reserved*. And this is the reason why Unparsed has been introduced. However, it is not possible to write XML content directly. Thus, we need to use the classes introduced in the previous section. Here is how one can store the first lines:

```
var header = Group(
           List(
              Unparsed("<?xml version=\"1. . ."),
              Unparsed("<!DOCTYPE html"),
              Unparsed("PUBLIC \"-//W3C//. . ."),
              Unparsed("\"http://www.w3. . . ."))))
```

The second problem is a little bit more involved – we need to find a way to read the contents of the user-supplied directory and then to store them in an appropriate XHTML group. Since Scala does not define any classes for file manipulation, we need to use Java's java.io.File class. This class is one that can be used to examine files and/or directories. Thus, we are going to use this class first to make sure that the user has supplied the name of an existing directory and only then to read its contents:

```
import java.io._
var path = args(0)
var dir = new File(path)
if ( dir.isDirectory() ) {
  var files: Array[String] = dir.list()
  var A:List[Elem] = Nil
  files.foreach(x => A =
    (Elem(null,"ul",Null,TopScope,Text(x)))::A)
```

Method isDirectory returns true if the instance is a directory. Similarly, method isFile returns true if the instance is a plain file. Method list returns an array of strings that contains the names of the files and directories contained in the directory that is represented by the corresponding object. The names will be stored in a Group structure, thus, we need to create a list whose elements will be Elem structures for each file and/or directory.

Exercise 5.2 Method `listFiles` returns an array of `File`s. Use this method to write a function that recursively traverses a directory and prints all files and directories and their contents.

The next thing to do is to store the body of the XHTML source to a variable:

```
var body =
   <html xmlns= . . .>
<head>
   <title>Directory {path}</title>
</head>
<body>
<h2>Directory {path}</h2>
<ul>
{new Group(A.reverse)}
```
. . . .

As was explained, the list that holds the file names is used to create a `Group`. But now we need to concatenate the header and the body of the XHTML content and for this the most natural choice is the creation of a `Group`:

```
var output = Group(List(header,body))
```

So far we have managed to create a structure that holds the whole XHTML content, however, we need to write this content into a real file. Again, we need to use some standard Java classes:

```
import java,io._
var out = new OutputStreamWriter(
          new BufferedOutputStream(
            new FileOutputStream("listdir.html")),"UTF-8")
```

Here `listdir.html` is the name of the output file and UTF-8 is the encoding of the output file. Method `write` of class `java.io.OutputStreamWriter` can be used to output the content. However, this method prints strings, not XML node structures! In order to solve this problem, we use Scala's `PrettyPrinter` class. An object of this class generates from any `Elem` object a printable string:

```
out.write(
   new PrettyPrinter(80,3).format(output))
out.flush()
out.close()
```

The two numbers denote the width and the indent of the resulting multiline string. Method `flush` is used to make sure that everything will be written to the file and nothing will remain in the computer's memory. And of course method `close` is used to close the output file.

5.4 XML input and output

Scala has two methods that can be used to input and output XML content directly from and to files. Module `XML` provides the methods `loadFile` and `save` for reading XML content from files and writing XML content to files. Method `loadFile` takes one argument, the name of a file, and creates an instance of `Elem`:

```
val x = XML.loadFile("listdir.html")
```

This method ignores document headers. In addition, if some string contains XML content, then one can use method `loadString` to create an `Elem` object from it.

Method `save` takes two arguments: the name of an output file and an instance of `Node` (`Node` is the abstract superclass of all Scala classes designed to represent XML content). A simple usage example of this method follows:

```
var z =
  <person>
     <name>Blaise</name>
     <surname>Pascal</surname>
  </person>
XML.save("persons.xml",z)
```

A complete XML document has a header, however, as we have seen in the previous section, it is not obvious how to handle headers (the standard XML header and the document type header). The XML library includes class `DocType`, defined in package `scala.xml.dtd`, which can be used to store headers. When instantiating this class we need to supply three values: a string that represents the document type, an instance of `ExternalID` (it can be either a `PublicID` or a `SystemID`), which is a comma separated list of public or system identifiers, and a sequence of internal subset declarations, which, in many cases, is just empty. For example, the following document type

```
<!DOCTYPE svg PUBLIC "-//W3C//DTD SVG 1.1//EN"
  "http://www.w3.org/Graphics/SVG/1.1/DTD/svg11.dtd">
```

is encoded in Scala as follows:

```
import scala.xml.dtd.*
val doctype = DocType("svg",
   PublicID("-//W3C//DTD SVG 1.1//EN",
            "http://www.w3.org/Graphics/SVG/1.1/DTD/svg11.dtd"),
   Nil)
```

It is now possible to use the `saveFull` method:

```
XML.saveFull("circle.svg", z, "UTF-8", true, doctype)
```

The third argument is the encoding of the output file and the fourth a boolean value that controls whether an XML declaration will be printed or not. In particular, if it evaluates to `true`, then the XML declaration is included. Method `write` takes the same arguments as method `saveFull`, except that the first argument must be a `java.io.Writer` (see previous section).

5.5 XML searching à la Scala

Scala provides methods and operators that mimic the capabilities provided by languages like XPath and XQuery. XPath is a language that can be used to navigate through elements and attributes in an XML document. XQuery is an extension of XPath version 2.0 and operates on the logical structure of an XML document. Scala's XML library defines two *projection* functions that are similar to XPath axes, that is, a path through the XML structure that makes use of particular relationship between nodes. In order to make clear what this means, let us start with a simple Scala command:

```
poem(i) =
<poem>
<title subtitle="In the Dark">Magic Everywhere</title>
<poet>Yannis Papadopoulos </poet>
<year>1942</year>
<stanza>
<verse> There's magic everywhere  </verse>
<verse> When I see your blue eyes </verse>
</stanza>
</poem>
```

Assume that one needs to create a new object (for example, an array of objects) that will contain the name of each poet and the title of each poem (in this section we will concern ourselves only with the extraction of the data). The first thing we need to do is to extract the nodes that contain the relevant data. The operators \ and \\ can be used to extract nodes from XML content. In particular, an expression of the form this \ "tag" extracts all the nodes that are labeled with tag. Thus, the following command

```
println(poem(0) \ "title")
```

will print the following:

```
<title>Magic Everywhere</title>
```

Remember that what is printed is a visual representation of the node and its content. Although this operator is quite useful, it does not produce exactly what we need – the text stored in the tags. The XML library defines the text method, which does exactly what we want. The following commands show how this method can be used:

```
var poem_title = (poem(i) \ "title").text
var poem_author = (poem(i) \ "poet").text
```

Obviously, these commands solve the problem of extracting information from XML content. If one wants to print subelements of a particular element, one can use the following idiom:

```
println(poem(i) \ "stanza" \ "verse")
```

The character _ is a wildcard "pattern." For example, the command

```
println(poem(i) \ "_")
```

will output the whole <poem>...</poem> structure. If a "tag" is prefixed with an @, then it refers to attributes with this name. For example, the command

```
println(poem(i) \\ "@subtitle")
```

will print In the Dark. The tag "@{uri}tag" should be used when a tag needs to be resolved in a namespace. Operator \\ differs from operator \ in that the former can find and extract nodes that are deep in the node hierarchy while the latter extracts information only from nodes on the first level. For example, the command

```
println(poem(i) \\ "verse")
```

will output the two verse nodes and the command

```
println(poem(i) \ "verse")
```

will output nothing.

Exercise 5.3 Examine the output produced by the following command

```
println(poem(i) \\ "_")
```

and explain why Scala produced what it has produced.

Suppose that we have a huge XML "database" of poems stored in a file. For example, we can assume that a huge number of <poem> elements are grouped together in a <poems> element as shown below:

```
<poems>
  <poem>
    <title>Magic Everywhere</title>
    . . . . . . . . . . . . . . .
  </poem>
  <poem>
    <title>Beautiful Life</title>
    . . . . . . . . . . . . . . .
  </poem>
  . . . . . . . . . . . . . . .
</poems>
```

An interesting question is how can we make queries to this "database." For example, how can we print all poets and poems which have been published after 1960? Provided that the "database" is stored in file poems.xml, the following code finds all poems that have been published after 1960 and prints the title and the poet of each such poem:

```
var poems=XML.loadFile("poems.xml")
for ( val poem <- poems \ "poem" ) {
  if ( (poem \ "year").text.trim.toInt > 1960 ) {
    var poet = (poem \ "poet").text
    var title = (poem \ "title").text
    println("\""+title+"\" by "+poet)
  }
}
```

Readers familiar with XQuery may see some resemblance between XQuery queries and this code.

Exercise 5.4 Write a Scala "query" that will print one time the name of each poet who has used the word *freedom* in one or more of their poems.

5.6 XML pattern matching

Since XML content is considered a legal Scala value, and since when performing pattern matching, a pattern can be any valid value, one may wonder whether it is possible to perform pattern matching when a pattern is some XML content. The answer is affirmative – real XML content can be used as a pattern. In addition, an XML pattern may include a standard Scala pattern, which, however, must be enclosed in curly brackets. In other words, when dealing with real XML content, curly brackets are used to interpolate Scala code in it, while in an XML pattern, the curly brackets can be used to interpolate Scala patterns in the XML content. Let us begin our discussion with a rather complex example that shows how to match an attribute:

```
var x = <a href="http://www.xyz.com">XYZ Law Firm</a>
var y = x match {
  case n @ <a>name</a> => n.attributes.get("href") match {
                             case None => "error"
                             case Some(x) => x + " " + name
                         }

  case _ => "error"
}
```

First note that we use the @ symbol. This is necessary since there is no way to match something inside the angle brackets, except of course the tags. Thus, if x is <a> tag, then variable n contains the whole HTML content. Also, note that between <a> and </a> there is a Scala pattern enclosed in curly brackets. Obviously, this is a very simple pattern that matches the sentence *XYZ Law Firm*. In conclusion, if the pattern is matched, then n matches the whole XML pattern and name the sentence between <a> and </a>. The expression on the right side of => is another match expression. Method get(*attr*) returns Some value if the specific tag contains a particular attribute; otherwise, it returns None. Note that the expression n.attributes.get("href") can be abbreviated as n.attribute("href").

In the previous example what goes between <a> and </a> is treated as a sequence of Nodes, however, if we want to treat them as a sequence of strings, we need a mechanism to access each string in the sequence. The code snippet that follows shows how to store all these strings in an array of strings:

```
var A = x match {
  case <a>{m}</a> => Pattern.compile("\\s+").split(
                        new PrettyPrinter(255,0).format(m))
  case _ => Null
}
A.foreach(println) //print each word on a single line
```

Here is an explanation of what the long expression does: the pretty printer object yields a string from a Node. This string is split into words, that is, substrings that are surrounded by spaces. Method split breaks a string where the particular pattern matches. If m was a sequence of Nodes, then we would have to use method formatNodes. Let us examine a similar problem to the one just described.

Assume that there is a tag that surrounds a sequence of other tags, that is, one has to handle XML content that looks like the content that is assigned to the following variable:

```
var z =  <h1><b>this</b> <i>is</i>
              <b>the</b> <u>night</u></h1>
```

A good question is: How can we process the individual tags that occur between <h1> and </h1>? First of all note that there are spaces between the various tags that will count as Nodes. Thus we need to filter out spaces. Thus, we should use pattern matching. Our general pattern must have the form p @ _* so that everything will be matched and the results will populate an array called p:

```
z match { case <h1>{p @ _*}</h1> =>
    p.foreach(k =>
      if (! Pattern.matches("^\\s+",k.text))
      println(k))}
```

Method matches takes two arguments – a pattern and a string. If the pattern matches the string, it returns true. Thus, the code above will print on separate lines each nonempty tag, which is exactly what we wanted. Assume now that we want to process the content of specific elements (for example, the content of element <b>). It seems that in order to proceed we need a new match expression. Not surprisingly, we can use a for comprehension to solve this problem. The code snippet that follows shows how this can be done:

```
z match {
    case <h1>{w @ _*}</h1> =>
      for (a @ <b>{text}</b> <- w)
        println(a+" contains \""+text+"\"")
}
```

Exercise 5.5 Use the XML pattern matching capabilities of Scala to transform <poems> into a valid HTML document.

6

GUI programming

Most "real" programs have a graphical user interface (GUI for short). Therefore, any serious modern programming language should provide tools for GUI programming. Scala provides such tools through the `scala.swing` package, which is an interface to Java's JFC/Swing packages. The ambitious goal of this chapter is to teach you how to build GUI applications in Scala.

6.1 "Hello World!" again!

Typically, most introductory texts on programming are written without any coverage of GUI programming. In addition, advanced texts on programming cover GUI programming only as a marginal or optional topic. The truth is that the most "useful" applications have a graphical user interface that allows users to interact with the application. This implies that GUI programming is more common than programming textbooks "assume." GUI programming is excluded by most texts because it is assumed that it is significantly harder than ordinary applications programming. Nevertheless, this is not true – it is true that GUI programming differs from conventional application programming, but being different does not make a methodology more difficult.

Creating simple GUI applications with Scala is relatively simple, however, one has to compile the source code of the application as it is not straightforward to create runnable GUI scripts. When compiling even a very simple GUI application, the Scala compiler will generate a number of `.class` files. This implies that if one wants to run this application, one needs to have all these files in a particular directory. Fortunately, it is possible to create a Java ARchive, which is a file format whose filename extension is `.jar`. Typically, a Java archive contains classes and associated metadata. One can create Java archives using the `jar` command line utility. The resulting Java archive is treated by Scala as a directory that contains

.class files. The following commands show what has to be done in order to compile and run an application that consists of many .class files:

```
$ scalac hello.scala
$ jar cvf hello.jar *.class
$ rm *.class
$ scala -cp hello.jar hello
```

The third command deletes all .class files from the current working directory. Having explained how to compile and run an application, it is time to construct our first GUI "application."

Figure 6.1 shows the code of a simple GUI application which when compiled and run will show a little window whose title will be *Greetings* and which will display the customary *Hello World!* message. The ouput produced by this program is shown in Figure 6.2.

As is obvious from the code in Figure 6.1, we have to use some Java classes directly in order to accomplish a number of tasks. Some may see this as a drawback, however, we strongly disagree with such a view. The main reason is that since Scala runs atop the JVM, it makes no sense to rewrite everything from scratch. One should be encouraged to use Java classes as long as they fit into the general programming

```
import scala.swing._

object hello extends SimpleGUIApplication {
  def top = new MainFrame {
    title = "Greetings"
    preferredSize = (200,100)
    val label = new Label {
      text = "Hello World!"
      font = new java.awt.Font("Verdana",
                                      java.awt.Font.BOLD,22)
    }
    contents = new GridBagPanel {
      var c = new Constraints
      c.gridwidth = java.awt.GridBagConstraints.REMAINDER
      add(label, c)
      background = java.awt.Color.yellow
      border = Swing.EmptyBorder(15, 15, 15, 15)
    }
  }
}
```

Figure 6.1 A Scala GUI "Hello World!" program.

GUI programming

Figure 6.2 Output generated by the code in Figure 6.1.

philosophy of Scala. Let us now turn our attention to the description of the code in Figure 6.1.

The important part of the code appears inside an `object` definition that extends class `SimpleGUIApplication`. This class should be used as a basis for most GUI applications. Any class extending this class should implement method `top`, since this is an abstract method. In addition, class `SimpleGUIApplication` includes all the necessary tools that initialize (for example, to inform the program that it has been loaded into the system), cause all subcomponents of this window to be laid out on the window, and, eventually, show the window.

Method `top` must return an instance of `Frame`, which is a superclass of class `MainFrame`. The advantage of returning an instance of `MainFrame` instead of a `Frame` is that the former quits the whole application when it is closed. Fields `title` and `preferredSize` are in fact getter/setter methods and can be used to set the title and the dimensions of the window. In fact, all *"fields"* are getter/setter methods. A `Label` is a *component* that creates a label. Again, `text` and `font` are not real fields, but correspond to getter/setter methods. With `text` one specifies the text that will appear on the label while `font` can be used to specify the font that should be used to render the text. Class `Font` is a standard Java class that defines a representation of a font. When initializing an object of this class we need to specify the name of a real font (Verdana in our case), the font style (`BOLD` in our case), and the font size. If we want the regular or the italic style, we should replace `BOLD` with `PLAIN` or `ITALIC`, respectively. The bold-italic style can be specified with the following sum:

```
java.awt.Font.BOLD + java.awt.Font.ITALIC
```

The value assigned to "field" `contents` is a container. In this example, `GridBag-Panel` is a container that contains only a `Label` component. The nonstandard field `c` becomes an instance of class `Constraints`. This field is very important since it contains information that is used by the container to place its components. The value `REMAINDER` means that the component is the last in a row. We will say more about component placement in a moment, when we present our next example. Method add is used to include a component in the container. This method takes two arguments – a component and an object containing constraints specific to this component. "Field" background can be used to set the background color of any component that supports it. The color can be either a predefined color (as the one used in the example in Figure 6.1) or a user defined color. For example, it is possible to define an RGB color with Color(r,g,b), where the arguments are numbers in range 0.0–1.0. An RGB color is produced by mixing "quantities" of *red*, *green*, and *blue*. Method Swing.EmptyBorder is used to set the width of each side of the border of the component. The four numbers specify the top, the left, the bottom, and the right edges, respectively. The example presented is simple and, in addition, it is the simplest possible static GUI application (i.e., it is a noninteractive application). A more elaborate static example is shown in Figure 6.3.

The example in Figure 6.3 shows how to deal with situations where more than one component is to be included in a container. Also, it shows how to load and display an image, something very important for many GUI applications. Let us start by explaining how one can include an image in an application. An image must be loaded and displayed inside a container and the simplest container is a Panel. In general, it is possible to have a container inside another container. Typically, images, after they have been read with Image.read, are stored as BufferedImages. Once an image is read and loaded, it must be displayed. For this reason we need to redefine method paintComponent. This method is invoked automatically when the system is ready to display a component and takes one argument which is an abstract class that allows an application to draw onto components. Method drawImage is invoked actually to "draw" the image. It is possible to specify explicitly the width and the height of the image as shown below:

```
drawImage(img, 0, 0, width, height, null)
```

The last argument will not concern us here. So, you can safely assume that it is always null. If we comment out the following line from the code in Figure 6.3

```
c.ipady = 100; c.ipadx = 100; c.weighty = 1.0
```

the result will not look as the screenshot shown in Figure 6.4. Instead, the image will appear as a tiny square. These "fields," and some others, can be used to fine-tune the appearance of a component in a container. Let us present them briefly.

In order to understand how the following "fields" affect the appearance of a particular component, please bear in mind that each component "lives" in a cell.

gridwidth and gridheight Specifies the number of cells in a row/column for the component's display area. REMAINDER should be used to specify that the component's

```scala
import scala.swing._
import java.awt.image._
import javax.imageio.ImageIO._

object fruit extends SimpleGUIApplication {
  def top = new MainFrame {
    . . . . . . . . . . . . . . . . . . . . . . .
    var image = new Panel {
      var img:BufferedImage = null
      try {
        img = javax.imageio.ImageIO.read(
                new java.io.File("strawberry.jpg"));
      } catch{
          case e : java.io.IOException => println("Error!")
      }
      override def paintComponent(g: java.awt.Graphics) {
        g.drawImage(img, 0, 0, null)
      }
    }
    contents = new GridBagPanel {
      var c = new Constraints
      c.gridwidth = java.awt.GridBagConstraints.REMAINDER
      add(label, c)
      c.ipady = 100; c.ipadx = 100; c.weighty = 1.0
      add(image, c)
      background = java.awt.Color.pink
      border = Swing.EmptyBorder(15, 15, 15, 15)
    }
  }
}
```

Figure 6.3 Displaying images in GUI applications.

Figure 6.4 Output generated by the code in Figure 6.3.

display area will be from `gridx` to the last cell in the row/column, while `RELATIVE` specifies that the component's display area will be from `gridx` to the next to the last cell in its row/column.

`gridx` and `gridy` By setting `gridy` we specify the cell at the top of the component's display area. For the topmost cell, `gridy = 0`. The value `RELATIVE` specifies that the component be placed exactly below the component that was added to the container just before this component was added. On the other hand, by setting `gridx` we specify the cell containing the leading edge of the component's display area. For the first cell in a row, `gridx = 0`. The value `RELATIVE` specifies that the component be placed immediately after the component that was added to the container just before this component was added.

`weightx` and `weighty` Specifies how to distribute extra horizontal/vertical space.

`anchor` If the component is smaller than its display area, then by setting this "field" we specify where to place the component. Possible values include `CENTER`, `North`, `NorthEast`, `East`, `SouthEast`, `South`, `SouthWest`, `West`, and `NorthWest`. When using any of these values, they must be specified as in the example below. Possible values are:

```
c.anchor = GridBagPanel.Anchor.CENTER
```

`fill` When a component's display area is larger than the component's requested size, then this field should be set in order to resize the component.

> `java.awt.GridBagConstraints.NONE` Do not resize the component.
>
> `java.awt.GridBagConstraints.HORIZONTAL` Only resize the component horizontally so as to fill its display area.
>
> `java.awt.GridBagConstraints.VERTICAL` Only resize the component vertically so as to fill its display area.
>
> `java.awt.GridBagConstraints.BOTH` Make the component fill its display area entirely.

`ipadx` and `ipady` These "fields" specify the internal padding of a component, that is, how much space to add to the minimum width/height of the component.

`insets` By setting this "field" we can specify the minimum amount of space between the component and the edges of its display area. The default value is

```
new java.awt.Insets(0, 0, 0, 0).
```

The four arguments specify the inset from the bottom, the left, the right, and the top.

6.2 Interactive GUI programming

Any useful GUI application should allow users to interact with it. Even in the simplest case, a GUI application should include a button which, when pressed, will terminate the application. This means that there has to be a way to *listen* to *events* and to *react* accordingly. Package `swing.event` defines classes that can be used to handle events. By default a GUI application listens to no event. Method `listenTo` should be used to make the application listen to the events that take place in the component that is its only argument. Once an application listens to events occurring in a certain component, we need to specify what to do with them. All we have to do is add a *reaction* to field `reactions`. This can be done with a command like the following one:

```
reactions += { case event => action }
```

Here *event* is a pattern that must match a class defined in package `swing.event` and *action* is any legal Scala command. For example, if we add the following button

```
val close_button = new Button {
  text = "Close Window"
  font = new java.awt.Font("Verdana",
                           java.awt.Font.PLAIN, 14)
}
```

to the application in Figure 6.1, then the following code

```
listenTo(close_button)
reactions += {
  case ButtonClicked(b2) => exit(0)
}
```

will make the application listen to events occurring on this button and, in particular, when the button is pressed, the window will close. Literal b2 plays no role here, but we will see in the next example that it can be used to distinguish seemingly identical events. Figure 6.5 shows the output of the modified application.

Figure 6.5 Output generated by the code in Figure 6.1 augmented with an interactive button.

Exercise 6.1 Modify the GridBagPanel of the code in Figure 6.1 so as to accommodate the additional button.

If you have tried the previous exercise, you may have noticed that the button goes exactly under the label, while in the screenshot shown in Figure 6.5 there is clearly some white space between the two components. This additional space can be inserted by adding an invisible component. There are two kinds of invisible components: glues and struts. A glue is a component which can be stretched either horizontally or vertically and is useful in cases where components have a maximum width or height, respectively. Methods Swing.HGlue and Swing.VGlue yield a horizontal and a vertical glue, respectively. On the other hand, a strut should be used to adjust the space between components. A strut takes an argument that forces the layout manager to leave a certain amount of space between two components. Methods Swing.HStrut and Swing.VStrut yield a horizontal and a vertical strut, respectively. Note that a horizontal strut has no height and no depth, while a vertical strut has no width. If you add the following commands

```
add(Swing.VStrut(20), c)
add(close_button, c)
```

just after the command add(label,c) in the code of Figure 6.1, you will get the result shown in Figure 6.5. The next example we will present is more complicated. In particular, we want to write a GUI application which will display a window with one label and two buttons – one of them will open a new window with some "help" information and the other one will shut down the application. In addition, the second window must display some text and it must also include a button which, when pressed, will close only this new window. Figure 6.6 shows how the first window should look.

There are two problems we need to solve in order to build this particular GUI application. The first problem was identified earlier: How can the compiler know

Figure 6.6 A window with a label and two buttons.

which event-handler corresponds to which component? In other words, how can
the compiler tell which button was pressed and activate the corresponding action?
The second problem is about the construction of the window: How can we create
a new fully-functional window?

The first problem can be solved by using method `equals`. This is a method that
all classes have and is used to compare the receiver object with the argument object
for equivalence – `x.equals(y)` is `true` if both `x` and `y` reference the same object.
The code that follows shows how we can solve our first problem:

```
listenTo(close_button)
reactions += {
  case ButtonClicked(b2) =>
    if(b2.equals(close_button)) exit(0)
}
```

Having a solution for the first problem, let us see how we can solve the second
problem.

When we say that a GUI application opens a new window, this means practically
that the application will create an instance of class `Frame`. Since `Frame` is a superclass of `MainFrame`, creating an instance of `Frame` should be a procedure almost
identical to the creation of a `MainFrame`. This is true and the only difference is
that for any instance of `MainFrame`, "field" `visible` is always set to `true`, while
this is not true for any instance of class `Frame`. If the value of this "field" is not
`true`, then the window is not visible. Thus, we always need to give the proper
value explictly to this "field." Figure 6.7 shows what needs to be done in order
to open a window when a button is pressed. In particular, we specify that a new
instance of a particular class should be created when this button is pressed. The
text is displayed in a `TextArea`, that is, a special component that can be used to
display and/or input text. "Field" `editable` should be set to `false` so the user
cannot edit the text contained in this component. "Field" `text` can be used to
specify the contents of this component. Similarly, method `append` takes one string
argument which is appended to the current contents of component. Finally, "fields"
`columns` and `rows` can be used to set the number of rows and columns a text area
may have.

The last problem we need to deal with is to find a way to close the new window
when the user requests. Method `dispose` is the method we need to invoke in order
to release all resources occupied by a particular window. The code in Figure 6.7
shows how we can assemble all these components to build our toy application.
Although we have revealed many of the secrets of GUI programming in Scala, still
we have not presented a *real* application. For this reason, in the next section we
show how to build a (simple) desktop calculator in Scala.

```scala
import scala.swing._
import scala.swing.event._
object hello extends SimpleGUIApplication {
  def top = new MainFrame {
    . . . . . . . . . . . . . . . . . . . . . . .
    }
    contents = new GridBagPanel {
      . . . . . . . . . . . . . . . . . . .
      c.gridwidth = java.awt.GridBagConstraints.RELATIVE
      add(help_button, c)
      c.gridwidth = java.awt.GridBagConstraints.REMAINDER
      add(close_button, c)
    }
    listenTo(help_button)
    reactions += {
      case ButtonClicked(b1) => new Frame {
        title = "Help Window"
        visible = true
        val close_button2 = new Button { text = "Close" }
        val help_text = new TextArea {
          editable = false
          text = "Click the «Κλείσιμο» button to . . ."
        }
        contents = new GridBagPanel {
          . . . . . . . . . . . . . .
        }
        listenTo(close_button2)
        reactions += {
          case ButtonClicked(b3) => dispose()
        }
      }
    }
    listenTo(close_button)
    reactions += {
      case ButtonClicked(b2) =>
        if(b2.equals(close_button)) exit(0)
    }
  }
}
```

Figure 6.7 A simple interactive GUI application with one label and two buttons – one shuts down the application and the other opens a new window.

6.3 Building a desktop calculator

In this section we will describe how to build a rudimentary desktop calculator, that is, we are going to describe how to build an application that will look like the one shown in Figure 6.8.

The first and easiest part is to design the GUI. Observe that the buttons must be placed as if they have been placed in a grid, which is the best arrangement for this particular application. A `GridPanel` is a container that arranges its components in exactly this way, thus, it is the ideal tool to arrange the buttons. Although there are several choices concerning the functionality of the display (for example, should or shouldn't it be user editable), we have opted to make it an instance of `Label`. Since the display has to be at least as wide as the panel that contains the buttons, we need to use another container that will include all components. The following code shows how one should pack the display and the buttons:

```
contents = new GridBagPanel {
  var c = new Constraints
  c.fill = GridBagPanel.Fill.Horizontal
  c.gridwidth = java.awt.GridBagConstraints.REMAINDER
  add(num_display, c)
  add(Swing.VStrut(20), c)
  c.fill = GridBagPanel.Fill.None
  add(buttons, c)
  border = Swing.EmptyBorder(30, 30, 30, 30)
}
```

The declaration of each button looks like the following declaration:

```
val cbtimes = new Button { text = "*" }
```

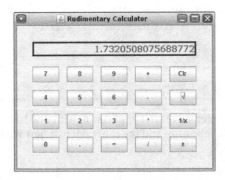

Figure 6.8 A rudimentary desktop calculator.

Once all buttons are declared, they must be packed into a grid container. The code that follows shows how this can be done:

```
var buttons = new GridPanel(0,5){
   hGap = 15
   vGap = 15
   contents += cb7
   . . . . . . . .
   contents += cbpm
}
```

First of all note how we add components to this container: we just "increase" the value of `contents`. Since components are placed on a grid and all componets occupy the same space, it makes no sense to specify constraints on the placement of components. The numbers in parentheses after `GridPanel` specify the number of rows and columns of the grid. If either number is equal to zero, then the system calculates the optimal number of rows or columns, respectively. "Fields" `hGap` and `vGap` are used to specify the horizontal and vertical space between the columns and the rows of the grid, respectively.

Exercise 6.2 Write down the definition of `num_display`.

Let us now see what should be done each time a number button is pressed. First of all, we cannot allow arbitrary long numbers. In other words, we demand that each number contains no more than a predefined number of symbols. As one should expect, each action depends on previous events or the lack of any previous event. Thus, if the calculator displays the digit zero, which should be displayed when the calculator starts or is being reset by pressing the `Clr` (clear) button, or if it displays the word error, which happens when, for example, one attempts to find the square root of a negative number, or if the button that was pressed previously is an operation button, then we need to clear the display. Otherwise, we just append a digit. This scenario can be implemented as follows:

```
listenTo(cb7) // corresponds to digit 7
reactions += {
  case ButtonClicked(b) =>
    if (b.eq(cb7) && (num_display.text.length < max_cols)) {
      tmp = num_display.text
      if (tmp == "0" || tmp == "Error" || opPressed) tmp = ""
      num_display.text = tmp.concat("7")
      opPressed = false
    }
}
```

The following fields are used to control the behavior of our calculator:

```
val max_cols              = 20
var isDecimal             = false
var tmp: String           = _
var leftOperand: Double   = _
var curr_value: Double    = 0.0
var isFirstOperation      = true
var previous_oper         = ""
var opPressed             = false
```

Field isDecimal is used to handle the button with the period:

```
listenTo(cbp) // corresponds to period
reactions += {
  case ButtonClicked(b) => // period
    if (b.eq(cbp) && (num_display.text.length < max_cols)) {
      tmp = num_display.text
      if (!isDecimal && tmp != "Error" &&
                          !tmp.contains(".")) {
        num_display.text = tmp.concat(".")
        isDecimal = true
      }
      opPressed = false
    }
}
```

Field leftOperand is used to store the left operand of an operation. The following code shows what should be done when the plus button is pressed:

```
reactions += {
  case ButtonClicked(b) =>
    if ( b.eq(cbplus) ) {
      tmp = num_display.text
      if ( tmp != "Error") {
        curr_value = java.lang.Double.parseDouble(tmp)
        if ( ! isFirstOperation ) {
          if (!leftOperand.isNaN)
            leftOperand = do_oper(previous_oper,
                            leftOperand, curr_value)
          if (leftOperand.isNaN)
            num_display.text = "Error"
          else
            num_display.text = leftOperand.toString
```

```
      }
      else {
        leftOperand = curr_value
        isFirstOperation = false
      }
      previous_oper = "+"
      opPressed = true
      isDecimal = false
    }
  }
}
```

Function do_oper is defined as follows:

```
def do_oper(oper:String, l:Double, r:Double): Double =
  oper match {
    case "+" => l+r
    case "-" => l-r
    case "*" => l*r
    case "/" =>  if (r == 0.0) Math.NaN_DOUBLE
                 else l/r
  }
```

It is interesting to see what should happen when we press the Clr button. Obviously, the calculator must return to its initial state, that is, the state it was in when we started the program:

```
reactions += {
  case ButtonClicked(b) =>
    if ( b.eq(cbclr) ) {
      num_display.text = "0"
      opPressed = false
      isFirstOperation = true
      isDecimal = false
    }
}
```

The following code shows what should be done when the square root button is pressed:

```
reactions += {
  case ButtonClicked(b) =>
    if ( b.eq(cbsqrt) ) {
      tmp = num_display.text
```

```
    if ( tmp != "Error") {
      curr_value = java.lang.Double.parseDouble(tmp)
      if ( curr_value < 0.0) {
        curr_value = Math.NaN_DOUBLE
        num_display.text = "Error"
      }
      else
        num_display.text = (Math.sqrt(curr_value)).toString
    }
    opPressed = true
  }
}
```

Programming project 6.1 Using the description of this section build your own calculator. Add more buttons that compute the trigonometric functions, logarithms, etc. In addition, add a button that can be used to close the calculator.

6.4 Simple graphics with Scala

The word graphics refers to the creation and/or the manipulation of pictorial data with the aid of a computer. In this section we will describe how one can write Scala code that is able to create pictorial data. Roughly, if one wants to draw something, it is necessary to define a *canvas*. As in Figure 6.3 on page 206, a canvas can be an instance of classes `Panel` or `BorderPanel` (see Section 6.8.3). The latter is a container that has a central component that takes most of the space and has other components that are placed on one of its four borders: north, east, south, and west. In addition, we need to redefine method `paintComponent` since this is the one that draws objects on the canvas. In order to make all these concrete, we will start with a simple example. In particular, we will construct a program that will allow the user to press the mouse button and then draw a circle having a radius of 5 pixels. The source code of this program is shown in Figure 6.9. Note that mouse events are handled in a different way.

For most applications an instance of `Graphics` can be used to solve most problems. However, there are cases that can be dealt with better using `Graphics2D`. This class, which is a subclass of `Graphics`, provides more sophisticated control over geometry, coordinate transformations, color management, and text layout. Although, we do not need these additional features for this particular example, still we show how it is possible to use it. The following command shows exactly what should be done:

```
val g2 = g.asInstanceOf[java.awt.Graphics2D]
```

```scala
object circle extends SimpleGUIApplication {
  def top = new MainFrame {
    var mouseX = 0; var mouseY = 0
    var mouseclicked = false
    title = "Draw Circle"
    preferredSize = (350,250)
    val canvas = new Panel {
      border = Swing.EmptyBorder(15, 15, 15, 15)
      opaque = false
      override def paintComponent(g: java.awt.Graphics) {
        val g2 = g.asInstanceOf[java.awt.Graphics2D]
        g2.setColor(java.awt.Color.magenta)
        g2.fill(new java.awt.Rectangle(350,250))
        g2.setColor(java.awt.Color.blue)
          if ( mouseclicked ) {
            g2.fillOval(mouseX, mouseY, 10, 10)
            mouseclicked = false
          }
      }
      listenTo(Mouse.clicks)
      reactions += {
        case MouseClicked(_, p, _, 1, _) => {
          mouseX = p.x
          mouseY = p.y
          mouseclicked = true
          repaint
        }
      }
    }
    contents = canvas
  }
}
```

Figure 6.9 A simple graphics example in which the user presses the mouse button
and in response it draws a little circle.

The value of "field" opaque controls whether all the bits of the component will be
painted or not. Method fill takes a *shape* and paints the area occupied by the shape
with the current color. There are many different shapes such as Polygons, Rectangles, etc. In this particular case, the rectangle is specified by its width and height.
In the most general case, it is specified by giving the coordinates of the upper-left
corner and the width and the height of the rectangle. Note that the origin of the

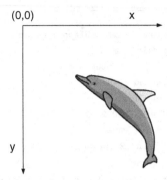

Figure 6.10 The standard coordinate system used in Scala/Java graphics.

coordinate system is at the upper-left corner of the component's drawing area. The *x* coordinate increases to the right, and the *y* coordinate increases downward, as shown in Figure 6.10. The top-left corner of a window is $(0,0)$.

If for some reason it is necessary to have a different coordinate system, one can use method `transform`. This method takes an instance of a class that represents an affine transformation. The following code snippet shows how to construct such an instance:

```
import java.awt._
var x = new geom.AffineTransform(m00, m10, m01, m11, m02, m12)
```

The user-defined field `mouseclicked` is set `false` in order to prevent the program from printing a dot on the screen. Method `fillOval` draws and fills an oval. Now, let us see how the program handles the mouse events.

First of all, note that we specify that the system should listen to a particular event category (for example, `Mouse.clicks`) and not to any event that may happen on a component. This event category should be used when the mouse is clicked, pressed, or released. In addition, the event categories `Mouse.moves` and `Mouse.wheel` should be used when the mouse enters, exits, moves, and drags, or when the mouse wheel moves, respectively. Each event can be handled one by of the following event handlers:

MouseButtonEvent*	MouseClicked*	MouseDragged[†]
MouseEntered[†]	MouseEvent[†]	MouseExited[†]
MouseMotionEvent[†]	MouseMoved[†]	MousePressed*
MouseReleased*	MouseWheelMoved*	

The patterns for the case classes with a * take four parameters: a `Component` (all components are subclasses of this class), in most cases it can be ignored, an instance of `java.awt.Point`, that is, a point in a two-dimensional space with members x and y, the third argument should almost always be ignored, the fourth is a number that corresponds to the number of mouse clicks (for example, for double-clicks it should be 2), and the fifth is a `Boolean` value that controls whether a pop-up component should rise or not. The patterns for the case classes with a [†] take as arguments the first three arguments that the patterns for the case classes with an * take, while a `MouseWheelMoved` pattern takes one more argument that corresponds to the amount that the mouse wheel was rotated (the number of "clicks").

When the user clicks the mouse, then the current mouse position is grabbed and the coordinates are stored in two variables, variable `mouseclicked` becomes `true`, and method `repaint` is invoked, The result of the invocation is to reexecute method `paintComponent`.

Exercise 6.3 Modify the code in Figure 6.9 so it prints the coordinates of the point instead of a bullet. Use the following method to *print* the coordinates on the canvas:

```
g2.drawString(string, x-coord, y-coord)
```

Although this example is quite instructive, still it does not show all the things one can do. The next example will reveal some other capabilities and it will show how one can solve problems in unexpected ways.

A simple paint-like application Let us now construct a simple paint-like application (i.e., an application that allows users to sketch simple curves, see Figure 6.11). Figure 6.12 shows the skeleton of the code[1] that was used to construct the application shown in Figure 6.11.

Figure 6.11 A simple paint-like application.

---

[1] The code is a Scala rewrite of the code of a Java applet which was published in "Introduction to Programming Using Java" by David Eck (see `http://math.hws.edu/javanotes`).

```
object sketcher extends SimpleGUIApplication {
   def top = new MainFrame {
      //"Global" members
      val canvas = new Panel {
         opaque = false; preferredSize = (width, height)
         override def paintComponent(g: java.awt.Graphics) {
            // Draw the contents of the window
         }
         def changeColor(y: Int) {
            //Change the drawing color after user  has
            // clicked the mouse on the color palette
         }
         def setUpDrawingGraphics {
            //Called when mouse is pressed and user clicks
            //on the drawing area.
         }
         listenTo(Mouse.clicks)
         reactions += {
            case MousePressed(_, p, _, _, _) => {
               //user has pressed the mouse anywhere
            }
         }
         reactions += {
            case MouseReleased(_, p, _, _, _) => {
               //user has released the mouse button
            }
         }
         listenTo(Mouse.moves)
         reactions += {
            case MouseDragged(_, p, _) => {
               //user moves the mouse while a mouse
               //button is held down
            }
         }
      }
      contents = canvas
   }
}
```

Figure 6.12 Scala skeleton code that implements the paint-like application shown in Figure 6.11.

The "global" members of the skeleton code in Figure 6.12 are fields that are used throughout the application. The following code snippet contains the definitions of all these "global" members:

```
val width        = 500  //width of the window
val height       = 450  //height of the window
var prevX        = 0    // previous mouse's X location
```

```
var prevY          = 0      // previous mouse's Y location
var colorSpacing = (height - 56) / 7
var dragging       = false //true while user is drawing
val BLACK          = 0;   val RED     = 1
val GREEN          = 2;   val BLUE    = 3
val CYAN           = 4;   val MAGENTA = 5
val YELLOW         = 6
var currentColor = BLACK //the color in use
var G2 : java.awt.Graphics2D = null
```

Field G2 is a graphics context that is used to draw the curve the user "draws." In addition, field colorSpacing is the distance between the top of one colored rectangle in the palette and the top of the rectangle below it. Each rectangle has a height that is equal to the value of this field minus three. Note that the *CLEAR* "button" is by default 50 × 50 pixels. Let us now describe what goes on inside each method.

Method paintComponent is redefined so as to draw the window of the application. Initially, all the available space is painted white. In addition, there is provision for the color palette and also there is some space that will cover the white area. This area is painted gray:

```
val g2 = g.asInstanceOf[java.awt.Graphics2D]
g2.setColor(java.awt.Color.white)
g2.fill(new
   java.awt.Rectangle(3, 3, width-59, height-6))
g2.setColor(java.awt.Color.gray)
g2.drawRect(0, 0, width - 1, height - 1)
g2.drawRect(1, 1, width - 3, height - 3)
g2.drawRect(2, 2, width - 5, height - 5)
g2.fill(new java.awt.Rectangle(width - 56,
              0, 56, height))
```

Method drawRect draws a rectangle (i.e., four perpendicular lines in a particular color). The next thing that must be done is to draw the *CLEAR* "button." This "button" is drawn at the lower right corner of the canvas. However, in order to make the button more realistic, we leave some space outside the "button" that is painted black. The last thing we have to do is to put the label on the "button";

```
g2.setColor(java.awt.Color.white)
g2.fill(new java.awt.Rectangle(width - 53,
            height - 53, 50, 50))
g2.setColor(java.awt.Color.black)
```

```
g2.drawRect(width - 53, height - 53, 49, 49)
g2.drawString("CLEAR", width - 48, height - 23)
```

Method drawString renders a string, the first argument, using the current font. The second and the third arguments refer to the coordinates of the left edge of the baseline where the first character is placed. The commands that follow draw the color rectangles:

```
g2.setColor(java.awt.Color.black)
g2.fill(new java.awt.Rectangle(width - 53,
            3 + 0*colorSpacing, 50, colorSpacing-3))
. . . . . . . . . . . . . . . . . . . . .
g2.setColor(java.awt.Color.yellow)
g2.fill(new java.awt.Rectangle(width - 53,
            3 + 6*colorSpacing, 50, colorSpacing-3))
```

Exercise 6.4 Complete the code snippet above.

The last thing that needs to be done is to draw a border around the color "button" that is currently active:

```
g2.setColor(java.awt.Color.white)
g2.drawRect(width-55,
    1 + currentColor*colorSpacing, 53, colorSpacing)
g2.drawRect(width-54,
    2 + currentColor*colorSpacing, 51, colorSpacing - 2)
```

Method changeColor is invoked when the user clicks on the color palette in order to change the pen's color. It has as its only argument the y-coordinate which is used to compute the color that was chosen by the user. Since all color "buttons" occupy the same space, one needs to divide the y-coordinate by colorSpacing to find which "button" was chosen:

```
val newColor = y / colorSpacing
if ( newColor >= 0 && newColor <= 6 ) {
  val g  = peer.getGraphics()
  val g2 = g.asInstanceOf[java.awt.Graphics2D]
```

Each class of the scala.swing package overrides "field" peer in order to provide direct access to the corresponding Java JFC/Swing class. The code that follows resets the border color of the previous color "button" and after setting the new color it changes the border color of the current color "button:"

```
g2.setColor(java.awt.Color.gray)
g2.drawRect(width-55, 1 + currentColor*colorSpacing,
            53, colorSpacing)
g2.drawRect(width-54, 2 + currentColor*colorSpacing,
            51, colorSpacing - 2)
currentColor = newColor //set new color!
g2.setColor(java.awt.Color.white)
g2.drawRect(width-55, 1 + currentColor*colorSpacing,
            53, colorSpacing)
g2.drawRect(width-54, 2 + currentColor*colorSpacing,
            51, colorSpacing - 2)
g2.dispose()
}
```

By invoking method `dispose` we free the corresponding graphics context and, consequently, release any system resources that it is using.

Method `setUpDrawingGraphics` is invoked when the user starts drawing. It just sets up the graphics context in the current color:

```
val g = peer.getGraphics()
G2 = g.asInstanceOf[java.awt.Graphics2D]
G2.setColor(currentColor match {
  case BLACK   => java.awt.Color.black
  case RED     => java.awt.Color.red
  case GREEN   => java.awt.Color.green
  case BLUE    => java.awt.Color.blue
  case CYAN    => java.awt.Color.cyan
  case MAGENTA => java.awt.Color.magenta
  case YELLOW  => java.awt.Color.yellow })
```

In this particular application, the user can press or release the mouse's buttons or the user can drag the mouse while a button is pressed. Let us first see what should happen when the user just presses the mouse's buttons. In the code that follows p holds the coordinates of the mouse the moment the mouse's button is pressed:

```
var x = p.x
var y = p.y
if ( ! dragging ) { // User is not drawing
  if ( x > width - 53 ) {
    if ( y > height - 53 )
```

```
      repaint            // Clicked on "CLEAR" button.
   else
      changeColor(y) // Clicked on the color palette.
}
```

Now let us see what should happen when the user clicks on the white drawing area. In order to draw a curve, the application needs to "remember" the previous coordinates of the mouse:

```
   else if (x > 3 && x < width - 56 &&
            y > 3 && y < height - 3) {
      prevX    = x
      prevY    = y
      dragging = true
      setUpDrawingGraphics
   }
} //if ( ! dragging )
```

The test is necessary to ensure that the user has clicked the mouse on the white area. Now let us see what should happen when the user releases the mouse's button. In the case that the user was drawing something, we assume that the user has finished. Of course, we may resume later but this is something that should not concern us here:

```
if ( dragging ) {
   dragging = false
   G2.dispose()
   G2          = null
}
```

The last thing we need to handle is the motion of the mouse while a mouse button is held down. If the user is drawing, the program should draw a line segment from the previous mouse location to the current mouse location:

```
if ( dragging ) {
   var x = p.x
   var y = p.y
   if ( x < 3 )            // Adjust the value of x,
      x = 3                // to make sure it's in
   if ( x > width - 57 )   // the drawing area.
      x = width - 57
   if ( y < 3 )            // Adjust the value of y,
      y = 3                // to make sure it's in
```

```
if ( y > height - 4 )   // the drawing area.
  y = height - 4
G2.drawLine(prevX, prevY, x, y)  // Draw the line.
prevX = x  // Get ready for the next
prevY = y  // line segment in the curve
}
```

Method `drawLine` draws a line in the current color from one point to another.

Exercise 6.5 Redesign the application window to make room for a *CLOSE* "button." In addition, modify the code so that the window closes when the user presses this new "button."

Programming project 6.2 Create a pen palette from which the user can choose pens with different strokes. Hint: Use method `setStroke` of class `Graphics2D`.

6.5 Creating pictorial data

We have already seen how to draw images on a canvas on the computer screen. However, we have not explained how to save graphical data directly to pictorial data or just image files. In fact, if these image files have a fairly simple structure, then it is relatively simple to create such files. In addition, it is not difficult to save graphical data in *common* image file formats like JPEG or PNG.

Let us start by showing how one can create simple image files. In [71], the author explained what is needed to save graphical data into PPM, PGM and PBM files. A PPM (Portable Pixel Map) image file can be used to create colorful images. The first four lines of a PPM file have the following form:

```
P3
#Optional comment
width height
maximum color value
```

The rest of the file contains pictorial data in nonbinary form, that is, the data are in a human readable form. In particular, for each image pixel there are three positive integers that denote its corresponding RGB color. The "maximum color value" must be less than 65536 and greater than zero. In order to store the data in binary form, one needs to change the header from P3 to P6. As a first exercise we will construct a program that will output a PPM image file depicting a chess-like board like the one shown in Figure 6.13.

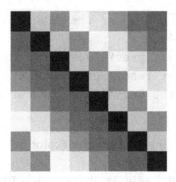

Figure 6.13 A colorful chess-board.

The code that follows creates the image shown in Figure 6.13.

```scala
val n = 8 // number of columns
var colors = Array( (0,0,139),      (144,238,144),
                    (0,191,255),    (250,250,210),
                    (240,230,140),  (205,133,63),
                    (255,20,147),   (160,32,240))
val width = 480
val out   = new java.io.FileWriter("board.ppm")
var m:Int = width / n
out.write("P3\n#Created with Scala\n480 480\n255\n")
for ( _ <- 0 to n-1 ( { //just loop n times
  for ( h <- 0 to m-1; w <- 0 to width - 1 ){
    out.write(((colors(w/m)._1).toString)+" ")
    out.write(((colors(w/m)._2).toString)+" ")
    out.write(((colors(w/m)._3).toString)+"\n")
  }
  // "rotate" colors to ensure each square is
  // colored with a unique color
  var t = colors(7)
  for (j <- 7 to 1 by -1)
    colors(j) = colors(j-1)
  colors(0) = t
}
out.close()
```

In order to create a PPM file with binary data, we first need to store the data with a FileOutputStream instead of a FileWriter and then to transform the header into raw bytes:

```
val out = new java.in.FileOutputStream("board.ppm")
out.write(("P6\n\n480 480\n255\n").getBytes())
```

Method getBytes encodes this string into a sequence of bytes using the platform's default character set. In addition, each of the tree output commands inside the repetition construct must be replaced with a command like the following one:

```
out.write(colors(w/m)._1)
```

Exercise 6.6 As it stands the program produces the same output all the time. However, it is not difficult to make the program draw as many squares in as many different colors as the number supplied as a command line argument. Implement this idea and make sure there are enough different colors!

A PBM (Portable BitMap) image file can be used to create black and white images. The first three lines of a PBM file have the following form:

```
P1
#Optional comment
width height
```

The rest of the file contains the pictorial data in nonbinary form. The data is a sequence of ones and/or zeros. Each digit represents the color of a pixel – ones represent black and zeros represent white. If the pictorial data are in binary form, then each byte represents the color of 8 pixels. In addition, the header of the file must be P4 instead of P1. Creating PBM files with nonbinary data is easy, but creating PBM files with binary data is rather tricky. We will show how to create such a file by implementing an algorithm described in [63]. The algorithm examines a bit within the binary representation of an integer and paints the corresponding pixel. In particular, if i and j are the coordinates of a pixel, then depending on the nth bit of the binary representation of $i^2 j$ the algorithm paints pixel (i, j) accordingly. The "chaos from bits" algorithm, as its author Clifford A. Pickover calls it, produces images like the one shown in Figure 6.14.

Let us now implement this algorithm. However, before proceeding we need to solve a few problems. First of all, we need to find out how to transform an integer number into a bit string, that is, a string that contains binary digits only. An "obvious" solution is to use method toBinaryString which yields the bit string value corresponding to this:

```
scala> 67.toBinaryString
res1: String = 1000011
```

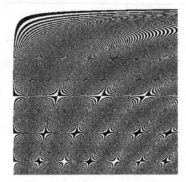

Figure 6.14 Chaos from bits.

Unfortunately, method `toBinaryString` generates strings that do not contain a fixed number of digits. So it is necessary to pad the string produced by this method with a number of zeros. Although this is a trivial task, the task of transforming eight bits into a byte is not trivial. Method `parseInt` of class `java.lang.Integer` takes two arguments, a string and an integer, and parses the string as a signed integer in the radix specified by the second argument. Thus the expression

```
java.lang.Integer.parseInt(bitString,2))
```

yields a signed byte (i.e., an integer in the range from -128 to 127) while what we need is an unsigned byte (i.e., a number in the range from 0 to 255). Given a signed byte b, the expression b & 0xFF yields the corresponding unsigned byte. Strictly speaking, it yields an `Int` in the required range. We now know all that is necessary in order to implement the "chaos from bits" algorithm. Figure 6.15 shows the Scala code that created the image shown in Figure 6.14.

A PGM (Portable Grey Map) image file can be used to create gray scale images. The first four lines of a PGM file have the following form:

```
P2
#Optional comment
width height
maximum gray value
```

Here "maximum gray value" is a number that must be less than 65536 and greater than zero. The number represents the number of different gray shades. Each pixel is "colored" with a number in the specified range. As in the previous cases, the data are nonbinary, while if we want binary data, then P2 has to be replaced by P5.

```
val out = new java.io.FileOutputStream("bitchaos.pbm")
out.write(("P4\n480 480\n").getBytes())
var k=0; var bits=""; val n = 5
for ( h <- 1 to 480; w <- 1 to 480) {
  k += 1
  var iprod = h*h*w
  var test2 = iprod.toBinaryString
  var pad   = ""
  for (_ <- test2.length  to 27)  pad += "0"
  test2 = pad + test2
  bits  = bits.concat(test2.charAt(n+7).toString)
  if (k == 8) {
    out.write((java.lang.Integer.parseInt(bits,2)) & 0xFF)
    k = 0; bits = ""
  }
}
out.close()
```

Figure 6.15 The code that created the image shown in Figure 6.14. Note that 27 is the number of digits of the binary representation of 480^3.

Exercise 6.7 Write a Scala program that will create a gray scale version of the image shown in Figure 6.13.

Exercise 6.8 There is a bug in the two programs presented in this section so far. Find the bug and fix the programs accordingly.

The term JPEG is a commonly used method of compression for photographic images. This compression method is used in a number of image file formats including JPEG/Exif (used by digital cameras, etc.) and JPEG/JFIF (used for storing and transmitting photographic images on the Web). The term PNG (Portable Network Graphics) refers to an open, extensible image format with lossless compression. Basically, the PNG format was designed to replace the older and simpler GIF format and thus it is widely used in the Web. Scala can read and write JPEG/JFIF and PNG files. In the rest of this section we will show how to create simple and complex images in these image formats.

Let us start with a simple example, which will form the basis of our explorations. The code snippet that follows shows exactly what is needed to create a JPEG file:

```
var rendImage = CreateImage
try {
  val file = new java.io.File("newimage.jpg")
  javax.imageio.ImageIO.write(rendImage, "jpg", file)
} catch {
```

```
    case e: java.io.IOException =>
      println("Could not create/write JPEG image.\nAboring.")
  }
```

To create a PNG file just replace jpg with png! Function `CreateImage` creates a `RenderedImage` object:

```
  def CreateImage: java.awt.image.RenderedImage = {
    // Create a buffered image in which to draw
    val bufferedImage =
      new java.awt.image.BufferedImage(width, height,
            java.awt.image.BufferedImage.TYPE_INT_BGR)
    // Create a graphics context for the buffered image
    val G = bufferedImage.createGraphics()
    // Draw graphics

    . . . . . . . . . . . . . . . . . . . . . . . .

    // Graphics context no longer needed so dispose it
    G.dispose
    return bufferedImage
  }
```

As an exercise, we will show how to draw the Mandelbrot set with Scala. We use the distance estimator method [62] to draw the Mandelbrot set. The skeleton of our code follows:

```
  var iter     = 0
  val overflow = 1.0e100
  var rendImage = drawMandelbrot
  val file     = new java.io.File("mandelbrot.jpg")
  javax.imageio.ImageIO.write(rendImage, "jpg", file)
  // Function drawMandelbrot
  // Function MSetDist
```

Figure 6.16 shows the code of function `drawMandelbrot` and Figure 6.17 shows the code of function `MSetDist` which is used in function `drawMandelbrot`. The generated image is shown in Figure 6.18.

The code presented above draws the Mandelbrot set quite fast which means that Scala can be used for scientific computation. Obviously, it is not enough to provide facilities for scientific computation, we need also to be able to deliver results really fast. Method `createGraphics` creates an instance of `java.awt.Graphics2D`, which can be used to draw into `this BufferedImage`.

```
def drawMandelbrot : java.awt.image.RenderedImage = {
  val XScreen = 1024; val YScreen = 1024
  val bufferedImage =
      new java.awt.image.BufferedImage(XScreen, YScreen,
              java.awt.image.BufferedImage.TYPE_BYTE_GRAY)
  val G          = bufferedImage.createGraphics()
  var iynew  = 0
  val pmin    = -2.2; val pmax = 0.7
  val qmin    = -1.5; val qmax = 1.5
  val DeltaP = (pmax-pmin) / (XScreen - 1)
  val DeltaQ = (qmin-qmax) / (YScreen -1)
  for ( np <- 0 to XScreen - 2 ) {
    var iy = 0
    var x  = pmin + DeltaP*np
    var D  = MSetDist(x,qmin)
    while (iy < (YScreen - 1)) {
      iynew    = iy + (Math.floor(Math.max(1.0,
                          Math.min(20.0, D)))).toInt
      var y    = iynew*DeltaQ + qmax
      var Dnew = MSetDist(x,y)
      if ( D <= 0.0 )
        G.setColor(java.awt.Color.black);
      else {
        var c = (iter % 15 +1) * 17
        G.setColor(new java.awt.Color(c,c,c))
      }
      G.drawLine(np, iy, np, iynew)
      iy = iynew
      D  = Dnew
    }
  }
  G.dispose
  return bufferedImage
}
```

Figure 6.16 Function drawMandelbrot.

6.6 Dialogs

A dialog window is one with an optional title and a border that is typically used
to take some form of input from the user or to notify the user with a message (for
example, a warning). The most simple form of a dialog is a confirmation dialog,
that is, a window that asks a user to confirm or to deny the execution of a particular
action. For example, if we replace the reaction part of the code that generates the

```scala
def MSetDist(cx : Double, cy : Double) : Double = {
  var xorbit = new Array[Double](MaxIterations)
  var yorbit = new Array[Double](MaxIterations)

  val MaxIter = 100; val huge = 1000.0;      vari      = 0
  var dist    = 0.0; var xder = 0.0;         var yder  = 0.0
  var temp    = 0.0; var x2   = 0.0;         var y2    = 0.0
  var x       = 0.0; var y    = 0.0;         xorbit(0) = 0.0
  yorbit(0)   = 0.0; iter = 1

  while ((iter < MaxIter) && ((x2+y2) < huge)) {
    temp            = x2 - y2 + cx
    y               = 2.0*x*y + cy
    x               = temp
    x2              = x*x
    y2              = y*y
    xorbit(iter)    = x
    yorbit(iter)    = y
    iter           += 1
  }
  if ( (x2+y2) > huge ) {
    xder       = 0.0
    yder       = 0.0
    var i      = 0
    var flag = false
    while ( ( i < iter ) && (! flag) ) {
      temp = 2.0*(xorbit(i)*xder-yorbit(i)*yder+1.0)
      yder = 2.0*(yorbit(i)*xder+xorbit(i)*yder)
      xder = temp
      flag = Math.max(Math.abs(xder),
                       Math.abs(yder)) > overflow
      i    += 1
    }
    if (! flag)
      dist = Math.log(x2+y2)*Math.sqrt(x2+y2)/
             Math.sqrt(xder*xder+yder*yder)
  }
  return dist
}
```

Figure 6.17 Function MSetDist which is used in function drawMandelbrot.

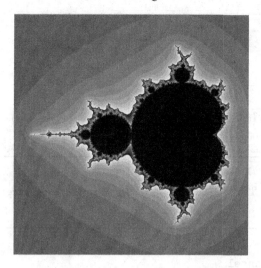

Figure 6.18 The Mandelbrot set as drawn with the distance estimator method.

window shown in Figure 6.5 on page 208 with the following code

```
reactions += {
  case ButtonClicked(b2) => {
    import Dialog._
    var s = showConfirmation(close_button,
                             "Are you sure?",
                             "Close Window",
                             Options.YesNo,
                             Message.Question,
                             null)
      if ( s == Result.Yes )
        exit(0)
  }
}
```

then when the user presses the "Close Window" button, a dialog window, like the one shown in Figure 6.19, will pop up.

Figure 6.19 A very simple dialog window.

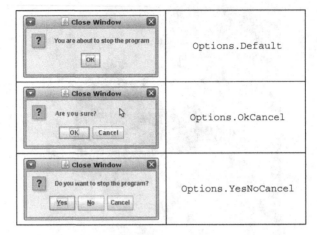

Figure 6.20 The effect of `Options.Default`, `Options.OkCancel`, and `Options.YesNoCancel`.

Method `showConfirmation` creates a window. The method takes several arguments. The second and the third argument correspond to the text that will appear on the window and the text that will appear as its label. The first argument is the parent component, that is, a component to which this window is attached. The last argument is an icon that can replace the preselected one. In this case the standard icon is a little square with a question mark. With the fourth argument one specifies the set of buttons that appear at the bottom of the window. There are three more possible values that can affect the set of buttons and these, as well as the results, are shown in Figure 6.20.

The fifth argument specifies the icon that should be displayed in the dialog window. Apart from `Message.Question` there are four more values whose effect is shown in Figure 6.21. The possible answers that method `showConfirmation` may return are `Result.Yes`, `Result.Ok`, `Result.No`, `Result.Cancel`, and `Result.Closed`.

The code presented at the beginning of this section is somehow unnatural, though correct. First of all we do not need to define the button separately and second there is no reason to define any reactions, at least in the way we have done so far. Instead we can add a component and its behavior to a special hash table that maps such components to constraints. The component is a button that is created using an alternative constructor, which expects an instance of class `Action`. However, in the code that follows, we indirectly use method `apply` of the corresponding `Action` object. This method takes two arguments: a string, which is the text that will be printed on the button, and a block of code, which will be executed whenever the button is pressed. In addition, as shown below, we modify or add properties to the newly constructed button.

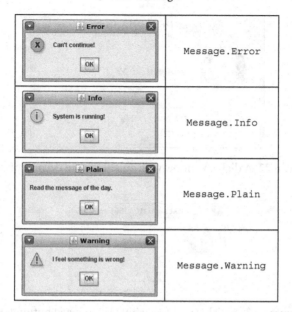

Figure 6.21 The effect of Message.Error, Message.Info, Message.Plain, and Message.Warning.

```
layout(new Button(Action("Close Window") {
    import Dialog._
    var s = showConfirmation(mypanel,
                             "Are you sure?",
                             "Close Window",
                             Options.YesNo,
                             Message.Question, null)
    if ( s == Result.Yes )
        exit(0)
}){ font = new java.awt.Font("Verdana",
            java.awt.Font.PLAIN, 14)}) = c
```

Here mypanel is the self type of a newly constructed GridBagPanel:

```
contents = new GridBagPanel { mypanel =>
```

As was noted above, if the last argument of showConfirmation is null, then a default icon decorates the window. However, we can choose to use a different icon. If the icon is a file on our computer's hard disk, then the icon can be specified as follows:

```
new javax.swing.ImageIcon("question.png")
```

For example, by replacing the expression of the previous example for null, we may get a dialog window like the one shown in Figure 6.22.

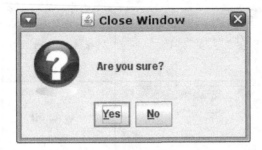

Figure 6.22 A dialog window with an alternative decoration icon.

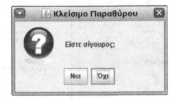

Figure 6.23 A dialog window with a customized button text.

If the icon file resides in a remote computer connected to the Internet, it is possible to use this image by letting the system resolve the URL and fetching the file. The following expression shows how this can be done:

```
new javax.swing.ImageIcon(
  new java.net.URL(
    "http://ocean1.ee.duth.gr/~apostolo/question.png")))
```

In many cases it is necessary to be able to customize what appears on the buttons. For example, when constructing a GUI application for Greek users, the buttons should look like the those of the dialog window shown in Figure 6.23. Method showOptions can be used to create such customized buttons:

```
var options = Array("Ναι", "Όχι")
var s = showOptions(mypanel,  "Είστε σίγουρος;",
        "Κλείσιμο Παραθύρου", Options.YesNo,
        Message.Question,
        new javax.swing.ImageIcon("question.png"),
        options, 1)
```

The text that should appear on the buttons is stored in an array which is passed as an argument to method showOptions. In fact, this array is passed as the seventh argument of the method while the value of the last argument corresponds to the button that will be highlighted (the first button corresponds to number zero, etc.).

Figure 6.24 An informative dialog pop-up.

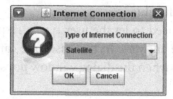

Figure 6.25 A dialog that can get user input.

Method showMessage should be used when we want just to display a message. If we replace the code above in the GUI application with the code that follows

```
showMessage(mypanel, "System will shutdown immediately!",
            "System Shutdown",Message.Info, null)
```

then when we press the button, a dialog window like the one shown in Figure 6.24 will pop up.

In certain cases it is useful to be able to get input from the user. For example, if one programs a network diagnostic tool, which needs to ask users to enter their network connection, then method showInput can be used to get input from the user. The code that follows can be used to create the dialog window shown in Figure 6.25:

```
val entries = Array("Analog", "ISDN",
                    "B-ISDN", "ADSL",
                    "SDSL", "VDSL",
                    "Cable", "Wireless",
                    "T-1 Lines", "T-3 Lines",
                    "Satellite")
var s = showInput(mypanel, "Type of Internet Connection",
            "Internet Connection", Message.Question,
            new javax.swing.ImageIcon("question.png"),
            entries, "ADSL")
s match {
  case Some(x) =>
    println("You have a "+x+" Internet connection.")
```

```
    case None    =>
      println("You have no Internet connection.")
  }
```

Method showInput returns a Some(*v*) value, if a value is selected or None if
Cancel is pressed. The entries appear as a pull-down menu from which the user
can choose a value. This value is returned when *OK* is pressed. The last argument
of the method is the default value.

In rare cases, one may need to let the user type a response instead of choosing
one from a set of possible answers. In this case, one can simply replace the sixth
argument with Nil and so when the dialog window pops up, the user can enter the
preferred value.

6.7 Menus

Typically, a menu is a list of options displayed on a window (for example, as a
pull-down window) and from which the user may make a choice. There are several
forms of menus and in this section we will present all the different forms of menus.

6.7.1 Radio buttons

A radio button is a type of GUI component that allows the user to choose only one
of a predefined set of options. Suppose we want to create a set of radio buttons.
Then the following code snippet should be used to create a set of radio buttons:

```
    val T  = new ButtonGroup
    val a1 = new RadioButton("a1")
    val a2 = new RadioButton("a2")
    . . . . . . . . . . . . . .
    val aN = new RadioButton("aN")
    val R = List(a1,a2,...,aN)
    T.buttons ++= R
    T.select(a1)
    val L = new BoxPanel(Orientation.Vertical) {
      contents ++= R
    }
    add(L,c) // or anything else that is suitable
```

Here BoxPanel is a panel that lays out its contents one after the other, either
horizontally or vertically. In the sample code above the orientation is vertical; for
horizontal orientation one must use Orientation.Horizontal instead. The next
thing we need to know is how to respond to a user selection in a radio button group.

Figure 6.26 A simple GUI application with a radio buttons group

Assume that a user has to press an ordinary button after selecting a radio button. Then the following code shows exactly how to program a response to a user selection:

```
layout(new Button(Action("Choose one") {
  T.selected.get match {
    case `a1` => . . . //action(s) for button a1
    . . . . . . . . . . . . . . . .
    case `aN` => . . . //action(s) for button aN
  }
})) = c
```

Here the patterns are stable identifiers, that is, patterns which in general are *paths* (i.e., parts of a named type like C.this or C.super.x) that end in an identifier. One should be careful and make sure that all a1,...,aN conform to the expected type of the pattern. As an exercise let us build a simple GUI application with a radio button group like the one shown in Figure 6.26. After the user has made a choice and has pressed the "Choose a team" button, a question is printed just under this button. The code that follows shows how to define the buttons:

```
contents = new GridBagPanel {
  var c = new Constraints
  c.gridwidth = java.awt.GridBagConstraints.REMAINDER
  add(label,c)
  val myfont = new java.awt.Font("Verdana",
                     java.awt.Font.PLAIN,18)
  val teams = new ButtonGroup
```

```
val chelsea = new RadioButton("Chelsea")
chelsea.background = java.awt.Color.lightGray
chelsea.font = myfont
. . . . . . . . . . . . . . . . . . . .
val manchesterUnited = new RadioButton("Manchester United")
manchesterUnited.background = java.awt.Color.lightGray
manchesterUnited.font = myfont
val radios = List(chelsea,arsenal,
                    liverpool,manchesterUnited)
teams.buttons ++= radios
teams.select(chelsea)
val myradios = new BoxPanel(Orientation.Vertical) {
  contents ++= radios
  background = java.awt.Color.lightGray
}
add(myradios,c)
```

And the code that follows shows what should be done in order to place the button in the panel and how to program the behavior of the application:

```
layout(new Button(Action("Choose a team") {
  teams.selected.get match {
    case `chelsea` => fan.text = "Are you a pensioner?"
    case `arsenal` => fan.text = "Are you a gunner?"
    case `liverpool` => fan.text = "Are you a red?"
    case `manchesterUnited` => fan.text =
                          "Are you a red devil?"
  }
}){ font = new java.awt.Font("Verdana",
              java.awt.Font.PLAIN, 14)}) = c
```

Exercise 6.9 Complete the code above and verify that it works in the expected way.

6.7.2 Check boxes

These are GUI components that allow users to make multiple selections from a number of options. For example, a restaurant menu can be easily described with check boxes. In order to show how to use check boxes, we will implement the (very simple) "calorie calculator" shown in Figure 6.27.

First of all we need to create an instance of class CheckBox for each check box:

```
val banana  =  new CheckBox("banana")
```

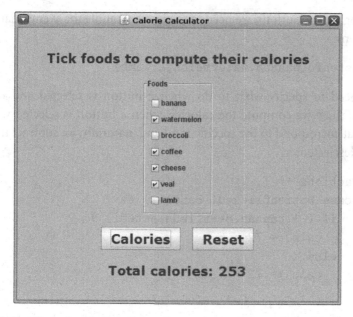

Figure 6.27 A "calorie calculator" that demonstrates the use of check boxes in Scala.

Once all check boxes have been defined, we need to place them in a panel. The best way is to define a special panel that will be included in the panel that includes all components:

```
var foods = new BoxPanel(Orientation.Vertical) {
    border = CompoundBorder(TitledBorder(
            EtchedBorder, "Foods"), EmptyBorder(5,5,5,10))
    banana.background = java.awt.Color.lightGray
    . . . . . . . . . . . . . . . . . . . . . . . . .
    contents.append(banana,watermelon,broccoli,
                    coffee,cheese,veal,lamb)
    background = java.awt.Color.lightGray
```

The check boxes will be enclosed in a compound border (i.e., a border that allows multiple border objects) with a title drawn in etched border style. In addition, we set the color of the background of each check box as well as the color of the background of the panel. Observe how we add all the components in the panel and compare it with the way we added the button group in the same panel:

```
contents.append(banana,watermelon,…,lamb)
```

After arranging the buttons, we need to see how to handle the events that occur on these buttons:

```
listenTo(banana,watermelon,…,lamb)
```

Next we need to specify what to do when a button is selected and when it is deselected. Since we compute the calories, when a button is selected we add the calories that correspond to the specific food and, naturally, we subtract them if the button is deselected:

```
reactions += {
   case ButtonClicked(`banana`) =>
     if ( ! banana.peer.isSelected() )
        cals -= 72
     else
        cals += 72

       . . . . . . . . . . . . . . .

   }
}
```

Method `isSelected` checks whether a given check box is selected or not. This method is defined in class `javax.swing.JCheckBox`.

The two ordinary buttons that are shown in Figure 6.27 become part of a box panel:

```
var mybuttons = new BoxPanel(Orientation.Horizontal) {
   contents.append(cal_button,Swing.HStrut(20),reset_button)
   background = java.awt.Color.lightGray
}
```

Although putting all the components together is easy and the reader should be able to write the corresponding code, we still believe it makes sense to show one more time how things should be done. The code snippet that follows shows how to put all the components together:

```
contents = new GridBagPanel {
   var c = new Constraints
   c.gridwidth = java.awt.GridBagConstraints.REMAINDER
   add(label,c)
   add(Swing.VStrut(20), c)
   add(foods, c)
   add(Swing.VStrut(20), c)
   add(mybuttons, c)
```

```
    add(Swing.VStrut(20), c)
    add(result_label, c)
    background = java.awt.Color.lightGray
    border = Swing.EmptyBorder(50, 50, 50, 50)
}
```

Now let us see what should happen when each of the ordinary buttons is pressed. In the case of the leftmost button, all we need to do is to display the total calories in the specially designated label:

```
listenTo(cal_button,reset_button)
reactions += {
  case ButtonClicked(b1) => if(b1.eq(cal_button)) {
    result_label.text = "Total calories: "+cals
  }
}
```

In the case of the reset button, we reset the value of the "global" field `cals`, then deselect all buttons, and make the text of the result label empty:

```
reactions += {
  case ButtonClicked(b2) => if(b2.eq(reset_button)) {
    cals = 0
    banana.peer.setSelected(false)
    . . . . . . . . . . . . . . .
    result_label.text = ""
  }
}
```

Method `setSelected`, which is defined in `javax.swing.JCheckBox`, should be used to deselect a selected check box.

6.7.3 Combo boxes

A combo box is a GUI component which is a combination of a drop-down list and a single-line text box, allowing users either to type a value directly into the control or to choose from the list of existing options. In Scala one can create combo boxes with a definition like the following one:

```
val cb1 = new ComboBox(List("b1","b2","b3","b4","5"))
```

Assume we have a number of combo box definitions. Then we could arrange them horizontally, one after the other, by including them in a `FlowPanel`. In the sample code below we use such a panel to arrange the combo boxes. Also, the code shows how to make the action listener listen to the events that occur on a combo box and how to handle these events:

```
val panel = new FlowPanel {
  contents += cb1
  . . . . . . . .
  contents += cbN
  reactions += {
    case SelectionChanged(`cb1`) =>
      label1.text = cb1.selection.item
      . . . . . . . . . . . . . .
    case SelectionChanged(`cbN`) =>
      labelN.text = "No " + cbN.selection.index +
                     " was pressed"
  }
  listenTo(cb1.selection,…,cbN.selection)
}
```

Note that we register cbM.selection and not cbM which is an instance of object ComboBox.selection. Also, "fields" item and index return the item selected and the index of the item selected (with zero being the first index). With this information, we can create a GUI application like the one shown in Figure 6.28. Let us see how we can construct such an application.

First of all we need to define a hash table with the correct answers:

```
var quiz = Map("Greece"  -> "Athens",
               . . . . . . . . . . . .
         "Canada"  -> "Ottawa")
```

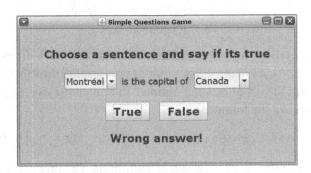

Figure 6.28 A simple GUI application that uses combo boxes.

Next we need to define various components. We start with the labels:

```
def top = new MainFrame {
  title = "Simple Questions Game"
  val prompt_label =
    new Label("Choose a sentence and say if its true")
  val answer_label = new Label("")
```

Let us define the combo boxes and some auxiliary members:

```
var capital   = "Athens"
var country   = "Greece"
val countries = new ComboBox(List("Greece",…,"Canada"))
val capitals  = new ComboBox(List("Athens",…,"Montreal"))
```

Now that the combo boxes have been defined we need to arrange them in a panel:

```
val questions = new FlowPanel {
  contents += capitals
  val connector =
    new Label(" is the capital of ")
  contents += connector
  contents += countries
```

Exercise 6.10 Enclose the combo boxes in a border, like the one in the previous example.

Once the combo boxes have been arranged, we need to specify how to handle the events that occur on them:

```
reactions += {
  case SelectionChanged('countries') =>
    country = countries.selection.item
  case SelectionChanged('capitals') =>
    capital = capitals.selection.item
}
listenTo(countries.selection,capitals.selection)
}
```

As is evident, we simply assign to the auxiliary members, the values selected by the user. The two buttons in the lower part of the application can be programmed easily:

```
val true_button   = new Button("True")
val false_button  = new Button("False")
```

```
val answer_buttons = new BoxPanel(Orientation.Horizontal) {
  contents.append(true_button,Swing.HStrut(20),false_button)
}
```

Exercise 6.11 All componenents and subpanels are arranged in a `GridBagPanel`.
Write the code that arranges all these components in the panel.

The last thing we need to take care of is what should happen when the user presses
either button. In the code that follows we have used a different coding technique
to show that one should experiment and not learn by heart all the programming
idioms presented in this chapter, unless, of course, it is absolutely necesary:

```
listenTo(true_button,true_button)
reactions += {
  case ButtonClicked(b) =>
    if ( b.eq(true_button) ) {
      if ( quiz(country) == capital )
        answer_label.text = "Correct answer!"
      else
        answer_label.text = "Wrong answer!"
    }
    else if ( b.eq(false_button) ) {
      if ( quiz(country) == capital )
        answer_label.text = "Wrong answer!"
      else
        answer_label.text = "Correct answer!"
    }
} // of new FlowPanel
```

Exercise 6.12 Add a label that will display how many correct and how many wrong
answers the player has given.

Especially for combo boxes it is possible to have images instead of strings. The
simple GUI application shown in Figure 6.29 demonstrates the use of images in a
combo box. Since creating such a combo box is not straightforward, we will explain
in detail what should be done in order to create similar combo boxes.

First of all we have to specify how the images will be loaded. As the following
code snippet shows, we use an instance of `ImageIcon` to create an icon and method
`resourceFromClassloader`, which is defined in `SimpleGUIApplication`, to
retrieve the pictorial data that are stored in an image file. This method translates a
string to an instance of `java.net.URL`, which can be consumed by `ImageIcon`. If
for some unpredictable reason the file that contains the image is not in the expected

Figure 6.29 A simple GUI application that uses combo boxes with images.

location, we need to include a fallback mechanism to prevent our program from crashing. And this exactly is the reason why the formation of the combo box is part of a try expression:

```scala
import javax.swing.{Icon, ImageIcon}
. . . . . . . . . . . . . . . . . . . . . . . .
val icon_menu = new FlowPanel {
val icons = try {
  List(new ImageIcon(
           resourceFromClassloader(
             "images/apples.jpg")),
  . . . . . . . . . . . . . . . . . . . . .
} catch {
  case _ =>
    println("Couldn't load images for combo box")
    List(Swing.EmptyIcon)
}
```

Object Swing.EmptyIcon stands for a no-image, that is, an image with no contents and no dimensions. However, in order to be absolutely sure that our application will not have to use the fallback mechanism, we can include the images in the final .jar file as shown below:

```
$ scalac comboIcons.scala
$ jar cvf comboIcons.jar *.class images
```

The following code initializes a combo box with icons:

```scala
val iconBox = new ComboBox(icons) {
  renderer =
    new ListView.AbstractRenderer[Icon, Label](new Label) {
```

```
def configure(list: ListView[_], isSelected: Boolean,
            hasFocus: Boolean, icon: Icon,
            index: Int) {
    component.icon = icon
    list.selectionBackground = java.awt.Color.green
    component.xAlignment = Alignment.Center
    if ( isSelected )
      component.border =
        Swing.LineBorder(list.selectionBackground, 3)
    else
      component.border = Swing.EmptyBorder(3)
  }
 }
}
```

As expected, when the user clicks on the image that is shown on the combo box, a drop-down menu emerges. As the user moves the mouse over the menu, the images are highlighted. "Field" renderer of ComboBox is of type ListView.Renderer which is a superclass of ListView.AbstractRenderer. This "field" is used to set the renderer for this combo box's items. The renderer that we are using provides a component that is responsible for item rendering and it assumes reasonable default settings. Method configure can be used to specify how images should appear when the mouse is over them. "Field" selectionBackground is used to store the background color of the drop-down menu where images are displayed. Similarly, selectionForeground is used to store the foreground color of the same drop-down menu. Method Swing.LineBorder draws a line as border in a specific color which is either user specified or system specified (i.e., there are two constructors). Note that for Swing.EmptyBorder it holds that

$$\text{EmptyBorder}(w) \equiv \text{EmptyBorder}(w, w, w, w).$$

The next thing is to add the combo box into the application's panel and to specify what should happen when the user makes a selection from the combo box. One should bear in mind that this has nothing to do with the appearance of the combo box:

```
contents += iconBox
reactions += {
  case SelectionChanged('iconBox') =>
    likes.text = "So you like " +
                  fruits(iconBox.selection.index) + "!"
  }
  listenTo(iconBox.selection)
}
```

The label likes is used to display the message " So you like....." Integrating the code that defines the label into a GUI application is easy and the reader should have no problem doing so.

Combo boxes are not the only components with icons, one can also create labels with icons. For example, the following definition creates a label with an image instead of some text:

```
val L = new Label("",
          new ImageIcon(
            resourceFromClassloader("I.jpg")),
          Alignment.Center)
```

Although the current version of Scala does not support the creation of buttons with icons, still it is very easy to define a new class that will create buttons with images. The easiest way to define such a class is to create a subclass of the Button class. The following definition shows how this can be done:

```
class ImageButton(icon: javax.swing.Icon ) extends Button {
  override lazy val peer: javax.swing.JButton =
    new javax.swing.JButton(icon) with SuperMixin
}
```

Remember that all GUI related classes are actually wrappers around Java's JFC/Swing classes, thus, trait SuperMixin is used to redirect certain calls from the peer to the wrapper and back.

If we replace the code that creates the button shown in Figure 6.1 with the following code

```
val close_button =
  new ImageButton(new ImageIcon(
    resourceFromClassloader("close_button2.jpg")))
```

then the result will look like the window shown in Figure 6.30.

Figure 6.30 A simple GUI application with a button that bears an image instead of some text.

Exercise 6.13 Class javax.swing.JButton can take a string and an icon, in this order, to create a button with an icon and an accompanying text. Define a Scala class that creates such buttons and test its usability.

6.7.4 Building a text editor with a menu bar and menus

Any nontrivial GUI application has a *menu bar*, that is, a bar where a number of *menus* are available. Typically, each menu is a pull-down window that offers a number of (different) choices to users. Class Frame defines "field" menuBar which should be used to define a menu bar. Typically, one can define a menu bar inside method top as follows:

```
menuBar = new MenuBar
```

The menu bar consists of individual menus and each individual menu consists of menu items. The next few commands show how to define a new menu and how to add menu items:

```
val aMenu        = new Menu("Sample Menu")
aMenu.contents += new MenuItem("Entry A")
aMenu.contents += new Separator
aMenu.contents += new MenuItem("Entry B")
```

As expected, the string argument is the corresponding title of each menu and menu item. Class Separator creates a horizontal line that separates menu items. In the most general case the constructor accepts orientation value, while the default value is Orientation.Horizontal. A rudimentary editor (see Figure 6.31) is the

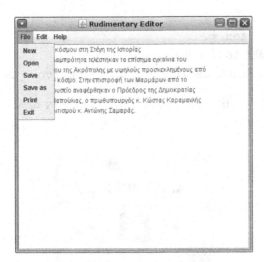

Figure 6.31 A rudimentary editor in Scala.

ideal example to demonstrate the use of menus, therefore, we will explain how to construct such an application.

The first thing we need to take care of is to define the component that will be used to edit and display the text. The best choice for this is a TextArea:

```
val editor = new TextArea {
  font = new java.awt.Font("UM Typewriter",
                           java.awt.Font.PLAIN, 12)
  columns = 40
  rows = 20
  editable = true
  text = ""
}
```

When using an editor one needs to be able to open a file, to modify its contents, and then to save the changes made. The capability to navigate the file system, and then to choose either a file or a directory from a list, or enter the name of a file or directory is provided by *file choosers*. Here is how one can define a file chooser:

```
val file_IO = new FileChooser(new java.io.File(".")) {
  fileSelectionMode = FileChooser.SelectionMode.FilesOnly
}
```

The argument of the constructor is the default directory from where the navigation of the file system begins. As should be obvious, a user can pick up only files not directories. The other possible values are FileChooser.SelectionMode.DirectoriesOnly and FileChooser.SelectionMode.FilesAndDirectories. We can use the file chooser to implement the expected functionality of the *Open* menu item from the *File* menu:

```
menu_file.contents += new MenuItem(Action("Open") {
  import io._
  if (file_IO.showOpenDialog(menuBar) ==
      FileChooser.Result.Approve)          {
    currentFile = file_IO.selectedFile
    editor.text = new String
    for (line <- Source.fromFile(currentFile).getLines)
      editor.append(line)
    backup = editor.text
  }
})
```

First of all, we are using class Action to program the behavior of the menu item. Next, we use FileChooser.showOpenDialog dialog to allow the user to select the file to be opened. The response FileChooser.Result.Approve means that the user has successfully chosen a file. The responses FileChooser.Result.Cancel and FileChooser.Result.Error are useful to check whether the user has not selected a file (for example, presses the *Cancel* button) or whether some error has happened, respectively. Method selectedFile returns the File that the user has selected. Class Source provides an iterable representation of input files and this is why we are able to use the file in a for comprehension. Method getLines returns string *iterator*, that is, a structure that allows the iteration over a sequence of elements, which in our case are the lines of the input file including the line ending character. Method Source.fromFile creates an iterator from, among others, a File. Member backup is user defined and it is used to check whether the contents have been modified since the last save operation took place.

Programming the behavior of menu item *Save* is more involved. We have to distinguish two different cases – one where the contents of the text area have not been saved before (i.e., the user has typed something) and one where the user has opened a file in order to modify it. The first case can be handled by the following code snippet:

```
menu_file.contents += new MenuItem(Action("Save") {
  if (currentFile == null) {
    if (file_IO.showSaveDialog(menuBar) ==
      FileChooser.Result.Approve)                    {
      currentFile = file_IO.selectedFile
      var out =
        new java.io.OutputStreamWriter(
          new java.io.BufferedOutputStream(
            new java.io.FileOutputStream(currentFile)))
      backup =  editor.text
      out.write(backup); out.flush(); out.close()
    }
  }
```

The user-defined member currentFile holds an instance of a File that corresponds to the file that has been opened or to the file to which the program has just saved data. If currentFile is null, then the user must choose the output file where the data will be stored. This is done with FileChooser.showSaveDialog, whose argument is the parent component of the component that invokes this method.

Exercise 6.14 If the user selects an existing file, the code overwrites the existing file without asking! Remedy this deficiency of the code. (Hint: Use method exists() of class File, which checks whether the file denoted by a class instance exists.)

If currentFile is not null, then the program will save the data to the file stored to this member:

```
    else {
      var out =
        new java.io.OutputStreamWriter(
          new java.io.BufferedOutputStream(
            new java.io.FileOutputStream(currentFile)))
        backup = editor.text
        out.write(backup); out.flush(); out.close()
    }
  })
```

When the user chooses *New*, the program must take care of the current contents (if any) of the text area:

```
  menu_file.contents += new MenuItem(Action("New") {
      check_on_exit(1)
  })
```

The user-defined method check_on_exit examines whether the text stored in the text area has been saved in a file. If this is not true, then a dialog window pops up and asks whether the user wants to save the file or not. Depending on the user's response the program saves the contents, discards them, or continues as if nothing happened. This functionality is implemented as follows:

```
  def check_on_exit(oper : Int) = {
    if ( backup != editor.text ) {
      import Dialog._
      var s = showConfirmation(menuBar,
        File is not saved,\n would you like to save it?",
        "Save File", Options.YesNoCancel,
                          Message.Question, null)
      if ( s == Result.Yes ) {
        if (file_IO.showSaveDialog(menuBar) ==
          FileChooser.Result.Approve)                   {
          currentFile = file_IO.selectedFile
          var out =
            new java.io.OutputStreamWriter(
```

```
            new java.io.BufferedOutputStream(
                new java.io.FileOutputStream(currentFile)))
          backup = editor.text
          out.write(backup); out.flush(); out.close()
        }
        cleanUp(oper) // remember: oper is the only
      }                // argument of this method
      else if ( s == Result.No )
        cleanUp(oper)
      }
   }
```

Method `cleanUp` is defined as follows:

```
def cleanUp(oper:Int) = {
  currentFile = null
  if (oper == 0 )
    exit(0)
  else {
    editor.text = ""
    backup = ""
  }
}
```

Now we can easily implement the menu item for *Exit*:

```
menu_file.contents += new MenuItem(Action("Exit") {
    check_on_exit(0)
})
```

Exercise 6.15 Implement the functionality of the *Close* menu item.

Printing the contents of the text area is very simple:

```
menu_file.contents += new MenuItem(Action("Print") {
    editor.peer.print()
})
```

Implementing the *Edit* menu, which includes the *Find* and *Find Next* menu items, is more involved but not difficult. Of course, one must bear in mind that we are building a rudimentary editor and not some full-fledged editing tool. In order to make searching general enough, we have opted to use regular expressions. Since the functionality of *Find Next* depends on the outcome of *Find*, we define the following two fields to be accessible by the code that implements the behavior of both menu items:

```
var p : java.util.regex.Pattern = null
var m : java.util.regex.Matcher = null
```

The easiest way to allow the user to enter the word (pattern) to be searched is by using an showInput dialog with an *empty* list of entries and no initial choice:

```
menu_edit.contents += new MenuItem(Action("Find") {
  val s = showInput(menuBar,
                    "Search text for:",
                    "Search text for a word",
                    Message.Plain, Swing.EmptyIcon,
                    Nil, "")
```

Once the user has closed the dialog window, we need to check whether some input has been provided:

```
if ((s.isDefined) && (s.get.length > 0)) {
```

Method isDefined returns true if s is not equal to None. In the case when we want to check whether an option value is None, we should use isEmpty. Method get returns the value of a particular option. Since we are sure that s is not None, there is no reason to use pattern matching to obtain its value. However, if we are not sure whether an option value is None, it is better to use getOrElse, if we insist on not using pattern matching. This method returns the value if the option value is nonempty, otherwise it returns its argument evaluated. Now that we are sure that the user has entered a "word," we prepare the pattern matcher to start searching the text stored in the text area:

```
      search_text = s.get
      p = Pattern.compile(search_text)
      m = p.matcher(editor.text)
      if (m.find())
        editor.caret.dot = m.start()
      else showMessage(menuBar, "Pattern not found!",
        "String not found",Message.Info, null)
    }
  })
```

Object caret is a wrapper around a Java class that implements the idea of a place within a document view (roughly, the part of a document that is visible to a user) where things can be inserted. Generally, we can say that a caret is the cursor and its position within the document is represented by "field" dot. If the pattern matcher finds a word that matches the pattern, then we move the cursor to the print where this word starts. Otherwise, we have to inform the user that there was no match. Menu item *Find Next* is easier to implement:

```
menu_edit.contents += new MenuItem(Action("Find Next") {
  if (m != null && m.find())
    editor.caret.dot = m.start()
  else
    m = null
})
```

If the user chooses this menu item while the pattern matcher has not been initialized, then we must ensure that our program will not crash. This is exactly the reason why we need to make sure that m is not equal to null. A better effect is achieved by coloring the cursor:

```
editor.peer.setCaretColor(java.awt.Color.blue)
```

In addition, we could use highlighting, but this requires extensive Java programming, so we skip it.

Exercise 6.16 Assume that the user will enter simple words not regular expressions. Implement the searching mechanism using method `indexOf` (see Section 2.14).

We have defined all menus and we have defined the text area that will hold the text, what is left is to put it all together. The good news is that for menu bars there is nothing special to be done: they are automatically included in the application once they are defined. Thus, we need a component that will contain only the text area. But we need a container that will allow users to scroll both horizontally and vertically. A `ScrollPane` is a component that can include at most one component that can be scrolled (i.e., scrolling makes sense):

```
contents = new ScrollPane { contents = editor }
```

Exercise 6.17 Implement the *Help* menu using appropriate dialogs.

The last thing we would like to say is that if we want our text editor to be copy and paste "aware," then we need to include at least the following commands in our final code:

```
var transferHandler = new javax.swing.TransferHandler("")
editor.peer.setDragEnabled(true)
```

6.8 Tabs

A tab is a navigation widget that, in the simplest case, allows users to switch between sets of *pages*, which contain GUI component. The real benefit of using tabs is that users do not have to open many different windows – they just need to open a new tab for each window. A simple GUI application with tabs is shown in Figure 6.32.

6.8.1 Simple tabs

The application shown in Figure 6.32 consists of five tabs, each of them showing a picture. Each tab is a TabbedPane.Page and, at the same time, it is a member of an instance of a TabbedPane. The entire tab structure is placed in a GridPanel:

```
contents = new GridPanel(1,1) {
    val tabs = new TabbedPane {
        import TabbedPane._
```

In this example we use labels to shows pictures. Thus, each picture is just a label. In order to achieve this we load the picture, as has already been described, and make it the value of "field" icon:

```
. . . . . . . . . . . . . . . . . . . . . . . .
    var picture3 = new FlowPanel {
        val pic = new Label
        pic.icon = new ImageIcon(
            resourceFromClassloader("pic3.jpg"))
        contents += pic
    }
```

Figure 6.32 A simple GUI application with tabs.

```
        pages += new Page("River in Summer", picture3)
        . . . . . . . . . . . . . . . . . . . . . . . .
    }
    contents += tabs
}
```

Object `TabbedPane.pages` is a structure similar to an array and it holds the tabs and can be used to append, remove, and insert tabs. Operator `+=` "appends" a tab; method `insertAt` takes two arguments – an integer and a tab – and inserts a tab at a specific position; method `remove` takes an integer and deletes a tab from a position that corresponds to its argument; and, finally, method `length` returns the number of tabs stored in the class instance.

6.8.2 User-disposable tabs

Typically, any application with tabs allows users to manipulate tabs. Therefore, it is much more useful to build an application with disposable tabs, much like the one shown in Figure 6.33. The example is a rewrite of an example presented in the "The Swing Tutorial" at Oracle's web site. This application does not include provision for inserting tabs but, as we will see, adding this functionality is almost trivial once one has managed to define user-disposable tabs.

As was explained above, there is provision for changing a tab panel (i.e., by removing a tab). However, what is missing are GUI components for the removal and/or insertion of tabs. Typically, applications that provide this functionality include a menu item for the insertion of tabs and a button on the tab title for removing the tab. In order to have this button, we need to redesign a new component to replace

Figure 6.33 An application with tabs with customizable "tips."

the default title component. The first part is not difficult, but if there is no way to replace the title component, it is almost useless. Fortunately, method setTabComponentAt, which is defined in class javax.swing.JTabbedPane, can be used to set a component that will be responsible for rendering the title for a specific tab. The skeleton of a class that defines such a component is shown in Figure 6.34. This

```
class ButtonTabComponent(val pane: TabbedPane)
      extends FlowPanel(FlowPanel.Alignment.Left) {
   opaque = false
   val label = new Label { // title of tab
      border = EmptyBorder(0,0,0,5)
      text   = pane.pages.apply(pane.pages.length-1).title
   }
   val button = new TabButton(Action("") {
      val i = pane.peer.indexOfTabComponent(
      ButtonTabComponent.this.peer)
      if ( i != -1 )
         pane.pages.remove(i) // remove tab
   })
   contents += label
   contents += button
   border    = EmptyBorder(2,0,0,0)
   class TabButton extends Button {
      def this(a: Action) = {
         this()
         action = a
      }
      . . . . . . . . . . . . . . . . . . . . . . . .
      override def paintComponent(g: java.awt.Graphics) {
         . . . . . . . . . . . . . . . . . . . . .
      }
      listenTo(Mouse.moves)
      reactions += {
         case MouseEntered(c,_,_) => . . . . . . .
         case MouseExited(c,_,_)  => . . . . . . .
      }
   }
   listenTo(Mouse.clicks)
   reactions += {
      case MousePressed(c, _, _, _, _) => . . . . . . .
   }
}
```

Figure 6.34 Skeleton of a class that defines a component that can be used to render the title of a tab.

class is quite interesting since it has a nontrivial primary constructor, it includes an inner definition and it shows how to handle mouse events. Although we have explained how to handle mouse events, we did not give examples that show how to handle mouse events that happen over specific components.

Class ButtonTabComponent defines a component that includes two other components: a label and a button. The label is used to display the title of the tab while the button is there for users who want to close a particular tab. The label gets its text from the title of the last tab inserted in the tab panel:

```
text = pane.pages.apply(pane.pages.length-1).title
```

The button bears an "X" mark which is drawn by paintComponent. The following commands are executed every-time a new instance of this class is created:

```
val mysize        = 17
preferredSize    = (mysize, mysize)
tooltip          = "close this tab"
border           = EtchedBorder
rolloverEnabled = true
peer.setUI(new javax.swing.plaf.basic.BasicButtonUI())
peer.setContentAreaFilled(false)
peer.setFocusable(false)
```

"Field" tooltip can be set to display a "tip" for a component. Method setUI of class javax.swing.JPanel sets the *look and feel* class instance that renders a component. The term look and feel refers to a distinctive platform-independent appearance and standard behavior for all components. If the argument of method setContentAreaFilled, which is defined in class javax.swing.Abstract-Button, is true, then the component's content area will be painted. Otherwise, the button will be transparent. Method setFocusable, which is defined in class java.awt.Component, controls whether the component will be focusable or not. The value of "field" rolloverEnabled determines whether rollover effects will occur or not. An example of a rollover effect is an image which changes when the mouse is over it. In our case, the rollover effect will be the change of color of the "X" mark on the button. The definition of the class is completed with the redefinition of method paintComponent:

```
override def paintComponent(g: java.awt.Graphics) {
  super.paintComponent(g)
  val g2 = g.asInstanceOf[java.awt.Graphics2D]
```

The first command is included so to make sure all other paintings will finish before we proceed with the painting described in this method.

```
if ( peer.getModel().isPressed() )
  g2.translate(1, 1)
```

Method getModel, which is defined in class javax.swing.AbstractButton, returns the state model that the button represents and method isPressed, which is defined in "trait" ButtonModel, indicates whether the button is pressed.

```
g2.setStroke( new java.awt.BasicStroke(2) )
g2.setColor( java.awt.Color.black )
```

Now we set the stroke and the color of the stroke that will be used to draw the "X." Method setStroke should be used to set the stroke and class java.awt.Basic-Stroke is used to create a stroke type. In this case we create a simple stroke whose width is 2 units.

```
if ( peer.getModel().isRollover() )
  g2.setColor( java.awt.Color.magenta )
```

This code snippet changes the color of the "X" mark when the mouse is over it. In particular, method isRollover returns true when the mouse is over the button.

```
val delta = 6
g2.drawLine(delta, delta, size.width - delta - 1,
          size.height - delta - 1)
g2.drawLine(size.width - delta - 1, delta, delta,
          size.height - delta - 1)
}
```

These commands draw the two lines that make up the "X" mark.

When the mouse is on the tip of a tab and is pressed, it should remove the tab from the panel. The following expression

```
pane.peer.indexOfTabComponent(ButtonTabComponent.this.peer)
```

computes the index of the current tab, that is, the tab over which the mouse is, or it returns −1 in case of error. And this index is used to remove the current tab in the definition of TabButton shown in Figure 6.34. The mouse events are handled differently. In all cases, what matters is the component over which the mouse is. If it is over the button, the border of the button is painted:

```
case MouseEntered(c,_,_) =>
  if (c.isInstanceOf[AbstractButton]) {
```

```
        val button = c.asInstanceOf[AbstractButton]
        button.borderPainted = true
    }
```

When the mouse is not over the button, then the border of the button will lose its painting:

```
    case MouseExited(c,_,_) =>
      if (c.isInstanceOf[AbstractButton]) {
        val button = c.asInstanceOf[AbstractButton]
        button.borderPainted = false
    }
```

The following code implements something that is obvious for a user but not always for a programmer – when the user clicks on the label, the program should make this tab the one in the foreground. This is something that is handled automatically (try the previous example and you will see what we mean), but from the moment we placed a label over it, things are not the same:

```
    case MousePressed(c,  _,  _,  _,  _) =>
      if (c.isInstanceOf[Component]) {
        val i = pane.peer.indexOfTabComponent(
          ButtonTabComponent.this.peer)
        if ( i != -1 )
          pane.selection.page = pane.pages.apply(i)
    }
```

By modifying the `contents` of the code, which produces the GUI shown in Figure 6.32, as shown below, we get the GUI shown in Figure 6.33:

```
    contents = new GridPanel(1,1) {
      val tabs = new TabbedPane
      . . . . . . . . . . . . . . . . . . . . . . . .
      tabs.pages += new Page("Montmartre", picture5)
      tabs.peer.setTabComponentAt(4, // index
                (new ButtonTabComponent(tabs)).peer)
      contents += tabs
    }
```

Exercise 6.18 Modify the code of the rudimentary editor, which was presented in Section 6.7.4, so to include support for tabs.

6.8.3 GUI lists, sliders, and split panes

So far we have seen only one way to change tabs – by pressing on the tab's tip. However, there are at least two more ways and we are going to describe them and show how to implement them. The first involes the use of *sliders* and the second GUI lists. A slider is a component that lets users select a value graphically by sliding a knob within a bounded interval. The slider can show ticks (both major and minor between the major ones). In addition, sliders can print text labels at any location along the slider track. A GUI list is a component that displays a list of objects (for example, text) and allows users to select one or more items. It is quite instructive to think of GUI lists as hyperlinks. The GUI application shown in Figure 6.35 demonstrates how one can use both sliders and GUI lists to change tabs in a GUI application with tabs. Let us see how we can implement this GUI application.

First of all we need to define the tab. The method we used in section 6.8.1 also works here, so we will not repeat it. The core of the code of the application is shown in Figure 6.36. Member `list` is an instance of `ListView` and it is used to display a sequence of `TabbedPane.Page`, which automatically builds a nonmodifiable instance of a list model. Module `ListView.selection` refers to the current item selection. Method `selectIndices` takes as argument an integer, which corresponds to a selection, and changes the current selection to this number. "Field" `intervalMode` should be used to get or set the selection mode for a GUI list. This "field" may assume three different values: `IntervalMode.Single` (only one list item can be selected at a time), `IntervalMode.SingleInterval` (only one contiguous interval can be selected at a time), and `IntervalMode.MultiInterval` (there are no selection restrictions as it is the default mode). The last thing is to

Figure 6.35 An application with tabs, sliders, and GUI lists.

```
contents = new BorderPanel {
  val list = new ListView(tabs.pages) {
    selection.selectIndices(0)
    selection.intervalMode = ListView.IntervalMode.Single
    import ListView._
    renderer = ListView.Renderer(_.title)
  }


  val center = new SplitPane(Orientation.Vertical,
                             new ScrollPane(list), tabs) {
    oneTouchExpandable = true
    continuousLayou    = true
    dividerSize        = 15
  }

  layout(center) = BorderPanel.Position.Center

  val slider = new Slider {
    min                = 0
    value              = tabs.selection.index
    max                = tabs.pages.size-1
    majorTickSpacing   = 1
    paintTicks         = true
  }
  layout(slider) = BorderPanel.Position.South

  listenTo(slider,tabs.selection,list.selection)
  reactions += {
    case ValueChanged(`slider`) =>
      if ( !slider.adjusting )
        tabs.selection.index = slider.value
    case SelectionChanged(`tabs`) =>
      slider.value = tabs.selection.index
      list.selection.selectIndices(tabs.selection.index)
    case SelectionChanged(`list`) =>
      if ( list.selection.items.size == 1 )
        tabs.selection.page = list.selection.items(0)
  }
}
```

Figure 6.36 The core of the code that produces the GUI application shown in Figure 6.35.

convert the sequence of titles of all tabs into renderer, something that the following command does:

```
renderer = ListView.Renderer(_.title)
```

The reader may have noticed so far that both the tabs and the GUI list are not yet part of the main application panel. Also, it should be evident that the main panel is split into two subpanels, separated by a *divider*. These are called *split panes*. The constructor of a SplitPane takes three "arguments": a value that corresponds to the pane's orientation, the left and the right components. "Field" oneTouchEx-pandable sets the *oneTouchExpandable* property. In other words, by setting this property, the divider component (i.e., the little vertical line shown in Figure 6.35) gets the two little arrows that make it possible to shrink and expand either side of the split pane. Also, "field" continuousLayout should be set to true if we want the two components to be continuously redisplayed and laid out during user intervention. If one wants to set the width of the divider, one should use "field" di-viderSize, whose value is an integer that denotes the width in pixels. In addition, "field" dividerLocation can be used to set the exact location of the divider. In fact, Scala uses the formula

$$\frac{\texttt{dividerLocation}}{\texttt{size.height} - \texttt{dividerSize}}$$

to compute the exact location of the divider, if Orientation.Vertical is the chosen orientation. Otherwise, the following formula is used:

$$\frac{\texttt{dividerLocation}}{\texttt{size.width} - \texttt{dividerSize}}.$$

In Scala, a slider is an instance of class Slider. "Fields" min and max are used to set/get the minimum and the maximum value supported by the slider, while field value should be used to set the slider's current value. Moreover, "fields" major-TickSpacing and minorTickSpacing should be used to set/get the major/minor tick spacing. Also, when "field" paintTicks is true, then ticks appear on the slider. If we want to add labels to certain ticks, we can do this fairly easy. For example, if we add the code that follows in the definition of slider

```
labels     = Map(0 -> new Label("Aut."),
                  1 -> new Label("Winter"),
                  2 -> new Label("Summer"),
                  3 -> new Label("Sea Shr."),
                  4 -> new Label("Mon/re"))
paintLabels = true
```

the output will look like the screenshot shown in Figure 6.37.

Figure 6.37 A application with a slider that has ticks and labels.

A `BorderPanel` is a component that can contain other components. There is always a central component that occupies most of the available space. Other components can be placed on the north, south, east, or west of this central component. Object `BorderPanel.Position` defines the five different positions: `North`, `South`, `West`, `East`, and `Center`. As is obvious from the code in Figure 6.36, method `add` is used to add components to a `BorderPanel` and it takes as arguments a component and its position.

There are three different kinds of events that may happen in our application: the user may slide the knob of the slider component, or the user may select a tab, or choose an element from the GUI list. Therefore, the application must *listen to* all these events and adjust itself accordingly. Let us see what happens in each case.

(i) When the application detects that the knob has changed position, case class `Value-Changed` detects this, then only when the knob stops will it return a number that corresponds to its position. Note that member `adjusting` is set to `true` when the knob moves and this is why we check whether it is `false`. In the end, the value of the slider, which is stored in member `value`, is used to set the current tab.

(ii) When changing a tab, we need to adjust the position of the knob and change the item selected in the GUI list.

(iii) In the case that the user selects from the GUI list, we make absolutely sure that only one item has been selected and only then set the current tab, which has as a side effect the adjusting of the knob.

6.9 More on text components

In Section 6.7.4 we used a `TextArea` component to build a rudimentary text editor. However, this is not the only text-based component – Scala supports simple text

Figure 6.38 A minimal application with a text and a password field.

and password fields. Roughly, a text field is a `TextArea` with only one line, while a password field is a text field where one can see that something was typed, but one cannot see the original characters. As in all previous cases, we will build a simple application in order to show the capabilities of both text and password fields. Figure 6.38 shows such a minimal application that mimics a login screen. Let us see how to construct this minimal application.

Let us start with the text field which is an instance of class `TextField`:

```
val user_field = new TextField {
  columns = 10
}
```

This definition can be abbreviated as follows:

```
val user_field = new TextField(10)
```

In other words, the length of the text field (stored in "field" `columns`) can be supplied directly to the constructor.[2] Similarly, we can either directly supply the contents of a text component or assign it to "field" `text`. By default "field" `editable`, which controls whether the text field is editable, is `true`. If one wants to ensure that the input given in a text field is valid (whatever this may mean), one should use "field" `shouldYieldFocus`. The value of this "field" can be any function that takes a string and returns a `Boolean`. Behind the scenes, when the editing is done, this function takes as argument the text of the text field and only if the function returns `true`, the *focus* can move to another component (roughly, one cannot use any other component unless the function returns true). The code snippet that follows shows

---

[2] The value of this "field" does not imply that the length of the user name will be ten or at most ten characters long! It just means that the user can see at most ten characters and this happens only if the font used has glyphs that are wide enough.

how we could make a text field accept only two particular strings as input:

```
shouldYieldFocus = (x:String) => (x == "apostolos"
                               || x == "αποστολος")
```

It is possible to impose further restrictions on the data that can be entered in a text field, but we will come back to this after we have discussed password fields.

Password fields are implemented by class PasswordField which, quite naturally, is a subclass of class TextField. Although one can give an initial value to a password field, it makes no sense to do so. But it makes sense to supply only a value for columns:

```
val pass_field = new PasswordField(10) {
  echoChar = ''
}
```

The value of "field" echoChar is of type Char and it is the character that appears when the user enters something in a password field. Method password returns an array of characters that contains the characters the user has entered in the password field.

Exercise 6.19 Write a complete Scala GUI application that implements the application shown in Figure 6.38.

When a user enters some text in a text field, there is only one way to tell when the user has finished – the user has to press the enter key. In our simple application the user will press the enter key after entering the password. Class EditDone detects this event and the code that follows shows how we handle events in this application:

```
listenTo(pass_field)
reactions += {actors/Actor.scala]
  case EditDone(`pass_field`) =>
    if ( user_field.text.length > 0  )
      if (user_field.text == user_name &&
          pass_field.password.deepMkString("") == password)
        error_label.text = "Welcome!"
      else
        error_label.text = "Incorrect username/password!"

}
```

Our code is very simple since we assume that there is only one user and, naturally, only one password. In addition, the password is stored unencrypted in a simple member something that is not safe at all (for more information about data encryption the user should consult the documentation of package java.secu-rity). Method deepMkString returns a string representation of an array. In the simplest case it takes only one argument which corresponds to a separator that will appear between array elements. Naturally, method toString is invoked to create a string representation of each element. In its most general form, method deepMk-String takes three arguments which are all strings. The first one is the argument with which the string representation will start, the third is the one with which the string representation will finish, and the second is a separator.

The code presented so far is certainly not realistic. Indeed, it lacks some features that will make it more realistic. First of all, our application prints an error message when the user fails to enter the correct combination of user name and password, but it does not print a message inviting the user to retry. Before presenting the other problem, let us see how we can solve this problem. In order to print the error message and then prompt the user to retry, we need to insert some code that will delay the appearance of the second message, or else only the second will appear. Putting a busy wait loop like the following one

```
var i = 0; while(i<300000) i+=1
```

between the commands that print the messages does not solve the problem (try it!). The simplest way to implement the required functionality is to use an actor (see Chapter 7 for details). Roughly, in the code that follows the commands form a block expression (i.e., a block that evaluates to an expression, see Section 7.1 for more details) that is executed in a different thread of execution. Putting it simply, this means that the commands that make up the block expression will be executed independently from the commands that precede or follow them. Here is the complete definition:

```
import scala.actors.Actor._
val delayGUI = actor {
  error_label.text = "Wrong Username/Password"
  Thread.sleep(2500)
  error_label.text = "Please retry."
}
```

Method sleep of class java.lang.Thread suspends execution for a given number of milliseconds. In conclusion, the net effect of the definition above is that the first command will be executed, then the thread will pause for 2.5 seconds, and, finally, the second command will be executed. But this is not enough: focus must go to the text field where the user name is entered while the previous user name must be cleared:

```
user_field.text = ""
user_field.requestFocus
```

Obviously, method `requestFocus` moves the focus to the component it is called from.

In many cases, we expect users to enter in a text field input of a particular type. For example, if one builds an application that processes income tax statements, then most fields will be numeric with at most two decimal digits. Thus, in order to reduce unnecessary checks, it would be far better to allow only certain kinds of characters to be entered in a particular text field. In Scala, this facility is available when using a `FormattedTextField`. Unfortunately, in order to use this class properly, one needs to know a lot about a good number of Java classes. Therefore, we will not use this solution. On the other hand, we are going to present a simpler solution which uses only Java's `MaskFormatter`. This class produces formatters that are built according to a string. This string may contain ordinary characters and the special formatting characters shown in Table 6.1. For example, the string "€ ### ##" could be used to create a text field that shows the Euro sign and where the user has to enter amounts less than 1000 €. As a design principle, we believe that

Table 6.1 *Special characters that may appear in a* `MaskFormatter` *mask*

Character	Description
#	Any valid decimal digit (i.e., `c.isDigit`, where c is a `Char` and method `isDigit` returns `true` if c is a decimal digit, will return `true`)
'	Escape character, used to escape any of the special formatting characters
U	Any letter character (i.e., `c.isLetter`, where c method `isLetter` returns `true` if c is a Latin, Greek, etc. letter, will return `true`), all lowercase letters are mapped to uppercase
L	Any letter character, all uppercase letters are mapped to lower case
A	Any letter or digit character
?	Any letter character. No transformations performed
*	Any character
H	Any hexadecimal digit (i.e., 0–9, a–f or A–F)

the direct use of Java classes in Scala code should be kept to a minimum. Therefore, we define this new `MaskFormatter` component so that the users of the class use Java classes only implicitly. The code that follows defines this class:

```
class MaskedTextField(format: String)
    extends TextComponent.HasColumns {
    var formatter : javax.swing.text.MaskFormatter = null
    try {
      formatter = new javax.swing.text.MaskFormatter(format)
    } catch {
      case e : java.text.ParseException =>
        println("bad formatter")
        exit(-1)
    }
    override lazy val peer: javax.swing.JFormattedTextField =
      new javax.swing.JFormattedTextField(formatter)
    def columns: Int = peer.getColumns
    def columns_=(n: Int) = peer.setColumns(n)
}
```

Method `text` is not defined since it is inherited from trait `TextComponent.Has-Columns` which is a "subclass" of class `TextComponent`. Note that trait `Text-Component.HasColumns` defines "field" `columns` as abstract and that is why we need to define it. Similarly, trait `TextComponent.HasRows` defines "field" `rows` as abstract and so any class extending it must explicitly define it.

6.10 Tables

A table is a GUI component that can be used to display data in a tabular form (for example, think of a spreadsheet, which is the archetypal application that displays data in a tabular form). Usually, one cannot modify the contents of any cell, but, optionally, program designers may allow users to edit the data. Obviously, the data displayed by a table are not part of the table as, for example, one can use the same table to display different sets of data.

A table can be constructed by creating an instance of class `Table`. In order to construct a table, we can supply either two arrays or two integers to the constructor. In the first case, the first array is actually an array of arrays of type `Any` that contains the data that are displayed in the table, while the second array contains the strings that are used as row names. In the second case, we create a table that contains

XML Display

First Author	Second Author	Third Author	Title	Subtitle	Publisher	Address	Year
Apostolos Syropo...	No Author	No Author	Hypercomputation	Computing Beyon...	Springer	New York	2008
Apostolos Syropo...	Antonis Tsolomitis	Nick Sofroniou	Digital Typograph...		Springer	New York	2002
Christos Loverdos	Apostolos Syropo...	No Author	Steps in Scala	An Introduction to ...	Cambridge Univer...	New York	2010
Απόστολος Συρόπ...	No Author	No Author	LaTeX		Παρατηρητής	Θεσσαλονίκη	1998
Απόστολος Συρόπ...	No Author	No Author	Στοιχεία προγραμ...		Παρατηρητής	Θεσσαλονίκη	2003
Απόστολος Συρόπ...	Νικόλαος Σωφρονί...	Δημήτριος Φιλίππου	Τεχ και ψηφιακή τ...	110 Ερωτήσεις και...	Εκδόσεις Ζήτη	Θεσσαλονίκη	1998

Figure 6.39 A typical table whose data come from an XML file.

$n \times m$ cells, where n and m are the first and second integer arguments, respectively. The table shown in Figure 6.39 was created using the first constructor whereas the data have been read from an XML file. The code that follows shows how the table was constructed:

```
def top = new MainFrame {
  title = "XML Display"
  val columnNames = Array("First Author",
                          "Second Author",
                          "Third Author",
                          "Title",
                          "Subtitle",
                          "Publisher",
                          "Address",
                          "Year")
  val table = new Table( (books.toArray), columnNames) {
    preferredViewportSize = new java.awt.Dimension(900,200)
  }
  contents = new ScrollPane { contents = table }
}
```

Class java.awt.Dimension is a class that encapsulates the width and height of a component in fields width and height, respectively. As a matter of fact "field" preferredSize gets instances of this class as values.

Exercise 6.20 The input file that contains the XML content has the following format:

```
<library>
  <book>
    <authors><author>A.B</author>…</authors>
    <title>Title</title>
    <subtitle>Subtitle</subtitle>
    <publisher>Publisher</publisher>
    <address>Address</address>
    <year>2010</year>
  </book>
    . . . . . . . . . . . . . . . . . .
</library>
```

By design there can be at most three `<author>` elements. The XML content will be loaded with the following command

```
var library = XML.loadFile("library.xml")
```

whereas it must be stored in the following array:

```
var books : List[Array[Any]] = Nil
```

Write the code that "populates" array `books`.

The definition of class `Table` is not really flexible. As it stands one cannot easily add or remove rows. So, we cannot easily transform our XML viewer into an XML editor. In order to be able to add/delete rows we need to be able to pass an `Array-Buffer` instead of an `Array`. Roughly, an `ArrayBuffer` is an array which can grow. The following interaction with the language interpreter shows the basic capabilities of `ArrayBuffers` (the output has been truncated for typographic reasons):

```
scala> import scala.collection.mutable._
import scala.collection.mutable._

scala> var A = new ArrayBuffer[Int]
A: scala.collection.mutable.ArrayBuffer[Int] = ArrayBuffer()

scala> A += 2 //append element

scala> A += 3

scala> A
res2: ArrayBuffer[Int] = ArrayBuffer(2, 3)

scala> A.+:(1) //prepend element
    scala> A
res2: ArrayBuffer[Int] = ArrayBuffer(1, 2, 3)

scala> A.remove(2) //remove element
res5: Int = 3

scala> A
res2: ArrayBuffer[Int] = ArrayBuffer(1, 2)
```

Alternatively, one could define a new *table model*. In general, the correct manipulation of tables demands a good knowledge of `javax.swing.JTable`, something that falls outside the scope of this book and so we stop here our presentation of tables and their capabilities.

6.11 Applets

An applet is a program written in any language that runs atop the JVM and which can be included in an HTML page, just like an image can be included in such a page. In order to view such a page, one needs to use a Java technology-enabled browser (by default most current browsers are Java technology-enabled). In order to include an applet in an HTML page, one needs to know the basics of the HTML <APPLET> tag. However, for our needs the following general form of the tag is enough:

```
<applet code="AppletSubclass.class"
    archive="custom.jar,scala-swing.jar,scala-library.jar"
        width="500" height="500">
</applet>
```

The attribute `archive` is used to specify the location of one or more Java archive files. In this particular example, we list the standard Scala library archives `scala-library.jar` and `scala-swing.jar`. Naturally, a better idea would be to bundle these libraries with the final archive (see appendix B for more details), but here we want to make things as simple as possible.

Building applets is similar to the construction of ordinary GUI applications. However, there are some differences. The skeleton code that follows shows the general structure of an applet:

```
class SkeletonApplet extends Applet {
  object ui extends UI with Reactor {
    override def init : Unit = { ... }
    override def start : Unit = { ... }
    override def stop : Unit = { ... }
  }
}
```

Abstract class `Applet.UI` declares the three methods shown above and provides a redefinition of "field" contents. Trait `Reactor` defines the methods `listen-To` and `deafTo` whose effect is to remove events from the event listener. Method `init` is called by the browser to inform the applet that it has been loaded into the system, method `start` is called to inform the applet that it should start its execution, and method `stop` is called to inform the applet that it should stop its execution. Typically, one should use `init` to initialize some variables, nevertheless, this is not necesary in most cases. So one can have the whole code of an applet in either the `init` or `start` method. However, there are cases where the two methods have different roles to play (for example, see Section 7.2).

Instead of presenting a simple applet, we have opted to present an applet that is a rewrite of the "jumping box" Java applet that comes with every version of the *Java Development Kit* (JDK). This way, readers with some experience in Java programming will be able to translate their applets easily in Scala, while readers with no familiarity with Java will see how to construct real applets. Figure 6.40 is a screenshot that shows this applet in action.

The "jumping box" applet implements a simple game where the user tries to hit with the mouse a square that moves on the panel. To make the game realistic, each user action is associated with a particular sound, while messages appear on the status bar (i.e., the bar that reads "HIT IT AGAIN! AGAIN!" at the bottom of the screenshot shown in Figure 6.40).

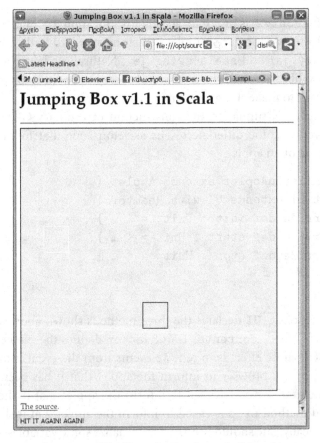

Figure 6.40 The "jumping box" as a Scala applet.

We will now reveal the code that implements this applet. First we need to define some auxiliary fields (variables):

```
private var mx      = 0
private var my      = 0
private var oldSize : java.awt.Dimension = null
private var onaroll = _
private var rnd     = new Random()
def init() = {
   onaroll = 0
}
```

The first two members hold the coordinates of the lower left corner to the square that the user tries to hit. The third member holds the size of the applet and the fourth one counts the number of times the square has been hit. As is obvious, method `init` does almost nothing! As was made clear above, the body of method `start` can replace the body of `init` and the result will be the same. The skeleton of the body of this method follows:

```
override def start() = {
   val canvas = new Panel {
      opaque         = false
      preferredSize = (500, 500)
      override def paintComponent(g: java.awt.Graphics) {
         . . . . . . . . . . . . . . . . . . . . . .
      }
      listenTo(Mouse.clicks)
      reactions += {
         case MousePressed(_, p, _, _, _) => {
            . . . . . . . . . . . . . . . . . . . .
         }
      }
      listenTo(Mouse.moves)
      reactions += {
         case MouseEntered(_,_,_) => repaint
         case MouseExited(_,_,_)  => repaint
         case MouseMoved(_, p, _) => {
            if ( (p.x % 3 == 0) && (p.y % 3 == 0) )
               repaint
         }
         case ComponentResized(_) => repaint
```

```
      }
    }
    contents = canvas
  }
```

Here ComponentResized is cached when the applet or, more generally, a component is resized. The only argument is the component that is resized. Other such events are described by the classes ComponentHidden, Component-Moved , and ComponentRemoved. The code that follows is the body of method paintComponent:

```
var newSize: java.awt.Dimension = getSize()
if (oldSize == newSize) { // Erase old box
  g.setColor(getBackground())
  g.drawRect(mx, my, (oldSize.width / 10) - 1,
          (oldSize.height / 10) - 1)
}
else {
  oldSize = newSize
  g.clearRect(0, 0, oldSize.width, oldSize.height)
}
// Calculate new position
mx = rnd.nextInt(999)  %
        (oldSize.width - (oldSize.width / 10))
my = rnd.nextInt(999) %
        (oldSize.height - (oldSize.height / 10))
g.setColor(java.awt.Color.black)
g.drawRect(0, 0, oldSize.width - 1, oldSize.height - 1)
g.drawRect(mx, my, (oldSize.width / 10) - 1,
          (oldSize.height / 10) - 1)
```

Method getBackground of class java.awt.Component gets the background color of a component. The code above erases the old square and redraws a new one in a new random position. The code that follows is executed every time the mouse button is pressed:

```
var x = p.x
var y = p.y
requestFocus
//determine if hit
if (mx < x && x < mx + getSize().width / 10 - 1 &&
```

```
        my < y && y < my + getSize().height / 10 - 1) {
    if (onaroll > 0) { //not first hit
      ( onaroll % 4 ) match {    //play a sound
        case 0 => play(getCodeBase(),"sounds/tulips.au")
        case 1 => play(getCodeBase(),"sounds/danger.au")
        case 2 => play(getCodeBase(),
                            "sounds/adaptOrDie.au")
        case 3 => play(getCodeBase(),
                            "sounds/NotCompleted.au")
      }
      onaroll += 1
      if (onaroll > 5)
        getAppletContext().showStatus(
          "You're on your way to THE HALL OF FAME:"
          + onaroll + "Hits!")
      else
        getAppletContext().showStatus("YOU'RE ON A ROLL:"
                                      + onaroll + "Hits!")
    } // end of "not first hit"
    else {  //first hit
      getAppletContext().showStatus("HIT IT AGAIN! AGAIN!")
      play(getCodeBase(), "sounds/that.hurts.au")
      onaroll = 1
    } // end of "first hit"
  } // end of "determine if hit|
  else { //miss
    getAppletContext().showStatus("You hit nothing at ("
      + x + ", " + y + "), exactly");
    play(getCodeBase(), "sounds/thin.bell.au");
    onaroll = 0
  }
  repaint
```

Method getSize of class java.awt.Component returns the size of a component
as an instance of java.awt.Dimension. Also, method getCodeBase returns the
URL of the directory that contains the applet. Method play reproduces the audio
clip that corresponds to the URL this method has as its argument. Currently, this
method can play only 8 bit, μ-law, 8000 Hz, one-channel, Sun ".au" files. In addition,
method getAppletContext determines the applet's context that allows the applet

to interact with the environment in which it runs. Finally, method `showStatus` takes a string as argument and "forces" the browser to show its argument in the statusbar.

Exercise 6.21 Implement the desktop calculator presented in Section 6.3 as a Scala applet.

6.12 Functional graphics

As is evident, the programming style employed in GUI programming is the imperative programming style. Unfortunately, it is a common belief that functional programming has no role to play in GUI programming and graphics. Fortunately, this is not true. For example, Conal Elliott has designed and implemented a purely functional system for making graphical images. This system, which is called *Pan* [20], is implemented as a Haskell library (a "domain-specific embedded language"). The following code snippet is a typical usage example that shows how one can draw an image like the one shown in Figure 6.41:

```
circles =   let blueCircle = colourRegion circle (0,0,1)
                redCircle  = colourRegion circle (1,0,0)
               blueCircle' = translate (-100, 0) blueCircle
               redCircle'  = translate (100, 0)  redCircle
            in  blueCircle' `over` redCircle'
```

In a nutshell, the `let` expression defines a scope that includes the expression specified in the `in` part. Obviously, `circles` holds an expression that is equal to what the `let` expression has computed.

   An interesting question is this: Can we implement a Pan-like system in Scala? Clearly, we can implement it as an *external* DSL using the library described in Chapter 4. However, it would be quite interesting to see whether one could implement it as an *internal* DSL based on the fact that the language can grow itself. Not so surprisingly, one can define such an internal DSL and the following code snippet

Figure 6.41 Output generated by an internal Scala DSL.

shows how we could use it:

```
val blueCircle = new colorRegion circle (0,0,1)
val redCircle  = new colorRegion circle (1,0,0)
blueCircle translate(-100, 0)
redCircle translate (100, 0)
blueCircle over redCircle
blueCircle.show
```

```
import java.awt.image.BufferedImage
import javax.imageio.ImageIO
import java.awt._
class colorRegion {
  private val imgtype = BufferedImage.TYPE_INT_ARGB
  var img = new BufferedImage(500, 500, imgtype)
  var g2 = img.createGraphics()
  private var ac = AlphaComposite.getInstance(
                       AlphaComposite.SRC_OVER, 0.5f)
  g2.setComposite(ac)
  private var transform = new java.awt.geom.AffineTransform
  def circle(c1 : Float, c2 : Float, c3 : Float) = {
    g2.setColor(new Color(c1,c2,c3))
    g2.fillOval(150, 150, 200, 200)
    this
  }
  def square(c1 : Float, c2 : Float, c3 : Float) {
    g2.setColor(new Color(c1,c2,c3))
    g2.fillRect(50, 50, 200, 200)
    this
  }
  def translate(c1 : Float, c2 : Float) {
    transform.setToTranslation(c1, c2)
    g2.setTransform(transform)
    this
  }
  def over(y: colorRegion) {
    g2.drawImage(y.img, 0, 0, null)
    this
  }
  def show {
    g2.dispose()
    ImageIO.write(img, "png", new java.io.File("funcG.png"))
  }
}
```

Figure 6.42 A class that implements a very simple GUI domain-specific language.

Figure 6.42 shows the definition of a class that provides the required functionality in order to make the code just presented meaningful. Class `java.awt.Alpha Composite` is used in order to make transparent the graphics generated by `Graphics2D`.

Exercise 6.22 Make the code of Figure 6.42 more functional by allowing expressions of the form

```
val blueCircle = blueCircle translate(-100, 0)
```

7
Concurrent programming

Today's computers have *multi-core* processors (i.e., integrated circuits to which two or more processors have been attached), which, in principle, allow the concurrent execution of computer instructions. In other words, today's computers are able to perform two or more tasks at the same time. Concurrent programming refers to the design and implementation of programs that consist of interacting computational processes that should be executed in parallel. In addition, concurrent programming is not only the next logical step in software development, but the next necessary step. Thus, all modern programming languages must provide constructs and libraries that will ease the construction of concurrent programs. Scala allows users to design and implement concurrent programs using either threads, or mailboxes or actors. Unfortunately, programming with threads is a cumbersome task, thus, concurrent applications in Scala are usually implemented using the actor model of programming.

7.1 Programming with threads: an overview

Roughly, a process is a program loaded into memory that is being executed. A *thread*, also known as a *lightweight process*, is a basic unit of processor utilization. Processes may include more than one thread while traditional processes include only one thread. Threads may effectively communicate but since they share a process's resources (for example, memory and open files), their communication is not without problems. Each Scala program has at least one thread while several other "system" threads take care of events in GUI applications, input and output, etc. The *main thread* of every application can be used to create additional threads as we will see below.

Threads can be constructed by creating instances of a class that either extends class Thread or mixes in with trait Runnable. Both belong to package java.lang. Class Thread defines method run which, in the most general case, does nothing

```scala
class PrintProgressMark(val mark: Char,
                             val delay: Int) extends Thread {
  private var mark_  = mark
  private var delay_ = delay
  private var i      = 0
  private val max    = 100
  override def run(): Unit =
    try {
      while (i <= max) {
        print(mark_)
        i += 1
        Thread.sleep(delay_)
      }
    } catch {
        case ex : InterruptedException => return
    }
}

object threadExample {
  def main(args: Array[String]) {
    new PrintProgressMark('+', 40).start
    new PrintProgressMark('*', 100).start
  }
}
```

Figure 7.1 Creating a threaded application by extending class Thread.

and exits immediately. Figure 7.1 shows how one can construct a threaded class by extending class Thread. This is a two-threaded program that prints at different rates one hundred times the symbols "+" and "*" and which is based on a Java program presented in [6].

Each thread is created by constructing an object of Thread or, in this case, an object of a class that subclasses Thread. Method start should be called when a thread is ready to run. In our case, the Thread objects are immediately ready to run. Method sleep suspends execution of a thread for a specific amount of time. The time is expressed in either milliseconds or milliseconds plus nanoseconds. In other words, this method takes either one or two arguments. In the first case, the argument is a time interval expressed in milliseconds while in the second case it is a time interval expressed in nanoseconds (milliseconds plus nanoseconds). Method sleep may throw an InterruptedException exception and this is the reason we have to use a try command. When this program runs, its output will look as follows:

++++++*++*++*++*++*++*++*++*++*++*++*++*++*+...

Note that where there is one "*" it is followed by either two or three "+" symbols.

```
class PrintProgressMark(val mark: Char,
                        val delay: Int) extends Runnable {
  private var mark_  = mark
  private var delay_ = delay
  private var i      = 0
  private val max    = 100
  override def run(): Unit =
    try {
      while (i <= max) {
        print(mark_)
        i += 1
        Thread.sleep(delay_)
      }
    } catch {
        case ex : InterruptedException => return
    }
}

object threadExample2 {
  def main(args: Array[String]) {
    var plus     = new PrintProgressMark('+', 40)
    var asterisk = new PrintProgressMark('*', 100)
    new Thread(plus).start
    new Thread(asterisk).start
  }
}
```

Figure 7.2 Creating a threaded application by using trait `Runnable`.

Exercise 7.1 Modify the code and make the first thread wait for 33 milliseconds and then compile and run the resulting code. What do you observe?

The code in Figure 7.2 shows how to convert the code shown in Figure 7.1 into an equivalent that uses trait `Runnable` instead. As is evident, the body of the class is not modified, but now we have to start each thread using a different sequence of commands. In particular, we first create two instances of class `PrintProgress-Mark` and then we allocate new `Thread` objects. In general, the expression

```
new Thread(Runnable target)
```

creates a new thread from an instance of a class that mixes in with trait `Runnable`. Also, it is possible to name a thread by supplying a string variable as the second argument of this class constructor.

In both examples presented so far the two threads do not interact. In fact, even if we add one or two or even more threads, nothing will change the essence of our application. However, things will get really interesting if two or more threads have

```
class cell (protected var contents : Int){
    private var ReadyToRead = true
    private var ReadyToWrite = false
                    var lock = new AnyRef
    def get() : Int =
      lock.synchronized {
          while ( !ReadyToRead ) lock.wait
          ReadyToRead  = false
          ReadyToWrite = true
          lock.notifyAll
          contents
      }
    def set(n: Int) : Unit =
      lock.synchronized {
          while ( !ReadyToWrite ) lock.wait
          ReadyToWrite = false
          ReadyToRead = true
          contents = n
          lock.notifyAll
      }
}
```

Figure 7.3 A "synchronized" version of a storage-cell.

to share some resources. For example, how should we handle two or more threads that share memory cells? In other words, how can we ensure that memory cells are not accessed simultaneously, to prevent data corruption? This and other similar problems have made the need for *synchronization* vital.

In order to show how synchronization works, we will present a relatively simple example – two threads that continuously update a memory cell like the one presented in Section 2.3.[1] In particular, assume that we define two threads where the first halves the contents of a cell while the second doubles the contents of the same cell. Then the question is how can we prevent the two threads from modifying the cell's value at the same time? The answer is shown in Figure 7.3.

In order to explain how these methods work, we need to say a few things about synchronization in general. First of all, each method must acquire a *lock* on the object in order to ensure that its contents are accessed by one thread at a time. Class AnyRef defines method synchronized, which should be used to acquire a lock on the object. This can be done by replacing the code of a method with a call to

---

[1] A similar example was presented by Ted Neward in his article entitled "Explore Scala concurrency," which is part of his "Busy Java developer's guide to Scala" series of articles. These articles are included in the technical library section of Java technology's part of IBM's developerWorks web pages. In fact, this and its companion article entitled "Dive deeper into Scala concurrency" are excellent additional reading.

this method that will take as argument the code of the original method. In the code shown in Figure 7.3 we did exactly this. A method may take as argument a *block expression*, that is, a sequence of commands and a final expression surrounded by curly brackets. Thus, the following is a valid Scala code snippet:

```
def A(x: Int) = 4*x
var y = A{println("Hello!"); 4}
```

When a lock is acquired on an object, this has to be temporary in order to allow other threads to acquire a lock. In other words, the execution of two synchronized threads must be *mutually exclusive*. Each thread owns its own locks and so it is not possible to have nested locks, that is, a synchronized method that is called from another synchronized method cannot block execution.

Although locking prevents threads from interfering with each other, still we need to have a procedure to communicate between threads. In the example of Figure 7.3 we have used a standard pattern that uses methods `wait` and `notifyAll` (or just `notify`). The first method may take as argument either a long integer or a long integer and a simple integer, or it may take no arguments. In all cases this method causes the current thread to wait until another thread invokes either method `notify` or method `notifyAll` for this object, or if it is specified with arguments, to wait until a specified amount of time has elapsed. The amount of time is expressed in either milliseconds or milliseconds plus nanoseconds. Methods `notify` and `notifyAll` wake up either a single thread or all the threads that are waiting on an object's *monitor*, correspondingly. Roughly, a monitor is an object's synchronization support mechanism. Naturally, there are many more details about monitors, but a full treatment of all these details is beyond the scope of this book. The interested reader should consult a more specialized book (for example, see [47]). But let us return to the description of the standard pattern.

A thread that is waiting should always execute a method that has to look like the following one:

```
def waitCondition() : α =
   lock.synchronized {
      while ( !condition ) lock.wait
      commands to be executed when condition is true
   }
```

The body of the method is synchronized in order to ensure, among other things, that once the **condition** becomes `true` it will remain so, at least until the method finishes. In addition, when the **condition** becomes `true`, the lock is automatically released. Finally, we are using a repetition construct because nothing guarantees that once a thread has been awakened the **condition** will become `true`.

Since our code handles both reading and writing requests, we need to notify waiting threads that our methods have completed their task when they have done so. The definition of the skeleton method that follows shows what should be done:

```
def changeCondition() : α =
    lock.synchronized {
        change values related to condition
        lock.notifyAll
    }
```

In code that involves many threads, one should use method notify only if one knows exactly what one is doing. In all other cases, it is advisable to use notify-All. In the code shown in Figure 7.3 we use two boolean variables that control the lock of each method. In this particular example, reading is the operation that is most readily available and this is the reason we have given to the two boolean variables the corresponding values. Now that we have defined our synchronized cell class, let us first define a class that reads the number stored in the cell and halves it:

```
class halveCell(c : cell) extends Runnable {
    override def run(): Unit = {
        var v = c.get //; println("H---> got "+v)
        for ( i <- 1 to 10) {
            c.set(v/2)   //; println("H---> send "+(v/2))
            v = c.get    //; println("H---> got "+v)
        }
        return
    }
}
```

By uncommenting the commented commands, the user can see the values received and dispatched by a thread that runs an instance of this class. The code that doubles the number stored in the cell follows:

```
class doubleCell(c : cell) extends Runnable {
    override def run(): Unit = {
        for ( i <- 1 to 10) {
            var v = c.get //; println("D---> got "+v)
            c.set(2*v)      //; println("D---> send "+(2*v))
        }
        return
    }
}
```

The careful reader may have noticed that any object of class halveCell will perform eleven read operations and ten writing operations while any object of class dou-bleCell will perform ten reading and ten writing operations in this order. This is necessary in order to avoid a situation that is known as a *deadlock*. In simple terms, a deadlock is a situation where there are two threads and each one waits for the other to complete in order to get a lock. Since neither thread can get a lock, neither one will be able to run. The following code completes our example and shows how the classes just presented can be used:

```
object threadExample3 {
  def main(args: Array[String]) {
    var c = new cell(16)
    new Thread(new doubleCell(c)).start()
    new Thread(new halveCell(c)).start()
  }
}NotEmpty
```

Exercise 7.2 Verify that by changing the body of method run of class halveCell as follows

```
      var v = c.get //; println("H---> got "+v)
      c.set(v/2)    //; println("H---> send "+(v/2))
```

the resulting program will fail to terminate.

Threads have been used extensively in applets that draw images or include animations. So the next step is to present such a usage example.

7.2 Animation with threads

The term *animation* refers to the rapid display of a sequence of images to create an illusion of movement. For instance, a full-blown feature-length movie and a simple animated GIF graphics file are examples of animation. Fortunately, with Scala we can do things that are better than a simple animated GIF but, on the other hand, it is not practical to try to produce a movie with Scala. In practical terms, Scala can be used to produce animations that are portable (for example, web-based applets or stand-alone programs). In this section we describe some thread-based animation techniques and apply them to create Scala applets only. Readers can use the same animation techniques to create stand-alone Scala programs.

Animation in Scala should always occur in a separate thread of execution. This way, users can interact with the animation program without perceptibly degrading performance. In practice, all we have to do is to mix in a module that extends abstract class `Applet.UI` with trait `Runnable` in addition to trait `Reactor` (the latter should be mixed in only if the applet is interactive). Then we define a thread variable that is started by method `start` and stopped by method `stop`. Method `init` is used to set up the graphical context. In order to demonstrate the animation techniques, we will show how to design an applet that will show a black line on which a yellow ball moves continuously from one edge of the line to the other.

Figure 7.4 shows the skeleton of an applet that implements the required functionality. The first four variables correspond to the coordinates of the starting

```scala
class Pulse extends Applet {
  object ui extends UI  with Runnable {
    var dotAx           = 15  //start X coordinate
    var dotAy           = 15  //start Y coordinate
    var dotBx           = 400 //end X coordinate
    var dotBy           = 15  //end Y coordinate
    var T : Thread      = null
    var currentX        = 0   //current X coordinate
    var currentY        = 15 //fixed Y coordinate
    var canvas : Panel  = null
    var dir             = 1 //LTR (1) and RTL (-1) direction
    var interval        = 5 //number of points to jump
    var lock            = new AnyRef

    override def init() = {
      canvas = new Panel {
        preferredSize = (dotAx + 30, dotBx + 30)
        opaque        = false
        override def paintComponent(g: java.awt.Graphics) {
          . . . . . . . . . . . . . . . . . . . . . . . . . .
        }
      }
      contents = canvas
    }

    override def start() = {
      . . . . . . . . . . . . . . .
    }

    override def stop() = {
      . . . . . . . . . . .
    }

    override def run(): Unit = {
      . . . . . . . . . . . . . .
    }
  }
}
```

Figure 7.4 Skeleton of a simple animation applet.

and ending points, respectively. There is also a variable that holds the current *x*-coordinate of the yellow bullet. The code that follows is the body of method `paintComponent`:

```
g.setColor(java.awt.Color.black)
g.drawLine(dotAx,dotAy,dotBx,dotBy)
g.setColor(java.awt.Color.yellow)
g.fillOval(currentX,currentY-7,15,15)
```

As should be obvious, the method draws a black line and then a yellow bullet. In other words, the line is drawn every time the bullet changes position. Figure 7.5 shows the definitions of methods `start` and `stop`. Method `run`, which is shown in Figure 7.6, is actually the one that controls the animation.

Method `run` checks whether the thread is alive and if it is, it paints the bullet and then computes the next position of the bullet. By increasing or decreasing the time the thread sleeps, the animation becomes slower or faster, respectively.

```
override def start: Unit =          override def stop: Unit =
  if (T == null) {                    if (T != null)
    T = new Thread(this)                T = null
    T.start
  }
```

Figure 7.5 Methods `start` and `stop` of the applet shown in Figure 7.4.

```
override def run(): Unit = {
  while ( T != null ) {
    canvas.repaint
    if (currentX == 0)
      dir = 1
    else if (currentX == dotBx)
      dir = -1
    currentX += dir * interval
    try {
      Thread.sleep(50)
    } catch {
        case ex : InterruptedException => return
    }
  }
}
```

Figure 7.6 Method `run` of the applet shown in Figure 7.4.

An annoying side effect in animations of the kind presented here is screen flicker. This phenomenon is more common on cathode ray tube (CRT) based computer screens while it is not completely alien on liquid crystal displays (LCD). Nevertheless, presenting a solution to this "problem" has as a side effect the demonstration of the generation of off-screen drawings. The reason is that screen flicker happens when cleaning the drawing area just before any new drawing operations are performed. Thus, to avoid this we create the image off-screen and when it is finished we replace the existing image with the new one.

To create an off-screen image one needs to invoke the drawing component's create-Image method. This method takes as arguments two integers. These numbers correspond to the width and the height of the drawing area. The method returns an instance of java.awt.Image. One can invoke this object's getGraphics method to get the image's graphics context.

If we want to modify the code of the previous applet to draw using off-screen graphics, we first need to declare some additional variables:

```
var offscreenImage : java.awt.Image    = null
var offscreenGraph : java.awt.Graphics = null
var appletDim : java.awt.Dimension     = null
var appletInsets : java.awt.Insets     = null
```

Method paintComponent should be modified as follows:

```
override def paintComponent(g: java.awt.Graphics) {
  offscreenGraph.setColor(getBackground())
  offscreenGraph.fillRect(0,0,appletDim.width,
                              appletDim.height)
  offscreenGraph.setColor(java.awt.Color.black)
  offscreenGraph.drawLine(dotAx,dotAy,dotBx,dotBy)
  offscreenGraph.setColor(java.awt.Color.yellow)
  offscreenGraph.fillOval(currentX,currentY-7,15,15)
  g.drawImage(offscreenImage,0,0,null)
  lock.synchronized {
     lock.notifyAll
  }
}
```

The last expression is necessary to inform all threads that all graphics operations have been completed. In addition, this expression overrides all relevant notifications that are automatically "broadcasted" by all relevant components. The code of method init concludes now with the following commands:

```
contents      = canvas
appletDim     = getSize()
appletInsets  = getInsets()
offscreenImage = createImage(appletDim.width,
                                appletDim.height)
offscreenGraph = offscreenImage.getGraphics()
```

The last difference between the code of this applet and that of the old one is in method run:

```
try {
  lock.wait
  Thread.sleep(10)
} catch {
  case ex : InterruptedException => return
}
```

As is evident, the only difference is that the method waits until the off-screen drawing is ready.

Exercise 7.3 Rewrite both applets as stand-alone applications.

7.3 Using mailboxes

Package `scala.concurrent` provides an abstraction layer over the "traditional" concurrency constructs that have been described so far. Needless to say, these "traditional" concurrency constructs are Java's legacy to Scala programmers!

A mailbox is a convenient mechanism that allows values to be passed from one object to another. Essentially, it is a mechanism that follows the spirit of object-orientation (i.e., the passing of messages between objects). A typical example of this value-passing procedure has been presented in Section 7.1. There we used locks to establish the synchronous passing of values from one object to another. In order to do the same thing with mailboxes, we need to define an instance of class `MailBox` which must be accompanied by two auxiliary classes. Class `MailBox` defines three methods – `receive`, `receiveWithin`, and `send`. The first method takes as argument a partial function which is used to evaluate any message that is delivered to the mailbox. However, the effect of the method is to wait until a message is delivered. Since one cannot always be sure whether a message will be actually delivered, method `receiveWithin` has been designed as the equivalent of `receive` that waits for a certain amount of time and not for ever. This method takes two arguments: an integer, which denotes the amount of time it has to wait, and a message handler, which again is a partial function. Roughly, method send places the message to be sent in a mailqueue if the receiver is not available; otherwise, the message is delivered to a mailbox.

The auxiliary classes play two different roles – one denotes that the mailbox is empty and the other denotes that the mailbox is not empty. Typically, these two cases can be covered by definitions like those that follow:

```
case class Empty()
case class Nonempty(v: value)
```

Figure 7.7 shows how one could rewrite class cell using mailboxes. Initially, we need to drop to the mailbox the value by which the class will be instantiated. When method get receives a Nonempty message, then it replaces the message with an Empty message and returns the value received. This means that there are two kinds of messages that correspond to the states of a mailbox (i.e., being empty or nonempty). Similarly, when the mailbox receives the empty message (i.e., when it is empty), a full message should be dropped to the mailbox. This is exactly what method set describes and the content of the message is the only argument of the method. If we replace class cell of Section 7.1 with the one presented here, then

```
import concurrent.MailBox

class cell(protected var contents : Int){
   private val mbox = new MailBox

   private case class Empty()
   private case class Nonempty(n : Int)

   mbox send Full(contents)//initialize

   def get():Int=
     mbox receive{
        case Nonempty(n)=>
          mboxsendEmpty()
          n
   }
   def set(n: Int): Unit=
     mbox receive{
        case Empty()=>
             mbox send Nonempty(n)
   }
}
```

Figure 7.7 Class cell rewritten in a message passing style.

the rest of the code will behave exactly the same way. However, it makes no sense to use threads directly in some parts of the code and to hide their usage in others. Thus, we will replace all direct uses of threads with other higher level constructs. Module concurrent.ops defines method spawn which is defined as follows:

```
def spawn(p: => Unit) = {
    val t = new Thread() { override def run() = p }
    t.start()
}
```

This means that one can delete the definition of classes doubleCell and halveCell and replace them with calls to method spawn with arguments the body of each class. In particular, class doubleCell can be replaced by the following method invocation:

```
import concurrent.ops._
spawn {
    for ( i <- 1 to 10) {
        var v = c.get //; println("D---> got "+v)
        c.set(2*v)    //; println("D---> send "+(2*v))
    }
}
```

Exercise 7.4 Complete the transformation of our simple application by replacing the definition of class halveCell with an invocation of method spawn. Uncomment the output commands and verify that the output generated by the initial application is comparable with the output generated by the application described in this section.

Neward in "Explore Scala concurrency" notes that "[o]ne drawback to the ops.spawn method is the basic fact that it was written in 2003 before the Java 5 concurrency classes had taken effect." Thus, it does not utilize new facilities introduced in Java in the meantime. As Neward suggests, it would not be difficult to rewrite this method using the new java.util.concurrent.Executor trait.

Programming project 7.1 Try to reimplement spawn using the Executor trait.

7.4 Actors: basic ideas

The actor model of concurrent computation has its roots in ideas that have been put forth by Carl Hewitt, Peter Bishop, and Richard Steiger [33]. Important milestones in the development of the theory include the work done by William Douglas

Clinger [14] and by Gul Agha [3]. Agha notes that "[a]n early precursor to the development of actors is the concept of objects in SIMULA" [3, p. 9] which means that actors are the most natural choice for coding concurrent applications with an object-oriented programming language. Thus, the inclusion of actors into the Scala programming language was a wise decision.

Actors are intercommunicating computational agents that operate concurrently. Each actor has a unique mail address and a sufficiently large mailbox, where messages appear in order of arrival. In addition, each actor is characterized by its behavior, which is a function of actions to be taken for incoming communication. In the simplest case, we can construct an actor by calling method `actor` of package `scala.actor`. In fact, we have used this procedure to construct an actor in Section 6.9. What we did not say there is that as soon as an actor is constructed, it starts operating as if a new thread has been started. As a first example, Figure 7.8 shows how one could rewrite the example shown in Figure 7.1 using actors only. Note that the number literal "2" is there since othewise Scala will complain that

```
import scala.actors.Actor._
object actorsExample {
  def main(args: Array[String]) {
    var max = 100
    var PrintProgressPlus = actor {
      var mark = '+'
      var i = 0
      while (i <= max) {
        print(mark)
        i += 1
        Thread.sleep(40)
      }
    }
    var PrintProgressTimes = actor {
      var mark = '*'
      var i = 0
      while (i <= max) {
        print(mark)
        i += 1
        Thread.sleep(100)
      }
    }
    2
  }
}
```

Figure 7.8 The example in Figure 7.1 rewriten in an actor style.

block must end in result expression, not in definition. Remember that the curly brackets delimit a block expression that must end with something that is not a definition or a declaration. Alternatively, we can define a class that subclasses trait `Actor`:

```scala
import scala.actors._
class PrintProgressMark(val mark: Char,
                        val delay :Int) extends Actor {
  private var mark_ = mark
  private var delay_ = delay
  private var i = 0
  private val max = 100
  def act: Unit = {
    while (i <= max) {
      print(mark_)
      i += 1
      Thread.sleep(delay_)
    }
  }
}
```

Method `act` of trait `Actor` is defined as abstract and this is why every class that subclasses class `Actor` must implement it. Method `start` can be used to start an actor. Thus, the following code shows how to create and a start an instance of class `PrintProgressMark`:

```scala
new PrintProgressMark('+', 40).start
```

Let us now show how to "translate" the thread-based animation applet, which was presented in Section 7.2, into an actor-based animation applet. First of all, object `ui` must not subclass trait `Runnable`. Next we need to define a "global" variable that will play the role of the animation thread:

```scala
var T : Actor = null
```

The last thing we need to do is to redefine method `start` as follows:

```scala
override def start() =
  if (T == null)
    T = Actor.actor {
      while ( T != null ) {
        if (currentX == 0)
          dir = 1
        else if (currentX == dotBx)
```

```
        dir = -1
        canvas.repaint
        currentX += dir * interval
        Thread.sleep(20)
      }
    }
```

In other words, the code of method `run` becomes the argument of method `Actor.actor`. Method `stop` stays as is!

The simple examples shown so far did not demonstrate the real capabilities of actors. Nevertheless, we have included them to show how one can construct and start actors. In the rest of this chapter we are going to discuss the real capabilities of actors.

7.5　Message passing with actors

The standard example of an interactive actor is the one where an actor receives messages (usually strings) and just prints them. The following interaction with Scala's interpreter shows how one can define and use such an actor:

```
scala> import scala.actors.Actor._
import scala.actors.Actor._

scala> val lousyActor = actor {
     |    receive {
     |        case msg => println("I got \""+msg+"\"")
     |    }
     | }
lousyActor: scala.actors.Actor = scala.actors.Actor$$
anon$1@107dcb

scala> lousyActor ! "Are you sure?"
I got "Are you sure?"
```

Method `receive`, which is the most typical message handler, takes as argument a partial function. This function takes arguments of any type. Method `!` sends asynchronously a message to the calling actor.

Assume that we want to create another actor that can handle many and different types of objects. For example, function `isNum` (see page 106) could be used as a basis for the construction of such an actor. Let us try to code this actor:

```
val lousyActor = actor {
  receive {
    case i : Int    => println("got the Int "+i)
    case l : Long   => println("got the Long "+l)
    case f : Float  => println("got the Float "+f)
    case d : Double => println("got the Double "+d)
    case x          => println("can't handle \""+x+"\"")
  }
}
```

If we try the following commands

```
lousyActor ! 3
lousyActor ! 4L
lousyActor ! 3.2
lousyActor ! 4.8D
lousyActor ! "help me!"
lousyActor ! 6
```

then our application will print *got the Int 3* and it will terminate! The reason for this behavior is that the actor has been programmed to receive one message and then to exit. Thus, we need to reprogram it so that it can receive and process messages repeatedly. In particular, we can use method loop that takes as argument the body of an actor and puts it in an infinite loop. Let us see how we can reprogram our actor:

```
val lousyActor = actor {
  loop {
    . . . same as above . . .
  }
}
```

If we try the previous commands, we will get all the expected responses, but the program will not terminate since it waits for ever. Thus, we need to decide when the actor will stop. In our case we can stop whenever a nonnumber is sent. This can be easily implemented by defining a boolean variable to control the loop:

```
var done = false
val lousyActor = actor {
  loopWhile (! done) {
    receive {
      . . . same as above . . .
      case x          => println("can't handle \""+x+"\"")
```

```
                              println("Aborting...")
                              done = true

                   }
             }
       }
```

Here we have used method `loopWhile` which takes as arguments a boolean expression and a series of commands. As expected, this method executes the commands as long as the boolean expression is true. By running the new code one observes that this new version of the actor will ignore completely the expression `lousyActor !` 6. Unfortunately, this is the price we have to pay for fixing the previous problem. On the other hand, we can inform the actor that a particular message is the last one so after processing it, the actor must terminate. Since we want essentially to send the same messages, all we have to do is to send instances of a more complex message that will include the messages as before and a termination reminder. In other words, we will send "structured" messages as shown below:

```
lousyActor ! new Tuple2[Any,Boolean](4L, false)
```

The following code shows how we should rewrite the actor in order to be able to handle these new kinds of messages:

```
val lousyActor = actor {
  var done = false
  loopWhile (! done) {
    receive {
      case (i : Int, b : Boolean)     =>
        println("got the Int "+i)
        done = b

      . . . . . . . . . . . . . . . .

      case (x, b : Boolean)           =>
        println("don't know what to do with \""+x+"\"")
        done = b
    }
  }
}
```

When this program is executed it will handle all cases and only then will it stop.

Method `!` is not the only one that can be used to send messages. Method `!!` sends a message and immediately returns an instance of classs `Future`, which represents the value of a reply. A `Future[α]` is an abstract class that has three abstract methods: `isSet`, `apply`, and `respond` which are inherited from class

Responder. In addition, method ! ! may get as argument a message plus a partial function which, in conjunction with the Future returned, can be used to post-process what the actor returns. In order to make clear what we mean, consider the following redefinition of our lousy actor:

```
var done = false
val lousyActor = actor {
  loopWhile( ! done ) {
    react {
      case i : Int     =>
        println("got the Int "+i)
        reply(0)

      . . . . . . . . . . . . . . .

      case None => println("I must quit!")
        done = true
      case x           =>
        println("don't know what to do with \""+x+"\"")
        reply(1)
    }
  }
}
```

Also, consider the following partial function definition:

```
val R : PartialFunction[Any,Unit] = {
  case 0 => println("proceeding")
  case 1 => lousyActor ! None
}
```

The commands that follow

```
var x = lousyActor !! (3, R)
x.apply
x = lousyActor !! (4L, R)
x.apply
x= lousyActor !! (3.2F, R)
x.apply
x = lousyActor !! (4.8D, R)
x.apply
x = lousyActor !! ("help me!!", R)
x.apply
lousyActor ! 6
```

will produce the following output:

```
got the Int 3
proceeding
got the Long 4
proceeding
got the Float 3.2
proceeding
got the Double 4.8
proceeding
don't know what to do with "help me!!"
I must quit!
```

Of course our example is totally useless, but it shows what is involved. Method `reply` is used to send back a message from an actor to its sender. Also, method `react` is a cheaper version of `receive`. In fact, `react` evaluates the message handler and only then it returns. If everything an actor is doing is included in the body of the message handler, it is better to use `react` instead of `receive` since the former consumes far less resources.

The real use of futures is in what is called *fork/join parallelism*. This is a parallel programming technique in which, as Douglas Lea notes, "problems are solved by (recursively) splitting them into subtasks that are solved in parallel, waiting for them to complete, and then composing results" [46]. The most typical application of fork/join parallelism is a parallel version of the merge sort algorithm. However, in order to keep things simple we will describe a simpler example. Assume that we want to compute the sum of the hundredth power of the numbers from 2 to 10. In order to compute the hundredth power of an integer we will use the following (simple) function:

```
def power(i : Int) : BigInt = {
  var p : BigInt = 1
  for ( i <- 1 to 100) p*= i
  return p
}
```

If we want to solve our problem in parallel, we need to find a way to compute powers in parallel. For this purpose we create a list that will include all these subproblems, then it will fire up all of them making them operate concurrently, and in the end it will sum up the results. How can we implement this idea? Easy! The following code snippet shows how:

```
val futures = for(i <- (2 to 10).toList)
                 yield future { power(i) }
val sum = (for (f <- futures) yield f()).reduceRight(_+_)
```

Roughly, method `future`, which is defined in module `Futures`, takes as argument a block expression that computes an expression of type $\hat{I}\pm$ and once it has been computed by some actor it is returned as a `Future`. Also, method `reduceRight` can be used by a list to compute the expression $a_0 \oplus (\ldots \oplus (a_{n-1} \oplus a_n) \ldots)$, where $\oplus$ is its only argument and a_i the elements of a list. Similarly, method `reduceLeft` computes the expression $(\ldots (a0 \oplus a1) \oplus \ldots) \oplus a_n$.

Exercise 7.5 André Barbé [7] has described the notion of fractal matrices, that is, matrices that are defined recursively from

$$E_{m+1} = E_1 \oplus E_m,$$

where E_1 is an $r \times s$ matrix of integers $e_1(i,j)$, $\le i \le r$, $0 \le j \le s$ and $A \oplus B$ is the bigsum operation between two matrices, that is, it is the matrix obtained by replacing each elelement $a(i,j)$ of A by matrix B while adding $a(i,j)$ to all elements of B. Define a function that given some matrix E_1 uses futures to compute E_n for some $n \ge 1$.

One may wonder what is the speed that is gained by this technique. We have "benchmarked" our program by modifying the code snippet presented above as follows:

```
val t = nanoTime
val sum = (for (f <- futures) yield f()).reduceRight(_+_)
println((nanoTime - t)* 1.0E-9)
```

We have found that on a dual core system the future-enabled version completes in 0.02014393 seconds, while the nonparallel version completes in 0.046899953 seconds. In other words, the parallel version is 2.33 times faster. Method `nanoTime` measures time elapsed since the program has started.

Method `!?` is another method that can be used to send messages to actors. This method sends messages and awaits a reply. Also, method `?` can be used to get the next message from an actor's mailbox. If for some reason we want to refer to an actor inside its definition, we should use method `self` which returns the currently executing actor.

7.6 Computing factorials with actors

Hewitt [32] has presented a noniterative implementation of factorial in his *PLASMA* notation, where PLASMA stands for *PLAnner-like System Modeled on Actors*. One of the implementations uses message passing and recursion. However, one can achieve the same effect using actor *replication* (i.e., by creating new instances of an actor that solve particular subproblems) and message passing. More specifically, an actor

```
import scala.actors.Actor
import scala.actors.Actor._

case class Val(a: Actor, n: Int)
case class Res(n: Int)
class Fact extends Actor {
   def act =
     react {
       case Val(a,0) => a ! Res(1)
       case Val(a,n) =>
          var p = new Fact
          p.start
          p ! Val(self,n-1)
          react { case Val(_, m) => a ! Val(a, n*m)
                  case Res(m)    => a ! Val(a, n*m) }
     }
}
```

Figure 7.9 A self-replicating actor that computes the factorial.

creates a copy of itself, sends a message to this subactor asking for the solution of
a subproblem of the whole problem, and when it receives the response from the
subactor, it composes the solution. Let us now see how this methodology would
work in the case where we want to compute the factorial of some number n. Initially,
an actor, say A_1, is created and the number n is passed to it. Actor A_1 receives the
message and creates a new actor, say A_2. A_1 sends to A_2 the number $n - 1$ as well as
its mail-address. When A_2 finishes, it sends back a number m which is multiplied
by n and A_1 sends it back to its creator. Clearly, in order to compute its result A_2
must create a copy of itself (i.e., a copy of A_1), etc. Let us now see how this idea is
implemented in Scala. Figure 7.9 shows the definition of a class that can be used
to compute the factorial of some number. Let us explain a few things regarding
this definition. First of all, there are two **react** blocks. The first one processes the
message received by the actor just after it has been created and the second receives
the message the newly created actor sends before it terminates. Also, the actors do
not receive and send plain numbers but instances of case classes. Class **Val** holds
an actor, which is used to send back a reply, and a number, which is the number
that is communicated between various instances of class **Fact**. The only exception
occurs when an instance of class **Fact** is asked to compute the factorial of zero. In
this case, it returns an instance of **Res**. This was necessary to prevent the actor from
looping for ever.

In order to use this class we need to define an actor that will create the first
instance of class **Fact**. The definition of such an actor follows:

```
var factorial = actor {
  react {
    case Val(a,n) =>
      var q = new Fact
      q.start
      q ! Val(self,n)
      react { case Val(_,f) => a ! Val(a,f) }
  }
}
```

Now we can use this actor to compute the factorial of some number:

```
factorial ! Val(self,6)
react { case Val(_, n) => println(n) }
```

The output of these commands will be the number 720, that is, the factorial of 6.

Exercise 7.6 Use this technique to implement a message-passing "algorithm" that computes the Fibonacci numbers.

So far it has been demonstrated how to use actor replication to compute the factorial of some number. Clearly, the next logical question would be whether it is possible to use only message passing to compute the same value. Not surprisingly, Hewitt [32] has shown that this is possible. Indeed, Figure 7.10 shows the definition of an actor that can compute the factorial of any number. The actor uses an accumulator to keep the result computed so far while it reduces a counter each

```
val loopActor = actor {
  var ResActor : Actor = null
  loop{
    react {
      case Val(_, acc, 1)     =>
        ResActor ! acc
        exit("done")
      case Val(a, 1, count)   =>
        ResActor = a
        self ! Val(self, count, count-1)
      case Val(a, acc, count) =>
        self ! Val(self, acc*count, count-1)
    }
  }
}
```

Figure 7.10 A purely iterative actor that computes the factorial of some number.

time the accumulator is multiplied. The first time the actor is used, we store the return address to a local variable which is used to deliver the result at the end of the computation. This actor sends messages that are instances of the following case class:

```
case class Val(a: Actor, n: Int, m: Int)
```

The following actor is something like a front-end to the actor shown in Figure 7.10:

```
var factorial = actor {
  react {
    case InitVal(a,0) => a ! InitVal(a, 1)
    case InitVal(a,1) => a ! InitVal(a, 1)
    case InitVal(a,n) =>
      loopActor ! Val(self,1,n)
      react { case f: Int => a ! InitVal(a,f) }
  }
}
```

This actor uses instances of the following case class:

```
case class InitVal(a: Actor, n: Int)
```

Again actor `factorial` can be used as in the previous example.

Exercise 7.7 Modify the actors presented to compute the Fibonacci numbers.

8

On paths and a bit of algebraic abstraction

It is quite probable that most of us are not *consciously* aware of an ever-appearing design pattern, which goes far beyond the design patterns in the normal sense of [24]. This pattern has to do with how we organize our data and, sometimes as a consequence, how we access these data. What we are talking about is the *hierarchical data organization* pattern that we can abbreviate in short as: *Hierarchies are everywhere*!

A file system is the canonical example of hierarchical organization. Its structure is a collection of files and directories, with the directories playing the role of containers for other files and/or directories. The Unix tradition has more to say about files, since the file system "pattern" has been extended to support other use cases than the traditional ones. For example, in Linux, /proc is a special mounted file system which can be used to view some kernel configuration and parameters. In fact, normal file system I/O calls can be used to write data into this special file system, so that kernel and driver parameters can be changed at runtime.

XML advocates will feel pleased to recognize that XML has been promoting such hierarchical organization. We are not sure how many of them were aware of the real essence of the general "Hierarchies are everywhere" pattern mentioned above, but the pattern itself is ubiquitous. Strangely enough, hierarchical databases have not survived, but probably XML strikes back on their behalf.

Windows users will be happy to recognize that their sacred Windows Registry falls into the described pattern category. They will be made more happy to recollect that the Registry existed even before XML. The Windows Registry can well be viewed as a special file system.

In modern enterprise Java-based applications, JNDI (Java Naming and Directory Interface) provides an excellent abstraction for hierarchical organization of data. With its support for multiple namespaces and pluggable namespace providers, its flexibility has a foundational value: so much so, that many enterprise developers often ignore its full potential.

The module and packaging systems of modern programming languages are another perfect example. For example, Java's hierarchical packages fit nicely into an underlying file system. In fact, when we see a Java package name, we instantaneously know where to look in the file system.

A parser generator, like the legendary yacc by Stephen Curtis Johnson, takes as input the description of a programming language in a notation similar to EBNF. A language grammar normally starts with a top-level nonterminal symbol and proceeds to depths of varying complexity. This is clearly a hierarchical organization, at the definition site of a language. At the processing site (at least for a compiler) or even at the execution site (i.e., for an interpreter), usually a program is represented by an Abstract Syntax Tree (AST).

The list of examples can continue almost indefinitely. So, hierarchies are everywhere and, as a consequence, file systems are everywhere. A fundamental notion in every hierarchical organization is that of a *path*. We use paths to designate where in the hierarchy something resides. Paths are naturally composed to create larger paths and can be deconstructed to simpler parts as well. In the following, we are inspired by the utility of paths in order to model them in Scala. In our discussion we use files to motivate things, since they are the foremost "client" of paths.

8.1 Path requirements

In a file system, paths designate where files reside. They are in effect the file location representations. Unfortunately, but not uncommonly, these representations vary across different implementations. The normal barrier between these implementations is the operating system. For example, while for a hierarchical representation there exists the common notion of a *root* point, the possible file system roots vary. The Unix tradition accepts a *slash* (/) as the only root of the file system, while in Windows we can have as many roots as the letters of the English alphabet, namely `A:\, B:\, C:\` and so on, not to mention the special *UNC*[1] paths that start with a double *backslash* (\\).

Also, another striking difference is the separation of a child-path from its parent. It is common knowledge and already evident from the above that / applies to Unix and \ applies to Windows. So a Unix path `/home/loverdos/Projects` may be something like `C:\home\loverdos\Projects` in Windows and, to make matters worse, a string representation of the latter should become "C:\\home\\loverdos\\Projects" because of the "escaping" character of the backslash, a tradition ranging back to at least C.

---

[1] UNC stands for *Universal Naming Convention*. Apart from Windows, the Samba software stack also uses it to represent network resource names.

Even before bothering with the previous incompatibilities, we should ask ourselves why model paths? After all, `java.io.File` handles all the underlying platform "difficulties" and can transform the paths correctly even if we are not in the "correct" platform. The following simple example, which was run under Windows in order to get the C drive as the file system root, reveals this fact:

```scala
scala> import java.io.File
scala> println(new File("/").getAbsolutePath)
C:\
```

The truth is that `File` models two concepts with just one implementation. The first one is the file path and the second is the file itself. We would like to separate the two concepts, so that they can be combined later only when necessary. We want to elevate the path to a first-class entity.

Working with relative paths can be tedious. There must already be a lot of source code lines that just concatenate strings to create relative paths:

```scala
System.getProperty("user.dir")
  + "/.m2/repository/"
  + GroupId.replace('.', '/') + "/"
  + ArtifactId + "/"
  + VersionId
```

The example above demonstrates some string concatenation to obtain the directory where the local copy of a *maven*-managed library resides (Apache Maven is a software project management and comprehension tool).

So how exactly do we expect to handle paths and what requirements do we wish to impose on a Path API? Which should be our guiding principles for the design? It seems logical to assume that paths should be

(i) typefull,
(ii) composable,
(iii) user-friendly,
(iv) platform independent,
(v) immutable.

By *typefull*, we mean that it is best to avoid using plain strings. Even if the low-level representation that either makes more sense or seems more obvious than the others is the `String`, do not expose strings at the user level directly. This has a couple of clear advantages.

(i) Method overloading works much better, since we do not have to count paths as strings and so the combinations of path and string parameters can be greater.

(ii) We hide the actual implementation behind a type, leveraging in this way the object-oriented encapsulation principle.

After all, paths have enough personality not to "condemn" them to strings!

Composable paths means that if we have two paths p_1 and p_2, we can form a third path $p_3 = p_1 \cdot p_2$. The composition operator $\cdot$ is nothing other than the ubiquitous slash / that combines path components in a traditional Unix shell. If we can write the slash operator directly in our code, then we can eliminate cumbersome string concatenation and this automatically gives us *user-friendly* paths.

Clearly, our code must be behaviorally equivalent, no matter what the underlying running environment is. Although running under the JVM certainly gives a sense of uniformity, the JVM itself has to communicate with the operating system at some point. There is the "opportunity" for an API to break and we actually need our path API to be *platform independent*.

Immutable objects have several advantages. In an epoch where the need for and fuss about concurrency constantly increases, designing with immutability in mind can be an asset for a software engineer. If your object has no complex business logic and simple state, consider adopting an immutable implementation. Paths seem to be very good candidates for this.

Also, in addition to the above, we would like the `String` representation of the paths to be normalized, especially when it comes to the appearance of (back)slashes. In particular, we will adopt the following requirements.

- Only the / character will be the separator of path elements.
- More than one consecutive occurrence of / will be collapsed to just one /.

The second requirement will be relaxed for the beginning of UNC paths and our convention is that in their normalized form they start with two slashes.

8.2 Path API

A first-cut, reasonable API for paths is given in Figure 8.1. A few of the provided methods are the following.

name This is, traditionally, the last part of the path. We just follow here the convention of the `java.io.File` API where the related method, following the JavaBeans convention, is `getName`.

fullName This is the `String` representation of the path and actually the value returned by the overridden `toString` method.

relative This method returns the relative part of a path, if it is an absolute one, or the path itself otherwise. For example, it should return home\loverdos\Projects for C:\home\loverdos\Projects and just home\Projects\Batchiera for home\Projects\Batchiera. Any root prefix is removed.

```
trait Path {
  def name: String
  def fullName: String
  def relative: Path

  def isEmpty: Boolean
  def isRoot: Boolean
  def isUNC: Boolean
  def isAbsolute: Boolean = !isRelative
  def isRelative: Boolean = !isAbsolute

  def /(that: String): Path
  def /(that: Path): Path

  def parent: Path

  def parts: List[String]

  def pathParts = parts.map(Path(_))

  override def toString = fullName

  override def hashCode = fullName.hashCode

  override def equals(any: Any) =
    any.isInstanceOf[Path] &&
      any.asInstanceOf[Path].fullName == this.fullName
}
```

Figure 8.1 A path API given as a `trait` with partial implementation.

isRoot This returns `true` if the path actually represents a file system root. For example, it must return `true` for / under Unix and for A:\, B:\, ..., Z:\ under Windows.
/ The two methods with this name are the means to compose paths.
parts This decomposes the path into a list of the path `String` elements.
pathParts As the implementation shows, this method takes the result of `parts` and transforms it into paths. The `Path(_)` factory call is made on the companion object, which we will start implementing shortly.

Notice also how we have implemented `isRelative` and `isAbsolute` by mutual recursion. A subclass of `Path` is expected to provide an alternative implementation for one of them, whichever is more suitable for the particular case.

8.3 Empty paths

Empty paths play a special role and are represented by `EmptyPath` in Figure 8.2. They arise when, for example, we ask for the parent of a root path. Our convention

```
object EmptyPath extends Path {
    def name = ""
    def fullName = ""
    def relative = this

    def isEmpty = true
    def isRoot = false
    def isUNC = false
    override def isAbsolute = false
    override def isRelative = false

    def parts = Nil
    def parent = this

    def /(that: String) = Path(that)
    def /(that: Path) = that
}
```

Figure 8.2 The implementation of `EmptyPath`.

is that the call of `parent` on the path representing `"/"` should return a special path
with an empty string as its name. Also, when composing any path with `EmptyPath`,
the latter is absorbed and the net result is the former. From Figure 8.2, there is one
point in the implementation of `EmptyPath` that we have not defined yet, and it is
the call `Path(that)` in method `/(that: String)`. We have already met `Path` in
the definition of the main trait but we need to present a few more implementation
bits before delving into the `Path` object.

8.4 Unix paths

Unix paths are the simplest. One could say that they adhere to the *canonical design*.
There is only one root and one type of absolute path, so the implementation is
rather straightforward and is shown in Figure 8.3. We are somewhat careful with
the implementation of methods `parent` and `paths`.

Regarding `parent`, when the path is the root (/) then, as discussed previously,
we get the `EmptyPath`. For all other cases, we must check where the last / resides.

- If there is no / in the string representation of the path,

    ```
    case -1 => EmptyPath
    ```

    then the empty path is the result.
- If / appears last in the very first position of the string,

    ```
    case 0 => new UnixPath("/")
    ```

```scala
class UnixPath(val fullName: String) extends Path {
  def relative =
    new UnixPath(
      if(isAbsolute)
        fullName.substring(1)
      else
        fullName
    )

  def parent =
    if(isRoot)
      EmptyPath
    else {
      fullName.lastIndexOf('/') match {
        case -1 => EmptyPath
        case  0 => new UnixPath("/")
        case  n => new UnixPath(fullName.substring(0, n))
      }
    }

  def name =
    fullName.substring(fullName.lastIndexOf('/') + 1)

  override def parts = {
    fullName.split('/') map {
      case "" => "/" // the root must be transformed
      case s => s
    } toList
  }

  def isUNC = false

  def isRoot = "/" == fullName

  def isEmpty = false

  override def isAbsolute = '/' == fullName.charAt(0)

  def /(that: String) = Path.combine(this, that)

  def /(that: Path) = Path.combine(this, that)
}
```

Figure 8.3 The implementation of UnixPath.

then the parent is the root. This is clearly the case, since if / is at zero index, then the path is in the form /somePath.

- Otherwise, for any position n of the last slash,

```scala
case 0 => new UnixPath(fullName.substring(0, n))
```

a substring up to n is what is needed to get the parent.

The implementation of `parts` exhibits some functional character:

```
override def parts =
  fullName.split('/') map {
    case "" => "/" // the root must be transformed
    case s => s
  } toList
```

First, we split the full name into parts, using / as the separator. We must keep in mind that `split` returns an array, so the transformation to a list is necessary. Then, we need to take care of the special nature of /. Let us see why with an example. If we split the string `"/usr/bin"` according to the same rule, then the result will contain an empty string at the beginning of the generated array:

```
scala> "/usr/bin" split '/'
res0: Array[String] = Array(, usr, bin)
```

Unfortunately, the three string parts in the generated array, do not correctly represent paths. There is a problematic empty string at index zero. Just to remedy the situation, we resort to a simple transformation, the one shown above, via the higher-order function `map`.

As a final note regarding the implementation of `UnixPath`, the composition methods

```
def /(that: String) = Path.combine(this, that)
def /(that: Path)   = Path.combine(this, that)
```

delegate to a method in the companion object.

8.5 Windows paths

Windows paths are a bit more complicated because of their variety. For our purposes, we will distinguish between

- simple paths, which we will represent using the `UnixPath` implementation,
- UNC paths for which we will implement a new `UNCPath` subclass of `Path`, and
- drive absolute paths, which start with something like `C:\`; our corresponding implementation is class `DriveAbsPath`.

In order to relate `UNCPath` and `DriveAbsPath`, we define a subclass of `Path`

```
trait WinPath extends Path
```

and make them subclasses of `WinPath`.

Exercise 8.1 Under Windows and to the best of our knowledge, there are two more cases one has to consider. In particular, there are directory relative paths, which are in the form \somePath and drive relative paths that look like C:somePath. Notice the missing drive letter in the former case and the missing backslash in the latter case. After studying the implementations we give for the path types mentioned above, implement these two missing path types. How is path composition affected?

8.5.1 Simple paths

If we would like to reuse the implementation of UnixPaths for simple (relative) Windows paths, of course we need to take care of the slash-backslash difference. For that reason, we will for now assume and later show how to implement our paths in some normalized form, where only forward slashes appear. There is actually no pragmatic problem with this approach, since we can easily verify that java.io.File under Windows, when given a path with forward slashes, will properly handle it as if they were backslashes:

```
scala> new java.io.File("C:/windows")
res0: java.io.File = C:\windows
```

Notice the automatic transformation of / to \ in the above interactive session, performed on a Windows machine.

8.5.2 UNC paths

The implementation of UNCPath is shown in Figure 8.4. As in UnixPath, the most interesting methods are parent and parts. For example, parent has to see where exactly the last / resides and break the path string representation accordingly. Also, parts checks whether the UNCPath just represents "//", in which case it is just a root.

We consider an UNCPath to be a root path if and only if the length of its string representation equals two. These two characters will be "//". Notice how we follow the general rule of normalized paths, according to which slashes are the sole path separators, regardless of the underlying platform.

8.5.3 Drive absolute paths

Drive absolute paths are implemented using DriveAbsPath in Figure 8.5. These paths always start with χ: (in their normalized form), where the variable χ denotes some character from A to Z and their lowercase counterparts. So a path is always at

```scala
class UNCPath(val fullName: String) extends WinPath {
  def isRoot = 2 == fullName.length

  def isUNC = true

  override def isAbsolute = true

  def isEmpty = false

  def name =
    fullName.substring(fullName.lastIndexOf('/') + 1)

  def relative = new UnixPath(fullName.substring(2))

  def parent = {
    if(isRoot)
      EmptyPath
    else
      fullName.lastIndexOf('/') match {
        case 1 => new UNCPath("//")
        case n => new UNCPath(fullName.substring(0, n))
      }
  }

  override def parts = {
    if(isRoot)
      "//" :: Nil
    else
      "//" :: fullName.substring(2).split('/').toList
  }

  def /(that: String) = Path.combine(this, that)

  def /(that: Path)    = Path.combine(this, that)
}
```

Figure 8.4 The implementation of `UNCPath`.

least three characters long. If it is exactly three characters long, then it is a root path:

```scala
def isRoot = 3 == fullName.length
```

The definition of `parent` follows the same philosophy as previously

```scala
def parent =
  if(isRoot)
    EmptyPath
```

```
class DriveAbsPath(val fullName: String) extends WinPath {
  def isRoot = 3 == fullName.length

  def isUNC = false

  override def isAbsolute = true

  def isEmpty = false

  def name =
    if(isRoot)
      ""
    else
      fullName.substring(fullName.lastIndexOf('/') + 1)

  def relative = new UnixPath(fullName.substring(3))

  def parent = {
    if(isRoot)
      EmptyPath
    else
      fullName.lastIndexOf('/') match {
        case 2 => new DriveAbsPath(fullName.substring(0, 3))
        case n => new DriveAbsPath(fullName.substring(0, n))
      }
  }

  override def parts = {
    if(isRoot)
      fullName :: Nil
    else
      fullName.substring(0, 3) ::
        fullName.substring(3).split('/').toList
  }

  def /(that: String) = Path.combine(this, that)

  def /(that: Path)   = Path.combine(this, that)
}
```

Figure 8.5 The implementation of `DriveAbsPath`.

```
else
  fullName.lastIndexOf('/') match {
    case 2 => new DriveAbsPath(fullName.substring(0, 3))
    case n => new DriveAbsPath(fullName.substring(0, n))
  }
```

and the same holds for the definition of `parts`

```
override def parts =
  if (isRoot)
    fullName :: Nil
  else
    fullName.substring(0, 3) ::
      fullName.substring(3).split('/').toList
```

8.6 Path factory

It is time to work out the implementation of the `Path` companion object. First, we will need a few utility methods.

```
object Path {
  implicit def string2path(path: String) = this(path)

  val isWindows =
    System.getProperty("os.name")
      .toLowerCase.contains("windows")

  def isDriveLetter(ch: Char) =
    'a' <= ch && ch <= 'z' || 'A' <= ch && ch <= 'Z'

  def isBackSlash(ch: Char) = '\\' == ch

  def isSlash(ch: Char) = '/' == ch

  def isAnySlash(ch: Char) = isSlash(ch) || isBackSlash(ch)

  def getSlashF(anySlash: Boolean) =
    if (anySlash) isAnySlash _ else isSlash _
}
```

Every Java Virtual Machine defines the `"os.name"` system property and under Windows its lowercase transformation contains the value `"windows"`.[2] We use this piece of information to recognize the underlying operating system. Also, we will obviously use `isDriveLetter` for paths under Windows.

---

[2] Lowercase here is usual practice when a programmer does not exactly remember the specification and just needs to be sure. Actually, under Windows XP, the exact value returned from `System.getProperty` is `"Windows XP"`.

The other methods are checks that decide whether a character is a slash or backslash. The last one, getSlashF is actually a method that returns a function. We can discover the exact type by using the interpreter:

```
scala> def getSlashF(anySlash: Boolean) =
 | if(anySlash) isAnySlash _ else isSlash _
   getSlashF: (Boolean)(Char) => Boolean
```

This just means that the result of getSlashF is a function from Char to Boolean values. The first parentheses, (Boolean), mean of course that getSlashF takes one Boolean parameter.

Question 8.1 If, in the above interpreter session, we issue the command:

```
val f = getSlashF _
```

in order to get a function version of method getSlashF, then what is the type of f?

But what is the purpose of getSlashF? The implementation clearly shows that it selects the proper check for a forward slash or backslash character. Furthermore, it seems to distinguish two cases.

- In the first case, which happens if and only if the input parameter is true, isAnySlash is selected as the slash check. Here, we use the term "slash" in its generalized meaning, so it may be either a forward slash or a backslash.
- In the second case, isSlash is selected as the slash check.

So, getSlashF is a kind of dynamic slash check. As we will see shortly, under Windows any slash, either a forward one or a backslash, counts as a path separator. Under Unix, the (forward) slash character is the only separator. Did you know that in Unix, this funny \/ directory can be created?

```
loverdos:~> mkdir funny; cd funny

loverdos:~/funny> ls -al
total 0
drwxr-xr-x    2 loverdos  staff      68 Jun 18 06:24 .
drwxr-xr-x+ 119 loverdos  staff    4046 Jun 18 06:24 ..

loverdos:~/funny> mkdir \\; ls -alF
total 0
drwxr-xr-x    2 loverdos  staff      68 Jun 18 06:24 ./
drwxr-xr-x+ 119 loverdos  staff    4046 Jun 18 06:24 ../
drwxr-xr-x    2 loverdos  staff      68 Jun 18 06:27 \/
```

Of course, we cheat a little here. The directory name is just \ and not \/. The /
part has been "created" by the F switch in `ls -alF`.

8.6.1 A few more utility methods

Since our path string representation is going to be normalized, we will need two
more utility methods:

- `removeRedundantSlashes` and
- `lastNonSlashIndex`

The second one starts from the end of the input string and discards any slash
characters:

```
object Path { // continued
  def lastNonSlashIndex(path: String, anySlash: Boolean) = {
    val isSlashF = getSlashF(anySlash)
    var index = path.length - 1
    while(index > 0 && isSlashF(path.charAt(index)))
      index -= 1
    index
  }
}
```

The second parameter, `anySlash`, is there to help pick up the correct slash-checking
method. The code above has an imperative feeling. A more functional approach
might look like:

```
object Path { // continued
  def lastNonSlashIndex2(path: String, anySlash: Boolean) = {
    val isSlashF = getSlashF(anySlash)

    def discoverIndex(index: Int): Int =
      if(index <= 0)
        -1
      else if(isSlashF(path.charAt(index)))
        discoverIndex(index - 1)
      else
        index

    discoverIndex(path.length - 1)
  }
}
```

Instead of searching via a `while` loop and decreasing a `var`, which is a mutating operation, we use a helper method that counts down until either it reaches the beginning of the input string or it finds the first nonslash character. No state is mutated and counting down is achieved via selective subtraction.

The imperative version is a bit smaller. In such cases, coding style is a matter of taste and heritage. A programmer coming from an object-oriented background may directly resort to the first version. Yet, for such a programmer, it may be a great opportunity to start thinking in a different style. Note that `discoverIndex` is tail recursive.

The other method, `removeRedundantSlashes`, is a bit more complicated than `lastNonSlashIndex`:

```
object Path { // continued
  def removeRedundantSlashes(
    path: String, startIndex: Int,
    endIndex: Int, anySlash: Boolean) = {

    val sb = new StringBuilder
    var index = startIndex
    var previousWasSlash = false
    val isSlashF = getSlashF(anySlash)

    while(startIndex <= index && index <= endIndex) {
      val ch = path.charAt(index)

      if(isSlashF(ch)) {
        if(!previousWasSlash) {
          sb.append('/')
          previousWasSlash = true
        }
      } else {
        sb.append(ch)
        previousWasSlash = false
      }

      index += 1
    }

    sb.toString
  }
}
```

What we do here is to track the place where we see a slash, remember consecutive slash positions and collapse consecutive slashes to one /. All other characters are just copied through. This is again an imperative algorithm.

But we could provide a more declarative approach. For example, the one-liner

```
x.replaceAll("[\\\/]+", "/")
```

can indeed remove redundant slashes of any kind, as can be seen by a quick experiment:

```
scala> "C:\\//usr///bin".replaceAll("[\\\/]+", "/")
res0: java.lang.String = C:/usr/bin
```

Exercise 8.2 Use the previous one-liner approach or some other of your choice to make the algorithm implementing `removeRedundantSlashes` more functional/declarative.

8.6.2 *The factory method*

The heart of the Path object is its `apply` method:

```
object Path { // continued
  def apply(path: String): Path =
    if("" equals path)
      EmptyPath
    else if(isWindows)
      parseWinPath(path)
    else
      parseUnixPath(path)
}
```

It simply consults the value of `isWindows`, in order to call the appropriate algorithm that will build a normalized path out of a string value. Of the two algorithms, `parseUnixPath` is, as expected, the most straightforward one:

```
object Path { // continued
  def parseUnixPath(path: String): UnixPath =
    parseSimplePath(path, false)

  def parseSimplePath(path: String, anySlash: Boolean) =
    new UnixPath(
```

```
removeRedundantSlashes(
  path,
  0,
  lastNonSlashIndex(path, anySlash),
  anySlash))
}
```

In order to parse a path under Windows and in accordance with our design, we must proceed from the beginning of the string on a character-by-character basis, until we have enough information for the type of path. The details are shown in Figure 8.6 and we analyze them briefly.

For the life of a call to parseWinPath, we always use true as the value to anySlash, since under Windows we assume that both / and \ are separators for

```
def parseWinPath(path: String) = {
  val len = path.length
  val ch0 = path.charAt(0)

  len match {
    case 1 =>
      parseSimplePath(path, true)

    case _ =>
      val ch1 = path.charAt(1)
      if(isAnySlash(ch0) && isAnySlash(ch1))
        new UNCPath(
          "//" +
          removeRedundantSlashes(
            path, 2, lastNonSlashIndex(path, true), true))
      else if(len > 2 &&
              isDriveLetter(ch0) &&
              ':' == ch1 &&
              isAnySlash(path.charAt(2))) {
        val prefix = path.substring(0, 2) // C:
        val rest = path.substring(2)
        val suffix = removeRedundantSlashes(
          rest, 0, lastNonSlashIndex(rest, true), true)

        new DriveAbsPath(prefix + suffix)
      } else
        parseSimplePath(path, true)
  }
}
```

Figure 8.6 Parsing a path under Windows.

path elements. The initial decision-making procedure is around the length of the input string. If the length is just one, then we delegate to `parseSimplePath`. Otherwise, meaning that the string is at least two characters long, we must see the exact character value at the initial positions.

If the first two characters are slashes, then an `UNCPath` is parsed

```
new UNCPath(
  "//" +
  removeRedundantSlashes(
    path, 2, lastNonSlashIndex(path, true), true))
```

and we manually preserve the initial `"//"`, since we do not want them to be absorbed or destroyed by a call to `removeRedundantSlashes`.

Otherwise, if the length is at least three characters, such that the initial three characters form an absolute drive designator in the form χ:\, then an `AbsDrivePath` is parsed

```
val prefix = path.substring(0, 2) // C:
val rest = path.substring(2)
val suffix = removeRedundantSlashes(
  rest, 0, lastNonSlashIndex(rest, true), true)

new DriveAbsPath(prefix + suffix)
```

and we are being careful to not put the whole input string through `removeRedundantSlashes` and `lastNonSlashIndex`.

Question 8.2 Can you spot the reason why we need to treat the input string specially?

8.6.3 Canonical paths

So far, the `Path` factory can handle any underlying operating system curiosities by selectively calling the appropriate internal method, either `parseWinPath` or `parseUnixPath`. But since the `UnixPath` implementation is the canonical one and a great deal of applications would expect to use paths outside their dominant environment, that is the file system, we provide one more factory method:

```
object Path { // continued
  object UnixPath {
    def apply(path: String): Path =
      if("" equals path)
        EmptyPath
```

```
       else
         parseUnixPath(path)
   }
 }
```

We are in effect saving a platform-specific decision, stating that the default Path implementation is that of UnixPath. The advantage of the new addition is that it gives us the opportunity to construct a UnixPath directly, if we know a priori that the semantics of the client code require that kind of construction and nothing more elaborate that would engage platform-specific decisions.

Giving a plausible example, imagine that we are under Windows, where UNCPaths apply and that we are manipulating URIs[3] via the java.net.URI API:

```
scala> import java.net._
import java.net._

scala> val uri = new URI("http:///path/resource")
uri: java.net.URI = http:///path/resource

scala> val path = uri.getPath
path: java.lang.String = /path/resource

scala> val uri2 = new URI("path")
uri2: java.net.URI = path

scala> val path2 = uri2.getPath
path2: java.lang.String = path
```

The interpreter session demonstrates that the path of a URI may start with a /. Let us assume that some client code manipulates the path part of a URI, translating it to an absolute path using a simple string concatenation

```
Path("/" + uri.getPath)
```

But now remember that we are under Windows, our library has created an UNCPath, since uri.getPath already starts with a /.

The above example is simple but the same simple, or rather innocent, thinking can lead to bugs. And if it *can*, then according to *Murphy's Law* it most certainly *will*.

---

[3] See RFC 2396 http://www.ietf.org/rfc/rfc2396.txt. The initials stand for Uniform Resource Identifier.

We always have to think of the path semantics we need when transforming strings to paths. The introduction of the `UnixPath` factory gives us one more alternative to take into account.

8.6.4 Combining paths

The truth is that there is a particular piece of code that has been repeated in a few places without any attempt on our part to factor it out in some `trait`. The last implementation part of Figures 8.3, 8.4 and 8.5 is *identical!*

```
def /(that: String) = Path.combine(this, that)
def /(that: Path)   = Path.combine(this, that)
```

In the companion object, the corresponding definitions are:

```
object Path { // continued
  def combine(a: Path, b: String): Path = combine(a, Path(b))

  def combine(a: Path, b: Path) =
    (a.isAbsolute, b.isAbsolute) match {
      case (_, true) => error(
        "Cannot concatenate path <%s>" +
        " with absolute path <%s>".format(a, b))

      case (_, false) => Path(a.fullName + "/" + b.fullName)
  }
}
```

The basic idea in the first `case` statement is that in a path composition p_1 / p_2, where p_1 is visually the *left* part and p_2 is the *right* part, p_2 cannot be an absolute path. In all other cases, we simply concatenate the full names using the normal / separator.

8.7 Notes on representation

It is obvious that for all `Path` subclasses we have chosen the full path name as the main representation. This is evident from the several constructor definitions:

```
class UnixPath(fullName: String) extends Path
class UNCPath(fullName: String) extends WinPath
class DriveAbsPath(fullName: String) extends WinPath
```

The corresponding type hierarchy is shown in figure 8.7.

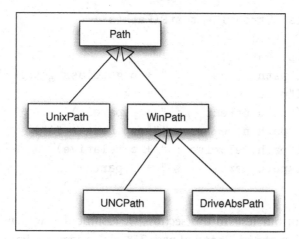

Figure 8.7 Basic implemented path hierarchy.

Choosing `fullName` as the primary representation simply means that all client-code operations using `fullName` directly are efficient.

8.8 Notes on visibility

Up to now, all the `trait` and `class` definitions are public. Normally, we would like the companion object `Path`, via its `apply` method, to be the only interface point to the path library: an external user should see only this factory method and none of the above constructors.

If we are certain that we have all the needed implementation classes and no class may subclass `Path` in the future, then we can make the `Path` trait a `sealed` one and, of course, provide the implementation of the subclasses in the same source unit. If we are not sure we are done with subclassing `Path`, then we can encapsulate all the definitions inside a package and then make the constructors of the subclasses of `Path` package-private. The two features can be combined, so that the only user-visible API for constructing a `Path` is the companion object:

```
package scalabook.path
...
sealed trait Path { ... }
...
class UnixPath private[scalabook.path](val fullName: String) ...
... etc ...
```

8.9 Testing paths

Let us define a couple of utility methods that will help us observe how several path characteristics are represented by our path library:

```
def testS(s: String) = testP(Path(s))

def testP(p: Path) {
    println("path.class     : " + p.getClass.getName)
    println("path           : " + p)
    println("path.parent    : " + p.parent)
    println("path.name      : '" + p.name + "'")
    println("path.relative : " + p.relative)
    println("path.parts     : " + p.parts)
}
```

For the rest of our tests in this section, we assume that we have imported the implicit definition `string2path` of page 318, via an `import Path._` statement.

8.9.1 User-friendliness

Implicits are our best friends:

```
scala> "usr" / "bin"
res0: scalabook.path.Path = usr/bin
```

The first string is "caught" by `string2path` and converted to a `Path`. After that, a normal call on method / of the newly created `Path` is issued.

We can even go a bit further and save one keystroke per path part:

```
scala> implicit def symbol2path(s: Symbol) = Path(s.name)
symbol2path: (Symbol)scalabook.path.Path

scala> testP('usr / 'bin)
path.class     : scalabook.path.UnixPath
path           : usr/bin
path.parent    : usr
path.name      : 'bin'
path.relative : usr/bin
path.parts     : List(usr, bin)
```

Equality works as expected (or is it not?):

```
scala> "/usr" / "bin" == "/usr/bin"
res1: Boolean = false
```

Shouldn't the two paths be equal? Well, the answer lies implicitly in our choice of words. Specifically, we are talking about *paths* but are we really dealing with paths here? A little more experimentation will provide us with the needed answers:

```
scala> val a = "/usr" / "bin"
a: scalabook.path.Path = /usr/bin

scala> val b = "/usr/bin"
b: java.lang.String = /usr/bin
```

So, a is a `Path` but b is a `String` and they cannot be equal, according to our definition of the `equals` method in Figure 8.1. The bottom line is that keeping in mind the *types* will make it a lot easier to reason about the *values*. If we had spotted that the path combination operator / produces values of type `Path` but `"/usr/bin"` is just a `String`, then everything would seem quite normal in the first place.

8.10 Algebraic abstractions

The compositional nature of paths should be more than evident right now. Thanks to the expressiveness of the Scala language, we have been able to define a special operator, /, that composes two paths *and gives another path as the result*. This operation of combining two objects and producing a third object of the same kind is ubiquitous, especially in mathematics: we can add, subtract, multiply real numbers. In Scala we can even define complex numbers that can behave like real numbers in writing algorithms with arithmetic operations such as the ones mentioned above.

Another characteristic of the composition is that just as with high-school algebra

$$(x+y)+z = x+(y+z)$$

for any numbers x, y, z, a similar property holds for paths, so that

$$(p_1/p_2)/p_3 = p_1/(p_2/p_3)$$

for paths p_1, p_2 and p_3. We can easily verify the latter:

```
scala> ( "usr" / "local" ) / "bin"
res0: scalabook.path.Path = usr/local/bin

scala> "usr" / ( "local" / "bin" )
res1: scalabook.path.Path = usr/local/bin
```

This very property of *associativity* alone is a rather important one and deserves special credit.

8.10.1 Semigroups

Informally, a *semigroup* is a collection of objects and an associative binary operation that we use to combine these objects. We saw what associativity means. A *binary operation* takes two objects of the same kind and produces a third object of the same kind. For the mathematically oriented, we can write it as

$$f : (A, A) \rightarrow A$$

where f is its name, although we have already met names like $\cdot$ as a general composition (or combination) operator and / for paths. For two objects a_1 and a_2, we usually write the act of the combination operator on them as $a_1 \cdot a_2$.

It is evident that paths[4] form a semigroup. Let us code a semigroup in Scala:

```scala
trait Semigroup[A] {
  def compose(a: A, b: A): A
}
```

We might be tempted to write it as

```scala
trait SemigroupOther[A] {
  def compose(that: A): A
}
```

but actually it is easy to be certain about exactly what we need. Remember that a semigroup is a collection of objects with some associative operation. The key phrase here is *collection of objects*: the definition of `SemigroupOther` clearly represents just *one* of these objects, since in `compose` only the second object is passed as a parameter, while the first is none other than the object-oriented `this`.

We could have adopted the second definition, in addition to the first one, renaming it properly and providing some extra machinery that does the actual work:

```scala
trait IamInASemigroup[A] {
  def composeWith(that: A)(semi: Semigroup[A]) =
    semi.compose(this, that)
}
```

Then an object of type `A` belonging to a semigroup can mix in `IamInASemigroup[A]` and the composition is achieved by providing an extra parameter, the actual semigroup.

---

[4] The careful reader might already be thinking that only relative paths guarantee that their combination will not fail.

But Scala can be more expressive than that, if we desire so. Let us say we have several predefined types of semigroups that we want to be used *implicitly*, instead of explicitly passing them around as parameters:

```
trait IamInASemigroup[A] {
  def composeWith(that: A)(implicit semi: Semigroup[A]) =
    semi.compose(this, that)
}
```

The `compose` operation may also be seen as `append`, as in the Haskell libraries or `Scalaz`, a library with a wealth of abstractions currently missing from the official Scala distribution.

Returning to our paths, the relevant semigroup can be coded as

```
object PathSemigroup extends Semigroup[Path] {
  def compose(a: Path, b: Path) = Path.combine(a, b)
}
```

Now the interesting design question arises: Should we have thought about it at the beginning and provided the actual implementation of `combine` inside `PathSemigroup` instead of the companion `Path` object? Well, yes! This is the essence of *algebraic thinking*: to start thinking about the *structure* of our objects (paths in this respect). The word structure here means the way our objects are organized and how their organization is revealed by the permitted operations.

The structure of a semigroup, as expressed by the needed associative operation, is a minimal one. Several other, more complicated "things" can be built *on* it or *independent of* it, if we wish to be precise about the meaning of our words.

8.10.2 Monoids

In our implementation of paths, there is one particular path that stands out. Let us again take a look at Figure 8.2 and consider the role of `EmptyPath`:

```
scala> val usrbin = "usr" / "bin"
usrbin: scalabook.path.Path = usr/bin

scala> EmptyPath / usrbin
res0: scalabook.path.Path = usr/bin

scala> EmptyPath / usrbin == usrbin
res1: Boolean = true
```

```
scala> usrbin / EmptyPath == usrbin
res2: Boolean = true
```

Regarding path combination, `EmptyPath` leaves the other operand unchanged. Using a near-mathematical notation, the property $p/EmptyPath = EmptyPath/p = p$ holds. Generally speaking, for a binary operation $\cdot$ and an object a, another element *id* such that

$$a \cdot id = id \cdot a = a$$

is called the *identity* object. We say *the* identity and not just *an* identity, because it can be proved that there is only one object with this particular property.

Now we are ready for the introduction of another algebraic structure. A *monoid* is a semigroup equipped with an identity. For example, the integers with addition as the binary operation form a monoid and the identity is the number zero. For integers with multiplication, the identity is the number one. Paths form a monoid with `EmptyPath` as the *identity path*.

We can code the relevant Scala abstraction as:

```
trait Monoid[A] extends Semigroup[A] {
    def ident: A
}
```

Alternatively, we can make a standalone definition for an identity abstraction

```
trait Identity[+A] {
    def ident: A
}
```

and then mix in the appropriate ingredients

```
trait Monoid[A] extends Semigroup[A] with Identity[A]
```

Returning to our paths problem domain, we need

```
object PathIdentity extends Identity[Path] {
    def ident = EmptyPath
}
```

and we define PathMonoid to reflect the new structure

```
object PathMonoid extends Monoid[Path] {
  def compose(a: Path, b: Path) = Path.combine(a, b)
  def ident = EmptyPath
}
```

9

Virtual files coming into existence

Continuing our investigations on path territory in Chapter 8, the natural evolution is to touch some of the actual *file* abstraction. As a historical note, complete operating systems have been built based on this abstraction, Plan 9 being one that used it quite extensively. Plan 9 was designed by, among others, Ken Thompson and Rob Pike who also designed UTF-8 [65]. Throughout the book, we are using files as they are defined and implemented by a standard Java Development Kit distribution for an obvious reason: they use a pragmatic approach and at the same time make a very successful utility for everyday programming. In this chapter, we will try to tickle a few of our brian neurons around this design.

The `java.io.file` class of the Java platform already provides a file abstraction, via the `java.io.File` class. Despite the official online documentation, which states that `File` is

An abstract representation of file and directory pathnames,

the implementation plays the dual role of handling both generic paths and their physical counterparts in the native file system. We have already treated path representation and composition. The most common mapping of paths to underlying system resources is that related to native files.

So, we will develop here a small library for accessing files. But, instead of just providing a Scala wrapper around Java's `File`, we will abstract away common operations. The goal is for the design to accommodate not only the *native* file system but also a variety of other *virtual* file systems. For brevity, from now on we will use the term *VFS* to denote a Virtual File System. Accordingly, the term *VFile* will denote a virtual file for some particular VFS.

Interestingly, the VFS notion and accompanying terminology is nowadays ubiquitous in operating systems. The idea probably originated in the 1980s as a necessity for the Solaris, an early precursor to OpenSolaris, kernel [41]. The development team needed a systematic way to handle both the local file system and the *Network File System* (NFS)[1] uniformly.

9.1 Types, requirements and API

9.1.1 Types

Our basic notions are those of the file system (VFS) and the type of files (VFile) a file system supports. For example, in Java the native file system is implicitly assumed by the java.io.File, which plays the role of a VFile. But it is better if we separate the two. Of course, there will be some connection – and we will shortly propose a plausible connection – but the design should reflect the fact that each one of the two serves a semantically distinct role.

A VFS abstracts away the underlying *storage medium*. The details of this medium may well constrain the way the respective VFiles function or the operations that they support. When a VFS is *attached* (or *mounted* in Unix parlance) to the system in read-only mode, then it is not possible to modify any file contained in it. Having the storage medium as the starting point, a VFile, on the other hand, is a provided entity. We expect that operations that deal directly with the underlying medium will be delegated to appropriate functionality in the VFS.

From the above discussion, one might go ahead and model a VFile as a VFS-dependent entity, reflecting this directly in the relevant type:

```
trait VFile[VFS]
```

But the truth is that although we clearly expect a VFS to play a fundamental role in the implementation, the most important user-viewable entity is that of a VFile. So, we express a VFS in terms of *what it provides*:

```
trait VFS[VFile]
```

for some type VFile that will support a virtual file API.

9.1.2 Design goals

Our requirements are modest. Although we intend to give a quite usable implementation, programming a full-fledged library is not our goal. Separation of concerns and type safety are certainly on the agenda. We achieve the first by the essential separation and, for what it is worth, the explicit representation of VFS and VFiles.

---

[1] NFS is a network file system protocol originally developed by Sun Microsystems. It was originally described in RFC 1094 at http://www.ietf.org/rfc/rfc1094.txt.

This is in contrast to the native Java API which blurs the distinction of a file system that implicitly exists and a native-only file abstraction.

As far as type safety is concerned, as shown above, we expect that each VFS type is related to a particular VFile type. Thus, VFS types are separated by what kind of files they provide. Generally, VFiles from different VFSs will not be compatible, unless of course they can be considered as such for the sake of generality. Just to give a practical example, let us assume that all the lower-level details of how we read bytes from and how we write bytes to a file are properly implemented. Then, providing a generic file copy operation where the source and target files cross the VFS boundary is not only legitimate but also desirable, at least as a first approximation. We say "as a first approximation" because lower-level implementation details of a file system may demand a more ad hoc approach.

In the following sections, we present our API and explain the rationale and expectations of the defined operations.

9.1.3 VFS API

The API is presented in Figure 9.1. Notice the declared type, in the spirit of our previous discussion:

```
trait VFS[T <: VFile[T]]
```

Of course, VFS[T <: VFile[T]] seems a bit more complicated than VFS[VFile] but we will come to that in detail after we present the VFile API. For now, the nontrivial, semantically, methods are as follows.

mkpath Given a string, the method returns a path interpretation for that string. This may sound unnecessary in that we could always directly call the path constructor Path(_), thus letting our path library handle the different underlying operating system (OS) semantics. But we are missing one point here: Path(_) can surely handle the OS semantics, although now we are one design layer above that. Our interest, having resolved the path issues, has shifted to some other functionality on top of the provided one. For this particular reason, it is wise to anticipate new semantics for the extra design layer.

roots This returns the file system roots. Here, we borrow the idea from file systems that have more than one root point. The accompanying root method just returns the zero-indexed root, which by convention we can call the default one.

container This returns the container of the VFS. A VFS, being virtual, can reside practically anywhere. If all those places can be captured by the ideas developed in this chapter, then we can expect that a *nested* VFS exists within some generic file, its

```
package scalabook.file

import scalabook.path.Path

object VFS {
  type AnyFile = VFile[_]
}

trait VFS[T <: VFile[T]] {
  def name: String

  def mkpath(name: String): Path

  def roots: List[T]

  def root = roots(0)

  def container: Option[VFS.AnyFile]

  def isContained = container.isDefined

  def newTempFile(prefix: String, suffix: String): T

  def newFile(path: Path): T

  def newFile(path: String): T = newFile(mkpath(path))

  def newFolder(path: Path) = newFile(path)

  def newFolder(path: String): T = newFolder(mkpath(path))

  def resolve(path: Path): Option[T]

  def resolve(path: String): Option[T] =
    resolve(mkpath(path))

  def contains(path: Path) = resolve(path).isDefined

  def contains(path: String) = resolve(path).isDefined

  override def toString = "VFS(" + name + ")"
}
```

Figure 9.1 The VFS API.

container. The type of that container is worth a comment:

```
type AnyFile = VFile[_]
```

The underscore in VFile[_] means that we do not actually care about the exact type. At any particular moment, where we use it, it is *some* type and in Scala it is called an *existential type*. Just because we do not name this type, we cannot explicitly reuse it. The conceptually derived method isContained is implemented using container by checking the returned Option value.

newFile This returns an object that represents a file. This is a fundamental method. Only the VFS knows what its files look like and how they behave, so the VFS is the canonical file factory. We need to make one comment on the method though. The semantics of whether the method actually creates a new file at the underlying storage medium or whether it just creates a virtual representation of such a file (a file-to-be) are up to the particular VFS implementation. For some VFSs it might be more relevant to return files that only exist, while for others new files are returned at will, independently of their existence. The java.io.File API belongs to the latter category.

Notice how we have two overloaded methods, one taking a Path as input type and a second taking a String. We have introduced the second one because of a design choice we made in the Path implementation. In particular our implicit definition

```
object Path {
    implicit def string2path(path: String) = this(path)

    def apply(path: String): Path = ...
}
```

in the path factory object will always convert a String to a Path if the definition is in scope. If only the version of newFile with the Path input parameter existed, then every client use of newFile with a string, as in

```
SomeVFS.newFile("somePath")
```

would result, by the compiler, in an equivalent call

```
SomeVFS.newFile(Path("somePath"))
```

This way we would lose the opportunity to let the VFS construct the path, using mkpath, which is exactly what the implementation of newFile with a String parameter does:

```
def newFile(path: String) = newFile(mkpath(path))
```

newFolder This returns an object that represents a folder. Although for the moment we do not distinguish programmatically between a file and a folder, we have two dimensions to consider:

(i) the user's intentions,

(ii) the underlying VFS implementation.

newTempFile This method returns a temporary file. Not all VFSs are required to implement this functionality.

resolve This provides an extra layer on top of newFile by actually resolving the underlying resource. If it does not exist, then the method returns None. The method contains is a convenient alternative. In the VFS trait, we have chosen to give a default implementation where contains is based on resolve but specific implementations may choose to override the definitions and express the relationship in the opposite direction.

Overall, we have factory methods for paths and files, discovery methods that provide a file only when it can be resolved in the underlying storage, and informational methods about the root structure of the file system. Under Windows, for example, the native file system has more than one root point.

9.1.4 VFile API

Let us now turn our attention to the VFile API, shown in Figure 9.2.

asNative This returns a virtual file as a NativeFile. The latter is the default implementation we give later regarding a native file system. This method should not attempt to do any transformation to a native file. Instead, it should wrap an existing NativeFile instance to an Option. It provides a convenient utility when the client code either knows it manipulates native files or this has been determined by a call to isNative.

isFile, isFolder These return true if and only if the VFile instance represents a file or folder respectively.

children This returns an Iterable of files (or folders) that exist under a particular virtual folder. Each virtual file returned is described by its complete path, that is its path includes its parent. This method resembles listFiles of java.io.File. The main difference is that we do not return an array or list but rather an Iterable. This is in accordance with usual practice, where we just iterate over the children of some folder and do whatever actions during the iteration step.

childrenNames This returns just the names of the virtual folder children. Implementations are free to compute the names either using children directly

```
children.map(_.name)
```

or using some other ad hoc and more efficient way.

```
package scalabook.file

import scalabook.path.Path

trait VFile[T <: VFile[T]] { self: T =>
  def path: Path

  def name = path.name

  def isNative = this.isInstanceOf[NativeFile]

  def asNative: Option[NativeFile] = None

  def exists: Boolean

  def isFile: Boolean

  def isFolder: Boolean

  def children: Iterable[T]

  def childrenNames: Iterable[String]

  def /(that: String): T

  def /(that: Path): T

  def inputStream: Option[java.io.InputStream]

  def outputStream: Option[java.io.OutputStream]

  override def hashCode = path.hashCode

  override def equals(any: Any) =
    any.isInstanceOf[VFile[_]] &&
    any.asInstanceOf[VFile[_]].getClass == this.getClass &&
    any.asInstanceOf[VFile[_]].path == this.path

  override def toString = path.toString
}
```

Figure 9.2 The VFile API.

/ This returns a new VFile whose path is the path of this VFile composed with the given
argument.

inputStream This method returns an optional `java.io.InputStream` if this is possible given the underlying implementation. Of course, for folders, the return value is
expected to be None.

outputStream Again, if the underlying implementation permits it and this is not a folder, this method returns a `java.io.OutputStream` or None otherwise.

Note also that the equality method is crafted so that only VFiles of exactly the same class and with the same paths are considered equal. Under these two assumptions, it could have been written as

```
override def equals(any: Any) =
  any.asInstanceOf[AnyRef].getClass == this.getClass &&
  any.asInstanceOf[VFile[_]].path   == this.path
```

Question 9.1 Why use the cast `AnyRef` in the above use of `asInstanceOf`?

But this approach or the one in Figure 9.2, are just simple proposals. For example, with both, we are ruling out cases where subclasses might have to participate in the equality relation. The three most important properties that the `equals` contract should have are reflexivity, symmetry and transitivity. Properly implementing the required contract of `equals`, which according to Java also affects the implementation of `hashCode`, can be tricky but not impossible [59].

Now that we have defined our basic concepts, let us look a little more closely at the exact types of VFS and VFile:

```
trait VFile[T <: VFile[T]] { self: T => ... }

trait VFS[T <: VFile[T]]
```

First of all, the type of VFS is a consequence of the type of VFile. For example, we could not have written just `VFile[T]` for any T, since T has to be a subtype of any type a VFile has. On the other hand, the type of `VFile` is defined somewhat recursively. The *actual expected* type of a virtual file is the T parameter, as we can see from the declaration `self: T =>`, where this is constrained to have type T. As in the case of VFS, T is a subtype of `VFile[T]`.

Let us sit back a little and think what we can do with such a kind of definition. How could we investigate such a case? Obviously, since ultimately a VFile will be represented by some concrete class, the type T will need to be fixed to something concrete too. So, we seek a known type `ConcreteFile` for a concrete VFile implementation with the following properties:

- it will satisfy the `self: T` constraint, and
- it will be a subtype of `VFile`.

As far as the first property is concerned, a concrete implementation class `ConcreteFile` obviously gives to this a type of the same name. So, up to now we have a partial definition:

```
class ConcreteFile <... to be filled in ...> {
    // The constraint self: ConcreteFile now holds explicitly
}
```

Now, the second property dictates that the concrete file must be a subtype of VFile, so by literally translating into pseudocode, we arrive at

```
class ConcreteFile extends VFile[χ]
```

where χ must satisfy, according to the VFile[T] definition, the property χ <: VFile[χ]. But we have already established that ConcreteFile <: VFile because of the extends keyword. So χ must actually be the same as ConcreteFile itself and the complete definition reads

```
class ConcreteFile extends VFile[ConcreteFile]
```

By this type handling, we make sure that the exact type of a VFile is present at the parent trait right from the beginning and properly respected in any descendant. This holds as long as we adhere to the convention of defining concrete implementation in the way we have shown for ConcreteFile.

We now proceed to implementing some very useful file systems and their corresponding files.

9.2 Native file system

The first implementation, as expected, is that of the native file system. The relevant VFS-descendant is shown in Figure 9.3 where we can see that we have aliased java.io.File with JavaFile. The implemented methods are as follows.

mkpath This just delegates to the path factory method on the already known Path companion object.

name This gives the file system name.

newFile This always creates a new NativeFile object, resembling in this respect the familiar Java coding practice of creating a java.io.File instance via the relevant constructor.

resolve This can be characterized as not that light weight, since it has to check native resources to see whether the file actually exists. This is a price to pay for the heavy semantics the method bears, anyway.

newTempFile This leverages the respective createTempFile implementation of JavaFile and in fact the number and type of parameter of the super method in trait VFS were inspired by the Java.io.File API.

```
package scalabook.file

import scalabook.path.Path
import java.io.{File => JavaFile}

object NativeFS extends VFS[NativeFile] {
  def mkpath(name: String) = Path(name)

  def name = "NativeFS"

  override def newFile(path: Path) = NativeFile(path)

  def resolve(path: Path) = {
    val file = newFile(path)
    if(file.exists) Some(file)
    else                    None
  }

  def newTempFile(prefix: String, suffix: String) =
    NativeFile(JavaFile.createTempFile(prefix, suffix))

  def roots = JavaFile.listRoots.map { root =>
    NativeFile(root) } toList

  def container = None
}
```

Figure 9.3 The implementation of the native VFS.

roots This is a simple wrapper around the native `java.io.File`.
container This just returns None, since we consider a native file system to be top-level.

`NativeFS` is an `object`. Representing it as a singleton seems a reasonable choice, although there are other use-cases where a singleton-based design might not be the most appropriate.

Question 9.2 Can you think of a case where it would be preferable to implement a native file system using multiple class instances instead of a singleton instance?

`NativeFile` here plays the dominant role and the class and companion object definitions are given in Figures 9.4 and 9.5 respectively. The methods of `NativeFile` are as follows.

asNative This just returns this instance wrapped as an `Option`.
/ This composes the paths and gives a new file. We take advantage of the path / operator to combine the path of this instance with the provided parameter.

```
package scalabook.file

import path.Path

class NativeFile(val path: Path) extends VFile[NativeFile] {
  private[this] lazy val nfile =
    new java.io.File(path.fullName)

  override def asNative = Some(this)

  def /(that: Path) = new NativeFile(this.path / that)
  def /(that: String) = new NativeFile(this.path / that)

  def exists = nfile.exists
  def isFile = nfile.isFile
  def isFolder = nfile.isDirectory

  def inputStream = if(isFile)
        Some(new java.io.FileInputStream(path.fullName))
  else None

  def outputStream = if(isFile)
        Some(new java.io.FileOutputStream(path.fullName))
  else None

  def children = nfile.listFiles match {
    case null  => Array()
    case array => array.map { file =>
      NativeFile(file.getPath)
    }
  }

  def childrenNames = nfile.list match {
    case null  => Array()
    case array => array
  }

  def nativeJavaFile = nfile
}
```

Figure 9.4 The implementation of the native VFile.

exists, isFile, isFolder These all consult a private field named **nfile**, which is a native Java **File** used internally by the implementation.

inputStream This uses a **java.io.FileInputStream** to give access to the bytes of the native file for reading purposes. Note that the method checks to see whether we indeed have a file and not a folder.

```
package scalabook.file

import path.Path

object NativeFile {
    def apply(nfile: java.io.File) =
        new NativeFile(NativeFS.mkpath(nfile.getPath))

    def apply(path: Path) = new NativeFile(path)

    def apply(path: String) =
        new NativeFile(NativeFS.mkpath(path))
}
```

Figure 9.5 The native file companion object.

outputStream This uses a `java.io.FileOutputStream` to give access to the bytes of the native file for writing purposes. As in the case of `inputStream` it is always the caller's responsibility to close this stream when it is no longer needed.

children This takes advantage of the `java.io.File`'s `listFiles` method but we need to be careful here. In fact, according to the Javadocs it returns

An array of abstract pathnames denoting the files and directories in the directory denoted by this abstract pathname. The array will be empty if the directory is empty. Returns **null** if this abstract pathname does not denote a directory, or if an I/O error occurs.

So, we map a possible `null` value to Scala's `Array()`, which is the empty array constructor

```
        case null => Array()
```

and any other "normal" result, which is an array, to another array that contains our desired objects, created from the native ones

```
    case array => array.map { file =>
        NativeFile(file.getPath)
    }
```

Of course, all the needed types, for example the type for the `Array()` constructor, are inferred by the scala compiler.

childrenNames This also uses a Java native API to obtain the needed names.

There is an extra method in `NativeFile` that does not exist in VFile: `nativeJavaFile`. It returns the underlying `java.io.File` as a convenience to client code that might need it. The necessity for this bonus method would not exist at all if our API was so complete as to provide at least all the functionality `java.io.File` provides. For example, just to name a few missing cases, currently there is no provision for actually creating the native resource related to a folder. There is also no provision for deleting the underlying file at the operating system level. In essence, we have not exposed methods like `java.io.File.mkdir` and `java.io.File.delete` respectively.

Programming project 9.1 Try to make the API more complete, exposing as much functionality as possible from the Java APIs. The ultimate goal is not to have to expose Java APIs anymore, as we did with the `nativeJavaFile` method. It is not mandatory that each Java method should be translated to an exact method in the new API. After all, the `java.io.File` API leaves a lot to be desired from a design perspective. Just to get an idea of how poor it is, the `delete` method mentioned above returns just a `Boolean` to indicate success or failure. It would be better for the user to get some idea of what exactly is going on in the case of failure, for example an exception might be more indicative of the execution status.

9.3 Memory file system

We now turn our attention to another implementation: a file system that resides completely in memory. But why would such an implementation be useful? The obvious reason is efficiency. If anything is kept in memory, then I/O operation becomes significantly faster. Another reason is runtime restrictions. It may not be uncommon that under certain conditions, an application does not have access to the native storage. Then a file-based API should use a memory file system. For example, applets (see secion 6.11) usually run under a restricted environment in the context of a web browser and they are not given access to the client disks. Last, but not least, a very good reason for a hacker is curiosity. If we have a VFS abstraction, how far can we go playing with it?

A compiler also presents a use case where a memory file system can be handy and in fact the Scala compiler uses some internal abstractions that enable it to work with in-memory files. Also, in today's highly dynamic JVM programming environments it is not uncommon to generate classes on-the-fly and then instantly load them in the space of an application. That *instant loading* can be achieved by using a memory file system.

It is evident from a walk-through of Figure 9.6 that we will need two separate abstractions for VFiles. A `MemoryFile` represents a file and a `MemoryFolder` represents an in-memory container of other `MemoryFiles` and `MemoryFolders`. As we will see shortly, both `MemoryFile` and `MemoryFolder` are derived from a parent trait, `MemFile`. But first, let us take a look at `MemFS`.

```
package scalabook.file

import scala.collection.mutable
import path.Path

class MemFS(val name: String) extends VFS[MemFile] {
  private[this] val MemRoot: MemFile =
    new MemoryFolder(this, Path.UnixPath("/"))

  protected[file] val cache =
    mutable.HashMap[Path, MemFile](MemRoot.path -> MemRoot)

  def mkpath(name: String) = Path.UnixPath("/" + name)

  def roots = MemRoot :: Nil

  override def root = MemRoot

  def container = None

  def newTempFile(prefix: String, suffix: String) =
    throw new UnsupportedOperationException

  override def newFolder(path: Path) =
    cache.getOrElseUpdate(path, new MemoryFolder(this, path))

  override def newFile(path: Path) =
    cache.getOrElseUpdate(path, new MemoryFile(this, path))

  override def resolve(path: Path) = cache.get(path)

  override def toString = "MemFS(" + name + ")"
}
```

Figure 9.6 The implementation of a memory VFS.

9.3.1 *Memory VFS*

The ingredients of MemFS are shown in Figure 9.6.

name This is the name of the MemFS. Note that we use a val declaration in the
  constructor, so that this field is visible outside the class.

MemRoot This is a value representing the sole root of the file system.

cache This is actually the backbone of our implementation. It is a Map from Paths
  to MemFiles. The design we have adopted favors storing full paths for all the files
  and folders of the in-memory file system. This is probably the most straightforward
  approach. But how then is the hierarchical nature of a VFS going to emerge? The

answer is: implicitly and by computation. Since we know the full names of all files, for each parent folder we can compute the contained children.

mkpath This constructs a new `Path` from a `String` with a slight departure from the implementation one would normally expect. Instead of feeding the `Path` factory with the bare path name, we prepend a `/`. The reason is that, by our convention, an in-memory file path has to be an absolute one. The memory file system does not track relative paths. Regarding the path semantics we follow for this implementation, it is clear from the use of the `UnixPath` factory that we use the canonical path representation introduced in Section 8.6.3.

root This is the one and only `UnixRoot`. Since this is common to all instances of `MemFS`, it would be a good idea to refactor it into some singleton object.

container This returns `None` just as with the native file system implementation. By convention, a `MemFS` is not contained anywhere.

newTempFile This is currently not implemented in our small library.

Exercise 9.1 Write an implementation for `newTempFile`. How would you generate random file names?

newFile This returns a file if and only if it exists in the cache. Recalling the discussion in Section 9.1.3 and the details of Figure 9.1 we see that this VFS implementation always creates a new underlying file or folder if it does not exist. But the reference implementation in Figure 9.6 is flawed.

Exercise 9.2 Can you spot the error? Provide a better implementation. Hint: The fact that one asks for a `newFolder` and the `cache` already contains some mapping with the same path does not necessarily mean that the contained mapping refers to a folder and not a file. Also do not forget to update the cache if needed.

newFolder This returns a folder if and only if it exists in the cache. The same semantics as with `newFile` hold here as well.

resolve This consults the `cache` if the path exists.

9.3.2 Memory files and folders

`MemFile` is the parent trait of `MemoryFile`. The former is defined as follows:

```scala
sealed trait MemFile extends VFile[MemFile] {
  protected def combined(
    memFS: MemFS,
    full: Path,
    endingSlash: Boolean): MemFile =

    memFS.resolve(full) match {
```

```
      case Some(file) =>
        file
      case None =>
        if(endingSlash)
          memFS.newFolder(full)
        else
          memFS.newFile(full)
  }
}
```

while the latter is given in Figure 9.7. The sole purpose of MemFile is to provide the method combined which takes care of path composition. The details, although easy to follow, are a bit more complex than what we have usually seen. The reason is twofold.

First, memory files and folders are separate entities and this is reflected by the particular memory file system implementation. Second, we need a way to inform our MemFS API that, given a String which represents a path, the requested VFile is a file or folder. The endingSlash last argument plays exactly this role. If its value is true, the API understands that the client code means folder instead of file.

Each MemoryFile is backed by an array of bytes for its storage. This array, bytes, is mutable, since we need to update every time client code appends bytes to the file. The most notable methods of MemoryFile are those regarding the input and output streams.

Creating an input stream is merely constructing a new byte array input stream. Creating an output stream is just a bit more involved, since we need to update the underlying byte array when the stream is closed. Of course, closing the stream is solely a responsibility of client code.

The in-memory folder, MemoryFolder is shown in Figure 9.8. The method that returns the children contained in the folder

```
def children =
  memFS.cache.values.filter(_.path.isChildOf(path)).toList
```

uses an unknown, so far, operation on paths, namely isChildOf. The requirement for ischildOf is that it must return true if the current path (this) is a path contained in the immediate children hierarchy of the passed argument. The signature needed is

```
def isChildOf(that: Path): Boolean
```

```
package scalabook.file

import scalabook.path.Path

class MemoryFile(memFS: MemFS, val path: Path)
        extends MemFile {

  private[this] var bytes = new Array[Byte](0)

  def exists = true

  def isFile = true

  def isFolder = false

  def children = Nil

  def childrenNames = Nil

  def /(that: String) =
    combined(memFS, this.path / that, that.endsWith("/"))

  def /(that: Path) =
    combined(memFS, this.path / that, false)

  def inputStream =
    Some(new java.io.ByteArrayInputStream(bytes))

  def outputStream =
    Some(new java.io.ByteArrayOutputStream {
      override def close = {
        super.close

        MemoryFile.this.bytes = this.toByteArray
      }
    })
}
```

Figure 9.7 The implementation of the in-memory file.

Exercise 9.3 Make an incremental modification to the definition of Path and implement isChildOf.

Exercise 9.4 Redesign MemFS so that cache is not needed as it is. Instead, take a hierarchical approach, where each MemoryFolder directly stores its children, so that information is kept in a more local manner.

```
package scalabook.file

import scalabook.path.Path

class MemoryFolder(memFS: MemFS, val path: Path)
        extends MemFile {

  def exists = true

  def isFile = false

  def isFolder = true

  def inputStream = None

  def outputStream = None

  def children =
  memFS.cache.values.
      filter(_.path.isChildOf(path)).toList

  def childrenNames = children.map(_.name)

  def /(that: String) =
    combined(
      memFS,
      this.path / that,
      that.endsWith("/"))

  def /(that: Path) =
    combined(
      memFS,
      this.path / that,
      false)
}
```

Figure 9.8 The implementation of the in-memory folder.

9.4 Zip file system

9.4.1 Preliminaries

We now develop a VFS implementation for zip (and jar) files. Actually, we are going
to use JDK APIs, so whatever can be processed by those APIs can be represented
as a zip file system by our implementation. Zip and jar files are ubiquitous. The
CLASSPATH is normally full of them. Modern applications, like OpenOffice.org

and Microsoft Office, in its latest version, both use disguised zip archives for their documents. We only have to open an .odt or a .docx file with a GUI archiver or just issue

```
$ unzip -l SomeDoc.odt
```

in the command line to discover that this is indeed the case.

A zip file system (ZipFS for short) is based on the existence of some other VFile, whose contents are interpreted as a zip archive. This VFile need not be a native one. In fact, since we now have a little VFS framework we will take advantage of it and give the ability to create a ZipFS from any virtual file. Our ZipFS is a read-only one. The intention is to keep the codebase to a minimum yet functional point.

We will not re-invent the wheel but will try to take advantage of existing JDK APIs. A guiding point is the java.util.zip.ZipFile class. If we take a look at its constructor from the Javadocs, we will see that the implementation of a java.util.zip.ZipFile is based on a java.io.File. So, it is clear that in order to reach generality, any VFile which will be used as the archive has to be transformed to a java.io.File or, in our library, to a NativeFile. The next utility method is almost inevitable:

```
package scalabook.file
import java.io._

object IOUtil {
  def copy(in: InputStream, out: OutputStream,
           closeIn: Boolean, closeOut: Boolean) {
    val buffer = new Array[Byte](4096)
    var count = in read buffer

    while (count > -1) {
      out.write(buffer, 0, count)
      count = in read buffer
    }

    if(closeIn)  in.close
    if(closeOut) out.close
  }
}
```

The above imperative loop must be almost everywhere on the Internet. The next group of utility methods build upon the previous definition:

```scala
package scalabook.file
import java.io.File => JavaFile
import VFS.AnyFile


object FileUtil {

  def createTmpFile =
    NativeFS.newTempFile("scalabook-vfs", "tmp")

  def copy[T <: VFile[T]](from: AnyFile, to: T): T = {
    IOUtil.copy(
      from.inputStream.get,
      to.outputStream.get,
      true,
      true)

    to
  }

  def materializeToNative(file: AnyFile): NativeFile =
    if(file.isNative)
      file.asNative.get
    else if(!file.exists)
      error("File %s does not exist".format(file))
    else if(file.isFolder)
      error("File %s is a folder".format(file))
    else
      copy(file, createTmpFile)
}
```

Remember that our goal is to create a NativeFile out of any kind of VFile. That is the role of materializeToNative. An efficiency check at the beginning of its definition makes sure that an already NativeFile will not be copied over to some other temporary NativeFile. Of the two other methods in object FileUtil, createTmpFile is a wrapper around our own VFS API and copy presents some interest regarding its T type. The constraint we use, T <: VFile[T], is the same trick as in the very definition of VFile. In effect, the method accepts any VFile-like type, since `AnyFile` is an alias for `VFile[_]`, and generates a file of the same specific type of the `to` parameter.

9.4.2 Zip VFS

Before delving into the implementation of `ZipFS`, we need to say a few words about the approach we take. The general idea is that on instantiation of a `ZipFS`, we load the archive and create a cache of its entries. But this is not such a straightforward approach as it may seem initially.

   The main problem is that in a zip archive, there may be missing directory entries. Unfortunately, when client code decides to open a zip archive it is too late to control what is and what is not within the archive, so our library code must cope with the situation. We remedy the missing directory entries case by introducing "fake" virtual folders. Just to make sure the hierarchy is correct, we even inject manually the root folder `/`. The hierarchy that we create is a canonical, Unix-like file hierarchy. We now introduce the `ZipFS` definition:

```
package scalabook.file

class ZipFS(source: AnyFile) extends VFS[ZipFile] {
  protected[file] val (nativeZip, path2file) = loadEntries

  private[this] def loadEntries() = {
    val tmpJavaNative =
      FileUtil.materializeToNative(source).nativeJavaFile

    val nativeZip = new JavaZipFile(tmpJavaNative)
    val path2vfile = new mutable.HashMap[Path, ZipFile]

    var entriesEnum = nativeZip.entries
    while(entriesEnum.hasMoreElements) {
      val nextEntry = entriesEnum.nextElement
      val entryPath = mkpath(nextEntry.getName)
      val zipFile = new ZipFile(this, entryPath, nextEntry)

      path2vfile(entryPath) = zipFile
    }

    // add non-existent folder entries
    val missingPaths = new mutable.HashSet[Path]
    path2vfile.foreach { case (path, _) =>
```

```
def mkAllPaths(path: Path, all: List[Path]): List[Path]
= {
  val parent = path.parent
  if(parent.isEmpty)
    path :: all
  else
    mkAllPaths(parent, path :: all)
}

mkAllPaths(path, List()).foreach { path =>
  if(!path2vfile.contains(path))
    missingPaths(path) = true
}
}

missingPaths.foreach{ path =>
  path2vfile(path) = new SyntheticZipFolder(this, path)
}

// add root
val rootFile =
  new SyntheticZipFolder(this, ZipFS.RootPath)
path2vfile(ZipFS.RootPath) = rootFile

(nativeZip, path2vfile)
  }
}
```

The method that does all the caching and detection of nonexistent directory entries
is loadEntries. First of all, we create a NativeFile – the one that will be used
to instantiate a java.util.zip.ZipFile – and store it in val tmpJavaNative.
The caching map is path2vfile. Next, we iterate over all entries and update the
caching map. This procedure gives us a global view of what is in the archive.

But we are not done yet, since we need to create any missing entries synthetically.
The nested utility method mkAllPaths takes a path as input and generates a List
of all the path's hierarchy. We then check this hierarchy of parent paths and record
any part that was not discovered when we iterated the archive entries

```
mkAllPaths(path, List()).foreach { path =>
  if(!path2vfile.contains(path))
    missingPaths(path) = true
}
```

This procedure that checks a path hierarchy is repeated for all the discovered paths of the archive, as we can see by the outer loop

```
path2vfile.foreach { case (path, _) =>
  ...
}
```

The loop is over the path2vfile map entries and, of course, from the entry tuple we only consider the path.

Finally, we store the ZipFS root manually

```
val rootFile = new SyntheticZipFolder(this, ZipFS.RootPath)
path2vfile(ZipFS.RootPath) = rootFile
```

and then return the tuple (nativeZip, path2vfile) which is stored in the ZipFS vals nativeZip and path2file respectively.

The remaining methods are the usual VFS methods that must be implemented.

```
class ZipFS...{ //continued
  def newTempFile(prefix: String, suffix: String) =
    error("Unsupported operation")

  def name = toString

  override def toString = "ZipFS(" + source + ")"

  def mkpath(name: String) = Path.UnixPath("/") / name

  def newFile(path: Path) =
    resolve(path).getOrElse(NoFile.as[ZipFile])

  override def resolve(path: Path) = path2file.get(path)

  def container = Some(source)

  override def isContained = true

  def roots = List(path2file(ZipFS.RootPath))
}
```

The ZipFS.RootPath value is given in the ZipFS object and we will also need to define NoFile.

9.4.3 *Zip VFS factory object*

Following our usual practice, we introduce a factory object.

```
package scalabook.file
import scalabook.path.Path

object ZipFS {
  val RootPath = Path.UnixPath("/")

  def apply(path: Path): ZipFS =
    new ZipFS(NativeFile(path))

  def apply(path: String): ZipFS =
    new ZipFS(NativeFile(path))

  def apply(vfile: AnyFile): ZipFS =
    new ZipFS(vfile)
}
```

9.4.4 *A VFile that does not exist*

During the implementation of ZipFS and in particular its newFile method the need has arisen to return a nonexistent VFile. We implement such a VFile in two steps:

```
package scalabook.file
import scalabook.path.Path

sealed class NoFileType extends VFile[NoFileType] {
  def path = Path("")
  def exists = false
  def isFile = false
  def isFolder = false
  def children = Nil
  def childrenNames = Nil

  private[this] def unsupported =
    throw new UnsupportedOperationException

  def /(that: String) = unsupported
  def /(that: Path) = unsupported
```

```
    def inputStream = unsupported
    def outputStream = unsupported

    override def equals(any: Any) = this == any

    def as[T <: VFile[T]] = this.asInstanceOf[T]
}
```

```
object NoFile extends NoFileType
```

In the first step, we define a concrete class with the proper type and make it sealed so that no client code can ever extend it. In the second step we use the sealed class to define a singleton. A VFile that does not exist has a uniform behavior across all cases and so there is no need to create new instances each time.

The above two-step procedure is necessary, since there is no way to satisfy the Scala type inferencer by trying to define the singleton directly:

```
scala> import scalabook.file._
import scalabook.file._

scala> object FooSingleton extends VFile[FooSingleton]
<console>:6: error: not found: type FooSingleton
       object FooSingleton extends VFile[FooSingleton]
                                         ^

scala> object FooSingleton extends VFile[FooSingleton.type]
<console>:6: error: illegal cyclic reference involving object
                                                  FooSingleton
object FooSingleton extends VFile[FooSingleton.type]
                                  ^
```

In Scala, singletons have their own type which is distinct from the type of the class they extend.

9.4.5 Zip VFile

A virtual zip file is tightly coupled not only to the container zip file system but also to the underlying native (at least as far as Java is concerned) entry in the actual archive:

```
package scalabook.file
```

```
class ZipFile(
  zipFS: ZipFS,
  val path: Path,
  entry: JavaZipEntry) extends VFile[ZipFile] {

  private[this] var childrenCache = List[ZipFile]()

  def inputStream =
    Some(zipFS.nativeZip.getInputStream(entry))

  def outputStream = None

  def children =
    if(!childrenCache.isEmpty)
      childrenCache
    else {
      val childrenBuffer = new mutable.ListBuffer[ZipFile]

    zipFS.path2file.foreach {
      case (tpath, tfile) =>
        if(tpath.isChildOf(path))
          childrenBuffer += tfile
    }

    childrenCache = childrenBuffer.toList
    childrenCache
    }
}
```

Exercise 9.5 Implement the rest of the `ZipFile` methods.

One more addition is that of `SyntheticZipFolder`. Recall that we create synthetic entries in the `ZipFS` cache for all missing directory entries of the archive. Instances of `SyntheticZipFolder` represent just these missing entries:

```
// in the same package
class SyntheticZipFolder(zipFS: ZipFS, path: Path)
    extends ZipFile(zipFS, path, null) {

  override def isFolder = true
}
```

10

Compositional file matching

10.1 Matching files

Now that we have all the file machinery, we can build a few abstractions based on them. First, our motivation is the recurring pattern of searching for files that match specific criteria. Those who feel more than comfortable working in the command line – and we refer, unless explicitly stated otherwise, to the Unix command line – must have issued this or a relevant command more than a few times:

```
$ find . -type d -maxdepth 1
./.git
./chapter-cas
./chapter-ep
./chapter-file
./chapter-path
./chapter-patterns
./chapter-proguard
```

The above command gives us all subdirectories of the current one. The -type d instruction means "keeps only directories" and -maxdepth 1 goes no further down the hierarchy than the current directory. For what it is worth, find is really a very helpful command. The reader is invited to search the Web for more information on the find utility.

Returning to the VFile API, the task seems almost straightforward. The children of a folder are already available, so we just need to pick the right ones:

```
scala> import scalabook.file._
import scalabook.file._

scala> val cwd = NativeFile(".")
cwd: scalabook.file.NativeFile = .
```

```
scala> cwd.children.filter(_.isFolder)
res0: Iterable[NativeFile] = Array(././.git, ./chapter-cas, ...)
```

The Scala one-liner `cwd.children.filter(_.isFolder)` is the equivalent of the shell one-liner `find . -type d -maxdepth 1`. The iteration procedure, which is inherent in the `filter` method, selects only those children that *match* the specific criterion expressed by `_.isFolder`. We could use a similar approach to select just the regular files instead of the folders and the object-functional nature of Scala, with its native support for higher-order functions, usually makes this or similar goals a oneline experience, or quite close to it, if typesetting constraints must be obeyed.

```
cwd.children.filter(f => f.isFile && f.name.endsWith(".sh"))
```

These higher-order functions, like `filter` that we are using here, are fundamental building blocks. These blocks act like small components ready to be composed by the programmer. All we need to do is provide them with the appropriate input. The input itself can be as simple as `_.isFolder` is or it can be the outcome of a more compositional approach, for example

```
f => f.isFile && f.name.endsWith(".sh")
```

as above.

We are actually talking about two kinds of composition here. The first one is related to the combination of higher-order functions. It does not appear in the previous examples but we have emphasized its significance. It is easy to picture a series of *function applications* using, for example, `map` and `filter` that can help us select the appropriate data with the appropriate type and this is the traditional bottom-up approach of functional programming:

```
cwd.filter(_.isFile).map(_.path)
```

The second kind of composition, the one that is explicit in the above examples of selecting the appropriate files, relates to the argument passed to `filter`. In the first case, which is just a simple one, the selection is based on a straightforward function, since our `_.isFolder` is nothing more than an on-the-fly definition of a function value. We can use the Scala interpreter to verify this intuition and check that the types and the functionality are as expected:

```
scala> val isFolderCheck = (f: NativeFile) => f.isFolder
isFolderCheck: (NativeFile) => Boolean = <function>
```

```
scala> cwd.children.filter(isFolderCheck)
res1: Iterable[NativeFile] = Array(././.git, ./chapter-cas, ...)
```

In the case where we try to match specific files we use the boolean *and* operator
&& in order to combine pieces of smaller functionality into one greater functional
block.

This is all great. It would be much more verbose to achieve the same effect using a
language without first-class functions. Java, for example, would require the explicit
– that is, on behalf of the programmer – introduction of an inner class instance
that we would have to pass to the analog of a `filter` method. Scala is concise and
compositional. Yet, we can do better.

10.2 A less procedural approach

We only have to keep in mind our original goal, which is *searching for files that
match specific criteria* and then try to put ourselves in the position of a potential
user: Why would a user of our library have to go through the two-step *procedure*
shown in Figure 10.1? Note our emphasis on the word *procedure*, which in the figure
is characterized by the series of actions, that is, method calls. Our intention is mixed
with implementation details that show how to obtain what we want, step-by-step.
Clearly, a more declarative approach that hides the calls to both `children` and
`filter` might be a more user-friendly line of attack. In effect, we are seeking better
syntax, something more direct, as shown in Figure 10.2.

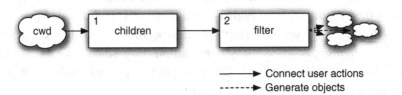

Figure 10.1 A two-step procedure to match a few files. The clouds depict virtual
files and the boxes indicate the actions necessary to get from the initial file to the
matched files. Any criteria used in the process are assumed to be part of the boxes
and are not shown.

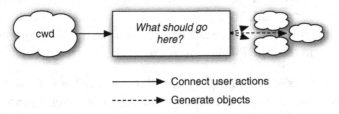

Figure 10.2 Seeking a more declarative approach to express the matching files
discovery process.

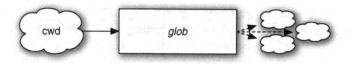

Figure 10.3 Substituting the two-step procedure for file matching with a shorter form.

Let us seek some inspiration from the idea of *glob patterns*.[1] Globbing is a functionality offered by several shells (that is, command line interpreters, like `bash` in Unix or `cmd.exe` under Windows) that deals with a particular form of pattern matching for file names and even whole paths. It is probable that anyone who has had experience writing commands in a shell, will have used the two most common patterns of a glob:

the question mark `?` denoting the appearance of any character just once and
the star `*` denoting the appearance of zero or more characters (any characters).

A couple of examples from the authors' disk drive, while working on this book:

```
$ ls *.tex
chapter-file.tex      chapter-path.tex      unicode-math-add.tex
chapter-iter.tex      scalabook.tex         unicode-math.tex

$ ls ?nicode*.tex
unicode-math-add.tex      unicode-math.tex
```

The patterns we can formulate based on globbing are not as powerful as regular expressions, but they are very handy on occasion. Everyday programming has proven them to be invaluable.

Now, it would be great just to say `cwd glob "*.scala"` and get all the files under `cwd` with a `scala` suffix in their names. Then, our little figure would look something like Figure 10.3.

Again, as in Figure 10.1, we are hiding any criteria that will be used while globbing. They are, in a way, *absorbed* in the globbing action. Initially, we used `find` and constrained it to a `maxdepth` of one. In our introduction of the glob patterns, we used the `ls` command, which by default operates to a maximum depth of one. Clearly, the ability of `find` to operate as deep as possible reflects a much different requirement than just listing the direct children of a folder. The difference in requirements is aligned with the fact that a simple, straight combination of `children` and `filter` cannot do the job for folder hierarchy depths of more than

---

[1] See the wikipedia entry at http://en.wikipedia.org/wiki/Glob_(programming). Under Unix, there is also the `fnmatch` C library call that tests whether a filename or pathname matches a shell-style pattern, that is a glob pattern.

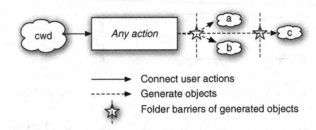

Figure 10.4 Describing a matching action on cwd that results in several objects not necessarily in the same folder. Note that we are explicit in showing the folder barriers of the generated file objects.

one. So, apart from the procedural versus declarative argument, we have yet one more reason to hide the exact sequence of actions behind a shorter, indicative form.

An even shorter syntactic alternative is almost suggesting itself by some visual inspiration. We will borrow the star * character from glob patterns and make it into a Scala operator. Using one * means that we search directly under a specific directory, so that

```
cwd glob "*.scala"
```

becomes

```
cwd * "*.scala"
```

We can go one step further and introduce a double star ** operator, meaning that our search extends to hierarchy depths of one or more. Using a modified form of our graphical notation, the general idea is given in Figure 10.4. Folder barriers are denoted with a star, so that files a and b are discovered directly under cwd, while file c is discovered further down in the file system hierarchy. Sometimes, it is not clear how the interplay between graphical notation and the standard API writing procedure (or the design process) evolves. For example, we could have started from the visual characteristics of the figure and introduced the star operator from there. In our times, with software complexity more evident than ever, a prominent tool for tackling it may be graphical notations that favor a compositional approach.

Clearly, there is no method glob or the newly introduced * anywhere in the definition of our VFiles. We will just keep in mind that it will most certainly have to be introduced at some part of our design. For the moment, let us concentrate on how to represent the criteria themselves. Our inspiration has been the glob patterns but, of course, these are special cases of more general "patterns" that can operate on types other than files as well:

```
package scalabook.file.matcher

trait Matcher[T] {
```

```
    def matches(t: T): Boolean
}
```

Then, a VFile matcher can be represented as `Matcher[VFile[_]]` or, since we have already introduced the type alias

```
type AnyFile = VFile[_]
```

in the VFS object, as just

```
type FileMatcher = Matcher[AnyFile]
```

The use of an existential type, via the wildcard-type nature of the underscore in the definition of `AnyFile`, is a design decision. The origin of this decision is in the definition of `matches` in trait `Matcher`. If type T of the supplied parameter corresponds to a file, then T will be in the form `VFile[A]`. But T is not reflected in the return type of `matches` and, as a consequence, the exact type of `VFile[A]` and therefore A is lost. No matter what the parameter is, only a `Boolean` survives. That is why our type alias for `FileMatcher` uses `AnyFile`. Using the rough equation

$$T = \text{VFile}[A]$$

as explained above for the parameter of `matches`, we actually instruct the Scala compiler to interpret it as

$$T = \text{VFile}[A] \text{ for some type } A$$

whose right-hand side, quite interestingly, translates directly to Scala as

```
            VFile[A] forSome { type A; }
```

It is time to write down an extension of `VFile` that incorporates the * operator for file matching:

```
package scalabook.file.matcher

class VFileWithStar[T <: VFile[T]](file: T) {
  import VFileWithStar.FileMatcher

  def *(matcher: FileMatcher): Iterable[T] =
    file.children.filter(matcher.matches)
}

object VFileWithStar {
  import scalabook.file.VFS.AnyFile
```

```
type FileMatcher = Matcher[AnyFile]

implicit def file2fileWithStar[T <: VFile[T]](f: T) =
    new VFileWithStar(f)
}
```

The `VFileWithStar` object is responsible for some book-keeping and extra flexibility, by defining the `FileMatcher` type and providing an implicit conversion from an instance of `VFile` to an instance of the the `VFileWithStar` class. The latter is an enriched version of `VFile` with the extra functionality of one-level file matching via the * method, which is trivially implemented using functional abstractions.

Note that

```
file.children.filter(matcher.matches)
```

is a shorthand for

```
file.children.filter(matcher.matches(_))
```

which can be further expanded to

```
file.children.filter(f => matcher.matches(f))
```

but, by now, we expect that the shortest form feels quite natural. It can be even shorter by writing it as `file.children filter matcher.matches`, that is in the form *object method parameter*.

So, in order to make use of the new machinery, we should properly import the implicit definitions; and we are saying *definitions*, since there is still a bit more stuff to program before delving into testing and experimentation.

In contrast to our reasoning for `FileMatcher` and the use of an existential type, a closer look at the `VFileWithStar` class shows a clear intention to preserve the exact type information of `VFile` by explicitly using the symbol for type T. The reason is the signature of method *, which is indicative of our expectations: a `FileMatcher` is expected to return the same type of file as that of the file used to construct an instance of `VFileWithStar`. For instance, trying to match virtual files under a zip file system should normally return zip virtual files, not native files, and this is a useful piece of information we do not want to discard.

10.3 Glob-style matching implementation

Towards our goal of implementing some concrete `FileMatcher`, we observe that a matcher for glob patterns can be thought of as a special `FileMatcher` that operates on just the path of a file:

```
package scalabook.file.matcher

trait FilePathMatcher extends VFileWithStar.FileMatcher {
  def matches(file: AnyFile) = matchesPath(file.path)

  def matchesPath(path: Path): Boolean
}
```

A straightforward implementation of this sort of matcher is one that inspects the file path extension:

```
package scalabook.file.matcher

class ExtensionMatcher(ext: String) extends FilePathMatcher {
  def matchesPath(path: Path) =
    path.extension.toLowerCase == ext.toLowerCase
}
```

Then, the glob-style matcher in Figure 10.5 is another special case of a `FilePathMatcher`. There are two things about the glob implementation that deserve a special remark. First, we use the prefix `Weak` for the class name to denote that we do not support full glob-style matching, in the lines of the Unix tradition. Only the simple file name matching is supported.

Exercise 10.1 Consult the Unix man page for the C function `fnmatch` in order to see the full potential of glob patterns. Under a Unix shell this is normally achieved by executing the command `man fnmatch`. The relevant piece of information can also be easily found on the Internet. Then augment the current glob pattern implementation borrowing ideas from `fnmatch`.

Second, we do not code any full-blown glob interpreter. Instead, in order to interpret a glob pattern, we leverage the power of regular expressions. We transform the pattern into a regular expression directly by following a few rules.

- We escape any backslash "\," period " .," bracket " [" and "]," dollar "$," parenthesis " (" and ")" and caret "ˆ," since they have special meaning in regular expressions.
- We are being careful first to escape backslash itself and then other characters, like the bracket, since otherwise it would be escaped twice.

```
package scalabook.file.matcher
import util.matching.Regex
import scalabook.path.Path

class WeakGlobMatcher(glob: String)
              extends FilePathMatcher {

  val globRE = new Regex("^(?i)" + glob
    .replace("\\", "\\\\")
    .replace(".", "\\.")
    .replace("[", "\\[").replace("]", "\\]")
    .replace("(", "\\(").replace(")", "\\)")
    .replace("*", ".+")
    .replace("?", ".?")
    .replace("$", "\\$")
    .replace("^", "\\^") + "$")

  def matchesPath(path: Path) =
    globRE.pattern.matcher(path.name).matches

  def toREString = globRE.pattern.toString

  override def toString = glob
}
```

Figure 10.5 A class implementing weak glob-style matching on file names.

- We transform the star "*" glob operator, which means *one or more appearances of any character*, to the equivalent regular expression form ".+."
- We transform the question mark "?" glob operator, which means *zero or one appearance of any character*, to the regular expression form ".?"
- We add a prefix of "^" and a suffix of "$," so that we subsequently match the whole input, that is the whole file name.
- We use the (?i) special construct, which instructs the underlying regular expression engine to be case insensitive. Alternatively, we can leave this piece off and just support case sensitivity as the default.

Method matchesPath uses the exposed val pattern of class Regex in order to obtain a proper matcher for the file name. Note that pattern is of type Pattern from the JDK package java.util.regex, so the code relies on Java features to work. Another implementation detail is that we construct a matcher each time we need to make a glob match against a file name. A few CPU cycles can be saved if we take advantage of the fact that a java.util.regex.Matcher can be reused.

Usually, Java programmers either forget about this behavior or are totally unaware of it. In any case, the relevant method of Matcher and the Java documentation is clear:

```
public Matcher reset(CharSequence input)
```

Resets this matcher with a new input sequence. Resetting a matcher discards all of its explicit state information and sets its append position to zero...

So, following the above recommendation, the code can be changed by renaming globRE to globREMatcher, so that it reflects its purpose better, then using one more call to get a matcher

```
val globREMatcher = new Regex("^" + glob
    .replace("\\", "\\\\")
    ...
    .replace("^", "\\^") + "$").matcher("")
```

and, finally, changing the implementation of matchesPath in WeakGlobMatcher to use the matcher instead of the pattern.

```
def matchesPath(path: Path) =
    globREMatcher.reset(path.name).matches
```

Now we have already introduced regular expressions in Section 2.15. Everything seems in place and ready for immediate use, yet the observant reader may think that we have crossed language borders or, phrasing it more realistically, that we have crossed library borders. Regex is a perfectly valid Scala class, yet our implementation has dived into plain Java territory by using Pattern and Matcher, both under the JDK package java.util.regex. Was that inevitable? Was that necessary?

Before discussing the reason for this, if any, let us consider the approach of using a pure-Scala API. Looking at Regex, the method findFirstIn is of interest and seems to fit the purpose:

```
def  findFirstIn(source : CharSequence): Option[String]
```

Return optionally first matching string of this regexp in given character sequence, None if it does not exist.

Returning to the glob matching problem, it is easy to see that if the glob pattern matches, then there is certainly a first match and it is clear that Some(x) will be returned by findFirstIn. Conversely, if findFirstIn returns Some(x), where x is the matching string, then obviously there was a match for our glob pattern! Once more, we change globRE and we patch matchesPath, so that now we stick to a pure-Scala API:

```scala
val globRE = new Regex("^" + glob
    .replace("\\", "\\\\")
    ...
    .replace("^", "\\^") + "$")

def matchesPath(path: Path) =
    globRE.findFirstIn(path.name).isDefined
```

10.3.1 *Remarks on a (non) pure-Scala implementation*

Returning to the questions, the digression from a pure-Scala approach was not entirely on purpose. We believe it reflects a real-world situation. There are several reasons why we might act similarly in other situations.

- We are so used to programming in Java that the necessary ingredients for an algorithm are almost seen in front of our eyes in JDK terms. This kind of behavior may persist even after one goes beyond the level of a *beginner Scala programmer*. Although there is no study to analyze the relevant behavior, a possible factor playing a key role is how much is the percentage of coding divided between Java and Scala.
- We are new to Scala programming, coming immediately from a Java background. As in the previous case, familiar classes from the JDK and relevant coding idioms are recalled easily and on-the-spot.
- The Scala library itself lacks the necessary features. This is not uncommon these days. In fact, one may argue that Scala still needs more libraries to reach a critical mass that would make it "feature-full." In such a case, we will inevitably have to resort either to the JDK or to some external Java library.
- The Scala library incorporates the necessary features, but in a not very satisfactory way. Here, *satisfactory* may mean different things to different people:
  fast
  well-designed
  thorough
  memory-efficient
  understandable
  to name a few. A combination of the above is also possible.

The "understandable" part is quite interesting. Scala, being an object-functional language, is different from current mainstream programming. A programmer who has been taught to think in a certain style or a particular language, may find it difficult to grasp the essence of this blend of object-oriented and functional programming. It may even feel "unnatural" during the very first steps. In those moments, techniques and code from a previous language, like Java, may come in handy.

So, it depends on the current state of Scala, on one's knowledge of the Scala platform and one's approach or even taste for programming. What can we do? One might be tempted to propose that the best overall advice to give is *go with a Scala implementation or contribute one to the community unless the feature is considered a lower-level one.* But in reality there are also other dimensions to consider. In fact, we have not yet mentioned *deadlines,* a scary fact of everyday professional programming. What if the deadline is tight, we know the feature exists in Scala but we are much more proficient in using an equivalent pure-Java library?

A pragmatic example is the Scala collections library. This deviates from the standard Java collections library, so that it can embrace the general programming style that Scala promotes. This is evident in the use of higher-order functions (HOFs) like `map` and `filter`. Since Scala provides such a comprehensive library, it is considered bad style to use Java collections when programming algorithms in pure Scala. Of course, the mix with pure Java implementation is inevitable when dealing with the real world, but exactly for that reason appropriate wrappers exist, which bridge the gap between the two worlds.

On the other hand, there are some features that can be considered lower level. These are either related to interfacing with the *native* world, meaning that the implementation is non-Java – probably something like C – or are considered fundamental building blocks that need not be duplicated. The interface `CharSequence` is the common parent of `String`, `StringBuffer` and `StringBuilder`, the ubiquitous Java classes. Even `java.nio.CharBuffer`, a core class in the Java New I/O (NIO[2]) standard library, implements it. So, it is natural to transfer this interface to our Scala coding practice. Yet, the truth is that time will tell exactly which coding patterns will survive.

10.4 Using glob-style matching

What we have so far is essentially an operator implementation to match against the files of a folder and proper abstractions that can handle virtual file matching. Concrete implementations of glob pattern matching took advantage of regular expression support, both in the Scala library and the JDK. The mini library is ready for a few tests. Let us assume that our current directory structure is

```
ls -al
-rwxr-xr-x  1 loverdos  staff    405 Jul  9 16:32 compile
-rwxr-xr-x  1 loverdos  staff     55 Jul  9 16:32 console
-rw-r--r--  1 loverdos  staff     37 Jul  9 16:32 console.bat
```

---

[2] The NIO library was introduced in Java version 1.4. It provides among other features the building blocks of more scalable network and file I/O than is possible with the traditional `java.io` API.

```
drwxr-xr-x   2 loverdos   staff     68 Jul  9 16:32 lib
drwxr-xr-x   5 loverdos   staff    170 Jul  9 18:47 project
drwxr-xr-x   4 loverdos   staff    136 Jul  9 16:32 src
drwxr-xr-x   7 loverdos   staff    238 Aug 17 15:12 target
-rw-r--r--   1 loverdos   staff  12511 Jul  9 16:32 test-1.jar
-rw-r--r--   1 loverdos   staff  11514 Aug 26 19:20 test-2.jar
-rw-r--r--@  1 loverdos   staff   1061 Aug 22 17:03 test-iter
-rw-r--r--   1 loverdos   staff    113 Jul  9 16:32 test.scala
drwxr-xr-x   6 loverdos   staff    204 Jul  9 16:32 uml
```

and move on to the Scala interpreter:

```
scala> import scalabook.file._
import scalabook.file._


scala> val cwd = NativeFile(".")
cwd: scalabook.file.NativeFile = .
```

Now, do we have any .scala files around? Let us see whether the * operator works:

```
scala> val cwdScalaFiles = cwd * "*.scala"
<console>:7: error: value * is not a member of
                    scalabook.file.NativeFile
       val cwdScalaFiles = cwd * "*.scala"
                               ^
```

But this can be easily remedied. First, we need to augment the VFileWithStar object with one more implicit conversion:

```
// continued
object VFileWithStar {
  implicit def glob2Matcher(glob: String) =
    new WeakGlobMatcher(glob)
}
```

Second, we need to import the implicit conversion and we are ready to try again.

```
scala> import scalabook.file.matcher.VFileWithStar._
import scalabook.file.matcher.VFileWithStar._


scala> val cwdScalaFiles = cwd * "*.scala"
cwdScalaFiles: Iterable[scalabook.file.NativeFile] =
  Array(./test.scala)
```

The true bug here was actually our absent-mindedness.

We can verify the correctness of the result, based on the previous directory listing. It is not necessary to reproduce the above directory structure exactly, which resembles a tiny part of the authors' hard disk, in order to test our library. In fact, using different directory layouts and different search patterns can generally help in catching bugs! Testing algorithms with other than the usual inputs can be advantageous in professional programming.

Two ingredients have helped in correctly interpreting the "query" cwd * "*.scala" and they are both in the VFileWithStar companion object. The first is the implicit conversion from a VFile[T] to a VFileWithStar class. The second is the implicit conversion from the string description of the query to a more type-full representation, which is WeakGlobMatcher in this case.

The test was on a native file. Normally, equipped with a virtual file system implementation at the core of our library, there will be no change with a zip file system as well. Using the same directory structure as previously, first we get an idea of the contents from the test-2.jar sample jar file:

```
$ jar tvf test-2.jar
     0 Wed Aug 26 19:20:28 EEST 2009 META-INF/
    60 Wed Aug 26 19:20:28 EEST 2009 META-INF/MANIFEST.MF
  1061 Wed Aug 26 19:18:04 EEST 2009 test.scala
 12511 Thu Jul 09 16:32:22 EEST 2009 test-1.jar
  1061 Sat Aug 22 17:03:06 EEST 2009 test-iter
```

Then we go into the jar file via our VFS abstractions:

```
scala> import scalabook.file._
import scalabook.file._

scala> import scalabook.file.matcher.VFileWithStar._
import scalabook.file.matcher.VFileWithStar._

scala> val jar = ZipFS("test-2.jar")
jar: scalabook.file.ZipFS = ZipFS(test-2.jar)

scala> val jarRoot = jar.root
jarRoot: scalabook.file.ZipFile = /

scala> jarRoot.children
res0: Iterable[scalabook.file.ZipFile] =
      List(/META-INF, /test-1.jar, /test.scala, /test-iter)
```

```
scala> val jarScalaFiles = jarRoot * "*.scala"
jarScalaFiles: Iterable[scalabook.file.ZipFile] =
                List(/test.scala)
```

It is rewarding and encouraging to see how the abstractions fit together. The same API unifies different implementations and the new features are uniformly "acquired." Sometimes, a new API makes us forget that standard facilities are still there, ready to be used. For example, once we have obtained a value for jarScalaFiles, we can combine it with more results:

```
scala> jarScalaFiles ++ (jarRoot * "*.jar")
res1: Collection[scalabook.file.ZipFile] =
        List(/test.scala, /test-1.jar)
```

Abstracting this away, so that it means "All the scala files plus other files whose type I will provide parametrically" should, by now, be easy in Scala:

```
scala> def scalaPlus(fm: FileMatcher) =
    |    jarScalaFiles ++ (jarRoot * fm)
scalaPlus: (FileMatcher)Collection[ZipFile]
```

We have omitted the fully qualified types of FileMatcher and ZipFile from the above output just in order to conserve space. Normally, the Scala interpreter will show them instead of the one-word abbreviations given above:

```
scala> scalaPlus("*.jar")
res2: Collection[ZipFile] = List(/test.scala, /test-1.jar)
```

Question 10.1 Why is the return type of scalaPlus a Collection?

There is more than one way to express the parametric concatenation of matched files. Let us assume we do not want to create a def in the interpreter session but we prefer a function as a value:

```
scala> val scalaPlus =
    |    (fm: FileMatcher) => jarScalaFiles ++ (jarRoot * fm)
scalaPlus: (FileMatcher) => Collection[ZipFile] = <function>
```

Once more, the result reassures us of the expressiveness of Scala.

Exercise 10.2 Provide the definition of a function value (val f = ...) that gives us all the Scala files directly under some folder, the folder being a parameter of the function.

There is also just one subtle point that can usually come up in three ways:

(i) out of pure curiosity at the abstract API level,
(ii) from a revelation, while experimenting in the interpreter,
(iii) from a real-world requirement.

The point in question is: What do we do if we need to combine searches from different virtual file systems? Can the API support this? If so, what are the types involved?

A closer look reveals that both the value of `jarScalaFiles` and the result of `jarRoot * "*.jar"` refer to `ZipFiles`. All we have to do is try with values that refer to results of different types. We recall that, in our examples, we have so far computed `cwdScalaFiles`, a collection of files at the native file system, and `jarScalaFiles`, a collection of files at the virtual jar file system. Here we use the term "collection" in its broad sense, although the actual types may be specified by the Scala `Collection` type. The interpreter is handy when we want to be reminded of the types:

```
scala> cwdScalaFiles
res3: Iterable[NativeFile] = Array(./test.scala)

scala> jarScalaFiles
res4: Iterable[ZipFile] = List(/test.scala)
```

Then, it just becomes a matter of a few keystrokes.

```
scala> cwdScalaFiles ++ jarScalaFiles
res5: Collection[
          VFile[_ >: NativeFile with ZipFile
                  <: VFile[_ >: NativeFile with ZipFile
                             <: ScalaObject
                  ]
          ]
    ] = Array(test.scala, test.scala)
```

We have pretty-printed the inferred type for better readability. Remember that `VFile` is actually defined as `VFile[T <: VFile[T]]` and that is why we see the nested `VFile` in the above interpreter session, where T has been replaced by `NativeFile with ZipFile`.

Question 10.2 What will be the result if we try to combine the two variables, `cwdScalaFile` and `jarScalaFiles`, using the ++ operator but with their order reversed?

```
package scalabook.file.matcher

trait Matcher[T] { outer =>
  def matches(t: T): Boolean

  def &&(other: Matcher[T]) = new Matcher[T] {
    def matches(t: T) =
      outer.matches(t) && other.matches(t)
  }

  def ||(other: Matcher[T]) = new Matcher[T] {
    def matches(t: T) =
      outer.matches(t) || other.matches(t)
  }

  def unary_! = new Matcher[T] {
    def matches(t: T) = !outer.matches(t)
  }
}
```

Figure 10.6 The extended definition of a matcher, which provides support for boolean composition.

10.5 Going boolean

Using the facilities of our small library, it is easy to define a query for matching, for instance, all .scala files. But what if we want to express more complex scenarios, like these?

- Match .scala *or* .jar files.
- Match .scala files whose name do *not* start with Test.

In essence, we are asking for matches that can be composed. Evidently, the emerging pattern is that of boolean expressions, which is ubiquitous in programming. So we need to provide support for boolean expressions at the matching level, which opts for an extension of Matcher[T].

Up until now, Matcher[T] only had one method, namely matches. The new definition is shown in Figure 10.6. Note how we use an explicit *self declaration* via the outer => construct. The reason is to be able to refer clearly and unambiguously to the enclosing Matcher instance from inside the new Matcher instances created on-the-fly from both methods && and ||. Apparently, method && is the boolean AND operator and method || is the boolean OR operator. The special syntax unary_! is there to tell the Scala compiler correctly that we want a unary operator, since method ! represents boolean NOT. In contrast to !, we say that both && and || are binary.

Now, let us start answering the scenarios at the beginning of the current section. Equipped with the new tools, programming looks more and more like fun. First, how about all the .scala or .jar files directly under the current folder?

```
scala> cwd * ("*.scala" || "*.jar")
res6: Iterable[scalabook.file.NativeFile] =
    Array(./test-1.jar, ./test-2.jar, ./test.scala)
```

Second, do we have any .scala files whose names do not start with test?

```
scala> cwd * ("*.scala" && !"test*")
res7: Iterable[scalabook.file.NativeFile] = Array()
```

The answer is in the negative.

If we know that we will usually work with particular kinds of files, a couple of mnemonic *shortcuts*, in the form of Scala vals, are handy:

```
scala> val WithScalaExtension: FileMatcher = "*.scala"
WithScalaExtension: VFileWithStar.FileMatcher = *.scala

scala> val WithJarExtension: FileMatcher = "*.jar"
WithJarExtension: VFileWithStar.FileMatcher = *.jar

scala> cwd * (WithScalaExtension || WithJarExtension)
res8: Iterable[scalabook.file.NativeFile] =
    Array(./test-1.jar, ./test-2.jar, ./test.scala)
```

The manual type annotations are here to assist the compiler in choosing the implicit conversion from a String to a generic type of Matcher for files, which is precisely what FileMatcher stands for. We know, via VFileWithStar, already imported in scope, that the only such implicit conversion is glob2Matcher.

10.5.1 Less redundancy

A quick look at Figure 10.6 reveals some redundancy regarding the definitions of the two binary operators. Indeed, they have exactly the same structure, the only difference being the use of the Scala built-in operators && and ||. This common structure can be easily abstracted away, resulting in tighter and aesthetically more pleasant definitions, as shown in Figure 10.7.

In fact, the situation helps us a little towards a more object-functional path. What we have are objects, which we wish to treat as values via their boolean composition. The object-oriented nature (the matchers being instances of a class) and the functional nature (the boolean values that can be composed) seem so nicely

```
package scalabook.file.matcher

trait Matcher[T] { outer =>
  def matches(t: T): Boolean

  def binop(other: Matcher[T],
                   op: (Boolean, Boolean) => Boolean) =
    new Matcher[T] {
      def matches(t: T) =
        op(outer.matches(t), other.matches(t))
    }

  def &&(other: Matcher[T]) = binop(other, _ && _)

  def ||(other: Matcher[T]) = binop(other, _ || _)

  def unary_! = new Matcher[T] {
    def matches(t: T) = !outer.matches(t)
  }
}
```

Figure 10.7 The alternative, more concise definition of a matcher.

interwound by design that an implementation on the same, object-functional, track would follow inevitably.

Yet, how successful an implementation is in this respect cannot be decided that easily. It is true we are experiencing the beginning of the object-functional era and as our experience along with the accumulated body of research and creative thinking grow, we will be able to tell with more accuracy. At least, proven object-functional patterns will emerge. Note that it took many years for the object-oriented design patterns to be clearly identified as such and then followed in enterprise computing cycles.

Returning to the problem at hand and Figure 10.7, the common structure of the binary boolean relations is abstracted by method `binop`. The conciseness of _ && _ and _ || _ expressions is appealing, although one might argue that, practically, we do not gain that much, since only two relations take advantage of the new syntax.

Question 10.3 Can you explicitly give the type of the _ && _ partial function?

Exercise 10.3 Currently, Figure 10.7 exploits the `binop` definition only for && and ||. Devise an implementation of the unary ! with the help of `binop`.

Exercise 10.4 Now that the functional nature of the approach has already surfaced, one might be tempted to encode it directly on our type hierarchy. Since what basically a Matcher[T] does, via its matches method, is to take a value of type T as input and give a value of type Boolean as output, one could define Matcher[T] as

```
trait Matcher[T] extends (T => Boolean)
```

which is equivalent to

```
trait Matcher[T] extends Function1[T, Boolean]
```

Explore this way of modeling.

10.6 Any level down the hierarchy

Looking back at figure 10.4 and our implementations from that point on, we observe that we have not passed the one folder barrier. Our matches are always one folder down the hierarchy but no further, and that is exactly what the star (*) operator of VFileWithStar does. We augment VFileWithStar with a double star (**) operator that descends the whole hierarchy at all levels and returns the matching files:

```
// continued
class VFileWithStar[T <: VFile[T]](file: T) {
    def **(matcher: FileMatcher): Iterable[T] = {
        def deep(f: T): Iterable[T] =
            f.children ++ f.children.flatMap(deep(_))

        deep(file) filter matcher.matches
    }
}
```

The workhorse is method deep. It is responsible for traversing the hierarchy at all levels and this is achieved by utilizing flatMap. The idea behind flatMap is to collect all the results and flatten them in a container which resembles the original. So, for each file, we obtain its children and for them we recursively obtain their children and concatenate the results. The rest of the job, that is returning a flattened Iterable of files, is done inside flatMap.

There is a catch, though, with the above approach. Note that, according to the last line of **, we first collect all the files and then we do the filtering. Over directory structures with a lot of files and folders, this can be very memory intensive, wasting resources that will be subsequently filtered out. At the expense of clarity, we can possibly patch the code to be more selective rather earlier during the traversing operation.

Exercise 10.5 Implement the aforementioned feature, in order to save memory resources. Hint: You must be careful not to reject folders as soon as possible, so some special treatment of them is needed. Will it be advantageous to use scala.Stream, so that the constructed lists are lazy? Explore possible alternatives with and without streams.

11

Searching, iterating, traversing

In Chapter 10 the goal was to match over a particular set of files, according to specific criteria. To this end we moved in two steps, first working one level down the folder hierarchy and then going deeper than the first level. In that second step, we walked over the filesystem tree, collecting all the possible files at once. We will now study this kind of "hierarchy walking" a little further. Our assumption is that we work over a tree structure.

For our exploration, we assume a general knowledge of the

- LIFO (Last-In First-Out) and FIFO (First-In First Out) notions,
- classical traversal or searching notions [68], such as breadth-first traversal, depth-first traversal, pre-order and post-order traversal.

11.1 Traditional knowledge

11.1.1 Iterables

The Java tradition dictates that we do iteration following the `Iterator` and `Iterable` interfaces, under packages `java.util` and `java.lang` respectively. An `Iterable` is the generator for `Iterators`, via its `iterator` method or, as the Java documentation specifies:

```
public interface Iterable<T>
```

Implementing this interface allows an object to be the target of the "foreach" statement.

Scala mimics this functionality with its `Iterable` and `Iterator` traits, both under the top-level `scala` package:

```
trait Iterable[+A] extends AnyRef
```

Collection classes mixing in this class provide a method `elements`, which returns an iterator over all the elements contained in the collection.

It is interesting to note that this pattern is ubiquitous. Microsoft's C# defines `IEnumerable`, which plays the same role as `Iterable`:

```
public interface IEnumerable<T> : IEnumerable
```

Exposes the enumerator, which supports a simple iteration over a collection of a specified type.

The idea, in all three languages, is to return an object that we can use to iterate over all the elements of the underlying collection. Also, while an `Iterator` is normally a one-off utility, an `Iterable` plays the role of a generator for iterators. So, referring to the Scala version, one can repeatedly call `elements` and always get a fresh object to work on. The usual programming pattern deals with some tedious code, like the following:

```
scala> val list = List(1, 2, 3, 4, 5)
list: List[Int] = List(1, 2, 3, 4, 5)

scala> val iter = list.elements
iter: Iterator[Int] = non-empty iterator

scala> while(iter.hasNext) println(iter.next);
1
...
5
```

11.1.2 Traversables

But we already know that Scala promotes another style of iteration, the one using the `for` construct:

```
scala> for(i <- list) { println(i); }
...
```

With this approach, we provide the `list` with a code block to execute for each one of its elements. Note that Java also provides a foreach construct which is syntactically similar to the above but is, in effect, translated by the compiler to equivalent code of the `hasNext/next` style. In this programming style, the programmer is not responsible for checking whether there are more items in the collection and for

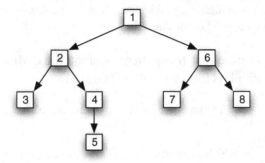

Figure 11.1 A test tree for studying iteration.

fetching the next one. Instead, the collection itself is responsible for these tasks, by providing the proper `foreach` method. The compiler just checks for the existence of the `foreach` method without the need for a class to conform to a particular trait.

The next version of Scala goes one step further in that it defines such a trait

```
trait Traversable[A] {
  def foreach[U](f: T => U): Unit
}
```

and makes it the *fundamental* trait which any collection class must implement. According to the relevant *Scala Improvement Document*:[1]

At the top of this [the collection] hierarchy, is trait `Traversable`. Its only abstract operation is ... `foreach` ...The operation is meant to traverse all elements of the collection and apply the given operation f to each element. The application is done for its side effect only; in fact, any function result of f is discarded by `foreach`.

11.1.3 *Test trees and expected search results*

In order to have a common language and setup, we assume we are interested in the tree shown in Figure 11.1. The easiest way to realize this tree is to create a directory structure that is an exact match. Under Unix, this can easily be accomplished in the command prompt:

```
$ mkdirhier 1/2/3 1/2/4/5 1/6/7 1/6/8
$ tree 1
```

---

[1] Scala Improvement Documents, or SIDs in short, describe the rationale, design, implementation and usage of a Scala feature. They are part of a process open to the community whose role is to promote the improvement of the language. The SID we refer to is number three, revision four.

```
1
|-- 2
|    |-- 3
|    `-- 4
|          `-- 5
`-- 6
     |-- 7
     `-- 8
```

What we did was to take advantage of the command `mkdirhier`, which is a variant of `mkdir` that also creates any intermediate directories if they do not exist. The input we provided to the command was a series of the tree paths that lead from the root (1) to each one of the leaves. Then, we used another useful command, `tree`, in order to visualize the newly created directory structure.

Depth-first search

The generic idea behind the *depth-first search* (DFS) is shown in Figure 11.2. We follow the paths from the parent to the last child, exploring paths to new children before exploring paths to siblings. For example, with the root node 1 under consideration, we first explore the children of node 2 before exploring 2's sibling, which is node 6. The three well known variations of DFS are pre-order, in-order and post-order DFS. Recall that we have presented these strategies in Section 3.1. However, for reasons of completeness, we analyze their respective behavior for our simple trees. Of course, these strategies can also be applied to graph.

Pre-order In pre-order DFS, any parent node is reported as found before any of its children. So, for the tree under study, a routine that does a pre-order DFS will

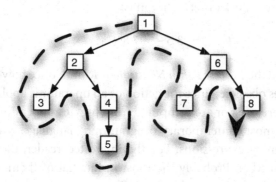

Figure 11.2 Generic idea behind the depth-first search.

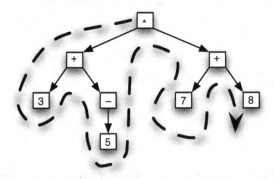

Figure 11.3 A possible abstract syntax tree, inspired by depth-first search.

report the nodes in this order: **1, 2, 3, 4, 5, 6, 7, 8**, which is just what we had in mind when naming the tree nodes in the first place!

In-order Assuming we are dealing with a binary tree, where a node normally has a *left* and a *right* child, an infix DFS will report first the left child, then the parent node and then the right child: **3, 2, 4, 5, 1, 6, 7, 8**. Of course, in our case, node 4 has only one child, 5, which we assumed to be the one on the right. The order produced by an in-order search, and the corresponding tree, resemble an Abstract Syntax Tree (AST) that a compiler generates while parsing source code. In fact, if we replace parent nodes with operators, the infix order of the nodes in Figure 11.3 resembles the expression:

$$(3 + (-5)) * (7 + 8).$$

Post-order A post-order DFS does in some sense the opposite of a pre-order search: it first reports the children and then their parent node. For example, the post-order outcome on our original tree is: **3, 5, 4, 2, 7, 8, 6, 1**. Accordingly, the previous expression written in post-order notation is:

$$3\,5 - + 7\,8 + *.$$

This is often called the *Reverse Polish Notation* or *RPN*. Notice how RPN renders the use of parentheses obsolete, since the action of an operator is applied only after the operands either pre-exist or are computed from previous operators. As a side note, it is evident that most contemporary programming languages prefer the in-order notation for defining expressions. For the interested reader, there are languages that are based on RPN. Probably the most influential of them all is Forth [35]. The Postscript [2] language, another RPN example, powers up a lot of the printers we use.

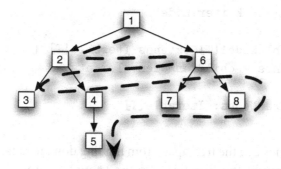

Figure 11.4 Generic idea behind the breadth-first search.

Breadth-first search

At the opposite end from DFS is *breadth-first search* (BFS), where we report siblings at the same tree level before other nodes at lower tree levels. The general idea is depicted in Figure 11.4, where we can recognize a zigzag route. Given that sometimes scientists give funny names to things, it is interesting that no one has yet named BFS as ZigZag Search (ZZS)! But it seems this is a privilege of physicists mostly, with their *quarks, colors, super-strings* etc. Using BFS, the nodes will be reported in this order: 1, 2, 6, 3, 4, 7, 8, 5.

We now proceed, in the following sections, to study a few design and implementation variations on iteration.

11.2 Iterating the hierarchy

11.2.1 *The shape of our data*

What is the most general programming interface one can come up with, in order to model iteration on tree nodes? There may be several answers. What we refer to is actually the data structure point of view: What is the *shape* of our data and how can that shape support iteration? Of course, this is just one of the possible questions. Others may include:

- What is the most efficient way to model iteration on trees?
- Is the way we model iteration coupled to the way we model our nodes?
- Should we model our data shape based on what we wish to do with our data?

These are all design dimensions we may need to take into account. Designing is hard. What is harder, though, is consciously to keep an agenda of the issues at stake, no matter whether we attempt to tackle them.

Returning to the original question, a visual clue from the several figures immediately results in the `IterableNode` trait:

```
package scalabook.iter.node

trait IterableNode1[T] extends Iterable[T] {
  def elements = childrenNodes.elements

  def childrenNodes: Iterable[T]
}
```

The role of each node in the tree, apart from holding domain data, is to point to its children. So, we model this directly, using the Iterable programming interface. The childrenNodes method is the one responsible for providing the children and the familiar elements method from Iterable simply delegates to it. The idea is to model nodes generically that act as placeholders of other nodes and this should be applied recursively.

We have probably made a mistake in our definition of IterableNode1. The first parent node, which is of the desired type IterableNode1[T], will give children of the type T; this is not convenient, since we would like to view all subsequent children as IterableNode1s as well. We can remedy the situation at once:

```
package scalabook.iter.node

trait IterableNode[T] extends Iterable[IterableNode[T]] {
  def elements = childrenNodes.elements

  def childrenNodes: Iterable[IterableNode[T]]
}
```

We could go on and implement the needed search algorithms in a generic fashion, based on the previous definition; but let us take a closer look at the innocent-looking IterableNode trait. What is its original purpose? It is, of course, to model our tree nodes. The motivating use case for searching over trees in this chapter comes from directory hierarchies. So, what this means is that at some place in the design of our VFS API we should have predicted the existence of IterableNode. This is already starting to feel like trouble.

Ths is not very much trouble in Scala though. Scala supports incremental, non-destructive modifications at the design level by employing the power of implicit conversions. If the type is not there, we can make it happen without touching existing source code.

```
package scalabook.iter.node

object IterableNode {
```

```
import scalabook.file.VFile

implicit def vfileAsIterableNode[T <: VFile[T]]
                        (f: T): IterableNode[T] =
  new IterableNode[T] {
    def childrenNodes =
      f.children.map(vfileAsIterableNode[T])
  }
}
}
```

Beware that this power comes with a price, as having too many implicits in scope can render the code not only less understandable but also incorrect.

We also use the implicit in its own definition, in order for the children to come out with the proper type. The `Iterable[T]` returned from method `children` of `VFile[T]` must be changed to `IterableNode[T]` but that is exactly what the implicit does, so we reused it as a normal method.

Subtle type inferring issues

· Note that in this direct usage of the implicit method, we must specifically annotate the call with type T, writing `vfileAsIterableNode[T]` instead of `vfileAsIterableNode`.[2] Actually, in the latter case the compiler will complain with something like:

```
IterableNode.scala:25: type mismatch;
found   : IterableNode[T(in method vfileAsIterableNode)]
required: IterableNode[(some other)T(in method
                                    vfileAsIterableNode)]
        f.children.map(vfileAsIterableNode)
                       ^
```

As the error message suggests, two type parameters with the same name T cannot be unified by the type inference procedure inside the Scala compiler, that is they cannot be proved to be the same type. Let us help the situation in understanding the error, first by avoiding the type parameter name clash. We introduce an auxiliary method

```
// object IterableNode
def auxiliary[S <: VFile[S]](f: S) = vfileAsIterableNode(f)
```

---

[2] The code compiles with a more verbose version as well: `f.children.map[IterableNode[T]](…)`.

and then we slightly change the definition of `vfileAsIterableNode` by replacing the nested call to `vfileAsIterableNode` with a call to `auxiliary`

```
// definition of vfileAsIterableNode

...

f.children.map(auxiliary)

...
```

Now the error becomes

```
IterableNode.scala:25: type mismatch;
found    : IterableNode[S]
required: IterableNode[T]
         f.children.map(auxiliary)
                        ^
```

and things are clearer in interpreting the error message: We must tell the Scala compiler that type S of `auxiliary` is the same as type T that appears in the definition of `vfileAsIterableNode`.

Exercise 11.1 In the above example, the compiler needed some extra assistance by having us provide an explicit type parameter. Devise a scheme, according to which method `vfileAsIterableNode` can be successfully compiled, without any type annotation in the `f.children.map` call chain. That is, we need a call like

$$f.children.map(\textit{something})$$

where *something* does not contain any type annotations.

Can we do better than wrapping?

No matter how powerful and time-saving implicits may be, the previous solution can be charged as guilty of over-wrapping. Indeed, that is the case. For every node in the hierarchy we create a wrapper, so it is as if we double the whole tree structure. If this is going to be – and *it is* – an a priori memory requirement for any searching algorithm, then we start off with a disadvantage, since we cannot even know what extra memory requirements the algorithm will have.

   Can we do better? If yes, how can we discover this better approach? Perhaps sitting back and thinking about our case a little bit might help. Let us inspect our facts. Some may seem or actually be trivial, others may not lead directly to an insight but experience reports reveal that *the very process[3] of just stating the known facts can be beneficial.*

---

[3] This technique can be transferred with success to other activities, like when trying to figure out where the most recent, ferocious bug of our application came from.

- There is a tree structure of nodes.
- Although not stated explicitly, we have silently assumed that nodes are of the same or similar nature. For example, all the previous figures depict nodes of two kinds:
  (i) either nodes that are plain numbers,
  (ii) or nodes that represent operators and operands.
  This assumption is directly reflected in the proposal of `IterableNode[T]`, where the type T characterizes the exact nature of similarity. T can be `Integer` for the nodes in Figure 11.1, it can be `Expr` for Figure 11.3, where `Expr` is some fictitious AST node type, and it can be a subtype of `VFile[T]` in our concrete file system example.
- As is typical in the usual implementation scenarios, a node will provide some way, that is some API, to expose its children. A `VFile`, for example, publicizes the `children` method. It is obvious that different kinds of nodes have different ways of providing their children, but the most important thing is the existence of such a facility.
- What do we want to do with the tree?
    Iterate over the nodes.
- What does *iterate over the nodes* mean?
    Iterate over them and their children.

11.2.2 Abstracting the ingredients

So, we have a set of similar nodes, the node as an entity can provide us with its children and we wish to iterate over all nodes. Could it all appear clearer now? Why not start from somewhere in the tree (the root actually), ask each node to provide its children and just report them all in the proper order? The *proper order* is the essence behind the different search variations, whether BFS or DFS (pre-order, in-order, post-order). It is a plausible strategy, so let us start abstracting over the ingredients.

Similar nodes

There is no special handling here, as the prescribed idea of type T parameter is the one to follow.

Children provisioning

We have stated that all kinds of nodes, that is nodes for each type T as given above, will have a way to expose their children. The only detail that remains in order to handle them uniformly, is to give a unifying API that does exactly that:

```
package scalabook.iter
```

```
trait NodeChildrenProvider[T] {
  def childrenOf(node: T): Iterator[T]
}
```

The crucial difference with the previous approach of IterableNode is that we do not impose any particular interface on the node type; instead, we take advantage of the fact that we can obtain the children and just enforce this property of the domain model in the unifying NodeChildrenProvider. Now, for each type of node there will be *one* NodeChildrenProvider and this will be valid for all instances of the same node type. The programming paradigm is completely different and the savings in memory are tremendous.

For example, a children provider for plain Java Files is coded as:

```
class FileChildrenProvider extends NodeChildrenProvider[File]{
  def childrenOf(file: File) = file.listFiles match {
    case null => Iterator.empty
    case array => array.elements
  }
}
```

where the unfortunate case of a Java API returning null instead of an empty array must be appropriately taken care of. Similarly, for our virtual files the encoding is straightforward:

```
package scalabook.iter
import scalabook.file.{NativeFile, VFile}

class VFileChildrenProvider[T <: VFile[T]]
  extends NodeChildrenProvider[T] {

  def childrenOf(node: T) = node.children.elements
}

object NativeChildrenProvider
  extends VFileChildrenProvider[NativeFile]
```

Iteration from the inside

Skeleton implementation Figure 11.5 presents a skeleton implementation of a tree iterator. Its basic ingredients are the following.

computeNext This is the actual workhorse of the algorithm. It returns true if and only if there is some node to report and sets _next according to the previous rule.

_next This holds the next node to be reported or None if there are no more nodes to report. It is declared **protected**, so that concrete implementations of NodeIteratorSkeleton can change its value. As a technical note, we could have used a **private** _next variable and have computeNext just return an Option[T]

```
package scalabook.iter

abstract class NodeIteratorSkeleton[T](
  start: T,
  provider: NodeChildrenProvider[T]) extends Iterator[T] {
  // None <==> no next value has been computed
  protected var _next: Option[T] = None

  protected def computeNext: Boolean

  def hasNext =
    if (_next.isDefined)
      true
    else
      computeNext

  def next =
    if(hasNext) {
      val result = _next.get
      _next = None
      result
    } else
      throw new NoSuchElementException
}
```

Figure 11.5 Skeleton implementation of a tree iterator.

to signify the existence or not of one more node, without altering any state. This point will be clearer when presenting the actual DFS and BFS implementations.

hasNext This consults the value of _next and in the case it is None it calls computeNext to obtain the next value.

next This simply returns the next node or throws an exception if there are no more nodes to iterate over.

One implementation detail about iterators, that new programmers usually ignore, is the fact that hasNext must not assume a subsequent call to next and vice versa. A good question to ask in order to get into the heart of the problem is: How will the iterator behave if we continuously call hasNext (next) without ever calling next (hasNext)? Although it is an abuse of the programming interface, one may insist on getting all the nodes out of the iterator by just calling next, until an exception is thrown, which will signal the end of iteration. So, ill-behaving clients may exist and our responsibility is to provide a robust implementation.

Keeping state We will implement our generic iterator using one of the DFS, BFS techniques. Discovering each node does not necessarily mean that we will immediately report it as the next item to return from the iterator. After all, such a decision

```
package scalabook.iter

trait NodeStore[T] {
  def addNode(node: T): NodeStore[T]

  def addChildrenOf(node: T,
                    provider: NodeChildrenProvider[T]
                   ): NodeStore[T]

  def remove: Option[T]
}
```

Figure 11.6 An abstract interface that models the idea of node buffering.

belongs to the internals of each search technique implementation. For example, in a post-order DFS, we discover a node but we report it only after all the subtree beneath it has been reported first.

So, it is clear we will need some sort of buffering, the main idea of which is captured by the programming interface in Figure 11.6. The operations needed are the following.

addNode This is responsible for storing the node offered as an input argument.

addChildrenOf This has the role of storing the children of a node. Why this is different than just calling addNode repeatedly will be covered shortly. Note that we use the concept of a NodeChildrenProvider. Implementations of NodeStore are expected to take advantage of the direct iterator provided by NodeChildrenProvider and pull the actual nodes directly, without any wrappers around them.

remove This checks to see whether there are any items stored and returns the first one, wrapped as Some (...), or None otherwise. The crucial detail here is what *first* means. The order in which we retrieve elements from the store is not necessarily the same as their insertion order. The usual data structure "suspects" named LIFO (Last-In First-Out) and FIFO (First-In First-Out) will play their role as well. As a preliminary observation, a LIFO backing store will be tied to a DFS implementation, while a FIFO store will be tied to a BFS implementation.

We will need two concrete implementations for NodeStore, namely LIFOStore and FIFOStore:

```
package scalabook.iter

class LIFOStore[T] extends NodeStore[T] {
  private var stack = List[T]()

  def addNode(node: T) = {stack = node :: stack; this}
```

```scala
def addChildrenOf(node: T,
                  provider: NodeChildrenProvider[T]) = {
  val children = provider.childrenOf(node).toList.reverse
  for (child <- children) addNode(child)
  this
}

def remove = stack match {
  case node :: rest =>
    stack = rest
    Some(node)
  case Nil =>
    None
}
}
```

The basic ingredient of `LIFOStore` is that of a stack, which we emulate here with an immutable `List`. `List` is an obvious candidate for a stack, since items are added at the head of the list and their access order is the reverse of their insertion order. Pattern matching in the implementation of `remove` makes the approach quite straightforward.

We also note the slight peculiarity of *reversing* the children iterator before inserting the children nodes into the stack. This is necessary, since we later want the children to pop-up in their normal order of appearance, which by convention is left-to-right. Figure 11.7 clarifies the situation.

If we do not reverse, then children 3 and 4, which will be seen in this order (left-to-right), are added (pushed actually) in the LIFO store in this order, so 4 will come on top. Later, when a node is removed from the store, 4 will be taken out before 3. If instead we add the children in reverse order, we will get the desired output order.

We should emphasize that this peculiarity is not in any way a needed *hack* just to get things done. The best way to see it is that we have entered one more constraint in the equation. How children are added into the store is just another parameter to

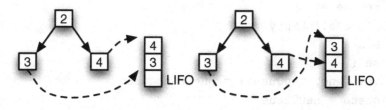

Figure 11.7

be abstracted over. In fact, different implementations will lead to other variations of iteration and this is the reason behind our introduction of the `addChildrenOf` method.

Exercise 11.2 After studying the material in this chapter, explore the above reasoning/suggestion.

For the `FIFOStore`, on the other hand, we directly use a `Queue`, which represents the canonical example of a FIFO data structure:

```scala
package scalabook.iter
import scala.collection.immutable.Queue


class FIFOStore[T] extends NodeStore[T] {
  private var queue = new Queue[T]

  def addNode(node: T) = {
    queue = queue.enqueue(node)
    this
  }


  def addChildrenOf(node: T,
                    provider: NodeChildrenProvider[T]) = {
    val children = provider.childrenOf(node)
    val buf = new collection.mutable.ListBuffer[T]

    for (child <- children) {
      addNode(child)
      buf += child
    }

    buf.clear
    this
  }

  def remove =
    if (queue.isEmpty)
      None
    else {
      val (end, newQueue) = queue.dequeue
      queue = newQueue
      Some(end)
    }
}
```

Pre-order depth-first iteration We are now ready for the implementation of a DFS that will help us iterate over the tree nodes in a pre-order fashion. The relevant code is shown in Figure 11.8. We keep internal the state about which nodes we have to explore, using the `toExplore` value, which is of `LIFOStore` type. The moment the `PreOrderDFS` iterator instance is created, we push the starting node, `start`, on the stack, since this is the first node to explore. Subsequent calls to `computeNext` will

```scala
package scalabook.iter

class PreOrderDFS[T](start: T,
                          provider: NodeChildrenProvider[T])
    extends NodeIteratorSkeleton(start, provider) {
    private val toExplore = new LIFOStore[T].addNode(start)

    protected def computeNext: Boolean = {
      toExplore.remove match {
        case nodeOpt@Some(node) =>
          _next = nodeOpt
          toExplore.addChildrenOf(node, provider)
          true
        case None =>
          _next = None
          false
      }
    }
}
```

Figure 11.8 Implementation of a pre-order, depth-first tree iterator.

```scala
package scalabook.iter

class BFS[T](start: T, provider: NodeChildrenProvider[T])
    extends NodeIteratorSkeleton(start, provider) {
    private val toExplore = new FIFOStore[T].addNode(start)

    protected def computeNext: Boolean = {
      toExplore.remove match {
        case nodeOpt@Some(node) =>
          _next = nodeOpt
          toExplore.addChildrenOf(node, provider)
          true
        case None =>
          _next = None
          false
      }
    }
}
```

Figure 11.9 Implementation of a breadth-first tree iterator.

pop the most recent node to explore off the stack, will add its children to the stack and then return the parent node. So, speaking rather informally, a parent is reported first, giving us the pre-order semantics. And since after the parent we immediately see its children, we have the depth-first property.

Breadth-first iteration Breadth-first iteration, which is shown in Figure 11.9, is remarkably similar to the pre-order, depth-first iteration of Figure 11.8. The only

```scala
package scalabook.iter

class PostOrderDFS[T](start: T,
                          provider: NodeChildrenProvider[T])
  extends NodeIteratorSkeleton(start, provider) {

  private[this] val toExplore =
                 new LIFOStore[T].addNode(start)

  private[this] var processed = Set[T]()

  protected def computeNext: Boolean =
    toExplore.remove match {
      case nodeOpt@Some(node) =>
        if (processed.contains(node)) {
          // a node is (post) processed only if
          // children are processed.
          _next = nodeOpt

          // this step keeps us memory efficient
          processed -= node
          true
        }
        else {
          // add again before children to obtain
          // the "post"-order property
          toExplore.addNode(node)
          toExplore.addChildrenOf(node, provider)
          processed += node

          computeNext
        }
      case None =>
        _next = None
        false
    }
}
```

Figure 11.10 Implementation of a post-order, depth-first tree iterator.

change is the use of a FIFO-based node store. Other than that, the code is, from a first principles point of view, identical to the respective pre-order DFS implementation. The power of abstractions clearly shines. In fact, most, if not all, textbooks and tutorials will point out the difference between LIFO and FIFO regarding DFS and BFS respectively, but fail to abstract over the children nodes addition operation.

Post-order depth-first iteration The implementation of a post-order, depth-first iterator is shown in Figure 11.10. One extra detail, compared to the pre-order implementation of Figure 11.8, appears here and it is related to the fact that we must remember which nodes have been processed. By "processed," we mean that all their children have been returned as the `next` iteration node. The relevant book-keeping is done via the `processed` variable of type `Set[T]`.

11.3 Traversing the hierarchy

So far, we have dealt with the ubiquitous `Iterable` and `Iterator` interfaces. Let us move our attention to the `Traversable` concept. As a quick reminder, it contains just one method, `foreach`:

```
package scalabook.iter

trait Traversable[A] {
  def foreach[U](f: T => U): Unit
}
```

Having led the way by resolving some fundamental issues regarding data representation in the previous section, the approach to implementing depth-first and breadth-first tree traversals is now more straightforward. Still, there are issues needing special care. For example, inspired by the utility of `NodeChildrenProvider`

```
trait NodeChildrenProvider[T] {
  def childrenOf(node: T): Iterator[T]
}
```

we may be tempted to write an analogous trait

```
trait TraversableProvider0[T] {
  def childrenOf(start: T): Traversable[T]
}
```

but in fact, this creates an extra requirement of possibly having to create a new `Traversable` for every invocation. Another issue is that it feels as if we are missing the idea behind `Traversable`, which is the provision of the `foreach` method. Why not encode it directly?

```
package scalabook.iter

trait TraversableProvider[T] {
  def foreach(start: T, f: T => Unit): Unit
}
```

What the above programming interface says, is: *give me a node and I will process all of its children using function f.* This is closer to the very spirit of `Traversable`.

A `TraversableProvider` for plain Java `Files` is

```
package scalabook.iter

object FileTraversableProvider
  extends TraversableProvider[File] {

  def foreach(start: File, f: (File) => Unit) {
    start.listFiles match {
      case null =>
      case array =>
        array.foreach(f)
    }
  }
}
```

and one for a virtual file is

```
package scalabook.iter

class VFileTraversableProvider[T <: VFile[T]]
  extends TraversableProvider[T] {

  def foreach(start: T, f: (T) => Unit) =
    start.children.foreach(f)
}
```

Pre-order depth-first traversal The implementation of a pre-order depth-first traversal is shown in Figure 11.11. The most interesting part is

```
        provider.foreach(start, foreach(_, f))
```

where we recursively call `TraversableProvider`'s `foreach` method.

```
package scalabook.iter

class PreOrderDFST[T](start: T,
                              provider: TraversableProvider[T])
  extends ToStringTraversable[T] {
  def foreach(f: T => Unit) = foreach(start, f)

  private def foreach(start: T, f: T => Unit) {
    f(start)
    provider.foreach(start, foreach(_, f))
  }
}
```

Figure 11.11 Implementation of a pre-order, depth-first tree traversal.

Exercise 11.3 Implement a nonrecursive version of the pre-order depth-first traversal.

Exercise 11.4 Implement the post-order depth-first traversal and the breadth-first traversal.

Exercise 11.5 Now that all the details are in place, implement the deep matching feature at the end of Chapter 10 using the new techniques.

11.4 Going on further

What are the differences between the two approaches (iteration, traversal)? How different or similar might they be? Are they the only approaches? What are the general concerns when iterating? Regardless of our investigation and findings in the previous sections, we attempt to name a few directions of interest in the following paragraphs.

User-directed versus collection-directed

Using the iterator is rather user directed. We, the users of the API, drive the whole process. We control when and whether to continue seeing the items, if more of them still exist. On the other hand, we have no control on the iteration itself with a `for`, unless of course we force some kind of an abnormal exit, via throwing an exception.

Is should be evident by now that using `hasNext` performs the iteration *externally*, while using `for` performs the iteration *internally*. It is a matter of who is responsible for doing it. Internal iteration is usually called *traversal*.

Procedural versus declarative nature

Using the iterator explicitly, via the `hasNext/next` idiom, has a procedural flavor. We always specify the exact steps to follow, that is `hasNext` and `next`, in order to iterate over the items. In contrast, we use `for` in a declarative style, by just giving the action to execute for each item in the collection. Since this feature is built into the compiler logic, the compiler does the appropriate transformations and calls on our part. These transformations, which amount to unrolling the iteration to specific method calls, are done mechanically, with one, bug-free algorithm.

Termination

Termination of the iteration is handled differently in the two cases. With the `hasNext/next` idiom, we are sure the iteration is over only when `hasNext` returns `false`. Since the iterator, as an object, must have some knowledge of the underlying structure of the items in order to hand them one-by-one properly to the user, it is responsible for closing any underlying resources. If this is not apparent, we can think of a `byte` iterator that takes its contents from a file. Now, a file is ultimately an operating system resource. The iterator, either on creation or lazily on first use of `hasNext` or `next`, opens the file for reading. This corresponds to reserving some operating system data structure, so that our application can use it to read bytes from the file. The question is, when is it appropriate to close the underlying resource represented by the opened file?

It is evident, by design, that such a decision cannot be made blindly. The iterator object cannot decide by itself to close the file, since it is not aware of how the user calls `hasNext/next`. But it will be safe for the iterator to release the underlying resource if the last call to `hasNext` returned `false`, since then it is known that no more bytes can be provided. The situation is far from satisfactory, since it relies on the user exhausting the iterator. Although this is normally what we do, the design relies on the good behavior of the client code. Clearly the approach does not scale. Even if the user is very careful and systematic with its own code, side effects always lurk around when using third-party libraries, and they could present themselves in unpredictable ways.

Fortunately, when the collection of items itself is responsible for the iteration, as is the case when using `for`, then it is up to the collection design to behave appropriately. The good news is that this can be programmed once in the code that implements the iteration and then all users can benefit for free.

Object-oriented or functional

Iteration with `hasNext/next` has been used traditionally in an object-oriented context, whereas the other form is ubiquitous in functional programming. It is believed that the latter is so because of the need to have closures in order to support traversal, but a simple remark breaks the argument: in an object-oriented context we could use interfaces. Instead of passing a closure around, we can pass the implementation of the interface but depending on the programming language we may have to take care of the free variables. In a language with support for closures, free variables are handled by the language itself, i.e., the compiler. It is just that closures make our programming experience a lot easier and certainly more concise.

Iteration strategy

Iteration has a linear feeling, although the underlying collection could be a graph. What we get is a series of items one after the other, but does this mean the underlying data structure is an array? What decides how to select the items that are given in the linear fashion expected by the iteration procedure? For a tree, there is, for example, breadth-first and depth-first traversals and the latter can be pre-order or post-order, to name just a few combinations.

Uniformity of implementation

Each collection has its own special characteristics. Structure is probably the most notable diverse feature and the one that normally dictates how iteration/traversal is going to be implemented. But abstraction has always been sought after and even favored in programming. The question is: Can we provide a general iteration/traversal implementation for which specific details regarding each collection can just be plugged in? What are the characteristics that can be abstracted over? How can we accommodate radically different structures (compare an array with an acyclic directed graph)?

Interchangeability between approaches

Software engineers with a mathematical background, a keen eye for abstractions, relevant experience or a functional-oriented background[4] tend to look for mathematical notions. These notions can be "algebraic properties," "duality" or "isomorphism" to name just a few. We might wonder, for instance: Can we derive one approach from the other? If that is the case, then we say that the approaches are isomorphic, that is there is always an algorithm so that given one of the approaches we can derive the other. So, what is the case with iteration and traversal?

Exercise 11.6 Derive a traversal-based implementation from an iterator-based implementation.

Exercise 11.7 *This is harder.* Derive an iterator-based implementation from a traversal-based implementation.

---

[4] These conditions need not necessarily be all true and they are by no means exhaustive.

12

The expression problem

12.1 Introduction

The expression problem, also known as the extensibility problem, refers to the situation where we need to extend the data types of a program as well as the operations on them, with two constraints: (a) we do not want to modify existing code and (b) we want to be able to resolve types statically. Thus, the essence of the expression problem lies in the type-safe incremental modification to both the data types and their corresponding operations, without recompilation and with the support/use of static typing.

At the heart of the expression problem is the Separation of Concerns principle. Since its inception about forty years ago by Edsger Wybe Dijkstra [19], the Separation of Concerns principle has been elevated to one of the cornerstones of software engineering. In plain words what it states is that when tackling a problem we have to identify the different concerns that apply to the specific problem and then try to separate them. By separating the concerns, we produce untangled, clearer code, thus reducing the software complexity and increasing maintainability.

Of course, separation of concerns is only half the truth. We can identify our concerns and successfully separate them, but at some point we will need to recombine them: after all, they are parts of the original problem.

So, what exactly do we separate and then recombine in the expression problem? Data and operations are two different dimensions. Incremental modifications to these dimensions should be done independently and in an extensible way. At any point, we should be able to recombine the independent extensions, so that modified data are combined with modified operations.

In the following, we will see how the expression problem appears in the setting of a common and well understood problem space: the design of an interpreter for a minimalistic expression language. We will study the problem by applying several techniques, using along the way several features of Scala. Our results are not conclusive, in the sense that we do not propose a certain way to handle the problem. The intention rather is to explore the design space and see alternative attacks. The section names are indicative of the respective approach. Also, unless stated otherwise, from now on the acronym *ExP* refers to the Expression Problem.

12.2 Data and operations

The requirements for our minimalistic expression language are that we need to model a set of operations over a set of data and we want to design both in an extensible way. Our data, which represent expressions, may come in the form of integer literals or combinations of other expressions, as for example in the case of the addition basic operation. Operations can be like the obviously needed evaluation or the string representation for each expression form. A grammar that describes the small language is the following:

```
expr ::= num | plus
plus ::= expr '+' expr
num  ::= <integer literal>
```

In order to study the expression problem, we will start by first omitting the definition for plus, which we will introduce as an extension. Also, we begin by supporting a basic eval operation and we will study progressively the incorporation of a new operation repr that generates a string representation of an expression. For the rest of the chapter, we will use the nouns *data* and *expression* interchangeably to denote the one dimension of the expression problem.

Data-centric decomposition

The straightforward object-oriented way to handle our expression language is to define a class representing our data and pack the needed operations as methods in the corresponding class, as shown in Figure 12.1.

Here, a `trait` abstractly defines the evaluation method signature and the concrete class NumD provides an implementation. Using this approach it is rather easy to extend our language with new kinds of expressions. For example, an expression representing the plus rule in the above grammar can be defined incrementally by PlusD.

Unfortunately, when a new operation is needed, the approach breaks down, since we have to modify every existing data class and add the new operation in its definition. As a side note, this modeling approach is in effect the Interpreter design pattern [24]. We can also call it the *object-oriented decomposition*.

```
trait BaseD { // our base data trait
  def eval: Int
}

class NumD(value: Int) extends BaseD {
  def eval = value
}

class PlusD(a: BaseD, b: BaseD) extends BaseD {
  def eval = a.eval + b.eval
}
```

Figure 12.1 Data-centric decomposition for the expression problem.

Operation-centric decomposition

Dual to the previous approach is the so-called operation-centric decomposition or *functional decomposition*. This may not seem so obvious from an object-oriented perspective but is again based on another pattern, the Visitor design pattern. The central idea is to make operations first-class citizens in our design by behaviorally separating them from the corresponding data. So, our expression language looks like this:

```
trait BaseD {
  def perform(op: BaseOp)
}

trait BaseOp {
  def compute(data: BaseD)
}

class NumD(val value: Int) extends BaseD {
  def perform(op: BaseOp) {...}
}
```

In effect, we have abstracted away any operation by defining a perform method. In the above design, our data, represented by BaseD, abstractly reference its operations by the op parameter of the perform method. At the same time, our operations, represented by BaseOp, abstractly reference the data they are applied to by the data parameter of their compute method. This gives the impression we have solved our problem by possessing a fully extensible design for both of our concerns: data and operations. It definitely seems like a huge success, but not quite so, as the following arguments reveal.

First of all, we have departed a little from the standard naming conventions of the Visitor design pattern, where the usual method names are `accept` when we are in the definition of data and `visit` when we are in the definition of the Visitor itself. The reason for this is to be semantically closer to our problem domain.

Then, taking into consideration our mappings `accept` → `perform` and `visit` → `compute`, according to the Visitor design pattern the typical implementation of any `accept`/`perform` method delegates to the *appropriate* `visit`/`compute` method of the visitor, as seen in Figure 12.2. This means the visitor needs to know the exact type of the data it is visiting, as demonstrated by the use of the `computeNumD` method.

Note the functional appeal of `EvalOp`: since the visitor's role is to evaluate expressions, we introduce an `apply` method. Having this feature, it is easy to instantiate

```
trait BaseD {
  def perform(op: BaseOp)
}

class NumD(val value: Int) extends BaseD {
  def perform(op: BaseOp) {
    op.computeNumD(this)
  }
}

trait BaseOp {
  def computeNumD(data: NumD)
}


class EvalOp extends BaseOp {
  var result: Option[Int] = None

  def apply(data: BaseD) = {
    data.perform(this)
    result.get
  }

  def computeNumD(data: NumD) {
    this.result = Some(data.value)
  }
}
```

Figure 12.2 Operation-centric decomposition for the expression problem.

```
object eval {
  def apply(data: BaseD) = new EvalOp()(data)
}

object repr {
  def apply(data: BaseD) = new ReprOp()(data)
}
```

Figure 12.3 Utility objects for operation-centric decomposition.

visitors and make on-the-fly computations over data:

```
scala> new EvalOp()(new NumD(4))
res0: Int = 4
```

Having this technique in our toolbox will be handy when we try to create more involved visitors, where computations may need to reuse other visitors. In fact, we can take advantage of functional Scala objects and define the small utilities of Figure 12.3. Also, we have used Option[Int] instead of Int as the type of result, so as to denote the absence of any value in case the visitor has not been used.

The real strength of the functional decomposition boils down to the fact that adding a new operation is merely adding a new visitor. After all, that is why we introduced visitors in the first place:

```
class ReprOp extends BaseOp {
  var result: Option[String] = _

  def computeNumD(data: NumD) {
    this.result = Some(data.value.toString)
  }
}
```

Exercise 12.1 Notice how the functional appeal of EvalOp is very ad hoc: it appears only in a concrete implementation of BaseOp and not in BaseOp itself. This means that, for example, the definition of ReprOp above should repeat the implementation of method apply in order to acquire the same functionality. Generify BaseOp using an "unknown" type for the result and implement apply in the base trait once.

Unfortunately, extensibility in the other dimension is cumbersome. New data mean new methods in every visitor, starting from the BaseOp trait and following down all the visitor hierarchy.

On notation

In order to study the expression problem in a consistent manner and follow the several examples with relative ease, we have made a few decisions on notation. First, as already described previously, there is a slight departure from standard Visitor nomenclature: we use `perform` instead of `accept` and `computeX` instead of `visitX` for some X representing a data type. Also, we name all data types with a D suffix: `BaseD`, `NumD` and so on. Finally, we name all of our operation types, that is Visitors, with an `Op` suffix in their names: `BaseOp`, `EvalOp` and so on.

Having this consistent notation, any code snippet can be mentally partitioned to its semantic parts rather quickly, without having to resort to the accompanying text right away. Also, we have kept the data naming the same for both the data-centric and the operation-centric approaches. Obviously, looking at the methods supported by `BaseD`, namely `eval` in the data-centric approach and `perform` in the operation-centric approach respectively, reveals the nature of the approach.

12.3 Data-centric approach with subclassing

We have mentioned that the data-centric approach does not work well with new operations because it needs modification of existing source code. Yet, the object-oriented way encourages the idea that new behavior can be added via subclassing, so we will try and see how far we can go with typical inheritance relationships. Let us encode the `repr` operation

```
trait ReprD extends BaseD {
  def repr: String
}
```

and immediately subclass our expressions to take advantage of it:

```
class ReprNumD(value: Int) extends NumD(value) with ReprD {
  def repr = value.toString
}
```

```
class ReprPlusD(a: ReprD, b: ReprD) extends Plus(a, b)
  with ReprD {
  def repr = a.repr + " + " + b.repr
}
```

A problem with this approach can be seen right away by noticing the constructor signature of `ReprPlusD`: its arguments are not just instances of `BaseD` but must be instances of the more specific type `ReprD`. This means that any `BaseD` instance we have cannot be used to create `ReprPlusD` instances. This is unfortunate: we may not have touched the source code of our `BaseD` trait but we cannot reuse pre-existing library code that generates instances of type `BaseD` and we cannot directly reuse instances of type `BaseD` produced by our code. These shortcomings are illustrated with the following example. Imagine that we have a library which was compiled before the introduction of the `Repr SomeD` data variants:

```
// This is part of a library. It is expected to return the
// tax percentage scale for my income.
def calculateTaxScalePercentage(income: BaseD): BaseD
```

Then the following yields an error:

```
scala> val myIncome = new Num(30000)
scala> val myTaxPercent = calculateTaxScalePercentage(myIncome)
scala> val fancyPlus = new ReprPlusD(new ReprNumD(1), myTaxPercent)
error: type mismatch;
 found   : NumD
 required: ReprD
  val fancyPlus = new ReprPlusD(new ReprNumD(1), myTaxPercent)
                                                 ^

one error found
```

Automatic instance transformations

The above issue could be resolved if we could have our code produce the correct instance type, namely `ReprNumD` instead of its super type `NumD`. We can achieve this automatically by employing Scala's implicits:

```
object AutoRepr {
  implicit def NumD2ReprD(n: NumD) = new ReprNumD(n.eval)
}
```

Of course, we will have to provide one implicit conversion per data type transformation. It would be desirable to have this generic transformation:

```
object AutoRepr {
  implicit def BaseD2ReprD(in: BaseD): ReprD = ??
}
```

but how can this be implemented in an extensible way?

Exercise 12.2 Explore this line of design. How can we define such a generic implicit? How can we provide refinements of this implicit, in order to cope with our model extensions? Do you see a repeating pattern here? In particular, isn't this exercise asking for an extensible way to define operations, in the form of implicits in this case? Is it possible that this line of design introduces the expression problem at another level of abstraction?

Another idea is to provide auxiliary constructors in the Repr*Some*D variants that take the respective base traits as parameters:

```
class ReprNumD(value: Int) extends NumD(value) with ReprD {
    def this(numd: NumD) = this(numd.eval)
    def repr = value.toString
}
```

Exercise 12.3 Notice how we have used numd.eval in the auxiliary constructor of ReprNumD above, instead of just numd.value. The latter will clearly not pass through the scala compiler, since it is not visible outside the definition of NumD. Explore this line of design that uses the call to eval instead of an explicit value getter in order to take advantage of the fact that eval is defined for all BaseD instances.

On the constructor of ReprPlusD

Let us take another look at the primary constructor of ReprPlusD

```
class ReprPlusD(a: ReprD, b: ReprD)
```

and ask ourselves what would happen if instead of ReprD we had just BaseD

```
class ReprPlusD(a: BaseD, b: BaseD)
```

The quick answer is, of course, it would not compile. Not because the constructor is erroneous, but we need the a and b instances to have a repr method, in order for the repr method of ReprPlusD to compile:

```
def repr = a.repr + " + " + b.repr
```

A somewhat trivial observation one may note, but actually a fruitful one. The question is: Can we constrain the constructor parameters in any way, so as to ensure they have a repr method and at the same time be BaseD instances?

Exercise 12.4 Try to model, in Scala, an answer to the above question. Hint: You may have to decide whether something stronger is needed than the abstractions we have used so far.

12.4 Operation-centric approach with subclassing

After using subclassing for the data-centric approach, it is tempting to try it for the case of operations as well. Let us say that we insert this new kind of data:

```
class PlusD(val a: BaseD, val b: BaseD) extends BaseD {
  def perform(op: PlusOp) {
    op.computePlusD(this)
  }
}
```

The required operation `PlusOp` and its concrete implementation `EvalPlusOp` are defined as follows:

```
trait PlusOp extends BaseOp {
  def computePlusD(data: PlusD)
}
```

```
class PlusEvalOp extends PlusOp {
  def computePlusD(data: PlusD) {
    this.result = Some(eval(data.a) + eval(data.b))
  }
}
```

Note how in the body of `computePlusD` we take advantage of the previously defined, in Figure 12.3, utility objects. If we try to compile class `PlusD` we will get an error:

```
error: class PlusD needs to be abstract, since method perform
       in trait BaseD of type (BaseOp)Unit is not defined
class PlusD(val a: BaseD, val b: BaseD) extends BaseD {
      ^
one error found
```

We have hit a wall! `PlusD` does not *properly* extend `BaseD` since it does not override method `perform`: it should have a parameter of type `BaseOp` instead of type `PlusOp`. This can be readily verified by using the `override` modifier

```
override def computePlusD(data: PlusD)
```

and then compiling the class:

```
class PlusD needs to be abstract, since method perform in trait
BaseD of type (BaseOp)Unit is not defined
class PlusD(val a: BaseD, val b: BaseD) extends BaseD {
      ^
```

```
method perform overrides nothing
override def perform(op: PlusOp) {
                 ^

two errors found
```

Instead, a type-cast can make the scala compiler happy:

```
class PlusD(val a: BaseD, val b: BaseD) extends BaseD {
  def perform(op: BaseOp) {
    op.asInstanceOf[PlusOp].computePlusD(this)
  }
}
```

Clearly, the implementation is not type-safe, since it applies as InstanceOf, casting the op object into something different from its definition type. Casting here is destructive and, by definition, circumvents the static type system.

> *"If anything can go wrong, it will"*

A general question may arise: Should we reject an implementation just because it applies casts? Should we stop pursuing our design further if it introduces casts at some point? Usually, casting is considered bad practice, especially in the context of a language with a rich and expressive type system, like Scala. Destructive cast applications, like the one seen previously, may lead to runtime errors and we do not want our application to fail suddenly, in a way that cannot not be predicted. In fact, if we think of Murphy's Law, it will most certainly lead to runtime errors!

On the other hand, casts may appear in the form of conditionals:

```
if(op.isInstanceOf[PlusOp])
  // do something using PlusOp
else if(op.isInstanceOf[SomeOtherOp])
  // do something else
```

The above operations are not destructive; yet it is widely known that they should be avoided, since they promote a non-object-oriented style. Consecutive ifs reveal a procedure style, while under object-orientation polymorphism should be preferred.

Generally speaking, it is not rare in the application libraries landscape, even after the advent of generics into the Java platform, to use type casts while implementing a library. The casts in the library are used to make the life of the application programmer easier. In effect, they *absorb* all the small unsafe details, making them invisible to higher layers, where a type-safe interface is provided. The following snippets from the Scala library implementation reveal exactly this fact:[1]

```
// from the implementation of scala.collection.immutable.HashMap
table(i) = copy(ltable(i).asInstanceOf[Entry])

// from the implementation of scala.collection.jcl.ArrayList
override def clone: ArrayList[A] =
  new ArrayList[A](
    underlying.clone().
      asInstanceOf[java.util.ArrayList[A]])

// from the implementation of scala.Seq
override def filter(p: A => Boolean): Seq[A] =
  super.filter(p).asInstanceOf[Seq[A]]
```

After all, *casts exist in our code just because the language allows them to.*

12.5 Generic operation-centric approach

So far, our approaches could have been tried in plain-old Java, even before the advent of generics. An interesting question arises of what we can expect if we pursue a design that employs generics in order to become more expressive. In particular, so far our "parameterization" relied on simply denoting the proper interface either for data or operations. We can call it first-order parameterization and its roots are in the support for polymorphism, inherent in every object-oriented language. Taking this a step further, we abstract away the needed interfaces as parameters of a generic type.

The basic idea is that since in the functional decomposition we have an extensibility issue regarding our data, we parameterize the data type with an operation type. As a consequence, the actual computations in the operation classes need to be parameterized, since their parameters are now parameterized data. Our first attempt:

```
trait BaseD[V <: BaseOp] {
  def perform(op: V)
}

trait BaseOp {
  def computeNumD[V <: BaseOp](data: NumD[V])
}
```

---

[1] The examples are from revision 16570 of the Scala subversion trunk repository.

```
class NumD[V <: BaseOp](val value: Int) extends BaseD[V] {
  def perform(op: V) {
    op.computeNumD(this)
  }
}

class EvalOp extends BaseOp {
  var result: Option[Int] = None

  def apply[V <: BaseOp](data: BaseD[V]) = {
    data.perform(this) // this is problematic!
    result.get
  }

  def computeNumD[V <: BaseOp](data: NumD[V]) {
    this.result = Some(data.value)
  }
}
```

immediately yields a compiler error:

```
error: type mismatch;
 found    : EvalOp
 required: V
    data.perform(this)
                 ^
```

```
one error found
```

The problem is that the `perform` method expects an operation of the generic type V, as can be seen from the definition of the `BaseD[V]` trait, but at the offending use site, `this` is of type `EvalOp`. Clearly, `this` is unrelated to V, at least as far as the compiler is concerned: there is no declaration anywhere that *fixes*[2] V to `EvalOp`.

The solution, due to Madst Torgersen [73], is to use a trick. Since `this` does not have the correct type, we can provide it using an extra parameter `self` of type V. The changes affect our `NumD` data and the operation definitions, as seen in Figure 12.4.

After this change, it is straightforward to add the new data `PlusD` in a statically type-safe manner

```
trait PlusOp extends BaseOp {
  def computePlusD[V <: PlusOp](data: PlusD[V], self: V)
}
```

[2] The wording is intentional. In particular, the alerted reader may well be anticipating *F*-bounds and type-constructor fixed points.

```
trait BaseOp {
 def computeNumD[V <: baseOp](data: NumD[V], self: V)
}

class NumD[V <: BaseOp](val value: Int) extends BaseD[V] {
 def perform(op: V) {
   op.computeNumD(this, textit{op})
 }
}

class EvalOp extends BaseOp {
 var result: Option[Int] = None

 def apply[V <: BaseOp](data: BaseD[V], textit{self: V}) = {
  data.perform(self) // self here has the correct type
  result.get
 }

 def computeNumD[V <: BaseOp](data: NumD[V], textit{self: V}) {
  this.result = Some(data.value)
 }
}

object eval {
 def apply[V <: BaseOp](data: BaseD[V], self: V) =
  new EvalOp()(data, self)
}
```

Figure 12.4 Operation-centric approach to ExP with generics and Torgersen's self parameter.

```
class PlusD[V <: PlusOp](val a: BaseD[V], val b: BaseD[V])
    extends BaseD[V] {
  def perform(op: V) {
    op.computePlusD(this, op)
  }
}


class EvalPlusOp extends EvalOp with PlusOp {
  def coputePlusD[V <: PlusOp](data: PlusD[V], self: V) {
    val ia = eval(data.a, self)
    val ib = eval(data.b, self)
    this.result = Some(ia + ib)
  }
}
```

Our code example has become a little more verbose but at least we have gained static type-safety by providing an extra parameter of the needed type.

12.6 Generic data-centric approach

Let us now turn to a somewhat dual design by trying to incorporate generics in a data-centric approach. The need for generics in this case will emerge from the simple data-centric approach of Section 12.3 and especially our remarks on the following constructor:

```
class ReprPlusD(a: ReprD, b: ReprD)
```

If, instead of ReprD we use BaseD, the problem, as discussed previously, is that we cannot call repr on a or b because repr does not exist in BaseD. But, ideally, we would like to have BaseD instances. How do we patch them in order to get the extra repr method? Our line of thought is the following.

- We want BaseD instances to have the extra repr method, which is defined in PlusD.
- The above means that we want BaseD instances to acquire features existing in subclasses of BaseD.
- Then, we ask how to "parameterize" BaseD in a way that guarantees the extra features.
- Let us choose T as the parameterization. Now, BaseD is "promoted" to BaseD[T]
- Following the previous points, T needs to have features of subclasses of BaseD. In OO terms, this means that T is a subtype of BaseD[T]

So, we have finally arrived at our basic definition:

```
trait BaseD[T <: BaseD[T]] {
   def eval: Int
}
```

In object-oriented terminology, subtyping constraints where the type to be bounded (BaseD in this case) is used in the constraint itself, are traditionally called *F-bounds* [12].

Equipped with the new constrained parameterization, the base definitions are seen in Figure 12.5 and the task is now to extend our model in the "difficult" dimension of operations. Choosing the string representation as our new operation, the data model is extended with the aid of ReprD

```
trait ReprD[T <: ReprD[T]] extends BaseD[T] {
   def repr: String
}
```

Notice how we now constrain the abstract type T to be a subtype of the data supporting the new operation repr, in accordance of course with the general

```
trait BaseD[T <: BaseD[T]] {
  def eval: Int
}

class NumD[T <: BaseD[T]](value: Int) extends BaseD[T] {
  def eval = value
}

class PlusD[T <: BaseD[T]](a: T, b: T) extends BaseD[T] {
  def eval = a.eval + b.eval
}
```

Figure 12.5 Generic, data-centric base definitions for the expression problem.

requirements of the F-bounds as introduced previously. The respective concrete implementations for NumD and PlusD are the fully type-safe extensions

```
class ReprNumD[T <: ReprD[T]](value: Int)
    extends NumD[T](value) with ReprD[T] {
  def repr = value.toString
}

class ReprPlusD[T <: ReprD[T]](a: T, b: T)
    extends PlusD[T](a, b) with ReprD[T] {
  def repr = a.repr + " + " + b.repr
}
```

Fixing the bounds

One consideration with this approach is that the *F*-bounds requirement makes our classes unfinished in their implementation. In order to create instances for our data, we need to fix the bounds to something concrete. In a rather informal way, an *F*-bound of the form

$$\text{type } F[\text{type } T <: F[T]]$$

resembles a *fixed-point equation*

$$x = f(x).$$

Like in the case of the equation, we seek *fixed types* or, in other words, we seek to find the "fixed-point" of the type in the bound, so that we can use nongeneric versions of that data type. This is achieved by subclassing:

```
trait FReprD
     extends ReprD[FReprD]

class FReprNumD(value: Int)
     extends ReprNumD[FReprD](value)

class FReprPlusD(a: FReprD, b: FReprD)
     extends ReprPlusD[FReprD](a, b)
```

Notice how, once again, Scala's design decision to provide a primary constructor saves us from extra keystrokes and unnecessary verbosity. In Java, we would have to provide an implementation for the constructor and in there issue a super constructor call.

12.7 OO decomposition with abstract types

While most object-oriented languages allow the definition of abstract or "virtual" operations, Scala advances one step further and allows us to declare *abstract types* as well. These are types given in the body of a class or trait that are not precisely specified: their exact definition can either be left totally unspecified or be constrained. We can take advantage of this scheme in the context of the expression problem but we have to decide on what to abstract: the data type or the operation type? In the present section we will deal with an object-oriented decomposition that abstracts over data, first presented by Odersky and Matthias Zenger [60].

Now, abstract types need an enclosing type and since we are modeling a small expression language with operations, we start like this:

```
trait BaseLang {
  type Data <: BaseD

  trait BaseD {
    def eval: Int
  }

  class NumD(value: Int) extends BaseD {
    def eval = value
  }
}
```

In these base definitions, we can see that the data type Data is unspecified but yet constrained to always be a subtype of trait BaseD. Although Data is not used anywhere else here, we anticipate that it will be the key idea when it comes to extending our base language with new operations.

Adding new data

Our approach, as can readily be seen, is not based on visitors. Thus, new data can be defined without difficulty. We could have included `PlusD` in `BaseLang` but it is easy to provide a new mini language with the extra data:

```
trait PlusLang extends BaseLang {
  class PlusD(a: Data, b: Data) extends BaseD {
    def eval = a.eval + b.eval
  }
}
```

The new language, `PlusLang`, enriches `BaseLang` with a representation of data addition. In the scope of `PlusLang`, the abstract type `Data` has no further refinement, so it retains the constraints of the base language, `BaseLang`, being a subtype of `BaseD`. By definition, `PlusLang` has all the data of `BaseLang` and, consequently, their operations.

One concern with the approach so far is that, since we base everything on top-level traits, we have nothing concrete to instantiate and use directly. Actually, the main issue is that the abstract type `Data` needs to be made equal to something known. For example, if we just try to make `PlusLang` concrete by defining an object

```
object PlusLang extends PlusLang {
  val n1: Data = new NumD(1)
}
```

the error is unavoidable

```
found    : NumD
required: Data
         val n1: Data = new NumD(1)
                            ^
one error found
```

To correct the situation, we make `Data` equal to `BaseD`

```
object PlusLang extends PlusLang {
  type Data = BaseD
  val n1: Data = new NumD(1)
}
```

and now we can use the newly created object without problem. What saved us previously was just the intentional type we gave to n1. In fact, if we try to compile without the n1 immutable value

```
object PlusLang extends PlusLang
```

the compiler gives no warnings or errors, but unfortunately we have rendered the object unusable for our purpose. The reason is exactly the fact that type Data has not been assigned a known value (BaseD in this case). A session with the interpreter sheds some more light:

```
scala> import PlusLang._
scala> val (n1, n2) = (new NumD(1), new NumD(2))
scala> val n3 = new PlusD(n1, n2)
<console>:8: error: type mismatch;
 found    : NumD
 required: Data
       val n3 = new PlusD(n1, n2)
                          ^

<console>:8: error: type mismatch;
 found    : NumD
 required: Data
       val n3 = new PlusD(n1, n2)
                              ^
```

So, the moral is we must not forget to fix the data type.

Adding new operations

The next step is to introduce a new operation. Since operations are built into the data types, we will have to create a new language for which the base type incorporates the new operation. Also, we must "patch" the already defined types of the base language with the new operation:

```
trait ReprLang extends BaseLang {
  type Data <: BaseD

  trait BaseD extends super.BaseD {
    def repr: String
  }

  class NumD(value: Int) extends super.NumD(value) with BaseD {
    def repr = value.toString
  }
}
```

We have explicitly declared that `BaseD` extends `super.BaseD`. The reason is that in Scala the new definitions simply shadow the previous ones and overriding is not the default option. For this, the `super` qualifier is needed in `ReprLang` to access the trait `BaseD` of the same name in `BaseLang`. Other than this technical detail, the enriched `BaseD` contains the new `repr` operation and the same is done with `NumD`.

Having defined the new operation, we can mix in the several languages to create variations of the desired functionality. For example, if we need a language that support both the `repr` operation and the `PlusD` data, we can mix in `PlusLang` and `ReprLang`:

```scala
trait ReprPlusLang extends PlusLang with ReprLang {
  class PlusD(a: Data, b: Data) extends super.PlusD(a, b)
                                  with BaseD {
    def repr = a.repr + " + " + b.repr
  }
}
```

and then use it right away

```scala
object FixedReprPlusLang extends ReprPlusLang {
  type Data = BaseD

  val n1: Data = new NumD(10)
  val n2: Data = new NumD(13)
  val n3: Data = new PlusD(n1, n2)
}

...
scala> println(FixedReprPlusLang.n3.repr)
res0: String = 10 + 13
```

Inside `ReprPlusLang`, the `Data` type refers to trait `BaseD` of `ReprLang`, so the parameters a and b already contain a `repr` method.

Exercise 12.5 So far, our operations return primitive types, for example, `Int` and `String`. Design a nondestructive `negate` operation with the following signature

```scala
def negate: Data
```

where `Data` is the abstract type used as previously. Note that the requirement is that `negate` does not just return an `Int` but an expression of our mini language. For example, a `NumD` instance is expected to return another `NumD` instance with the underlying `Int` value negated.

12.8 Operation-centric decomposition with abstract types

We now turn to the dual approach, again leveraging abstract type members in the context of trait-based expression languages that are extended in order to provide the extra functionality. Our base language is defined in Figure 12.6. The extension

```
trait BaseLang {
  type Operation <: BaseOp

  trait BaseD {
    def perform(op: Operation)
  }

  trait BaseOp {
    def computeNumD(data: NumD)
  }

  class NumD(val value: Int) extends BaseD {
    def perform(op: Operation) {
      op.computeNumD(this)
    }
  }

  class EvalOp extends BaseOp {
    this: Operation =>

    var result: Option[Int] = None

    def apply(data: BaseD) = {
      data.perform(this) // this is Operation
      result.get
    }

    def computeNumD(data: NumD) {
      this.result = Some(data.value)
    }
  }

  def newEvalOp(): EvalOp with Operation

  object eval {
    def apply(data: BaseD) = newEvalOp()(data)
  }
}
```

Figure 12.6 Base language for an operation-centric decomposition of the ExP with abstract type members.

direction is now that of the operations, so the relevant type `Operation` abstracts over the possible operations:

```
trait BaseLang {
  type Operation <: BaseOp

  ...
```

The most important thing to notice is the use of an explicit *self-type* in the definition of class `EvalOp`:

```
class EvalOp extends BaseOp {
  this: Operation =>

  ...
```

This way we constrain the type of any instance of `EvalOp` actually to be a subtype of our abstract type `Operation`, which is absolutely necessary for the following code inside `EvalOp` to type check:

```
def apply(data: BaseD) = {
  data.perform(this) // this is Operation
  result.get
}
```

Actually, this is a point where Scala's expressiveness really shines. Had we not used the explicit self-type, `this` would just be of type `BaseOp` and not of type `Operation`, as expected by the signature of method `perform` in `BaseOp`. The situation is similar to the one we faced in the context of the *generic operation-centric approach* developed in Section 12.5. There, the trick of an extra `self` parameter with the correct type was used. Here, we constrain, *by design*, instances of `BaseOp` to be instances of `Operation` and we let the compiler enforce this constraint and either accept our program or complain accordingly.

Exercise 12.6 Explore the design decision of using self-types in the context of the *generic operation-centric approach*. Can we employ self-types to avoid the extra `self` parameter that we used in Section 12.5 in order to achieve type safety? Feel free to disembark from the approach established in Section 12.5 if it is the only way to experiment with self-types. Generally speaking, with Scala, feel free to experiment in any direction that seems suitable. The language is so expressive that even slight deviations from established knowledge may either lead to interesting results or at least provide a rewarding (in itself) working path.

Also, in Figure 12.6 an abstract factory method is provided, namely `newEvalOp`, that will be used to create, on demand, new instances of the evaluation operation. The return type mixes `EvalOp` with `Operation` so that the self-type of `EvalOp`'s definition is correctly respected. The `eval` object is a convenient functional wrapper around `EvalOp`'s apply method. A concrete implementation that respects the above remarks is:

```
object FixBaseLang extends BaseLang {
  type Operation = BaseOp

  def newEvalOp() = new EvalOp // Operation is fixed now
}
```

Adding new operations

We normally expect that the addition of new operations poses no difficulties. For example, the familiar string representation operation can be modeled as follows:

```
trait ReprLang extends BaseLang {
  class ReprOp extends BaseOp {
    this: Operation =>

    var result: Option[String] = None

    def apply(data: BaseD) = {
      data.perform(this)
      result.get
    }

    def computeNumD(data: NumD) {
      this.result = Some(data.value.toString)
    }

    def newReprOp(): ReprOp with Operation

    object repr {
      def apply(data: BaseD) = newReprOp()(data)
    }
  }
}
```

Again, the explicit self-type reference is mandatory, in order to preserve the correct semantics, and we have used the same recipe with the factory method `newReprOp` and the functional object `repr`.

Exercise 12.7 Create a second operation extension and provide a combination of the two operations by a proper mixin.

Adding new data

We now turn to the normally difficult dimension, since we are in an operation-centric approach, of adding new data. Actually, the case is rather easy, as the following implementation of the `expr ::= expr '+' expr` grammar rule shows:

```scala
trait PlusLang extends BaseLang {
  type Operation <: BaseOp

  trait BaseOp extends super.BaseOp {
    def computePlusD(data: PlusD)
  }

  class PlusD(val a: BaseD, val b: BaseD) extends BaseD {
    def perform(op: Operation) {
    op.computePlusD(this)
    }
  }

  class EvalOp extends super.EvalOp with BaseOp {
    this: Operation =>

    def computePlusD(data: PlusD) {
    this.result = Some(eval(data.a) + eval(data.b))
    }
  }
}
```

Exercise 12.8 Provide a combination of a data extension with an operation extension.

12.9 Summary

We have presented the expression problem, which we believe is a fundamental design issue any software engineer should be aware of. Our analysis of the design space is based on research papers by Torgersen [73] and Odersky and Zenger [60]. While tackling the problem, we have progressively used language features existing in plain Java to more advanced features of Scala. The latter reveal the undeniably rich expressiveness of the Scala language. In order to follow the examples presented in this chapter more easily, we have used a common language that models our problem domain, namely a small expression language. In this direction, the naming of our traits and classes is consistent across all of the presented attacks on the expression problem.

In our opinion, the essence of the expression problem reveals a fundamental need: to come up with expressive designs that can model it; designs that should be based on reusable and extensible components. Several questions emerge and one of them is: Since patterns play a fundamental role in modeling the problem (either the Interpreter or Visitor), can we provide reusable and extensible pattern implementations that can be tailored to our needs? Can we provide patterns as a generic library that can be further customized?

13

A computer algebra system

Symbolic computation refers to the use of machines, such as computers, to manipulate mathematical content (i.e., equations, expressions, etc.) in symbolic form and deliver a result in this form. A classical example of such a system is one that can *compute* the derivative of a function expressed in some symbolic form (i.e., `sin(x)+1`). In this chapter we will explain why symbolic computation is interesting and what it can achieve, and then we are going to present a simple system that can differentiate functions.

13.1 Mechanical symbol manipulation

In the beginning of the twentieth century, the great German mathematician David Hilbert asked whether it would be possible to devise a method to solve mechanically any *diophantine* equation, that is, any polynomial equation with integer coefficients. In other words, he asked whether it is possible to solve any diophantine equation by dully following a clerical procedure. In fact, Hilbert was dreaming of a fully mechanized mathematical science. Unfortunately for Hilbert it has been shown that one cannot construct a general algorithm to solve any diophantine equation.[1] A consequence of this proof was that the dream of a fully mechanized mathematical science was not feasible. Nevertheless, certain problems of mathematics can be solved by purely mechanical methods. For example, it has been demonstrated that certain operations like differentiation and integration can be performed mechanically. In general, such systems are known as *symbolic computation* or *computer algebra* systems.

Mathematica™ and Maple™ are two very popular symbolic computation systems that are used by many people almost every day. A key factor of the success

---

[1] The reader interested in the details of this and related issues should consult a specialized book (for example, see [72]).

of these systems and other similar systems is that they can quickly solve problems that people cannot easily solve with pencil and paper. For instance, although all science students learn how to differentiate and integrate functions, still many of them have difficulty finding the derivative and especially the indefinite integral of some functions. Of course, there are much more difficult problems that can be solved relatively easily with symbolic computation systems, but these will not concern us here. In addition, it is known that such systems employ techniques traditionally employed in Artificial Intelligence, thus, they seem to exhibit some sort of intelligence. Again, whether this is indeed intelligence or not is something that will not concern us here.

Systems of symbolic computation are similar to modern programming language processors. First of all, they read strings that belong to some language (for example, a language describing functions). Second, they transform these strings into an internal representation (for example, some sort of parse tree). After this, they transform the input using transformation and rewrite rules. In the end, they ought to deliver their result in a form that is at least as readable as the strings of the input language. For example, if someone uses a system that differentiates functions, when one enters

$$(\sin(x))\verb|^|2 + 4,$$

the system should produce output that has at least the following form:

$$2*\sin(x)*\cos(x).$$

Let us now outline what are the steps involved in the construction of a rudimentary symbolic computation system.

First of all, we need to describe precisely the grammar of the input language. Here we have two choices: to define an external DSL or an internal DSL. To keep things simple, we have opted to define an external DSL. Next we need to decide how to get input and how to process it. The simplest solution is to have an interactive system that takes one expression at a time, processes it, and produces output. As expected, the program should stop when the user presses an end-of-input character.

13.2 The grammar

In most cases users expect new systems to be able to understand input in some standard form. For example, it is quite realistic to expect that a system that performs symbolic differentiation will be able to understand input in either TEX's notation or the notation employed in most programming languages. Again to keep things simple, we will use a subset of the notation employed by most programming languages. In addition, since most common programming languages do not include an exponentiation operator, we have opted to use the one used in BASIC, a very popular programming language of the 1980s:

```
Expression    = Term { ( "+" | "-" ) Term }
Term          = Factor { ( "*" | "/" ) Factor }
Factor        = Primary { "^" Primary }
Primary       = Number | "x" | ( "-" | "+" ) Expression
                | "(" Expression ")" | Function
Number        = Integer | Float
Integer       = Digit { Digit }
Digit         = "0" | "1" | "2" | ... | "8" | "9"
Function      = FunctionName "(" Expression ")"
functionName  = "sin" | "cos" | "ln" | ...
```

Exercise 13.1 Write down the production rule for floats.

Exercise 13.2 Write down a parser for the grammar above.

Although the language described by the grammar above is reasonable, still it is counterintuitive! For example, when mathematicians want to write "two times ex," they write $2x$ and not $2 * x$. In other words, we need to eliminate the multiplication operator for the sake of simplicity. One way to achieve this is to modify the corresponding derivation rule as follows:

```
Term            = Factor { MulOp Factor }
MulOp           = OptionalTimes | "/"
OptionalTimes   = "*" | OptionalSpaces
OptionalSpaces  = Empty | Space OptionalSpaces
```

Exercise 13.3 Modify the parser of Exercise 13.2 so as to include the additions suggested above.

13.3 Basic data model

As in other similar cases, we need to define a case class hierarchy that will reflect the syntax of expressions. At the top of the hierarchy, we need a sealed abstract class for obvious reasons:

```
sealed abstract class Expr
```

Next we need to define classes that will handle the various syntactic entities that belong to syntactic class `Primary`. First we need to define a module that will handle variables:

```
case object Chi extends Expr
```

We have decided not to distinguish numbers and so to have only one class for numbers:

```
case class Num(num: Double) extends Expr
```

Our system needs to be able to deal with unary operations (for example, $-x$) and binary operations (for example, $x + 2 * x$). Also, in order to handle the one-variable functions (for example, $\sin(x)$, $\tan(x)$, etc.), a special case class is needed for this as well:

```
case class UnOp(operator: String, operand : Expr)
                  extends Expr
case class BinOp(operator: String,
              Left: Expr, Right: Expr) extends Expr
case class Fun(name: String, arg: Expr) extends Expr
```

If we want to introduce more features, then we can augment this hierarchy accordingly.

Although it is not difficult to see how functions can be represented by instances of classes of this hierarchy, still we believe it is instructive to present a few examples:

- x becomes `Chi`,
- `x + 1` becomes `BinOp("+", Chi, Num(1))`, and
- `sin(2 * x)` becomes `Fun("sin", BinOp("*", Num(2), Chi)`.

In addition, the expresion `2 * x + 1` must be represented as

```
BinOp("+", BinOp("*", 2, Chi), Num(1))
```

and not as

```
BinOp("*", Num(2), BinOp("+", Chi, Num(1))
```

since the precedence of multiplication is higher than that of addition.

13.4 Experimenting with the data model

Although we have decided to design an external DSL, still it is quite instructive to see how we could implement an internal DSL. First, we need to redefine class Expr as follows:

```
sealed abstract class Expr {
    // overloading for use in Scala Interpreter
    def +(other: Expr) = BinOp("+", this, other)
    def -(other: Expr) = BinOp("-", this, other)
```

```
        def *(other: Expr) = BinOp("*", this, other)
        def /(other: Expr) = BinOp("/", this, other)
        def unary_-() = UnOp("-", this)
        def unary_+() = this
    }
```

In addition, we need to redefine class Chi – it is completely unnatural to type Chi. A better solution is the following singleton object:

```
    case object χ extends Expr
```

Now the following code snippet

```
    var y = χ + χ
    println(y)
```

will print the expression BinOp(+,χ,χ) on our computer screen. However, the code snippet

```
    var x = χ + 2
    println(x)
```

will make Scala complain that there is a *type mismatch; found : Int(2), required: this.Expr*. Clearly, we have not instructed Scala how to mix χs with numbers. As expected, an implicit conversion (see Section 3.6.3) will do the job:

```
    implicit def IntToExpr(i: Int) = Num(i)
```

Now the previous code will print the string BinOp(+,χ,Num(2.0)) on our computer screen.

Similarly, we need to define singleton objects like the following one for all functions that our system is supposed to understand:

```
    case object sin(override val arg: Expr) extends
            Fun("sin", arg)
```

Note the override val modifiers for the argument, needed to define the singleton correctly.

13.5 Basic operations

13.5.1 Finding the derivative of a function

Finding the derivative of a function in most cases is a straightforward task. Nevertheless, there are few cases like $(\sin x)^{\cos x}$ where the way to go is not that obvious. In calculus, if f is a function of one variable, say x, then df/dx denotes its derivative. Table 13.1 shows how one can find the derivative of some basic functions and some

Table 13.1 *Derivatives of basic functions and combinations of functions*

$$\frac{dc}{dx} = 0 \qquad\qquad\qquad \frac{d(u^n)}{dx} = nu^{n-1}\frac{du}{dx}$$

$$\frac{dx}{dx} = 1 \qquad\qquad\qquad \frac{d(\sin u)}{dx} = \cos u\frac{du}{dx}$$

$$\frac{d(-u)}{dx} = -\frac{du}{dx} \qquad\qquad \frac{d(\cos u)}{dx} = -\sin u\frac{du}{dx}$$

$$\frac{d(u+v)}{dx} = \frac{du}{dx} + \frac{dv}{dx} \qquad\qquad \frac{d(e^u)}{dx} = e^u\frac{du}{dx}$$

$$\frac{d(uv)}{dx} = u\frac{dv}{dx} + v\frac{du}{dx} \qquad\qquad \frac{d(u^v)}{dx} = vu^{v-1}\frac{du}{dx} + u^v\frac{dv}{dx}\ln u$$

$$\frac{d(cu)}{dx} = c\frac{du}{dx} \qquad\qquad \frac{d(\ln u)}{dx} = \frac{1}{u}\frac{du}{dx}$$

$$\frac{d\left(\frac{u}{v}\right)}{dx} = \frac{v\frac{du}{dx} - u\frac{dv}{dx}}{g^2} \qquad\qquad \frac{d(a^u)}{dx} = a^u\frac{du}{dx}\ln a$$

$$\frac{d(\sin^{-1} u)}{dx} = \frac{\frac{du}{dx}}{\sqrt{1-u^2}} \qquad\qquad \frac{d(\cos^{-1} u)}{dx} = -\frac{\frac{du}{dx}}{\sqrt{1-u^2}}$$

combinations of functions. Although this table is by no means complete, it includes the necessary information for our little programming project. For a complete list of all (?) possible cases, one should consult any standard calculus textbook (for example, see [67]).

Let us define a function that can compute the derivative of a given function:

```
def D(g: Expr) : Expr = g match {
  case Num(_) => Num(0)
  case Chi     => Num(1)
  case UnOp("-",u) => UnOp("-",D(u))
  case BinOp("+", u, v) => BinOp("+", D(u), D(v)
  case BinOp("*", u, v) => BinOp("+", BinOp("*", u, D(v)),
                                      BinOp("*", v, D(u))
  . . . . . . . . . . . . . . . . . . . . . . . . . . .
  case Fun("sin", u) => BinOp("*", Fun("cos", u), D(u))
  case Fun("cos", u) => BinOp("*", UnOp("-",
                               Fun("sin", u)), D(u))
```

```
    case Fun("ln", u) => BinOp("*", BinOp("/", Num(1), u),
                                   D(u))
    case Fun("e", u) => BinOp("*", Fun("e", u), D(u)
    . . . . . . . . . . . . . . . . . . . . . . . .
    case _ => print("Can't handle this function!\n")
  }
```

Exercise 13.4 Using Table 13.1 complete the code above.

Although the output produced by function D is correct, it is cluttered up with useless "information." For example, when x+1 is fed to D, the result will be

$$\text{BinOp}("+", \text{Num}(1), \text{Num}(0)),$$

which is correct but not what people would expect. This means that we have to simplify the result produced by this function.

13.5.2 *Simplifying an expression*

Before proceeding with the definition of a function that does the actual simplification, let us see what kind of simplifications can be performed.

First of all, we need to get rid of zeros and ones in additions and multiplications, respectively. Also, we need to remove all double negation signs. Furthermore, we need to simplify some standard expressions like $\sin^2 u + \cos^2 u$. The following function implements these ideas:

```
    def simplify(g: Expr) : Expr = g match {
      case Fun(s, e) => Fun(s, simplify(s))
      case UnOp("+", e) => simplify(e)
      case UnOp("-", Num(n)) => Num(-n)
      case UnOp("-", UnOp("-", e)) => simplify(e)
      case UnOp("-", e) => UnOp("-", simplify(e))
      case BinOp("+", Num(0), e) => simplify(e)
      case BinOp("+", e, Num(0)) => simplify(e)
      case BinOp("-", e, Num(0)) => simplify(e)
      case BinOp("-", Num(0), e) => UnOp("-", simplify(e))
      case BinOp("*", Num(0), e) => Num(0)
      case BinOp("*", e, Num(0)) => Num(0)
      case BinOp("*", Num(1), e) => simplify(e)
      case BinOp("*", e, Num(1)) => simplify(e)
      case BinOp("/", e, Num(1)) => simplify(e)
```

```
    case BinOp("+", BinOp("*", Num(n), e),
                    BinOp("*", Num(m), e)) =>
                    BinOp("*", Num(n+m), simplify(e))
    . . . . . . . . . . . . . . . . . . . . . . . . . . . .
    case BinOp("+", BinOp("^", Fun("sin", _), Num(2)),
                    BinOp("^", Fun("cos", _), Num(2)) => 1
    . . . . . . . . . . . . . . . . . . . . . . . . . . . .
    case BinOp(op, L, R) => BinOp(op, simplify(L),
                                    simplify(R))
}
```

Exercise 13.5 Complete the code above.

13.5.3 *Pretty-printing expressions*

Although the expression BinOp(*,Num(2.0),χ) is far more readable than the expression

$$\text{BinOp}(+,\text{BinOp}(*,\text{Num}(2.0),\chi),\text{Num}(0.0))$$

we are sure readers would prefer to see something like 2*x on their computer screen. Thus, it is almost mandatory to define a function that will pretty-print expressions. The easiest way to code a pretty-printer is to yield a string representation of each type of expression and, in certain cases, to surround subexpressions in parentheses:

```
def pretty_printer1(e: Expr) = e match {
  case Chi            => "χ"
  case Num(n)         => n.toString
  case UnOp(op, e)    => op + "(" + pretty(e) + ")"
  case BinOp(op, a, b) => "(" + pretty(a) + ") " +
                          op + " (" + pretty + ")"
  case Fun(name, e)   => name + "(" + pretty(e) + ")"
}
```

Let us test our pretty-printer. The string x * (2 + x) will be represented by the following expression:

$$\text{BinOp}("*", \text{Chi}, \text{BinOp}("+", \text{Num}(2), \text{Chi}))$$

By feeding this expression to the function just defined, we will get the following string which will be transformed by pretty to

$$(x) * ((2.0) + (x))$$

Unfortunately, this is not pretty at all! In the case of a complex expression, the result will be cluttered with parentheses. A way to solve this problem is to take into account the precedence of the various operators involved. First of all let us define a function that *computes* the precedence of the various operators:

```
def binPrec(op: String) =
  op match {
    case "+" => 1
    case "-" => 1
    case "*" => 2
    case "/" => 2
    case "^" => 3
    case _ => error("Unknown binary operator: " + op)
  }
```

As is evident, the bigger the return value the higher the precedence of the operator. Unary operators are handled separately:

```
def unPrec = 4
```

Now these functions can be used to compute the precedence of an expression which is equal to the precedence of the operator of the expression. However, since variables, functions, and numbers do not involve an operator, we assume that these symbols behave like unary operators. Thus our function should be defined as follows:

```
def precedence(e: Expr) =
  e match {
    case BinOp(op, _, _) => binPrec(op)
    case _               => unPrec
  }
```

Next we need to use these functions in order to decide whether a subexpression must be enclosed in parentheses when it is printed. The idea is very simple – we compute the precedence of a subexpression and if its precedence is less than the precedence of the operator, then we enclose the subexpresion in parentheses. The following functions implement this idea for binary operators:

```
def combineBinary(op: String, a: Expr, b: Expr) = {
  val aPrec  = precedence(a)
  val bPrec  = precedence(b)
  val opPrec = binPrec(op)
  var aStr   = pretty_printer(a)
  var bStr   = pretty_printer(b)
```

```
      if (aPrec < opPrec)
        aStr = "(" + aStr + ")"
      if (bPrec < opPrec)
        bStr = "(" + bStr + ")"
      aStr + " " + op + " " + bStr
    }
```

And the following functions implement the same idea for unary operators:

```
    def combineUnary(op: String, e: Expr) = {
      val eStr = pretty(e)
      op + (
        if (precedence(e) < unPrec)
          "(" + eStr + ")"
        else
          eStr
      )
    }
```

Now, it is straightforward to define function `pretty_printer`:

```
    def pretty_printer(e: Expr) =
      e match {
        case Num(x)        => x.toString
        case Chi           => "x"
        case BinOp(o,l,r)  => combineBinary(o,l,r)
        case UnOp(o,u)     => combineUnary(o,u)
        case Fun(n,e)      => n + "(" + pretty_printer(e) + ")"
      }
```

The reader may have noticed that we have tackled the pretty-printing problem by dividing the task into smaller subtasks and solving the subtasks first. The complete solution is then a synthesis of the smaller solutions. One can say that this is a typical example of the divide-and-conquer programming methodology.

Exercise 13.6 Change the definition of expressions, so that each expression type defines its precedence. For example, one could redefine Expr as follows:

```
    sealed abstract class Expr {
      def precedence: int
    }
```

13.6 Putting it all together

Now that we have solved all the subproblems involved (we assume that the reader has constructed the parser of Exercise 13.2), we can proceed and complete our programming project. Again, we need to use some standard Java classes to handle input:

```
// Expr class hierarchy
// Parser and function definitions
import java.io.BufferedReader,InputStreamReader
val input = new BufferedReader(
                new InputStreamReader(System.in))
var line = input.readLine
while( line != null ) {
   var result = SymbComp.parseAll(SymbComp.expr, line)
   if ( result.successful) {
      var parseTree = result.get
      var der = simplify(D(parseTree))
      println(pretty_print(der))
   }
   line = input.readLine
}
```

Field System.in is an instance of class java.io.InputStream that corresponds to the standard input. An InputStreamReader is a way to go from byte streams to character streams: it reads bytes and decodes them into characters using a specified character set (a Unicode character set by default). Finally, a BufferedReader can read text from a character-input stream while being able to buffer input so as to provide for the efficient reading of characters and whole lines.

Exercise 13.7 Use the following idiom to process input:

```
import scala.io._
import java.lang._
for (line <- Source.fromInputStream(System.in).getLines) {
   Process input
}
```

Method fromInputStream creates an iterator from an instance of class java.io.InputStream.

13.7 Functions of more than one variable

Assume that we want to extend our system so as to be able to compute partial derivatives. First of all, we need to replace the definition of Chi with something more flexible. In particular, we need to define a class that can be parametrized, such as the following:

```
abstract class Expr
case class Var(name: String) extends Expr
. . . . . . . . . . . . . . . . . . . . .
```

Obviously, we need to rewrite the definition of function D to reflect this change. In addition, function D needs to have a second argument that will correspond to the variable with respect to which it will differentiate its first argument. The last change in the code regards the handling of class Var. In general, if x and y are independent variables, then the partial derivative of y with respect to x is zero and the partial derivative of x with respect to x equals one, or more compactly

$$\frac{\partial y}{\partial x} = 0 \quad \text{and} \quad \frac{\partial x}{\partial x} = 1.$$

The skeleton code that follows shows how we have implemented the changes just described.

```
def D(g: Expr, x: String ) : Expr = g match {
    case Num(_) => Num(0)
    case Var(y) => if y==x then Num(1) else Num(0)
    case UnOp("-",u) => UnOp("-",D(u,x))
    case BinOp("+", u, v) => BinOp("+", D(u,x), D(v,x)
    . . . . . . . . . . . . . . . . . . . . . . .
    case _ => print("Can't handle this function!\n")
}
```

Exercise 13.8 Implement the missing cases in the previous function definition.

If we want to compute the partial derivative of some function $f(x,y)$ first with respect to x and then with respect to y, we need to use an expression like the following:

```
D( D( F, "x" ), "y" )
```

13.8 Summary and further reading

In this chapter we have used Scala's facilities to design and implement a simple algebraic system. The approach taken for differentiation is straightforward and probably rather familiar to some readers. In fact, it is common practice to do it in this way in programming courses teaching Prolog and/or functional programming languages.

Symbolic computation is a field of its own. Mathematicians have found particularly beautiful ways to differentiate functions symbolically and numerically, and one such approach is based on dual numbers. Dual numbers are like complex numbers, i.e. $(a, b) = a + db$, with the difference that the *dual unit* d (the analog of the *imaginary unit* i) has the property $d^2 = 0$ instead of the usual property $i^2 = -1$. Basic arithmetic with dual numbers goes like this:

$$(a_1, b_1) + (a_2, b_2) = (a_1 + a_2, b_1 + b_2)$$
$$(a_1, b_1) - (a_2, b_2) = (a_1 - a_2, b_1 - b_2)$$
$$(a_1, b_1) * (a_2, b_2) = (a_1 a_2, a_1 b_2 + b_1 a_2)$$
$$(a_1, b_1)/(a_2, b_2) = \left(\frac{a_1}{a_2}, \frac{a_1 b_2 - b_1 a_2}{a_2^2} \right).$$

The fact that $d^2 = 0$ means that $d^n = 0, \forall n > 1$, so in the Taylor series expansion of $f(x + d)$, where f is a function, an infinity of terms *do not survive*, thus leaving us with $f(x + d) = f(x) + f'(x)d$, where $f'(x)$ is the derivative of f with respect to x, that is df/dx. This is a remarkable property: it means that with just algebra, we can compute the derivate of a function!

Exercise 13.9 Define dual numbers in Scala and implement their arithmetic as defined above. Then write an algorithm for differentiation of polynomials that takes into account the above property. The Maclaurin series for any polynomial is the polynomial itself, so we can symbolically produce their derivative.

Our main symbolic manipulation has concentrated on differentiation but one should expect a computer algebra system to treat integration as well. Unfortunately, as opposed to the exact differentiation rules, integration does not enjoy such a generic treatment. Nevertheless, the set of known functions that are integrated exactly is not small.

The domain of symbolic manipulation is vast. The reader is invited to consult any general textbook in the field for more details (for example, see [29]). In addition, we suggest the excellent overview of the field of symbolic integration by the late Manuel Bronstein [10].

Appendix A

Multimedia processing

The term *multimedia* refers to the integration of multiple forms of media, including text, graphics, audio, video, etc. For example, an audio file is a typical example of a media file. Typically one needs a *codec* to encode and/or decode a digital data stream. In most cases, codecs are native libraries and this why it is not trivial to use them. In addition, many common media codecs are proprietary, which poses yet another obstacle in the creation of media applications. A simple solution is to use the Java Media Framework (JMF). This includes native libraries for many common codecs that include codecs for the reproduction of MP3 files, QuickTime files, etc. The following simple program shows how to program a trivial MP3-player using the JMF:

```
import java.io.File
import javax.media.Manager
import javax.media.Player

object playmp3 {
  def main(args: Array[String]) {
    val n = args.length
    if (n > 1 || n ==0 )
      println("Usage: mp3player <file>")
    else {
      try {
        val myMp3File: Player =
          Manager.createPlayer(
            new File(args(0)).toURI().toURL())
        myMp3File.start()
      } catch{
```

```
        case e : Exception => e.printStackTrace()
      }
    }
  }
}
```

The essence of the code just presented is the few lines inside the `try` command. In a nutshell, we create a new player capable of playing an MP3 file that is stored in a file whose name is supplied as a command line argument. We create an instance of `java.io.File` to generate an object that will be used by the player. Method `toURI` constructs a URI from an abstract representation of a file while method `toURL` creates a URL. Escaping characters that are illegal in URLs is done if these methods are invoked in this order. Once the new player is constructed, one can start playing the MP3 audio file.

Unfortunately, the JMF is not up-to-date and a better solution would be to use native libraries. For example, one can use the `libmpg123`, which was developed by Michael Hipp and Thomas Orgis. An easy way to do this is to use the Java Native Access framework. Access framework (`https://jna.dev.java.net/`). But we do not plan to explain how this can be done. Readers are very welcome to use all these tools to implement a simple MP3 player.

Appendix B

Distributing a Scala application along with Scala itself

B.1 Introduction

Let us assume that we have programmed our Scala application and the next major task is to provide it for download, so that people may try it. What are our options? In fact, there are several parameters to consider. One such parameter relates to whether we will use an installer creator in order to make a click-and-go executable. Providing an installer is quite common if indeed what we have is an application and less common if our product is just a library. Another parameter to consider is what assumptions we make on the requirements for the end-user's client machine. In this appendix we will concentrate on that last point and in particular what to do if a Scala installation at the client's machine is not always a true assumption (an assumption that not always evaluates to true).

End users are lazy, even lazier than developers. Distributing an application to an end user is different from distributing it to a developer. Scala is not at the moment an integrated part of any operating system and so we cannot rely on the user's open mind, curiosity and even a tendency for language exploration in order to assume that Scala is installed at people's computers. So how do we cope with that?

We will show a technique to incorporate all the needed runtime services of Scala inside one's application, so that when we distribute the application, we distribute the relevant part of Scala as well, in just one package. Of course, the trivial way would be just to copy the contents of the Scala-provided Java Archives (jar) inside our application jar file. This way, though, we would not take advantage of great open-source projects that are better suited for the job of automatically deciding which parts to include and, as a consequence, we would miss the opportunity to familiarize ourselves with these projects.

B.2 Enter proguard

Proguard[1] is an open-source program that can shrink, optimize, obfuscate and preverify Java classes.

- *Shrinking* is achieved by removing unused fields, methods and even whole Java classes.
- Several *optimizations* can be performed, such as constant expression evaluation, unused code removal, variable allocation reduction and many others.
- *Obfuscation* prevents reverse engineering by stripping off any debugging information and by transforming names (such as package and class names) to incomprehensible character sequences.
- *Preverification* is a feature related to JDK 6. When a class is loaded by the JVM, it is verified for correctness. This is something that may slow down the whole class-loading procedure. JDK 6 introduced the feature according to which verification can be done by the compiler and stored at special attributes inside the compiled class file. This piece of information can be discovered during class-loading, thus saving time and space.

Proguard defines an intuitive and easily mastered configuration language that we can use to tailor its execution to our needs, at a level of fine granularity. Using an example directly from its documentation, we can preserve all applets in a jar file with the following configuration option:

```
-keep public class * extends java.applet.Applet
```

B.3 Requirement and candidate application

Of all the proguard features, the one we are interested in now is shrinking. Our requirement is that given a jar file containing our application, we wish to generate a new archive which will, in addition to the application, include all the needed class files from a Scala distribution.

As a test application, we will use a handy script, shown in Figure B.1. The figure actually contains a skeleton, the missing parts of which we will fill in shortly. The script is intended as a command line utility, named *findcmd*, which takes a series of names as arguments and searches the executable PATHs for programs that match the name. A straightforward use of the script would be:

```
$ findcmd exe
--- exe --->
/opt/local/bin:
    gzexe, kfmexec, kioexec, luceneindexer, msgexec, msiexec
/usr/bin:
    execsnoop, gzexe, mpiexec, sandbox-exec
```

[1] http://proguard.sourceforge.net/

```
// script: findcmd.scala
import java.lang.System
import java.io.File
import java.util.regex.Pattern

val Path = System.getenv("PATH")

val PathSep = File.pathSeparator

val CASE_I = Pattern.CASE_INSENSITIVE

val pathFolders = Path.split(PathSep).toList
  .map(new File(_)).filter { file =>
    // Keep only non-empty directories
  }

val names = args map (_.toLowerCase)

names foreach { name =>
  println("--- " + name + " --->")
  var counter = 0
  pathFolders foreach { folder =>
    val children = folder.list
    val found = children filter { child =>
      // Keep files that match the input args
    }

    if(found.size > 0) {
      if(folder.getAbsolutePath.indexOf(" ") > -1) {
        println("\"" + folder + "\":")
      } else {
        println(folder + ":")
      }
      println("  " + found.mkString(", "))
    }
    counter += found.size
  }

  println()
}
```

Figure B.1 Application skeleton to package using proguard.

```
/usr/texbin:
  texexec
```

Here, we have searched for executables in the PATH that contain the string "exe." The command was actually executed in one of the authors' MacBook, with the *macports* suite installed under folder /opt/local.

Now let us complete the implementation. After splitting up the PATH according to the platform's path separation character (semicolon ";" for Windows and colon ":" for Unix variants), the first implementation "hole" has to do with keeping only those PATH elements that are directories and actually contain some files:

```
val pathFolders = Path.split(PathSep).toList
  .map(new File(_)).filter { file =>
    // Keep only non-empty directories
    file.isDirectory && (
      file.listFiles match {
        case null => false
        case _    => true
      }
    )
  }
```

The second missing implementation part, and the most interesting one, selects only the nonempty directories in the PATH:

```
val found = children filter { child =>
  // Keep files that match the input args
  child.toLowerCase.indexOf(name) > -1 ||
  Pattern.compile(name, CASE_I).matcher(child).find
}
```

What we do first is to see whether the name given in the command line is a substring of a file name. If this fails, then we go for a more general regular expression check. The whole search is case insensitive, as can be seen from both the code that transforms all command line arguments to lower case,

```
val names = args map (_.toLowerCase)
```

and the use of a case-insensitive regular expression pattern,

```
Pattern.compile(name, CASE_I)
```

Now that the implementation is complete, the script can be run using

```
$ scala findcmd.scala NAME
```

We are almost complete before delving into proguard configuration and execution details, except from one missing detail: we need a jar file containing the compiled code of our script. To this end, the scala executable can be very handy with its wealth of command line options. In particular, we will use the following two options.

-Xscript name This compiles the input file as a script, wrapping the scala code into an object with the given *name*.

-savecompiled This instructs the compiler to save (into a jar) the compiled classes.

So, we call

```
$ scala -Xscript findcmd -savecompiled findcmd.scala
```

and the result is a jar with the compiled classes of our script

```
$ ls -l findcmd.{scala,jar}
-rw-r--r--  1 loverdos  staff  9096 Jun  3 15:25 findcmd.jar
-rw-r--r--  1 loverdos  staff  1113 Jun  3 15:11 findcmd.scala
```

In addition to our own jar, we will need one more: `scala-library.jar` that comes with every Scala distribution. Normally we can find it under *SCALA_HOME*/`lib`, where *SCALA_HOME* denotes the location where Scala is installed. So, before we move to the next step, let us just copy this jar to our working folder, i.e. where `findcmd.jar` has been generated.

B.4 Proguard configuration

The corresponding Proguard configuration is shown in Figure B.2. As you can see, the configuration Domain Specific Language is primarily made of commands that start with a dash, like -injars. Let us explain those commands one-by-one.

-injars This takes a parameter which is the file location of a jar file. This file is assumed as part of our application and will be included in the final jar. The first use has to do with our, just generated, script jar. The second use regards the scala library classes that we want to incorporate in the final jar. The extra (`!META-INF/**`) specification means that we do not wish to include any entries from the `META-INF` directory of `scala-library.jar`. The exclamation mark ! has the familiar *not* semantics.

-outjars The parameter here is the output jar, the one we will distribute, containing our script and all the necessary Scala runtime classes.

-libraryjars Here we give any Java runtime dependency, so that standard classes referenced or used by either our code or the Scala library can be discovered. These dependencies mentioned here will not be included in the final jar, but are assumed to exist at any machine that will run our application. This is normally the case, since Java tends to be ubiquitous. After all, our exercise in this appendix assumes that Java, at least, is installed.

Notice how we parametrically define the location of the Java runtime libraries, using the `<java.home>` property. Also, there is a subtle configuration point, regarding the exact location and name of the libraries under the `<java.home>` directory hierarchy. The libraries given in Figure B.2 are in fact valid for a *MacOS X* machine, referring

```
# file: findcmd.pro
-injars findcmd.jar
-injars scala-library.jar(!META-INF/**)

-outjars findcmd-pro.jar

-libraryjars <java.home>/../Classes/classes.jar
-libraryjars <java.home>/../Classes/ui.jar

-dontoptimize
-dontobfuscate

-dontpreverify

-ignorewarnings

-keepclasseswithmembers public class * {
    public static void main(java.lang.String[]);
}

-forceprocessing
```

Figure B.2 Proguard configuration used to produce a standalone application.

to a JDK distributed and maintained by Apple. For the rest of the world (Windows, Linux, etc.), the standard conventions of a SUN JDK apply and the entry should read like this:

```
-libraryjars <java.home>/lib/rt.jar
```

-dontoptimize, -dontobfuscate These just reflect our intentions to do only shrinking.

-dontpreverify We instruct proguard that we are not interested in preverification.

-ignorewarnings This command is needed whenever it is safe to ignore any warnings and produce the output jar file regardless of their appearance. Unfortunately, for the moment, a lot of warnings are generated when processing our Scala application, so the command is mandatory.

-keepclasseswithmembers Without this command, no useful output will be produced. In effect, we inform proguard which classes we want to be included in the final archive. Then, proguard computes all transitive dependencies automatically.

-forceprocessing This command is just used for debugging purposes. In order not to compute resources, proguard detects if the output jar file is newer (in the underlying file system) than the configuration file and in such a case does not even proceed with its processing. By using -forceprocessing, we make our intentions clear that we always want proguard to do its normal processing.

B.4.1 *Running proguard*

The first line of the configuration in Figure B.2 is a comment (this is exactly what the hash character # indicates) where we denote the file name of our configuration. Assuming this file is in the same place as findcmd.jar and scala-library.jar and that the executable proguard is in the PATH, it is easy to produce the output jar like this:

```
$ proguard @findcmd.pro
ProGuard, version 4.4 beta2
Reading program jar [.../findcmd.jar]
Reading program jar [.../scala-library.jar] (filtered)
... output from proguard ...
Preparing output jar [.../findcmd-pro.jar]
...

$ ls -l findcmd*.{scala,jar}
-rw-r--r-- 1 loverdos staff 435595 Jun 4 14:59 findcmd-pro.jar
-rw-r--r-- 1 loverdos staff   9096 Jun 3 15:25 findcmd.jar
-rw-r--r-- 1 loverdos staff   1113 Jun 3 15:11 findcmd.scala
```

As a side note, from the source script file to the compiled jars files the file size has a clear tendency to increase. But how much?

```
scala> def dp(a: Double, b: Double) = 100.0 * (b - a) / a
dp: (Double,Double)Double

scala> dp(1113, 9096)
res0: Double = 717.2506738544474

scala> dp(9096, 435595)
res1: Double = 4688.863236587511
```

So the results are roughly 717% and 4689%!

B.5 Trading space for time

We have shown how to produce a standalone jar file, containing a Scala application and all the Scala runtime facilities needed to run the application. Our example was based on a Scala script. Some may ask: Doesn't it feel redundant to create a *fat* jar file just in order to run a script? Why not run it directly using scala? One plausible answer to this question is: *time*. Running java directly is faster than running scala.

Exercise B.1 We have tested the above assumption with JDKs 1.5 and 1.6 and Scala version 2.7.4.final. Can you verify the results? How much faster is using java than using scala?

Appendix C

Working with the compiler and the interpreter

In this appendix, we show how to use both the Scala compiler (scalac) and the Scala interpreter (scala) by experimenting with their command line arguments. Part of our presentation is based on the man pages coming with every Scala distribution. For our exposition, we assume a Unix terminal.

Scala is a scalable language. Marketing-wise this is mentioned quite frequently. The good news is that Scala is indeed scalable in many ways and, after all, there is no harm in advertising features that already exist. One such dimension of scalability has to do with the provided tools and how they can be used to increase the overall experience of programming in Scala. We will see that the features provided give a pleasant feeling that the language "grows" to our needs.

For the following, we assume that Scala is installed under a folder denoted by the value of the environment variable SCALA_HOME. Under Unix, this value is obtained by $SCALA_HOME, while under Windows this is obtained by %SCALA_HOME%. It is good practice to set this variable, since other applications that use Scala may depend on it.

C.1 The Scala compiler

The compiler is the workhorse of the whole platform. Even the interpreter uses it internally in order to give the impression of a scripting environment. As expected, it is packed with a wealth of command line options. Using scalac with no options and parameters informs us of all the options. The outcome is given in Table C.1. In the following, we describe the functionality provided by the majority of the options.

Version of scalac

For all our examples, we use scalac version 2.7.7.final:

```
$ scalac -version
Scala compiler version 2.7.7.final -- Copyright 2002-2009,
LAMP/EPFL
```

Table C.1 *The options of scalac, as reported when we call the executable with no command line arguments*

Option	Description
`-g:<g>`	Specify level of generated debugging information (none, source, line, vars, notailcalls)
`-nowarn`	Generate no warnings
`-verbose`	Output messages about what the compiler is doing
`-deprecation`	Output source locations where deprecated APIs are used
`-unchecked`	Enable detailed unchecked warnings
`-classpath <path>`	Specify where to find user class files
`-sourcepath <path>`	Specify where to find input source files
`-bootclasspath <path>`	Override location of bootstrap class files
`-extdirs <dirs>`	Override location of installed extensions
`-d <directory>`	Specify where to place generated class files
`-encoding <encoding>`	Specify character encoding used by source files
`-target:<target>`	Specify for which target object files should be built (jvm-1.5, jvm-1.4, msil)
`-print`	Print program with all Scala-specific features removed
`-optimise`	Generate faster bytecode by applying optimizations to the program
`-explaintypes`	Explain type errors in more detail
`-uniqid`	Print identifiers with unique names for debugging
`-version`	Print product version and exit
`-help`	Print a synopsis of standard options
`-X`	Print a synopsis of advanced options
`@<file>`	A text file containing compiler arguments (options and source files)

Debugging Info

Option −g lets the user decide how much debugging info will be generated into `.class` files.

none This instructs scalac to not generate any debugging information.

source This instructs scalac to generate only the source file attribute, which is a special attribute encoded in the resulting `.class` file.

line This instructs scalac to generate source and line number information.

var This instructs scalac to generate source, line number and local variable information.

notc This instructs scalac to generate all of the above information but without performing tail-call optimization.

Warnings

Option -nowarn is used to suppress warnings. For example, a source file named testwarn.scala with the following code

```
package testopt

class testwarn {
  def check[T](x: T) = x match {
    case _:Array[T] => "Array[T]"
    case _ => "something else"
  }
}
```

produces a warning when compiled

```
$ scalac testwarn.scala
warning: there were unchecked warnings;
         re-run with -unchecked for details
one warning found
```

but we can suppress the warning as instructed

```
$ scalac -nowarn testwarn.scala
<no-actual-output from scalac>
```

Verbosity

Option -verbose is used when we want to inspect what the compiler is doing. For example, adding a -verbose to the previous command line generates a series of lines:

```
$ scalac -nowarn -verbose testwarn.scala
[Classpath = …]
[loaded directory path … in 10ms]
[loaded class file scala-library.jar … in 9ms]
[parsing testwarn.scala]
[parser in 75ms]
[loaded class file … (scala/Predef.class) in 48ms]
[namer in 95ms]
[typer in 146ms]
```

```
[superaccessors in 11ms]
[pickler in 14ms]
[...
[Generate ICode from the AST in 90ms]
[wrote ./testopt/testwarn.class]
[total in 795ms]
```

This option is interesting since it provides an internal look at what the compiler does. In fact, scalac is built around a flexible and open architecture. The compiler runs in several phases, like *parsing* (which generates an Abstract Syntax Tree representation, AST for short, of the source files), *typing, intermediate code generation* (the ICode that we can see in the output) and final *bytecode generation* for the JVM. Anyone can write plugins that manipulate the Abstract Syntax Tree.

Deprecation

Option -deprecation is a boolean one, accepting these values: on, off, yes and no. Deprecated APIs should be marked as such by using the @deprecated annotation.

Unchecked warnings

The idea behind the -unchecked option is to inform the user about conditions related to type erasure. As is well known, the JVM does not preserve type parameters for generics, so that the generic type List[T] of Scala or, for example, type java.util.List<T> of Java is lost when compiling into bytecodes. Using our sample code in testwarn.scala, we can compile with -unchecked and observe the extra information that scalac provides:

```
$ scalac -unchecked testwarn.scala
testwarn.scala:5: warning: abstract type T in type pattern is
unchecked since it is eliminated by erasure
            case _:Array[T] => "Array[T]"
                    ^
```

Class paths

Option -classpath provides the same functionality as the counterpart in Java's compiler, javac . Usual rules for path separation apply, for example the use of a colon under Unix and semicolon under Windows. If no class path is specified, then the current directory is assumed to be the one and this is in alignment with javac .

Option -bootclasspath should provide a class path that will be used to locate the standard Scala classes, as for example scala.List .

Input and output

We can give multiple or alternative source file paths with the relevant -sourcepath option. In the case when we need to specify a particular folder where scalac will place the generated .class files, then option -d is handy. It takes one parameter, the destination folder. Also, if our source files are stored with an encoding other than the default, then we can use option -encoding.

Compilation target

The target platform (back-end, in compiler terminology) for which code is generated can be given with the -target option. Currently valid values are jvm-1.5, jvm-1.4, msil, cldc. The first two refer, of course, to a JVM environment. Target msil refers to a .Net environment, while the acronym cldc comes from "Connected Limited Device Configuration," which forms the basis of the Java Platform for devices with constrained resources.

If no value is given in the command line, then jvm-1.5 is assumed. Soon, support for JDK 1.4, via the jvm-1.4 value, will be completely dropped, since JDK 1.4 has already reached its End of Service Life.

Explain type errors

Option -explaintypes instructs the compiler to generate a sequence of statements, showing the exact decisions that led to a type error. For example, let us assume we have a file named testtyperr.scala with the following contents:

```
package testopt

class testtyperr {
  val intList = List(1)
  val strList: List[String] = intList
}
```

Clearly, this is totally flawed. We cannot assign an integer list to a string list, since there is no subtype relation between List[Int] and List[String]. Let us see what the compiler has to say:

```
$ scalac -explaintypes testtyperr.scala
testtyperr.scala:5: error: type mismatch;
 found    : List[Int]
 required: List[String]
   val strList: List[String] = intList
                               ^

 List[Int] < List[String]?
   Int < String?
     <notype> < java.lang.String?
     false
     <notype> < java.lang.String?
     false
   false
 false
false
one error found
```

The compiler is given the assignment

```
val strList: List[String] = intList
```

For this to succeed, the type of the value we try to assign to strList must be either
the exact type of strList, that is List[String], or a subtype of it. Since the
given value is of type List[Int], scalac tries to see whether[1]

```
List[Int] < List[String]
```

Now, since the actual generic type of lists, as specified in the Scala core library, is
List[+A], which is covariant in its type parameter, it would be sufficient to have

```
Int < String
```

But, clearly, this does not hold and so scalac complains with a type mismatch
error.

Advanced options related to compiler phases

Following the tradition of the Java compiler, which provides a set of "nonstandard"
options, scalac provides a similar set of "advanced" options, as they are described

---

[1] Note that in these debug messages, scalac is a bit inconsistent with what operator represents subtyping.

Table C.2 *A subset of the advanced options of scalac*

Option	Description
-Xcheck-null	Emit warning on selection of nullable reference
-Xcheckinit	Add runtime checks on field accessors, Uninitialized accesses result in an exception being thrown.
-Xdisable-assertions	Generate no assertions and assumptions
-Xlog-implicits	Show more information on why some implicits are not applicable
-Xno-uescape	Disables handling of Unicode escapes
-Xnojline	Do not use JLine for editing
-Xplugin:<*file*>	Load a plugin from a file
-Xplugin-disable:<*plugin*>	Disable a plugin
-Xplugin-list	Print a synopsis of loaded plugins
-Xplugin-require:<*plugin*>	Abort unless a plugin is available
-Xpluginsdir <*path*>	Location to find compiler plugins
-Xprint:<*phase*>	Print out program after <*phase*> or "all"
-Xprint-pos	Print tree positions (as offsets)
-Xprint-types	Print tree types (debugging option)
-Xprompt	Display a prompt after each error (debugging option)
-Xresident	Compiler stays resident, files to compile are read from standard input
-Xshow-class <*class*>	Show class information
-Xshow-object <*object*>	Show object information
-Xshow-phases	Print a synopsis of compiler phases
-Xsource-reader <*classname*>	Specify a custom method for reading source files
-Xscript <*object*>	Compile as a script, wrapping the code into object.main()
-Xwarninit	Warn about possible changes in initialization semantics

whenever we execute `scalac -X` on the command line.[2] Most of the options are presented in Table C.2. Here we will mainly discuss options related to compiler phases.

The Scala compiler is organized as a composite component that is executed in phases and it defines several subcomponents that are responsible for each one of these phases. We have already seen a few of the phases when examining the output of the -verbose option, where we met phase names like *namer*, *typer* and *pickler*.

---

[2] As a side note for Unix users, the options are printed in the standard error stream, instead of the standard output stream, so in case we want to pipe through some command line filter, we need to make an indirection, as in `scalac -X 2>&1`.

We can obtain a list of all the available phases by using the -Xshow-phases option:

```
$ scala -Xshow-phases
namer, typer, superaccessors, pickler, refchecks, liftcode,
uncurry, tailcalls, explicitouter, erasure, lazyvals,
lambdalift, constructors, flatten, mixin, cleanup, icode,
inliner, closelim, dce, jvm, sample-phase
```

Providing a description of the purpose and inner workings of all these phases is beyond the scope of this book. More information can be found at the Scala web site.

After parsing, the source code is transformed to an intermediate AST representation. Each phase then transforms this abstract syntax tree, potentially altering information on the symbols the tree contains, augmenting the tree with extra nodes or pruning existing nodes. In the case that we wish to see how the compiler "sees" our initial program after some particular phase, then we have to include option -Xprint:<phase> in the command line.

Let us examine possible outputs from -Xprint:<phase> for our test input file, named testprintphase.scala, which contains the following code:

```
// file: testprintphase.scala
package testopt

object testprintphase {
  def factorial(x: Int): Int =
    if(x <= 0) 1 else x * factorial(x - 1)

  val list = List(0, 1, 2, 3)
  val map  = list map factorial
  val sum  = map reduceLeft(_+_)
}
```

For the sake of presentation, we avoid explicit typing, especially when using higher-order functions like map and reduceLeft. Explicit typing of the factorial method is necessary, since the Scala type inference algorithm requires it whenever we define a recursive method.

Using -Xprint:namer The namer phase is responsible for declaring compiler internal symbols from our source code:

```
[[syntax trees at end of namer]]
// Scala source: testprintphase.scala
package testopt {
```

```
final object testprintphase extends scala.ScalaObject {
  def <init>() = {
    super.<init>();
    ()
  };

  def factorial(x: Int): Int = if (x.$less$eq(0))
    1
  else
    x.$times(factorial(x.$minus(1)));

  val list = List(0, 1, 2, 3);
  val map = list.map(factorial);
  val sum = map.reduceLeft(((x$1, x$2) => x$1.$plus(x$2)))
  }
}
```

A few short notes of interest.

- Method `<init>` is the constructor of the underlying class.
- In the implementation of `factorial`, the call `x.$less$eq(0)` uses the internal, compiler-related name for the method equivalent of the `<=` operator.
- Operators are generally transformed into the equivalent method names, i.e., the multiplication operator `*` is transformed to a call to method `$times`. Respectively, the subtraction operator `−` is transformed to a call to method `$minus`.
- The compiler transforms `reduceLeft(_+_)` to

```
reduceLeft(((x$1, x$2) => x$1.$plus(x$2)))
```

The strange-looking names with the dollar signs are synthetic names generated on-the-fly by scalac. According to the Scala Language Specification[57]:

The "$" character is reserved for compiler-synthesized identifiers. User programs should not define identifiers which contain "$" characters.

Using -Xprint:typer The next phase, `typer`, is responsible for type inference. It makes sure that the types a programmer has defined in the source code are correct and tries to find, from local coding context, missing types. The output is now a bit lengthier:

```
[[syntax trees at end of typer]]
// Scala source: testprintphase.scala
```

```
package testopt {
  final object testprintphase extends java.lang.Object
                                    with ScalaObject {
    def this(): object testopt.testprintphase = {
      testprintphase.super.this();
      ()
    };

    def factorial(x: Int): Int = if (x.<=(0))
      1
    else
      x.*(testprintphase.this.factorial(x.-(1)));

    private[this] val list: List[Int] =
      scala.List.apply[Int](0, 1, 2, 3);

    <stable> <accessor> def list: List[Int] =
      testprintphase.this.list;

    private[this] val map: List[Int] =
      testprintphase.this.list.map[Int]({
        ((eta$0$1: Int) =>
          testprintphase.this.factorial(eta$0$1))});

    <stable> <accessor> def map: List[Int] =
      testprintphase.this.map;

    private[this] val sum: Int =
      testprintphase.this.map.reduceLeft[Int](
        ((x$1: Int, x$2: Int) => x$1.+(x$2)));

    <stable> <accessor> def sum: Int =
      testprintphase.this.sum
  }
}
```

This output certainly looks more noisy than the previous one. The parts related to our discussion on types are clearly all the definitions (list, map, sum) where explicit typing information has been added by the typer phase of scalac. For instance, the type of the anonymous function _+_, which we use as a parameter to reduceLeft in order to add two list elements, is seen by scalac as if the programmer had typed

```
(x$1: Int, x$2: Int) => x$1.+(x$2)
```

The above is a function of two Int arguments, producing an Int result.

Other advanced options

Plugin options We can extend scalac by writing plugins. These compiler plugins are software components that can be injected between the several compiler phases and whose role is to provide some new functionality. The plugins take advantage of internal scalac API and so they must be compiled against the scala-compiler.jar that comes along with the Scala distribution. In contrast, normal, everyday applications mostly use the scala-library.jar. All these jars can be found under folder $SCALA_HOME/lib. From Table C.2, all the plugin-related options start with -Xplugin.

Disabling assertions Assertions, that is conditions that are checked and for which an exception is thrown if not found to hold, are enabled by default. If we use option -Xdisable-assertion, then we may get a slight performance gain, since a runtime check is omitted. The usual recipe is to enable assertions as long as an application or library is in development and testing phase and then disable them when going into "production" mode. Everyday practice, however, shows that people usually do not follow this advice and prefer to retain assertions all the time.

Compiling as a script Sometimes it is very convenient to write our little script in the most straightforward way and then use the -Xscript option to have the compiler wrap it as a normal Scala object. We have already used this technique in Appendix B, where the small findcmd script was simultaneously wrapped as an object and saved as jar file.

We must take special care to not include a package definition in the script, like in the following case:

```
// file: testscript-err.scala
package testopt
println(args.toList)
```

since, then, the compiler will complain

```
$ scalac -Xscript printargs testscript-err.scala
!!!
discarding <script preamble>
(fragment of testscript-err.scala):1: error: illegal start of
```

```
definition
package testopt
       ^

one error found
```

The correct way to achieve the same functionality is to have a simpler script

```
// file: testscript.scala
println(args.toList)
```

and then use all the machinery scalac provides to inject the information we need:

```
$ scalac -Xscript testopt.printargs testscript.scala

$ ls testopt/
printargs$$anon$1.class printargs$.class   printargs.class

$ scala testopt.printargs Hello World
List(Hello, World)
```

Notice how, instead of using a simple name, `printargs`, we used a fully qualified name, `testopt.printargs` and scalac automatically translated that to a packaged declaration for the newly created object.

Exercise C.1 What if in file `testscript.scala`, we used the name `argv` instead of `args`? Take advantage of the previously mentioned option `-Xprint:<phase>` (pick a phase here, although `namer` will be enough) to see what scalac is actually doing under the hood. Also, try to verify the packaged declaration of object `printargs`.

The private/experimental −Y options

Besides `−X` options, scalac also accepts a limited set of experimental or *private* options, starting with `−Y` and shown in Table C.3. They are either meant to be used by the compiler development team for debugging or are considered experimental. In any case they are subject to change without any notice. Nevertheless, as we will see, they can be very useful.

Using `−Ybrowse:typer` This pops up a graphical application that shows the abstract syntax tree generated by scalac after successfully parsing the input file. For example, using `testprintphase.scala` we can see the graphical representation in Figure C.1.

Without going into technical details regarding the inner workings of scalac, on the left part of the figure we can see highlighted a `ValDef`, that is, a value definition, corresponding to our `val list = List(0, 1, 2, 3)`. On the right there is

Table C.3 *A subset of the private options of scalac*

Option	Description
-Ybrowse:*<phase>*	Browse the abstract syntax tree after *<phase>*
-Ydebug	Output debugging messages
-Ydead-code	Perform dead code elimination
-Yinline	Perform inlining when possible
-Ylog:*<phase>*	Log operations in *<phase>*
-Ylog-all	Log all operations
-Yshow-trees	Show detailed trees when used in connection with -print: phase
-Yskip:*<phase>*	Skip *<phase>*
-Ystatistics	Print compiler statistics
-Ystop:*<phase>*	Stop after phase *<phase>*

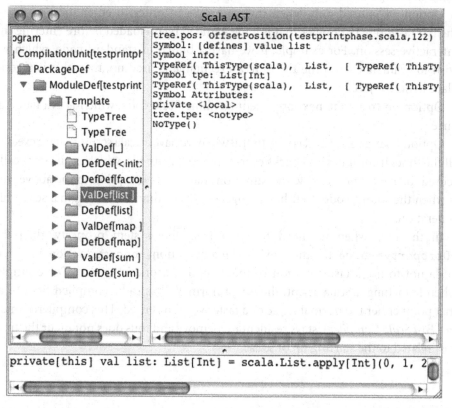

Figure C.1 Using option -Ybrowse on file `testprintphase` after `typer` phase.

information on the symbols involved and at the bottom we can see the respective source code fragment with types.

C.2 The Scala interpreter

The Scala interpreter inherits all command line options from scalac. This is easy to understand, since the underlying implementation makes heavy use of the compiler. When running the interpreter, using the scala command, we either specify a script file or object to run, along its arguments, or we enter an interactive shell. There are a few interpreter-specific options that we can pass.

Option -howtorun takes as values one of script, object or guess. If we use the first, then the provided parameter denotes a script file. If we use the second, then the provided parameter denotes an object name that will be pulled from the class path and run subsequently. The third, guess, means that the interpreter will do its best to guess the situation.

Option -i is used only when invoking scala in order to enter the interactive shell. It takes one parameter that is a file name to be preloaded before entering the interactive session. For example, if we have a bunch of standard code, which we wish to evaluate every time the scala executable is fired up, then this is a good place to do the job.

Option -e treats the next argument as inline Scala code, which is evaluated at once.

Option -savecompiled is very useful when we have a Scala script that we execute all the time. It compiles and packs everything to a .jar file, which is automatically reused the next time we issue the same command. The exception to the above rule is when the source code itself has changed *after* the time of the original script file generation.

In the case when we need to set a Java-wide system property, then the -Dproperty=value notation exists. Finally, option -nocompdaemon instructs Scala not to use a faster version of the compiler, if one is needed. For example, when launching a Scala script, the script normally has to be compiled first, so at that point either the normal scalac or a faster version is used. This compiler, named fsc (*Fast Scala Compiler*), stays resident in memory and thus does not incur the time cost related to the starting up of scalac.

Appendix D
Scala's grammar

In this section we present Scala's grammar in EBNF. The grammar is divided into two parts. In the first part, we present the grammar of lexical entities while in the second part we present the rest of the grammar. Apart from some small typographical adjustments, the grammar is identical to the one presented in the *The Scala Language Specification Version 2.7*.

D.1 Lexical entities

```
upper           =  "A" | ... | "Z" | "$" | "_" |
                      Unicode category Lu
lower           =  "a" | ... | "z" |
                      Unicode category Ll
letter          =  upper | lower |
                      Unicode categories Lo, Lt, Nl
digit           =  "0" | ... | "9"
opchar          =  "all other characters in range \u0020-\u007F
                      and Unicode categories Sm, So except
                      parentheses ([]) and periods"

op              =  opchar {opchar}
varid           =  lower idrest
plainid         =  upper idrest
                |  varid
                |  op
id              =  plainid
                |  "`" stringLit "`"
idrest          =  {letter | digit} ['_' op]

integerLiteral  =  (decimalNumeral | hexNumeral | octalNumeral)
```

```
                              ["L" | "1"]
decimalNumeral    =    "0" | nonZeroDigit {digit}
hexNumeral        =    "0" "x" hexDigit {hexDigit}
octalNumeral      =    "0" octalDigit {octalDigit}
digit             =    "0" | nonZeroDigit
nonZeroDigit      =    "1" | ... | "9"
octalDigit        =    "0" | ... | "7"


floatingPointLiteral
                  =    digit {digit} "." {digit}
                             [exponentPart] [floatType]
                  |    "." digit {digit} [exponentPart] [floatType]
                  |    digit {digit} exponentPart [floatType]
                  |    digit {digit} [exponentPart] floatType
exponentPart      =    ("E" | "e") [ ("+" | "-") ] digit {digit}
floatType         =    "F" | "f" | "D" | "d"


booleanLiteral    =    "true" | "false"


characterLiteral  =    "'" printableChar "'"
                  |    "'" charEscapeSeq "'"


stringLiteral     =    '"' stringElement '"'
                  |    '"""' multiLineChars '"""'
stringElement     =    printableCharNoDoubleQuote
                  |    charEscapeSeq
multiLineChars    =    ['"'] ['"'] charNoDoubleQuote


symbolLiteral     =    "'" idrest


comment           =    "/*" "any sequence of characters" "*/"
                  |    "//" "any sequence of characters up to end of line"


nl                =    "new line character"
semi              =    ";" | nl {nl}
```

D.2 The rest of the language

```
Literal           =    ["-"] integerLiteral
                  |    ["-"] floatingPointLiteral
                  |    booleanLiteral
                  |    characterLiteral
                  |    stringLiteral
```

```
                        |   symbolLiteral
                        |   "null"

QualId          =   id {"." id}
ids             =   id {"," id}

Path            =   StableId
                |   [id "."] "this"
StableId        =   id
                |   Path "." id
                |   [id "."] "super" [ClassQualifier] "." id
ClassQualifier  =   "[" id "]"

Type            =   InfixType "=>" Type
                |   "(" ["=>" Type] ")" "=>" Type
                |   InfixType [ExistentialClause]
ExistentialClause = "forSome" "{" ExistentialDcl
                        {semi ExistentialDcl} "}"
ExistentialDcl  =   "type" TypeDcl
                |   "val" ValDcl
InfixType       =   CompoundType {id [nl] CompoundType}
CompoundType    =   AnnotType {"with" AnnotType} [Refinement]
                |   Refinement
AnnotType       =   SimpleType {Annotation}
SimpleType      =   SimpleType TypeArgs
                |   SimpleType "#" id
                |   StableId
                |   Path "." "type"
                |   "(" Types ["," ] ")"
TypeArgs        =   "[" Types "]"
Types           =   Type {"," Type}
Refinement      =   [nl] "{" RefineStat {semi RefineStat} "}"
RefineStat      =   Dcl
                |   "type" TypeDef
                |
TypePat         =   Type

Ascription      =   ":" InfixType
                |   ":" Annotation Annotation
                |   ":" "_" "*"

Expr            =   (Bindings | id | "_") "=>" Expr
                |   Expr1
```

```
Expr1                  =  "if" "(" Expr ")" {nl} Expr [[semi] else Expr]
                       |  "while" "(" Expr ")" {nl} Expr
                       |  "try" "{" Block "}" [catch  "{" CaseClauses "}"]
                          ["finally" Expr]
                       |  "do" Expr [semi] "while" "(" Expr ")"
                       |  "for" ("(" Enumerators ")" | "{" Enumerators "}")
                          {nl} ["yield"] Expr
                       |  "throw" Expr
                       |  "return" [Expr]
                       |  [SimpleExpr "."] id "=" Expr
                       |  SimpleExpr1 ArgumentExprs "=" Expr
                       |  PostfixExpr
                       |  PostfixExpr Ascription
                       |  PostfixExpr "match" "{" CaseClauses "}"
PostfixExpr            =  InfixExpr [id [nl]]
InfixExpr              =  PrefixExpr
                       |  InfixExpr id [nl] InfixExpr
PrefixExpr             =  [ ("-" | "+" | "~" | "!") ] SimpleExpr
SimpleExpr             =  "new" (ClassTemplate | TemplateBody)
                       |  BlockExpr
                       |  SimpleExpr1 ["_"]
SimpleExpr1            =  Literal
                       |  Path
                       |  "_"
                       |  "(" [Exprs [","]] ")"
                       |  SimpleExpr "." id
                       |  SimpleExpr TypeArgs
                       |  SimpleExpr1 ArgumentExprs
                       |  XmlExpr
Exprs                  =  Expr {"," Expr}
ArgumentExprs          =  "(" [Exprs [","]] ")"
                       |  [nl] BlockExpr
BlockExpr              =  "{" CaseClauses "}"
                       |  "{" Block "}"
Block                  =  {BlockStat semi} [ResultExpr]
BlockStat              =  Import
                       |  ["implicit" | "lazy"] Def
                       |  {LocalModifier} TmplDef
                       |  Expr1
                       |
ResultExpr             =  Expr1
                       |  (Bindings | (id | "_") ":" CompoundType)
                          "=>" Block
```

```
Enumerators         =  Generator {semi Enumerator}
Enumerator          =  Generator
                    |  Guard
                    |  "val" Pattern1 "=" Expr
Generator           =  Pattern1 "<-" Expr [Guard]


CaseClauses         =  CaseClause { CaseClause }
CaseClause          =  "case" Pattern [Guard] "=>" Block
Guard               =  "if" PostfixExpr


Pattern             =  Pattern1 { "|" Pattern1 }
Pattern1            =  varid ":" TypePat
                    |  "_" ":" TypePat
                    |  Pattern2
Pattern2            =  varid ["@" Pattern3]
                    |  Pattern3
Pattern3            =  SimplePattern
                    |  SimplePattern { id [nl] SimplePattern }
SimplePattern       =  "_"
                    |  varid
                    |  Literal
                    |  StableId
                    |  StableId "(" [Patterns [","]] ")"
                    |  StableId "(" [Patterns ","]
                                   [varid "@"] "_" "*" ")"
                    |  "(" [Patterns [","]] ")"
                    |  XmlPattern
Patterns            =  Pattern ["," Patterns]
                    |  "_" *
TypeParamClause     =  "[" VariantTypeParam {"," VariantTypeParam} "]"
FunTypeParamClause  =  "[" TypeParam "," TypeParam "]"
VariantTypeParam    =  [ ("+" | "-") ] TypeParam
TypeParam           =  (id | "_") [TypeParamClause]
                                   [">:" Type] ["<:" Type] ["<%" Type]
ParamClauses        =  {ParamClause} [[nl] "(" "implicit" Params ")"]
ParamClause         =  [nl] "(" [Params] ")"
Params              =  Param {"," Param}
Param               =  {Annotation} id [":" ParamType]
ParamType           =  Type
                    |  "=>" Type
                    |  Type "*"
ClassParamClauses   =  {ClassParamClause}
                          [[nl] "(" "implicit" ClassParams ")"]
```

```
ClassParamClause  =  [nl] "(" [ClassParams] ")"
ClassParams       =  ClassParam {ClassParam}
ClassParam        =  {Annotation} [{Modifier} ("val" | "var")]
                        id ":" ParamType

Bindings          =  "(" Binding {"," Binding ")"
Binding           =  (id | "_") [":" Type]


Modifier          =  LocalModifier
                  |  AccessModifier
                  |  "override"
LocalModifier     =  "abstract"
                  |  "final"
                  |  "sealed"
                  |  "implicit"
                  |  "lazy"
AccessModifier    =  ("private" | "protected") [AccessQualifier]
AccessQualifier   =  "[" (id | "this") "]"
Annotation        =  "@" SimpleType {ArgumentExprs}
ConstrAnnotation  =  "@" SimpleType ArgumentExprs
NameValuePair     =  "val" id "=" PrefixExpr
TemplateBody      =  [nl] "{" [SelfType] TemplateStat
                          {semi TemplateStat} "}"

TemplateStat      =  Import
                  |  {Annotation [nl]} {Modifier} Def
                  |  {Annotation [nl]} {Modifier} Dcl
                  |  Expr
                  |
SelfType          =  id [":" Type] "=>"
                  |  "this" ":" Type "=>"
Import            =  "import" ImportExpr {"," ImportExpr}
ImportExpr        =  StableId "." (id | "_" | ImportSelectors)
ImportSelectors   =  "{" {ImportSelector ","}
                          (ImportSelector | "_") "}"
ImportSelector    =  id ["=>" id | "=>" "_"]
Dcl               =  "val" ValDcl
                  |  "var" VarDcl
                  |  "def" FunDcl
                  |  "type" {nl} TypeDcl
ValDcl            =  ids ":" Type
VarDcl            =  ids ":" Type
FunDcl            =  FunSig [":" Type]
FunSig            =  id [FunTypeParamClause] ParamClauses
TypeDcl           =  id [TypeParamClause] [">:" Type] ["<:" Type]
PatVarDef         =  "val" PatDef
```

```
                       |  "var" VarDef
Def               =  PatVarDef
                       |  "def" FunDef
                       |  "type" {nl} TypeDef
                       |  TmplDef
PatDef            =  Pattern2 {"," Pattern2} [":" Type] "=" Expr
VarDef            =  PatDef
                       |  ids ":" Type "=" "_"
FunDef            =  FunSig [":" Type] "=" Expr
                       |  FunSig [nl] "{" Block "}"
                       |  "this" ParamClause ParamClauses
                          ("=" ConstrExpr | [nl] ConstrBlock)
TypeDef           =  id [TypeParamClause] "=" Type
TmplDef           =  ["case"] "class" ClassDef
                       |  ["case"] "object" ObjectDef
                       |  "trait" TraitDef
ClassDef          =  id [TypeParamClause] ConstrAnnotation
                          [AccessModifier] ClassParamClauses
                          ClassTemplateOpt
TraitDef          =  id [TypeParamClause] TraitTemplateOpt
ObjectDef         =  id ClassTemplateOpt
ClassTemplateOpt  =  Extends ClassTemplate
                       |  [[Extends] TemplateBody]
TraitTemplateOpt  =  Extends TraitTemplate
                       |  [[Extends] TemplateBody]
Extends           =  "extends" | "<:"
ClassTemplate     =  [EarlyDefs] ClassParents [TemplateBody]
TraitTemplate     =  [EarlyDefs] TraitParents [TemplateBody]
ClassParents      =  Constr {"with" AnnotType}
TraitParents      =  AnnotType {"with" AnnotType}
Constr            =  AnnotType {ArgumentExprs}
EarlyDefs         =  "{" [EarlyDef {semi EarlyDef}] "}" "with"
EarlyDef          =  {Annotation [nl]} {Modifier} PatVarDef
ConstrExpr        =  SelfInvocation
                       |  ConstrBlock
ConstrBlock       =  "{" SelfInvocation {semi BlockStat} "}"
SelfInvocation    =  "this" ArgumentExprs {ArgumentExprs}
TopStatSeq        =  TopStat {semi TopStat}
TopStat           =  {Annotation [nl]} {Modifier} TmplDef
                       |  Import
                       |  Packaging
                       |
Packaging         =  "package" QualId [nl] "{" TopStatSeq "}"
CompilationUnit   =  ["package" QualId semi] TopStatSeq
```

References

[1] Abadi, M., and Cardelli, L. *A Theory of Objects*. Monographs in Computer Science. New York: Springer, 1996.

[2] Adobe Systems Incorporated. *PostScript Language Reference Manual*, 3rd edn. Reading, MA: Addison-Wesley, 1999.

[3] Agha, G. *Actors: A Model of Concurrent Computation in Distributed Systems*. Cambridge, MA: MIT Press, 1986.

[4] Alagić, S., and Arbib, M. A. *The Design of Well-Structured and Correct Programs*. New York: Springer, 1978.

[5] Armstrong, J. *Programming Erlang: Software for a Concurrent World*. Raleigh, NC: Pragmatic Bookshelf, 2007.

[6] Arnold, K., Gosling, J., and Holmes, D. *The Java Programming Language*, 4th edn. Reading, MA: Addison-Wesley, 2006.

[7] Barbé, A. Artistic design with fractal matrices. *The Visual Computer* 9, 6 (1993), 233–238.

[8] Barclay, K., and Savage, J. *Groovy Programming: An Introduction for Java Developers*. San Francisco, CA: Morgan Kaufmann, 2007.

[9] Barendregt, H. P. *The Lambda Calculus: Its Syntax and Semantics*. Amsterdam: Elsevier Science, 1985.

[10] Bronstein, M. *Symbolic Integration I: Transcendental Functions*, 2nd edn. Berlin: Springer, 2005.

[11] Burge, W. H. *Recursive Programming Techniques*. Reading, MA: Addison-Wesley, 1975.

[12] Canning, P., Cook, W., Hill, W., Olthoff, W., and Mitchell, J. C. F-bounded polymorphism for object-oriented programming. In *FPCA '89: Proceedings of the Fourth International Conference on Functional Programming Languages and Computer Architecture, London, 1989*. New York: ACM, 1989, pp. 273–280.

[13] Cardelli, L., and Wegner, P. On understanding types, data abstraction, and polymorphism. *ACM Computing Surveys* 17, 4 (1985), 471–523.

[14] Clinger, W. D. Foundations of Actor Semantics. Tech. Rep. AITR-633, Computer Science and Artificial Intelligence Lab, Massachusetts Institute of Technology, Cambridge, MA, 1981.

[15] Cook, B., and Launchbury, J. Disposable memo functions. In *Proceedings of the June 1997 Haskell Workshop, Amsterdam, 1997*.

[16] Cox, B. J., and Novabilsky, A. *Object-Oriented Programming: An Evolutionary Approach*, 2nd edn. Reading, MA: Addison-Wesley, 1991.

[17] Curry, G., Baer, L., Lipkie, D., and Lee, B. Traits: an approach to multiple-inheritance subclassing. In *Proceedings of the SIGOA Conference on Office Information Systems, Philadelphia, PA, 1982.* New York: ACM, 1982, pp. 1–9.

[18] Dahl, O.-J., and Nygaard, K. SIMULA – an ALGOL-Based Simulation Language. *Communications of the ACM* **9**, 9 (1966), 671–678.

[19] Dijkstra, E. W. *Selected Writings on Computing: A Personal Perspective.* New York: Springer, 1982.

[20] Elliot, C. Functional images. In *The Fun of Programming,* J. Gibbons and O. de Moor, Eds., Basingstoke: Palgrave Macmillan, 2003, pp. 131–150.

[21] Field, A. J., and Harrison, P. G. *Functional Programming.* Workingham: Addison-Wesley, 1988.

[22] Flanagan, D., and Matsumot, Y. *The Ruby Programming Language.* Sebastopol, CA: O'Reilly Media, 2008.

[23] Flatt, M., Krishnamurthi, S., and Felleisen, M. Classes and mixins. In *POPL '98: Proceedings of the 25th ACM SIGPLAN-SIGACT Symposium on Principles of Programming Languages, San Diego, CA, 1998.* New York, ACM, 1998, pp. 171–183.

[24] Gamma, E., Helm, R., Johnson, R., and Vlissides, J. *Design Patterns: Elements of Reusable Object-Oriented Software.* Boston, MA: Addison-Wesley Longman, 1995.

[25] Gibbons, J. Origami programming. In *The Fun of Programming,* J. Gibbons and O. de Moor, Eds., Basingstoke Palgrave Macmillan, 2003, pp. 41–60.

[26] Gibbons, J., and de Moor, O., Eds. *The Fun of Programming.* Basingstoke: Palgrave Macmillan, 2003.

[27] Goldberg, A., and Robson, D. *Smalltalk-80: The Language and its Implementation.* Reading, MA: Addison-Wesley, 1983.

[28] Gosling, J., Joy, B., and Bracha, G. S. G. *The Java Language Specification,* 3rd edn. Reading, MA: Addison-Wesley, 2005.

[29] Grabmeier, J., Kaltofen, E., and Weispfenning, V., Eds. *Computer Algebra Handbook.* Berlin: Springer, 2003.

[30] Harold, E. R., and Means, W. S. *XML in a Nutshell.* Sebastopol, CA: O'Reilly, 2004.

[31] Hejlsberg, A., Torgersen, M., Wiltamuth, S., and Golde, P. *The C# Programming Language,* 3rd edn. Reading, MA: Addison-Wesley, 2008.

[32] Hewitt, C. Viewing control structures as patterns of passing messages. *Artificial Intelligence* **8**, 3 (1977), 323–364.

[33] Hewitt, C., Bishop, P., and Steiger, R. A universal modular ACTOR formalism for artificial intelligence. In *Proceedings of the Third International Joint Conference on Artificial Intelligence.* San Francisco, CA: Morgan Kaufmann, 1973, pp. 235–245.

[34] Hutton, G., and Meijer, E. Monadic parsing in Haskell. *Journal of Functional Programming* **8**, 4 (1998), 437–444.

[35] International Standards Organisation. *Information Technology – Programming Languages – Forth,* 1st edn., March 1997. ISO/IEC 15145:1997.

[36] Jacobs, B. *Categorical Logic and Type Theory.* Amsterdam: Elsevier Science, 1999.

[37] Jones, N. D., Gomard, C. K., and Sestoff, P. *Partial Evaluation and Automatic Program Generation.* Hemel Hempstead: Prentice Hall International, 1993.

[38] Jones, S. P. *Haskell 98 Language and Libraries: The Revised Report.* Cambridge: Cambridge University Press, 2003.

[39] Jones, S. P., Marlow, S., and Elliott, C. Stretching the storage manager: weak pointers and stable names in Haskell. In *Implentation of Functional Language 1999,* P. Koopman and C. Clack, Eds., *Lecture Notes in Computer Science,* volume 1868. Berlin: Springer, 1999, pp. 37–58.

[40] Kaehler, T., and Patterson, D. *A Taste of Smalltalk.* New York: W. W. Norton, 1986.

[41] Kleiman, S. R. Vnodes: An Architecture for Multiple File System Types in Sun UNIX. In *Proceedings of the USENIX Summer Conference, Atlanta, GA, 1986*. Berkeley, CA: USENIX Association, 1986, pp. 238–247.

[42] Knuth, D. E. Structured programming with goto statements. *ACM Computing Surveys* **6**, 4 (1974), 261–301.

[43] Koschmann, T. *The Common Lisp Companion*. New York: John Wiley & Sons, 1990.

[44] Lambek, J., and Scott, P. *Introduction to Higher Order Categorical Logic*. Cambridge: Cambridge University Press, 1986.

[45] Lawvere, F. W., and Schanuel, S. H. *Conceptual Mathematics: A First Introduction to Categories*. Cambridge: Cambridge University Press, 1997.

[46] Lea, D. A Java Fork/Join Framework. In *JAVA '00: Proceedings of the ACM 2000 Conference on Java Grande, San Francisco, CA, 2000*. New York: ACM, 2000, pp. 36–43.

[47] Lea, D. *Concurrent Programming in Java*, 2nd edn. Reading, MA: Addison-Wesley, 2000.

[48] Liskov, B. H., and Wing, J. M. Behavioral subtyping using invariants and constraints. Tech. Rep. CMU-CS-99-156, School of Computer Science, Carnegie Mellon University, Pittsburgh PA, 1999.

[49] Lutz, M. *Programming Python*, 3rd edn. Sebastopol, CA: O'Reilly Media, 2006.

[50] Mac Lane, S. *Categories for the Working Mathematician*, 2nd edn. Graduate Texts in Mathematics. New York: Springer, 1998.

[51] Meijer, E., Fokkinga, M., and Paterson, R. Functional programming with bananas, lenses, envelopes and barbed wire. In *Functional Programming Languages and Computer Architecture*, J. Hughes, Ed., Lecture Notes in Computer Science, volume 523. Berlin: Springer, 1991, pp. 124–144.

[52] Meyer, B. *Eiffel: The Language*. Englewood Cliffs, NJ: Prentice-Hall, 1991.

[53] Moggi, E. Notions of computation and monads. *Information and Computation* **93** (1991), 55–92.

[54] Moon, D. A. Object-oriented programming with flavors. In *OOPLSA '86: Conference Proceedings on Object-Oriented Programming Systems, Languages and Applications, Portland, OR, 1986*. New York: ACM, 1986, pp. 1–8.

[55] Moors, A., Piessens, F., and Joosen, W. An object-oriented approach to datatype-generic programming. In *WGP '06: Proceedings of the ACM SIGPLAN Workshop on Generic Programming, Portland, OR, 2006*. New York: ACM, 2006, pp. 96–106.

[56] Morrisett, G., Walker, D., Crary, K., and Glew, N. From system F to typed assembly language. *ACM Transactions on Programming Languages and Systems*, **21** 4 (1999), 528–569.

[57] Odersky, M. *Scala Language Specification, v. 2.7*, 2009.

[58] Odersky, M., Altherr, P., Cremet, V., Dragos, I., Dubochet, G., Emir, B., McDirmid, S., Micheloud, S., Mihaylov, N., Schinz, M., Stenman, E., Spoon, L., and Zenger, M. An overview of the Scala programming language. Tech. Rep. LAMP-REPORT-2006-001, École Polytechnique Fédérale de Lausanne (EPFL), Lausanne, Switzerland, 2006. Electronic document available from the Scala homepage.

[59] Odersky, M., Spoon, L., and Venners, B. *Programming in Scala*. Mountain View, CA: Artima, 2008.

[60] Odersky, M., and Zenger, M. Independently extensible solutions to the expression problem. In *FOOL 12, The Twelfth International Workshop on Foundations of Object-Oriented Languages, Long Beach, CA, 2005*.

[61] Oliveira, B. C., and Gibbons, J. Scala for Generic Programmers. In *WGP '08: Proceedings of the ACM SIGPLAN Workshop on Generic Programming, Victoria, Canada, 2008*. New York: ACM, 2008, pp. 25–36.

[62] Peitgen, H.-O. Fantastic deterministic fractals. In *The Science of Fractal Images*, H.-O. Peitgen and D. Saupe, Eds. Berlin: Springer, 1988, pp. 169–218.

[63] Pickover, C. A. *Computers, Pattern, Chaos and Beauty*. New York: St. Martin's Press, 1990.

[64] Pierce, B. C. *Types and Programming Languages*. Cambridge, MA: MIT Press, 2002.

[65] Pike, R., and Thompson, K. Hello World or Καλημέρα Κόσμε. In *Proceedings of the Winter 1993 USENIX Conference, San Diego, CA, 1993*. Berkeley, USENIX Association, 1993, pp. 43–50.

[66] Reiser, M., and Wirth, N. *Programming in Oberon*. New York: ACM, 1992.

[67] Ryan, M. *Calculus for Dummies*. Indianapolis, IN: Wiley, 2003.

[68] Skiena, S. S. *The Algorithm Design Manual*, 2nd edn. London: Springer, 2008.

[69] Steele, Jr., G. L. Growing a Language. *Higher-Order and Symbolic Computation* **12** (1999), 221–236.

[70] Stroustrup, B. *The C++ Programming Language*, 3rd edn. Reading, MA: Addison-Wesley, 1997.

[71] Syropoulos, A. Στοιχεία προγραμματισμού στην Perl (*Elements of Perl Programming*). Thessaloniki: Paratiritis Editions, 2003. In Greek.

[72] Syropoulos, A. *Hypercomputation: Computing Beyond the Church–Turing Barrier*. New York: Springer, 2008.

[73] Torgersen, M. The expression problem revisited – four new solutions using generics. In *ECOOP 2004 – Object-Oriented Programming, 18th European Conference, Oslo, Norway, June 14–18, 2004*, M. Odersky, Ed., Lecture Notes in Computer Science, volume 3086. Berlin: Springer, 2004, pp. 123–143.

[74] Ungar, D., and Smith, R. B. SELF: The power of simplicity. *Lisp and Symbolic Computation* **4**, 3 (1991), 187–205.

[75] Wadler, P. How to replace failure by a list of successes. In *Proc. Conference on Functional Programming Languages and Computer Architecture*, Lecture Notes in Computer Science, volume 201. Berlin: Springer, 1985, pp. 113–128.

[76] Wadler, P. Comprehending monads. *Mathematical Structures in Computer Science* **2** (1992), 461–493.

[77] Wirth, N. Modula – A programming language for modular multiprogramming. *Software – Practice and Experience* **7** (1977), 3–35.

[78] Wirth, N. *Compiler Construction*. Harlow: Addison-Wesley, 1984.

Name index

Subject index

<-, 49
=>, 36, 66, 114, 119, 121
F-bound, 416

abstract
  class, 96, 134, 142
  field, 134
  method, 134, 204, 271, 297
access modifier
  private, 26, 39
  private[], 90
  private[this],, 90
  protected, 39
actor, 15, 269, 295–306
algorithm
  quicksort, 69
animation, 289–293, 297–298
annotation, 108
  @BeanProperty, 94
  @cloneable, 94
  @deprecated, 92
  @inline, 94
  @native, 94
  @noinline, 94
  @remote, 94
  @serializable, 94
  @throws, 94
  @transient, 94
  @unchecked, 108
  @volatile, 94
Apache Maven, 209
applet, 275–280, 289–293, 297–298

binary search tree, 98
block expression, 269, 287

C function, 367
call by-name, 13, 121, 157
call by-value, 121
case class, 95–102, 122, 134
casting, 411
  destructive, 411
  non-destructive, 411

category theory, 164–165
character
  NULL, 24
  ; (semicolon), 33
  _ (underscore), 30, 45, 70, 103, 198
check box, 240–243
class
  Action, 234, 251
  Any, 19, 138, 144, 145, 271
  AnyRef, 19, 26, 138, 145, 169, 286
  Applet.UI, 275, 290
  Array, 274
  ArrayBuffer, 274
  BorderPanel, 216, 266
  BoxPanel, 238
  Button, 208, 249
  ButtonClicked, 208
  CheckBox, 240
  ComboBox, 243, 248
  Component, 218
  ComponentHidden, 278
  ComponentMoved, 278
  ComponentRemoved, 278
  ComponentResized, 278
  concurrent.MailBox, 293
  Constraints, 204
  EditDone, 268
  Enumeration, 141
  Exception, 36
  Failure, 183
  FileChooser, 251
  FlowPanel, 243
  FormattedTextField, 270
  Frame, 204, 210, 211, 250
  Future, 300
  GridBagPanel, 204
  GridPanel, 212, 257
  instantiation, 25, 42
  java.awt.AlphaComposite, 282
  java.awt.BasicStroke, 261
  java.awt.Component, 260, 278, 279
  java.awt.Dimension, 273, 279
  java.awt.Font, 204

Printed in the United States
by Baker & Taylor Publisher Services